Comparative Public Policy

To

Beautiful Beth
and
All Our Children

Comparative Public Policy

Patterns of Post-war Transformation

Francis G. Castles

Professor of Political Science in the Research School of Social Sciences, Australian National University, Australia

Edward Elgar
Cheltenham, UK • Northampton, MA, USA

Published by
Edward Elgar Publishing Limited
Glensanda House
Montpellier Parade
Cheltenham
Glos GL50 1UA
UK

Edward Elgar Publishing, Inc.
6 Market Street
Northampton
Massachusetts 01060
USA

Paperback edition 1999

A catalogue record for this book
is available from the British Library

Library of Congress Cataloguing in Publication Data
Castles, Francis Geoffrey, 1943–
    Comparative public policy : patterns of post-war transformation/
    Francis G. Castles
        Includes bibliographical references.
        1. Policy sciences. 2. Political planning. 3. Comparative
        government. I. Title
    H97.C39 1998
    321'6—dc21   98–13443
                                                       CIP

ISBN 1 85898 816 0 (cased)
       1 85898 823 3 (paperback)

Printed and bound in Great Britain by
Biddles Ltd, Guildford and King's Lynn

Contents

List of figures

List of tables

Prefatory note and acknowledgements

This book started out as a kind of valedictory exercise designed to bring together findings on the many comparative public policy topics on which I have written in the past two decades. It has ended up as an attempt to write a comprehensive account of post-war public policy development in the OECD region based on a systematic analysis of data covering more than 30 years for 21 nations and 12 policy areas. All the material and all the findings are entirely new and several of the topics are ones on which I have not previously written. Although the book contains many tables and statistical findings, it has been designed to be accessible to a wide audience of those interested in the huge changes that have occurred in the economies, societies, polities and policies of Western nations since World War II.

The scholars, colleagues and, in many cases, friends who have given me advice or read parts of the manuscript come from many disciplines and many countries. Their names are as follows: Klaus Armingeon, Martin Baldwin-Edwards, Gugliano Bonoli, Jeff Borland, Frank Brennan, Steve Dowrick, Paul Dugdale, Diane Gibson, Bob Goodin, Janet Gornick, John Goss, Barry Hindess, Karl Hinrichs, Simon Jackman, Frank Jones, Raja Junankar, Hans Keman, Michael Laver, Stephan Leibfried, Peter McDonald, Deborah Mitchell, Max Neutze, Julia O'Connor, Ann Orloff, Phillip Pettit, Sue Richardson, Manfred Schmidt, Beth Seddon, Michael Shalev, Duane Swank, John Uhr and Bruce Western.

It is my hope that this book will prove suitable as a text in comparative public policy analysis. If it does, I shall have reason to be grateful to a group of Australian National University Public Policy students who were willing to risk taking a class in which I taught this material as I wrote it. They were: Shah Alam, Jande Bande, Robin Brown, Marilyn Chalkley, Xiaolin Li, Susan Pitt and Huaichuan Rui.

I would like to thank my research assistant, Joshua Ryan, who prepared the figures in Chapters 4–7, my colleagues in the Research School for their forbearance and my secretaries Jeannie Haxell and Mary Hapel for their many kind services. Finally, my greatest thanks go to my wife, Beth Seddon, who endured my distracted state in the year it took to write this book.

FRANCIS G. CASTLES

1. Making sense of post-war public policy

OBJECTIVES AND APPROACHES

This book uses a comparative research strategy to make sense of the ways in which the economic, social and political transformations of the post-World War II epoch have impacted on the outcomes of public policy in the advanced, industrial, nations of Western capitalism. As tables in the next two chapters demonstrate, the past half century has seen change on a massive scale amongst these nations. The economy has been transfigured by a more than twofold increase in real incomes, based on a massive growth in productivity and a major expansion of international trade. Social changes have included a shift from agriculture and manufacturing to services, a continuation of the trend – already well under way in the late nineteenth and early twentieth centuries – of movement from rural to urban residence and a dramatic process of population ageing. In the political arena, notable contrasts with the inter-war period have been the universal acceptance of liberal democratic institutions, the emergence of a new social and political agenda for women, the acknowledgement of parties of the Left as normal parties of government and, in some countries, the institutionalization of a consensual relationship between labour and capital.

As tables in subsequent chapters show, over the same period the ambit of public policy has also been greatly transformed. This is most readily measured in terms of the overall size of the public sphere and the range of areas in which it intervenes. Governments in the advanced countries spend, tax and consume goods and services on nearly twice the scale that they did in the early post-war years. A major reason for this expansion has been the growth of the welfare state, with social security, health and education spending in the typical OECD nation now amounting to around 30 per cent of national income. Nor does the welfare state define the outer limits of modern public policy. Over the post-war period, the state has intervened in areas formerly seen as almost exclusively realms of private interest, and today it is commonplace for governments and electorates to regard issues relating to the labour market and the domestic sphere as matters of major policy concern. As we shall see, a transformed conception of the choices open to women in the spheres of work and the family has been an important factor contributing to such changes. The broad reach of modern public policy does not stop with the deliberate actions of government. No less important are the wider repercussions of the extended role of the state, which have been seen by some commentators as undermining the efficient functioning of economy and civil society more generally. An important objective of later chapters of this book is to subject such claims to critical scrutiny.

That change has been the order of the day in the post-war era does not mean that it has proceeded at the same pace in all advanced nations. On the contrary, there was very substantial variation in the economic, social and political starting-points from which these countries embarked on the process of post-war modernization and no lesser variation in the speed of their ensuing development. Exactly the same is true of the policy arena. In the immediate post-war era, there were nations already well on the way to being advanced welfare states in social security spending terms and others where Keynesian labour market policies were already reasonably well developed. These nations contrasted with others where the role of government remained essentially that of the nineteenth-century 'nightwatchman state': to defend external borders and to maintain internal security. Again the trajectory of policy transformation has varied from country to country, with immediate post-war policy laggards sometimes becoming leaders, whilst former policy innovators have, on occasions, stagnated. Further important objectives of this book are to describe the extent of policy transformation in different countries and to show why that transformation has been more pronounced in some of them than in others.

That post-war changes in economy, society and politics are somehow connected to changes in the nature and scope of public policy is not in doubt. However, what does divide social science commentators on these developments is the nature of the linkages they see as crucial. Economists tend to see the functioning of the economy as the main engine of policy transformation. An early economistic view of public policy development was Adolf Wagner's (1877) 'law of increasing state activity', which suggested that, as nations became wealthier, a greater proportion of their national product would be spent by government (Larkey, Stolp and Winer, 1981). At present, we are in the midst of a heated academic debate on whether the globalization of national economies has imposed constraints on domestic economic policy-making, requiring governments to curtail domestic public expenditures (see both Keohane and Milner in Milner and Keohane, 1996; Hirst and Thompson, 1996; Boyer and

Drache, 1996). Sociologists have been no less concerned with the impact of economic change, but have tended to regard it as an aspect of a wider process of modernization, which includes changes in occupational structure, urbanization and demographic processes of population ageing (Wilensky and Lebeaux, 1958; Kerr, 1960).

Economic and sociological views have in common a perspective which sees policy change as primarily a consequence of socio-economic transformation. In contrast, political scientists have tended to regard political institutions and political ideologies as key factors shaping policy outcomes (see Castles and McKinlay, 1979; Schmidt, 1996a). This latter perspective certainly does not view socio-economic modernization as irrelevant, but rather as a process providing ideologically predisposed parties with the means to initiate new policy programmes within limits circumscribed by the institutional configurations within which they operate. In contradistinction to socio-economic perspectives, the political science view insists that we take account of cross-national variation in trying to understand policy change. While socio-economic factors influence policy in individual countries over time, institutional structures are often invariant and the impact of party is more often cumulative than immediate. Because this is so, it is often difficult to establish the role of politics in shaping policy on the basis of a single country's immediate history. But institutions differ as between countries. Some have federal structures, some are unitary; some have special requirements for constitutional change, whilst others do not. Party rule also differs as between countries – in terms of numbers of parties typically represented in the legislature, the size of diverse ideological tendencies and their relative dominance over time. Thus, in order to assess the possible impact of these factors, it is necessary to compare policy outcomes in different nations.

Because the process of policy transformation has differed from country to country and because some factors implicated in that process can only be studied by focusing on cross-national variation, this book is explicitly comparative in approach. It is important, however, to emphasise that, whilst an attempt to comprehend the role of political factors in the determination of policy outcomes presupposes a comparative approach, such an approach does not necessarily presuppose institutional or ideological explanations. Politics varies across nations, but so too do degrees of economic and social development. For example, compare Portugal and the USA, the two countries which, over the whole span of the post-war era, are probably the least alike of the 21 advanced nations featuring in our analysis. Apart from political differences (for the first half of the period, Portugal was a dictatorship, with no free trade unions or political parties), Portugal started out the period with a real per capita

national income less than one sixth that of the USA, with an urban population proportionately less than a third the size and a service sector
proportionately less than half the size. The sorts of questions this book
seeks to answer are whether such sources of variation account for
observed differences in levels and changes in public policy outcomes in
these nations and which of them has had the greatest impact. The
answers are not predetermined, nor are they the special preserve of any
one academic discipline.

A comparative approach becomes an interdisciplinary approach for
three obvious reasons. First, hugely complex policy processes are most
unlikely to have singular determinants. So the answer to the question of
which of the various kinds of differences between countries have had an
impact on policy outcomes is likely to be 'more than just one of them'.
Second, there is absolutely no guarantee that the factors influencing
policy will be invariant over time. An argument drawn from the analysis
which follows suggests that levels of female labour force participation
and of fertility were reciprocally linked in the immediate post-war
decades, but not thereafter. As we shall show, this change can best be
understood in terms of a transformation in the trade-off between work
and family premised on feminist ideas, which has made welfare benefits
for working mothers pivotal to population replacement levels of fertility
in the 1990s. In the study of the determinants of policy outcomes, context
often matters a great deal. Third, there is absolutely no reason to suppose
that different kinds of policy outcomes will have the same determinants.
It has often been assumed that the aspect of ideological partisanship
which has been most influential in shaping the role of the state has been
the emergence of strong parties of the political Left, but, as we shall see,
there are areas in which the roles of rightist and Christian Democratic
parties have been no less pivotal. Because the determinants of policy are
likely to be many, to change over time and to vary from policy area to
policy area, an approach to policy change from a single disciplinary perspective is likely to miss much of the action.

The approach taken by this book is comparative and interdisciplinary.
It is also more broadly focused than is often the case in the comparative
public policy literature. Because policy changes over time, we examine
policy outcomes at a number of different time-periods and we also
explore the determinants of change over time. Because policy areas vary
and the repercussions of policy change are potentially extensive, we
examine policy outcomes and their impacts across a wide range: the big
aggregates of spending and taxing, expenditures on components of the
welfare state, the determinants of labour market outcomes and areas
which have featured only marginally in the comparative public policy lit-

erature hitherto, such as home ownership, fertility and divorce. To ignore variation over time and across policy areas is to tell the story of post-war public policy in a manner which is incomplete and potentially misleading.

The conjunction of an approach which is simultaneously comparative, interdisciplinary and so broad-ranging is bound to attract the charge of superficiality from some quarters. In the sense that the story offered here does not focus on the inherently complex detail and context of particular policy areas, this criticism is not wholly unwarranted, but our objective of making sense of half a century's policy change nevertheless argues strongly for a focus on the big picture and its major components rather than on the detailed nuances of any particular policy area or policy development. To understand the factors shaping policy outcomes in the post-war era, we need to comprehend patterns of association between variables, patterns of change over time and patterns of interconnection between policy areas. Disciplinary approaches tend to supply such patterns by imposing the perspectives and theories of their disciplines on the topics they study. For reasons already suggested, such approaches are inappropriate to our subject-matter. The sorts of patterns we wish to comprehend are those of difference and similarity between diverse policy areas (are the factors shaping cross-national variation the same across different policy areas?), patterns over time (have there been important changes in the factors determining cross-national policy variation?) and patterns that reflect linkages across policy areas (is variation in one area of policy a determinant of variation in other policy areas?). To locate such patterns, to answer such questions and, in doing so, to identify the broad trajectories of post-war public policy development, demands an approach that is not narrowly restricted to any one area of policy or to any particular period of time.

STRUCTURE AND CONTENT

The focus of this study is 21 nations which, by the 1990s, were all industrialized, relatively affluent and democratic. They are countries which can sensibly be compared because they have many basic things in common (Dogan and Pelassy, 1990). The countries comprise all the major nations of Western Europe, the states of European settlement in the New World (the USA and Canada) and the Antipodes (Australia and New Zealand), together with the only nation, whose citizens were of non-European extraction, to make major progress towards modernization prior to World War II, namely Japan. These 21 countries are all long-term members of the Organization for Economic Co-operation and Development

(OECD), which is highly relevant from the point of view of this study, since the OECD has become by far the most important source of standardized data on public policy outcomes and most aspects of economic performance for this group of nations. Indeed, for the period in which we are interested here, one may reasonably refer to the 21 nations figuring in this study as 'the OECD nations', with the only three countries omitted being Luxembourg and Iceland, on grounds of small population size (less than half a million), and Turkey, on the grounds that it does not qualify as an advanced nation and that its democratic status remains more than somewhat precarious.

This latter disqualification raises the question of the appropriateness of including amongst our group three other nations which have themselves only recently become affluent and which have experienced periods of non-democratic rule in the post-war period. These three nations are the so-called 'new democracies' of Greece, Portugal and Spain. It is only very recently that researchers have focused on how the public policy experience of these countries compares and contrasts with that of other advanced Western nations (see Leibfried, 1993; Castles, 1995; Ferrera, 1996; MIRE, 1997). Earlier researchers had either explicitly argued against including these nations in comparative studies or, more commonly, simply ignored them. Where explicit, this neglect was justified in terms of the weakness of public sector intervention in Southern Europe, the absence of economic development on a scale comparable to the rest of Europe, the lack of or instability of democratic institutions and, in many cases the clinching argument, the sometimes conspicuous gaps in these countries' national accounts data for early periods and considerable doubts about the quality of the data that were produced.

These arguments are no longer valid. The countries of Southern Europe remain amongst the least affluent of the OECD group, but certainly can no longer be described as underdeveloped. Moreover, democracy is now more than two decades old in all three nations, and with democracy, and subsequently membership of the European Community (EC), has come a substantial growth of government, which has had amongst its effects the routine production of national accounts data comparable to those of the other OECD nations. So it is now possible to include these countries – and extremely valuable to do so. The methods we use to make sense of policy outcomes depend for their validity on the number of cases under examination, so that increasing the grouping under investigation from 18 to 21 represents a quite real increment in our capacity to comprehend the kinds of factors driving post-war policy development. However, because doubts must remain about the comparability of the countries of the New Southern Europe prior to the 1980s, we also note instances where our interpretation might be different in the absence of data for these countries.

In Chapters 2 and 3, we begin our analysis of these 21 nations by describing and discussing the major factors which have been identified in the comparative public policy literature as determinants of the trajectory of policy development in the post-war era. Since many of these factors simultaneously feature as core components of the social science disciplines' descriptions of the developments most salient in the economic, social and political transformation of these nations in the post-war period, this account also serves as the basis for a kind of interdisciplinary snapshot of the broad features of that transformation. It should be noted, however, that while these factors are those which have been most generally associated with policy outcomes, they are not the only ones featuring in our subsequent analysis. Other factors include ones specific to particular policy areas and policy outcomes themselves, for, as we shall see, one of the more interesting findings of this research is the extent to which choices in one policy area can shape outcomes in another.

In order to serve as a basis for systematic comparison, our analysis of the factors highlighted in Chapters 2 and 3 is, for the most part, structured according to a standard format. With only a few exceptions, the data in these chapters and in the subsequent ones examining different policy outcomes are provided for three standard time-points – 1960, 1974 and the early 1990s – and for change over the entire period. The rationale for each time-point is quite straightforward. The year 1960 is the first for which the OECD produces consistent and coherent data for most of the countries under examination here. Whilst for a few topics use could be made of alternative series that go back earlier, there are often major gaps in these series for the earliest periods. Moreover, where OECD data are the standard source for subsequent time-points, there are also serious problems of data continuity in using other and longer time-series. For these reasons, our study of the post-war era commences in 1960, although, where relevant, we note developments occurring between the termination of World War II in 1945 and the chosen start date for our analysis.

The mid-point for the study, 1974, is chosen as a marker for the end of what has variously been described as the 'Golden Age' of Western capitalism (Maddison, 1991) or the 'Golden Age' of welfare state expansion (Esping-Andersen, 1996). The first oil shock was the watershed event dividing economic boom from economic gloom. After 1974, growth rates declined, unemployment and inflation increased and governments became progressively less comfortable with financial commitments to policy development entered into in more expansive times. Inflation apart, this remains a fair enough description of the 'present discontents' of most OECD nations, providing us with no significant economic milestone that would serve as termination point for our inquiry. Thus the main criterion for particular cut-off points in the early 1990s is the latest availability of data in respect of each type of policy outcome. That does not make our finishing point an arbitrary one. The final, much delayed, act of World War II was the pulling down of the 'Iron Curtain' dividing Eastern and Western Europe. Hence the early 1990s provide an appropriate marker for the end of the post-war era and an appropriate vantage point from which to take stock.

The analysis in Chapters 2 and 3 covers a wide range of topics and the discussion is necessarily of a summary kind. Chapter 2 focuses on the economy and society. It examines the legacy of World War II, economic performance, trade expansion, urbanization, changes in the occupational structure, the ageing of the population and the nature of religious differences. Chapter 3 examines political institutions and ideologies. It discusses the process of democratization, manifestations of class politics, the changing balance of power between parties of the Left and Right, and the manner in which institutional structures variously moderate class conflict, impede change and create the basis for supranational policy-making. In addition, a final section of Chapter 3 seeks to assess the degree to which the various economic, social and political processes reviewed in Chapters 2 and 3 are interconnected. The analysis of each topic dealt with in these chapters starts from a summary table, generally providing data for all 21 countries and, where possible, for all three time-points. In each case, we give some account of the phenomenon for which the data provide a measure, suggest reasons why it has been seen as relevant to public policy development and note the main features of variation amongst countries at particular time-points and over the period as a whole.

An important aspect of this latter analysis is the identification of differences between groups of nations defined in terms of common cultural, historical and geographical features. These 'families of nations' (see Castles, 1993), which correspond substantially to the borders of what appear to be quite clearly identified cultural zones (Inglehart, 1997), constitute a preliminary organizing device allowing us to contrast cases in such a way that some of the factors underlying the character of their policy outcomes become more apparent. To facilitate contrasts of this kind, all the basic data tables in subsequent chapters are ordered in terms of the groupings identified below.

- An English-speaking family including Australia, Canada, Ireland, New Zealand, the United Kingdom and the USA. This group is united by language and common political and legal traditions consequent on historical ties with Great Britain. Within the group is a further sub-group of European settler nations of the New World and the Antipodes.

- A Scandinavian or, more properly, Nordic family consisting of Denmark, Finland, Norway and Sweden. The history of these nations has been closely interlinked throughout the past millennium, they have a common legal tradition and, Finland apart, they have languages which are closely akin.

- A continental Western European grouping of Austria, Belgium, France, Germany, Italy and the Netherlands. Language is not an element of commonality for this grouping, but a historical legacy of dynastic links, cultural (particularly religious) similarities and policy diffusion have created some real basis of likeness. In a sense, this family was given concrete form by the fact that, with the exception of Austria, and together with Luxembourg, these nations were the founding members of the European Community in the mid-1950s.

- A Southern European family consisting of Greece, Portugal and Spain. These countries lack the identity given by a common history or language, but possess many affinities as part of the ancient Mediterranean cultural world. As noted previously, they also have many features in common in virtue of the lateness of their economic, social and political modernization.

Only two of our 21 nations fail to find a place in these families of nations: Switzerland and Japan. The Swiss case is certainly unusual in a variety of ways, but Switzerland's non-inclusion in the family groupings here is essentially arbitrary. Another account, pointing to commonalities in history, language, decentralized political structures and, possibly, institutional modes of conflict resolution, could lead to the identification of a German-speaking family of nations, of which Switzerland would be a member (see Castles, 1993). Japan really is a one-off case in our sample of nations, since it is the only instance of a country of non-European antecedents to become an advanced capitalist democracy in the period under review here. Possibly, in some future study of policy development, conducted perhaps only a few decades down the track, Japan may appear as the first of a new family of newly industrialized countries (NICs) in Asia or, if the focus is East Asian, and the definition cultural, as part of a family of nations building its identity around 'the common language of Confucianism' (Goodman and Peng, 1996, 195).

Chapters 4 to 7 focus on policy outputs and outcomes. Throughout this study, we use the term 'policy outcome' as a shorthand way of referring to both the outputs of government programmes in the form of spending totals and the real outcomes of policies in the sense of what actually happens to people. Of course, outputs are designed to lead to outcomes – social security expenditures to provide a livelihood for those without income, health and educational expenditures to cater for the needs of the sick and the young – but sometimes the translation is far from perfect and it is always important to stress the distinction when we wish to query the adequacy of the policy in question. In this study that is not our main purpose and the term 'policy outcome' is used throughout. It is, nevertheless, worth keeping in mind that the chapters dealing with taxing and spending and with the welfare state are really analysing governmental outputs, whilst the later chapters on the labour market and on the way in which policy impinges on the sphere of the personal are more concerned with outcomes in the stricter sense.

Chapter 4 deals with the big aggregates of spending and taxing which may be seen as defining the reach of the state: the total outlays of government, the total receipts (mostly tax revenues) of government and civilian public consumption expenditure on goods and services. The focus of our inquiry in this chapter is on the causes of the growth of big government in the latter half of the twentieth century. Because the welfare state is much the largest single component of government spending, Chapter 5 looks at the three major programmes of the welfare state separately: social security income transfers, health expenditures and education expenditures. Chapter 6 focuses on labour market outcomes: male and female labour force participation and unemployment. How much purchase governments actually have on labour market outcomes is a matter of debate, because in this arena government programmes are factors which indirectly shape the decisions of millions of individuals rather than, as in the case of spending and taxing, directly spelling out the entitlements and obligations of citizens. Nevertheless, with the post-war advent of Keynesian economic policies, the functioning of labour markets has become an area in which outcomes are widely regarded as a responsibility of government.

Home ownership, fertility and divorce, the topics examined in Chapter 7, are also areas of human activity in which the impact of government is largely indirect. These are realms of the personal which are rarely thought of in policy terms at all, but in which the actions of governments are often highly significant. All governments regulate housing tenure and, if only implicitly, favour one form of tenure over another. Housing cannot be ignored by governments because it is so central to the life of citizens who typically spend about as much on shelter as they do on taxes to pay for the welfare state. Citizens and, therefore, governments are no less concerned with matters pertaining to family law and population growth. Since World War II, virtually all Western governments have responded to popular pressure to introduce or reform existing divorce laws. Nor is there anything new in a concern by governments over population policy. Once this was a matter mostly raised in connection with a nation's preparedness to fight wars. Today, when the fertility rate in many advanced countries is well below the rate required to maintain current population levels, and when low fertility also contributes to an ageing population, with all its attendant implications for government expenditure, population policy is a topic which seems likely to preoccupy Western governments more and more.

Quite apart from the direct interventions of government, the topics dealt with in Chapters 6 and 7 are an integral part of post-war policy transformation because government expenditure policies, in a manner which is not always fully anticipated by those who formulate them, often significantly influence labour market choices and personal behaviour. Policy choices in one area impact on policy choices in another, or policy choices in one area transform another into an area of policy concern. Examples we shall encounter in later chapters include the way in which the encouragement of private home ownership facilitates male labour force withdrawal, the role of government employment in increasing female labour force participation, and the manner in which parental benefits designed to promote female employment have led to higher levels of fertility. However, while we seek to map out some of these ways in which policy choices impact on one another, we are also concerned to dispel more mythical characterizations of the role of government in the latter half of the twentieth century. Big government and the welfare state are frequently criticized as undermining the will to work and as destroying traditional moral values. As we shall see, such blanket characterizations are far too simplistic. Public policy has clearly played an important role in reshaping both the labour market and the realm of the personal, but is very far from being the source of all contemporary problems in these areas.

Just as in Chapters 2 and 3, the later chapters on policy outcomes are built around summary tables providing data concerning differences between our 21 countries in 1960, 1974, the early 1990s and with respect to change over the period as a whole. The methods of analysis by which we examine the degree of association between the economic, social and political factors discussed in Chapters 2 and 3, and the policy outcomes that are the subject of later chapters, are discussed in the final sections of this introductory chapter. These methods allow us to identify a range of factors which the evidence suggests are closely linked to cross-national variation in policy outcomes at particular periods during the post-war era and with patterns of policy development over time.

Chapter 8, our concluding chapter, looks across the broad range of policy outcomes analysed in the book with the aim of locating patterns of policy development. Without the prior analysis, it is impossible to summarize the content of this concluding chapter. All we can do is note the kinds of questions we shall be trying to answer. Do different policy areas march to the beat of a single drum? In other words, can we identify commonalities in the factors associated with different policy outcomes? Are there commonalities over time as well as between policy areas? If not, what new factors have come to the fore over this period and why? Over time and across policy areas, have the nations we are studying become more similar? In other words, is it possible to identify a pattern of postwar policy convergence? Having identified ways in which nations generally have become more alike, does anything remain of the notion that some nations have special affinities by virtue of culture, history and language? Or, to put it another way, does locating a country as a member of a particular family of nations tell us anything of significance about that country's policy development? Lastly, we seek to establish whether the findings arrived at here have a bearing on arguments concerning the role of the state in the new millennium. Viewed in terms of contemporary critiques of the role of state, and the recent success of parties with a rhetoric of reducing its size, it is important to ask whether the emergence of big government in the post-war era was an aberration or represents the permanent shape of things to come.

These are not new questions. They raise issues which have been central to the emergence of a sub-discipline of comparative public policy, which has sought to use cross-national analysis as a means of inquiring into the causes and consequences of the growth of the post-war state. Earlier answers have tended to be based on narrowly focused research into the determinants of discrete areas of public policy. We would argue that conclusions as to the character of the post-war policy transformation are likely to be more firmly grounded if they rest on a wide-ranging and comprehensive analysis of policy outcomes of the kind provided in this study.

LOGIC AND METHOD

The comparative approach employed in this study is not just a matter of focusing our attention on the differences and similarities characterizing some 20 countries. Comparison simultaneously supplies us with a logic which assists in identifying patterns of association between policy outcomes and the factors which influence them. As we have already noted, there are many rival accounts of the determinants of policy change and our task is to identify those which seem to be most convincing. Comparing nations offers us a logic for doing this analogous to other research strategies designed to establish causal inferences (King, Keohane and Verba, 1994). In the social sciences, we cannot easily conduct experiments, but we can use the experience of other nations to provide what may be regarded as 'natural experiments'. To the degree that these countries are similar across a wide range of fundamental attributes (a real experiment requires a complete matching of attributes), we may infer that any remaining differences are related to each other. To take an example relevant to a later topic of discussion, we may argue that higher rates of divorce are likely to be, in some measure, a consequence of the shift from a gender division of labour typical of industrial production to the less rigid patterns associated with services production. There is a variety of ways in which this hypothesis might be tested, but one could involve a comparison between countries differing in the extent to which they possess an occupational structure dominated by services. The logic here is simple: if, in most cases where services employment is high, divorce is also high and if, in most cases where services employment is low, divorce rates are also low, we may conclude that we have established the existence of some sort of association or correlation between these two phenomena.

The confidence we have in the existence of that relationship depends on at least three factors. First and foremost, the relationship must make sense in terms of our theoretical understanding of the mechanisms through which the occupational structure could impact on family relationships. The remaining considerations are more practical. One is a question of what we mean by 'most cases'. Clearly our confidence depends on whether 'most cases' means a bare majority of cases or virtually all the cases. If the former, we may not be all that convinced that the association located is much more than an outcome of chance. If the latter, we may feel that an inference of some sort of causal relationship is appropriate, that is, we may feel justified in arguing that occupational structure is amongst the factors leading to higher levels of divorce. The other important question is how many cases are being compared. For any degree of apparent association between variables, the greater the number of cases in which the association is manifested, the greater will be our confidence that the association located is not fortuitous. So the essential logic of what we are seeking to do in this study is to assess the strength of hypotheses concerning the factors impacting on public policy outcomes in as large a group of nations as possible. What defines the possible in this context is the existence of sufficient similarity between the cases to make them comparable. The study here is limited to advanced democratic states. However, its conclusions are based not on a necessarily idiosyncratic selection of cases, but on all those for which there are adequate data.

Seeking to compare many cases creates difficulties in analysing data. When only a few cases are examined, data manipulation is relatively straightforward. If divorce rates are high in two nations in which services employment predominates and low in two countries where it does not, it is not difficult to arrive at preliminary conclusions. When the number of cases is substantially larger, and the association to be located is less than clear-cut, what is going on becomes far more difficult to disentangle. In the real world, outcomes are not unambiguously related to any single factor, so that no one-to-one correspondence of variables is identifiable. The difficulty is compounded by the fact that almost invariably the association between variables is masked by the 'noise' provided by other, and often unknown, factors also associated with the outcome under investigation.

Under these circumstances, the usual methodology for tackling comparative research involves the use of various statistical techniques. Such techniques make it possible to identify which variables are associated and which are not, and provide criteria for assessing the strength of the relationships so revealed. The problem with such methods is, of course, that the conclusions arrived at on such a basis are not readily accessible to those unversed in the techniques themselves. That poses a huge difficulty for a book like this, where some kinds of statistical manipulation of data serve as valuable means of cutting through the complexity of the relationships with which we are concerned, but, at the same time, where the use of such methods makes it difficult for all but a small portion of those interested in the character of these relationships to follow the argument.

Because this book is written out of the conviction that making sense of post-war patterns of public policy development is a topic of broad general interest, a very real effort is made here to improve the accessibility of the account provided. The book is written with three kinds of audience in mind. First, there are those with no statistical training of any kind who find numerical analysis profoundly off-putting. For this audience, a conscious attempt has been made to design the body of the text of subsequent chapters in such a way that it will be comprehensible to those with no statistical skills. Although the book contains many comparative tables and a number of statistical appendices, the main emphasis throughout is on providing a verbal account which can be understood with minimum reference to technical concepts. In addition, the policy analysis chapters seek to give an indication of the strengths of different relationships through figures which give a graphical dimension to otherwise quantitative findings. Obviously, those lacking a statistical background will have to take on trust that the account given of the statistical findings is fair and accurate, but, that apart, there is no reason why such readers should find it unduly difficult to follow the argument.

The second audience is a readership which comes to the material with a considerable prior statistical background. For this readership, the statistical apparatus required to support the arguments offered in this book is provided by a number of summary statistical measures to be found in the comparative tables in each chapter, by correlation matrices in the appendix to Chapter 3 and by correlations reported together with the figures in subsequent chapters. Most crucially, it is provided in the statistical appendices to be found at the end of these later chapters, which provide statistical models showing which sets of variables are most closely associated with policy outcomes at each time-point and for change over time.

Finally, there is likely to be a third audience of those without statistical training, which, nevertheless, wishes to find out what the statistical measures used here signify without having to invest too heavily in learning statistical techniques. For this last readership, what now follows is a brief and non-technical account of the nature of the statistical measures that appear in the later comparative tables, correlation matrices and figures. In addition there is an appendix at the end of this chapter which seeks to explain as simply as possible the meaning of the statistical measures in the later appendices.

Apart from in technical appendices, the only places in this book where numbers are to be encountered unadorned by verbal description are in the various comparative tables in the text. Much of what is contained in the tables requires no statistical aptitude of any kind. Look at any comparative table in Chapters 2 through to 7 and the main substance of what you will find will be constituted by values of particular measures of economic, social and political variables and of public policy outcomes for our 21 nations at the three designated time-points and for change over time. In all cases, these values are expressed in terms of commonly understood units of variation including US dollars per capita, percentages of national product or of the labour force, rates per 1000 of the population and so on. These measures offer the simplest possible descriptions of cross-national similarities and differences in policy outcomes and of the factors commonly seen as influencing them.

Only the last three lines of each table provide statistical measures of any kind. These are as follows:

- The first line provides the *mean* of the cases included in the comparison, which is simply the arithmetic average of the values for all the countries for which data are available (that is, the sum of all the values divided by the number of cases). Obviously, knowing what the mean of the cases is for a number of time-periods allows us to establish the most basic dimensions of the trajectory of change for the variable in question, that is, whether values are becoming larger or smaller over time.

- The second line provides the *correlation* between the 1960 value of the variable being compared and either subsequent values or subsequent change. A correlation is a basic measure of the degree of association between two variables which varies between +1.0 and –1.0. A high number, that is, one nearer +1.0 or –1.0 than to zero, indicates a reasonably strong relationship. The '+' or positive sign indicates that the greater the value of one variable, the greater the value of the other. A '–' or negative sign indicates that the greater the value of one variable, the lesser the value of the other. When, in our basic comparative tables, we look at the correlation between the value of a variable in 1960 and at later dates, we are offering a measure of the extent to which the cross-national variation at the later dates corresponds with the variation at the beginning of the period. This is one kind of indicator of whether any major change has taken place, with high positive values indicative of little fundamental transformation in the pattern of variation observed. Another indicator is provided by looking at the correlation between 1960 values and subsequent change. A positive sign here indicates that the countries which had the higher values of the variable in 1960 tended to be those in which the value increased most thereafter. A negative sign indicates that the countries which had the lower values in 1960 were those in which the values tended to increase most, a process often described as catch-up.
- The final line of each table reports the *coefficient of variation* of the cases. This measure provides a summary indicator of the degree to which the cases being compared differ from one another. The coefficient of variation allows us to contrast the extent of variation amongst cases at different time-points on a relative or standardized basis which takes account of the fact that the mean value of the variable may change over time. This allows us to assess the extent of divergence and convergence of cases over time, since an increased coefficient of variation is the same as saying that the cases have become less alike and a diminished coefficient that they have become more alike. It is most important to emphasize that the information provided by correlations between 1960 values and subsequent change over time and that provided by changes in the coefficient of variation over time are quite different. The first pertains to the relationship between the initial values of a variable and the subsequent trajectory of change in that variable, whereas the second involves a contrast between initial and subsequent values in terms of their variation from a mean which itself may have changed appreciably. Thus when, in coming chapters, we talk of *catch-up* and *convergence*, we are identifying different phenomena. Laggards may be catching up with leaders in absolute terms, but that does not necessarily mean that countries are converging and becoming more alike in relative terms.

Together these statistical measures provide us with some relatively simple tools for describing the trajectory of development of the most important economic, social and political factors of the post-war era and of the public policy outcomes on which they have had an impact. The correlation matrices in the appendix to Chapter 3 do a rather different job of showing us the extent to which the economic, social and political factors are themselves interconnected at different times. The correlations reported in these matrices are just like those appearing in the second last line of the comparative tables. They measure the degree of association between pairs of variables – affluence and urbanization, occupational structure and age structure of the population and so on. As in the comparative tables, positive correlations indicate that a high value of one variable goes along with a high value of another, whilst negative correlations indicate that high values of one are associated with lower values of the other. Correlation coefficients also appear quite frequently in the text of later chapters as simple indications of the strength of the relationship between a given pair of variables (otherwise known as a bivariate relationship), but, in these instances, the strength of each relationship is also reported verbally.

Apart from correlation coefficients and the other simple statistics to be found in the comparative tables, the results of a somewhat more complex statistical technique known as multiple linear regression analysis are reported in the later appendices. This technique permits us to model the relationships associated with particular outcomes, with the term 'multiple' referring to the fact that the regression equations used are seeking to sort out the relationship between many variables simultaneously, and the term 'linear' referring to the assumption used in this modelling technique that greater or lesser values of one variable will be directly proportional to greater or lesser values of another variable. Not all relationships between variables are linear, and at one or two points in our subsequent analysis we shall note the presence of curvilinear relationships: ones where the relationship between two variables changes at some point in the distribution, producing not a straight-line (linear) relationship between them but a U-shaped curve. To give a simple example, if public expenditure increases in direct proportion to how rich a country is, the relationship is linear. On the other hand, if, as countries initially become richer, they spend more, but then, as they grow richer still, they spend less, the relationship is curvilinear.

Multiple regression analysis seeks to establish the relationship between a so-called 'dependent' variable and a number of so-called 'independent' variables. 'Dependent' here simply designates that the variable in question is that for which we are seeking to provide an account, whilst the 'independent' variables are those which we believe may together or separately provide such an account. Here, of course, the purposes of our inquiry dictate that policy outcomes are the dependent variables for our analysis, whilst the economic, social and political factors in terms of which we describe the transformation of the post-war era figure largely as the independent variables. In each section of the later chapters, we provide verbal accounts of the factors located as being significantly related to the policy outcomes in question and a numerical, but not statistical, estimation of what that relationship means in real terms. The appendices provide technical details of the statistical findings for those with the background to understand them, whilst the appendix at the end of this chapter offers some simple guidance as to the definition of the concepts encountered in those later appendices.

PROBLEMS AND CHOICES

A few final points should be made about the status of the account of the development of post-war public policy being offered here. Readers without much background in statistics need to be clearly aware that the apparent precision of numbers can make a statistical approach seem more scientific than it sometimes is in reality. This is particularly true here, since almost none of the statistical research in the comparative public policy area conforms to the standard assumptions of statistical analysis as applied in most other fields. Classical hypothesis testing using statistical methods estimates the probability that a sample of cases is representative of a parent population. To have confidence that this is so generally depends on having samples many times larger than the 21 cases studied here. It is, moreover, quite obvious that these 21 cases are in no sense a real sample, but actually represent an almost complete enumeration of the population of countries under examination. In other words, the relationships identified here are descriptions of the actual associations located in the data rather than estimates of relationships likely to be found in a population from which a sample has been drawn (see Western and Jackman, 1994). This has advantages and disadvantages. It means that the relationships we identify are real, but it also means that conventional tests of statistical confidence cannot have the same meaning that they have in other areas of statistical research. We report such test statistics in statistical appendices to later chapters, but regard them simply as measures of the relative salience of the terms featuring in our models.

In addition to these problems of statistical inference, the descriptions of the associations between variables produced by such an analysis must be regarded as approximate. With only 21 cases and a large number of theories purporting to account for most aspects of policy variation, it is impossible to specify complete models comprising different independent variables for each of the factors we have reason to believe might be implicated in a given set of outcomes. Most studies deploying small numbers of cases get around this problem by only reporting on a rather limited range of hypotheses from the literature, but this disingenuousness by omission scarcely solves the problem. Our own solution is not necessarily more satisfactory from a statistical viewpoint, although it is more honest. In our subsequent discussions of the factors related to public policy outcomes, we report correlation coefficients for all the variables which our discussion of relevant hypotheses has suggested might be related to such outcomes. However, the multiple regression models reported in the appendices seek to maximize levels of explained variance, whilst simultaneously including only terms which are statistically significant. This simplification makes it possible to report clear-cut findings derived on the basis of an objective criterion, but it means that the models themselves merely represent which of the wide range of such hypotheses best fit the observed variation amongst the cases. Inevitably, such a procedure implies that the models are, to some greater or lesser degree, misspecified, but, we would argue, not necessarily more so than those based on an incomplete consideration of the full range of hypotheses in a particular area.

This choice of a research strategy is by no means the preferred one in this literature. On the contrary, the thrust of much recent work in the comparative public policy field has been to focus narrowly on particular policy areas and to utilize more and more complex statistical methods to explore an ever wider range of more specific hypotheses concerning the determinants of outcomes in that area. The preferred technique for such studies has been pooled time-series regression, which promises to overcome the problem of 'too few cases and too many theories' by counting as separate instances outcomes in the same country in different years. On this basis, 30 years of data for 21 countries gives you 630 cases. Much of this work has been analytically challenging and, to its great credit, it is this approach which has finally overcome the tendency in the literature to counterpose mutually exclusive accounts premised on the primacy of particular explanatory paradigms (good instances are Hicks and Swank, 1992 and Huber, Ragin and Stephens, 1993). Nevertheless, there have to be serious doubts about a technique which violates yet another basic statistical assumption, in this instance that the cases under investigation are independent of one another, and whose results often seem largely dependent on the particular methods used to correct for that difficulty (see Stimson, 1985; Beck and Katz, 1995).

So instead of adopting a narrow focus on our subject-matter, we have chosen to accept the limitations imposed by a restricted number of cases, but to seek to remedy that deficiency in two ways. The first is to be quite explicit about the fragility of the research methods employed throughout this literature and to regard the findings produced by statistical modelling as the results of a preliminary sorting process, informing us about combinations of variables which fit together to produce possible accounts of the phenomenon with which we are concerned. Whether the set of variables which maximizes the level of explained variance in a particular sample at a particular date will always provide the correct account is quite another matter. What such a model usually does do is to identify one or more factors which appear basic to any coherent account, whilst confronting us with a possible way in which factors could be combined to make sense of what was happening in a particular policy area at a particular time. Such accounts – a no less appropriate word is *stories* – need to be interrogated in terms of our wider understanding of policy development in this and other areas. Sometimes this process leads to more realistic specifications of our original models and, where this occurs, these modified findings are reported in notes to relevant appendices. In this way, the statistical findings reported in this book are part of an iterative process leading to a growing understanding of the interrelationship of the many factors contributing to policy development in the post-war era. They are where the analysis begins rather than where it ends.

The second way in which we seek to overcome the inherent limitations of statistical modelling in this field is by consciously embracing a broader perspective. Earlier we noted that one of the things that distinguishes this book is its attempt to make sense of post-war public policy development by looking at a much wider range of areas than has hitherto been the case in this literature. The argument for such an approach can now be seen to be methodological as well as substantive. The compelling reason for adopting a wider perspective in this or any other area of comparative research is that the most convincing evidence for the existence of strong relationships amongst variables occurs where relationships can be identified as occurring repeatedly across time and/or across cognate areas of human activity. Such recurrent patterns of relationships, even if discerned with the fuzziness inherent in a research design resting on only 21 cases, may provide evidence as to the forces shaping policy in so far as they allow us to observe the outcomes of large numbers of natural experiments instead of just a few. Rather than focus all our research energy on the data collection and the methodological refinement required to establish the correlates of a single policy outcome across both space and time in the manner of pooled time-series analysis, what we seek to do here is to use a variety of relatively simple statistical techniques to provide the basis for an analysis which can map out the factors associated with a very wide range of different policy outcomes observed at different time-points. Instead of artificially inflating the number of cases under investigation, this approach provides us with a plethora of diverse opportunities to observe the interplay of the many factors shaping policy outcomes. If post-war public policy development does manifest recurrent patterns of the kind suggested here, it is likely to be an approach of this latter kind that has the most immediate prospects of showing what they are.

APPENDIX 1.1   UNDERSTANDING REGRESSION EQUATIONS

The material in this appendix is designed to help those unacquainted with the statistical techniques of regression analysis to understand the tables that are to be found in the appendices to Chapter 4–7. This guidance itself appears as an appendix in order to honour the promise of the last section that material in the main body of the text will be accessible to all readers irrespective of their knowledge of statistics. Even so, what we say here is very far from being couched in the technical language of statistics. It is an attempt to explain simply what the numbers in later appendices are saying. If, however, you choose not to read this appendix further nor to look at later ones, you will still not find it difficult to follow the story presented in this book, because everything that matters for the story is told in words as well as in equations.

The best way to give an account of what the statistics we present are all about is to give an example with exactly the same format as in later appendices. The example below is of an equation or model which seeks to provide an account of the factors (the independent variables) associated with differences in sickness benefit expenditures (which is the dependent variable) in our 21 nation in 1993.

Example: Sickness benefit expenditures in 1993

	Coefficient	Standard error	t-value
Intercept	0.475		
Federalism dummy	–0.557	0.176	3.16
1950–early 1990s			
Left cabinet seats	0.012	0.004	3.207
Adj. R^2 = 0.51			

Sources and notes: Sickness benefit expenditures measured as a percentage of GDP from OECD (1996d), *Social Expenditure Statistics of OECD Member Countries* (provisional version), Paris. Federalism dummy from Table 3.5; 1950–early 1990s (1993) Left cabinet seats calculated from the same source as Table 3.3. 21 cases in regression. This analysis is only offered as an example of the way in which statistical results are presented in this volume and there is no further discussion of cross-national variation in sickness benefits. For further research on this topic, see Kangas (1991).

What follows is a plain language account of the unfamiliar terms in the example above.

- *Intercept*. This is the predicted value (0.475 per cent of GDP) of the dependent variable (sickness benefits) where the values of the independent variables are zero (that is, where a country is not federal and has experienced no left-wing governement in the post-war period).
- *Coefficient*. This expresses the predicted impact of the variables under consideration. Dummy variables take the values one and zero and here federal countries are assigned a value of one. So –0.557 simply means that federal countries have 0.557 per cent of GDP *less* (remember the minus sign) sickness benefit expenditure than non-federal nations. 1950–early 1990s Left cabinet seats measures the average percentage of cabinet seats held by parties to the Left in that period and the coefficient of 0.012 simply means that for every 1 per cent of seats there was 0.012 per cent *more* GDP spent on sickness benefits in 1993. Hence Sweden, with an average of 76 per cent Left cabinet seats in the post-war era, is predicted to have 0.912 per cent of GDP more sickness benefit spending than the USA, which had no Left government (i.e. 76 × 0.012 = 0.912). The USA is also a federal country but Sweden is not, so that the total predicted difference between the USA at one extreme and Sweden at the other is 1.469 (i.e. 0.557 + 0.912).
- *Standard error*. This is a measure of the likely error in estimating the coefficient. For confidence in the estimate of the coefficient, the standard error should be less than half the value of the coefficient. In the table above, standard errors are around a third of the values of the coefficients.
- *t-value*. A summary statistic expressing the degree of confidence in the predicted relationship. t-values of 2 or more denote statistically significant relationships. We use t-values of 2 as our minimum cut-off point for including variables in our models. As noted in the text above, the kind of statistical analysis commonly found in the comparative public policy literature does not rest on inferences from a sample to the population from which it is drawn and, under these circumstances, the use of such measures of statistical confidence is somewhat problematical.
- *Adjusted R^2*. This states the degree to which the equation as a whole accounts for the variation in the dependent variable. It can be expressed in percentage terms. The figure here means that together federalism and leftist government account for 51 per cent of the cross-national variation in sickness expenditures in our 21 nations in 1993.

Readers to whom all or most of these terms are new won't take in these explanations all at once. For those who want to follow the equations in later appendices, I suggest you read through the material here each time you get to a new appendix. After only a few repetitions, you will find you have a very fair idea of the story told by each set of equations.

2. Economy and society

INTRODUCTION

Making sense of the very substantial changes that have occurred in public policy outcomes over the past half century requires that we locate such changes in the context of the no lesser transformation that has taken place in the basic parameters of Western societies in the post-war era. This chapter and the next seek to do that in two ways. The first is to examine aspects of these nations' economies, their societies and political systems, and to identify similarities and differences between them at various points in time and over time. The second is to offer an initial survey of theoretical accounts linking various types of societal transformation to various kinds of policy change. These two tasks are closely related. Theory provides us with a range of alternative hypotheses concerning the forces driving policy development. Acquiring an understanding of the similarities and differences between nations in respect of the major parameters of economic, social and political development constitutes an important first step in establishing how well these hypotheses fit the facts.

The discussion in these chapters focuses on the big picture rather than on minute detail. In part, such an approach is necessitated by the scale of what we are trying to do. Surveying half a century of economic, social and political change in just two chapters does not make it possible to dwell on the historical particularity of individual cases, but only allows the identification of patterns, shapes and trajectories of development. Were our interest in the minutiae of policy, such an approach would clearly be much too coarse-grained. However, the sort of policy changes we are interested in here are also large in scale: growth in the reach of the state, the emergence of the welfare state, substantial movements of labour force aggregates and major changes in the personal sphere. Comparative public policy research, at least as it has developed so far, has been largely a matter of trying to offer a convincing account of how one set of big pictures is connected to another set.

For those coming to this kind of research with a sociological background there will be a temptation to see a large part of the subject-matter

of both Chapter 2 and Chapter 3 in terms of the model of societal transformation proposed by modernization theory. In this account, major
economic, societal and political changes over a span of time far longer
than that under examination here are seen as being so closely interlinked
as to constitute a single process. Seen from this perspective, there is, in
effect, just one big picture. In this story, which is at the core of the sociology discipline's depiction of the course of change in the modern era, the
linkages with trajectories of public policy development are no less strong.
In broad brushstroke, the revolutionary overthrow of the *ancien régime*
together with the rise of the industrial mode of production fostered
urbanization and wealth creation on a new scale and set in motion occupational and demographic change. Together, these forces reshaped the
nature of political participation and political demands, leading ineluctably
to a massive extension of the role of the state. Although this picture allows
of different starting dates for societal modernization in different nations,
the remainder of the account is of basic similarities in pattern: of nations
embarked on a singular process of transformation, pursuing a more or
less common trajectory of change and in the process becoming more and
more alike (see Inkeles, 1981). The post-war era is generally regarded as
the period in which this process comes to fruition, when all the countries
we are dealing with here complete their transition to full modernity.

This view of the modernization process is not uncontested, even
amongst sociologists. Moving from the abstractions of theory to the
national differences revealed by comparative analysis makes the notion of
a singular process more problematic. In the words of what is, perhaps, the
most insightful sociological history of the post-war era, it suggests that
there may be diverse 'routes to and through modernity' (Therborn, 1995,
5). The data to be found in the comparative tables in this chapter and the
next make it possible for us to question some crucial implications of
modernization theory. They allow us to ask whether the post-war period
has been one in which the countries which started out behind in respect
of various economic, social and political factors have been catching up
with former leaders, whether there has been a general process of convergence amongst the advanced nations, and the extent to which change in
respect of one set of factors has been associated with change in another.
Establishing whether the basic thrust of post-war transformation has
pushed most nations along similar trajectories of development or
whether change has been compatible with continuing national diversity
provides much of the context required for understanding the character of
the forces impacting on public policy development in the post-war period.

The division between this chapter (Economy and society) and the next
(Institutions and ideology) marks the conventional boundary between

socio-economic and political accounts of public policy development. However, as already noted in Chapter 1, it would be quite inappropriate to regard the boundary as one between mutually exclusive versions of reality. On the one hand, the modernization thesis, which we seek to interrogate across these chapters, sees politics and policy as an integral part of a unilinear process originating in socio-economic development. On the other, a rejection of the notion of a single trajectory of socio-economic transformation should not be taken to imply that ideology and institutions explain everything. The position we start from here is that, in order to make sense of post-war policy development, it is vital to understand change across all these dimensions: economic and social as well as ideological and institutional.

A significant school of thought in the comparative public policy literature sometimes labelled itself the 'politics matters' school. This assertion of the consequentiality of politics was once extremely valuable as an antidote to the prevailing orthodoxy that policy was merely a function of socio-economic forces, but should never have been read as implying the no less absurd proposition that only politics matters. This study approaches its subject-matter on the basis of the intellectually daunting, although probably quite realistic, assumption that, in order to construct a comprehensive account of post-war policy transformation, potentially *everything matters*. Thus the distinction between economy and society and institutions and ideology is for convenience of exposition only. It helps us to categorize the factors that are important before we seek to combine them in novel ways to account for different varieties of policy outcomes.

THE LEGACY OF WORLD WAR II

A feature common to much quantitative research in both the modernization and 'politics matters' modes is a certain blindness to history. Comparative public policy analysis is itself a child of the post-war era, but, with exceptions found mainly in researches utilizing historical or qualitative approaches (see Rimlinger, 1971; Heclo, 1974; Flora and Heidenheimer, 1981; Weir and Skocpol, 1985; De Swaan, 1988; Baldwin, 1990), it often seems largely unaware of the world before its birth. The main reason for this neglect of the past is, of course, that research using quantitative methods has found it extremely difficult to obtain any purchase on a pre-war world in which governments did not see it as their responsibility to produce routine data of the kind that comparativists now rely on. However, even in the absence of such data, it is possible to say something about the policy impact of the single most important precursor of post-war policy outcomes, World War II itself.

World War II reshaped economy and society. Countries were forced to re-engineer their industries for military rather than domestic production. Prospects of future economic growth were sacrificed to investment in weapons of mass destruction. Patterns of international trade were disrupted and much diminished. Women became full-time workers in the factories so that men might leave for the battle fronts. Demographic structures were distorted as men died on the battlefield and those who were left behind chose not to bring children into a terrifying world. The war had a no lesser impact in the arena of public policy. Post-war change can be used as a benchmark. In recent decades, the main focus of comparative public policy research has been on what has been portrayed as an unparalleled expansion of the state, giving rise to a 75 per cent increase in public spending in the 35 years after 1960 (see Table 4.1 below). Yet, in just six years, between 1939 and 1945, in so far as rather fragmentary data permit sensible estimates, many of these nations experienced public spending increases of comparable or even greater dimensions (for comparative data, see Mitchell, 1992; for the British case, see Dunleavy, 1989).

Nor was this increased spending only for military purposes. As one of the few quantitative studies on the wartime experience points out, this was a period in which social security spending grew very markedly in many countries, a development which may be attributed to a greater willingness to share risks under circumstances of uncertainty (Goodin and Dryzek, 1987). Expenditures of whatever kind were, in any case, only the tip of the iceberg. For the duration of the war, manpower was almost totally at the command of the state, with youthful, adult, male cohorts generally conscripted for military service and older ones directed into vital war work. Production was highly regulated and consumption tightly controlled through strict systems of rationing. World War II repeated the experience of World War I, but on a larger scale, demonstrating that the era of 'total war' was, by the same token, an era of total public policy.

The end of 'total war' did not mean the end of a public policy shaped by the experience of war. On the one hand, the wartime experience had accustomed governments to a more interventionist role, so that the tasks of running a welfare state, which had seemed beyond most governments in the 1930s, now seemed almost routine (see De Swaan, 1988, 224). By much the same token, the fact that the wartime experience accustomed citizens to high levels of taxation has been seen as the basis for a 'displacement effect' enabling post-war governments to fund their increased spending for social purposes (Peacock and Wiseman, 1961; cf. Henrekson, 1993). On the other hand, with the termination of history's most destructive war came the challenge of getting nations back on a peacetime footing. For the non-European members of the Allied coalition, this was substantially a matter of demobilization: of returning the economy to its former uses and of getting men out of uniform and back into the factories, often at the cost of the employment prospects of women. For Britain, although also amongst the victors, it meant the larger task of rebuilding an economy almost wholly exhausted by the war effort, whilst for the defeated nations under military occupation, and the nations which had suffered under former Axis occupation, it meant a comprehensive process of reconstructing shattered economies, flattened urban infrastructures and, sometimes, entire political systems. Even for the countries which had been neutral, there was the challenge of rebuilding economies which had experienced six years of virtual autarky.

Demobilization apart, in all these tasks of post-war reconstruction governments were the key actors, elaborating policy responses variously shaped by the extent of wartime damage, their own interventionist proclivities and, for the former Axis powers, by the differing demands of the forces of Allied intervention. Government responses to the tasks of post-war reconstruction also shaped labour market decisions and personal choices in the domestic sphere. As we shall later see, in some countries the enormity of the task of post-war reconstruction led to higher levels of female labour force participation. In others, it is possible that women's retreat from the labour force was one of the factors contributing to the post-war 'baby boom'. Thus the question for this study is not whether the war had a major impact on policy outcomes, but whether that impact was sufficiently lasting to show up in an analysis of levels and changes in outcomes which only systematically uses data for a period starting in 1960.

To make it possible for us to explore that possibility in later chapters, Table 2.1 provides two different measures of the way in which the wartime experience impacted on these nations. The first measure, labelled 'war impact', seeks to capture the severity of the wartime experience in destroying the fabric of society and, hence, to provide an indication of the size of the task of post-war reconstruction. The war impact scale has four values. It gives a score of 0 for the countries which were non-combatants during the war, 1 for the countries which were in the victorious Allied coalition, 2 for countries occupied by Axis forces during the course of the war and 3 for the defeated Axis nations. The characterizations underlying this scale are very simple. The non-combatant countries are seen as suffering the least disruption because they did not suffer loss of life or property as an immediate consequence of hostilities. Like the non-combatant nations, the Allies were not occupied by hostile forces, but victory had very real costs in lives and national resources. In general, the occupied nations suffered greater dislocation than the Allies because their sovereignty was abrogated and their territory fought over to varying degrees. Finally, the Axis powers

Comparative public policy

Table 2.1   War impact, real national income per capita and economic growth rates, 1937–50

Country	War impact	1937	1950	Growth rate: 1937–50
Australia	1	500	6678	3.3
Canada	1	515	6380	3.5
Ireland	0	347	2730	1.8
New Zealand	1	745	6667	1.9
UK	1	637	5395	−0.5
USA	1	707	8772	3.1
Denmark	2	566	5263	0.9
Finland	3	277	3506	1.6
Norway	2	385	4358	1.4
Sweden	0	449	5807	2.6
Austria	3	220	2930	1.1
Belgium	2	359	4433	2.8
France	2	344	4045	2.6
Germany	3	475	3421	−4.6
Italy	3	181	2743	2.3
Netherlands	2	457	4532	0.8
Greece	2	200	1409	−1.6
Portugal	0	127	1208	1.3
Spain	0	278	1913	3.0
Switzerland	0	427	6813	3.1
Japan	3	224	1430	−1.1
Mean		401	4306	1.4
Correlation with 1937			0.86	0.12
Coefficient of variation		43.05	48.28	

Source and notes: War impact is operationalized as described in the text. Clark (1957) published estimates of both 1937 and 1950 national income per head of the population. The 1937 data, expressed in Clark's international units are from that source. The data for 1950 are from Summers and Heston (1991) and are for real gross domestic product (GDP) per capita in constant dollars (expressed in international prices, base 1985). These data are given in preference to Clark's figures, in order to be consistent with the GDP data for the rest of the post-war period in Table 2.2. 1937–50 average annual growth rates are calculated by the author on the basis of Clark's original figures.

were both occupied and defeated, whilst, to varying degrees, their constitutional and domestic policy autonomy were constrained by Allied control during the early post-war years. Of course, there are shadings at the edges. We have already noted that Britain was more economically depleted than other Allied nations and some occupied countries had a far worse war than others, with Greece, arguably, at one extreme and Denmark at the other. In general, though, the higher the score on the scale, the worse the wartime experience and more formidable the task of post-war reconstruction.

The second method we use to measure the repercussions of the wartime experience employs the only available source (Clark, 1957) for pre-war national income levels for all the countries in our sample in order to calculate these countries' economic growth rates for the period 1937–50 (for method of calculation see sources and notes to Table 2.1 and Castles, 1991). These data appear in the final column of Table 2.1 and provide a picture which partly coincides with the assumptions built into the war impact variable, but which also demonstrate other forces at work. For instance, as one might expect, the overseas English-speaking nations generally did very well in economic terms during this period because they suffered no direct infrastructure damage. However, New Zealand is an exception, foreshadowing that country's subsequent long-term decline in economic performance. Several of the non-combatant countries had relatively high wartime growth rates, but Portugal and Ireland, stranded on the European peripheries, in a world in which trade links were disrupted, manifested a less buoyant performance. At the other end of the spectrum, Germany and Japan, the leading Axis powers, had still not recovered their 1937 positions by 1950, but the same was also true of Britain and Greece. Italy, which shifted from the Axis to the Allied side during the course of the war, experienced a higher level of economic growth than the other defeated nations. Amongst the occupied nations, we find considerable variability in performance, with Belgium, at one extreme, growing very rapidly, whilst the Netherlands, at the other extreme, recovered far more slowly.

What is quite clear, however, is that the overall pattern of economic development that occurred over the wartime period was rather different from that assumed by modernization theory. The modernization thesis highlights the importance of processes of catch-up and convergence. Neither are evident from the statistics in Table 2.1. In fact, the modest correlation of 0.12 between the level of real national income per capita in 1937 and subsequent economic growth shows that, during the course of World War II and its immediate aftermath, the economies of the richer nations were actually growing somewhat faster than those of the poorer nations. Given that the richer countries in 1937 were the English-speaking settler states, this is not really surprising. Moreover, the slightly increased coefficient of variation for real national income per capita in 1950 shows that the wartime experience had actually made these 21 countries somewhat less alike in economic terms during these years.

Most interestingly of all, there is strong evidence to suggest that this divergent pattern of economic development was not a wartime aberration, but represented the continuation of a trend dating back into the late nineteenth century (for relevant data on 16 of these nations, see Maddison, 1991, 130). Thus it would appear that, whilst many nations were becoming more economically developed over the course of the first half of the twentieth century, there is little support for the notion that a more general process of economic modernization was taking place prior to World War II. In the next section, we examine economic performance after 1950 in order to see whether modernization theory provides a more satisfactory account of the development trends manifested by the post-war economy.

POST-WAR ECONOMIC GROWTH

For most commentators, the characterization of post-war change as a radical transformation derives from the unprecedented pace of post-war economic growth in the decades from 1950 to the mid-1970s. For the period 1950–60, the average growth rate of real gross domestic product (GDP) per capita for our 21 nations was 3.3 per cent per annum and, between 1960 and 1974, it accelerated further to 4.1 per cent. Thereafter, growth slowed appreciably to 1.7 per cent per annum for the period 1974–92. Over the entire period from 1960 to the early 1990s, the figure was the 2.8 per cent per annum shown in the final column of Table 2.2. Per capita growth of GDP was, to a considerable degree, a reflection of an increased rate of growth in productivity measured in terms of real output per worker, which, for these same countries, was 3.8 per cent per annum both in the 1950–60 and 1960–74 periods, declining to 1.5 per cent between 1974 and 1990. The result of growth rates as high as those of the earlier post-war decades was a massive increase in average per capita incomes and productivity levels, with a threefold increase in both over the four decades after 1950. The figures cited above are all calculated from Summers and Heston (1991), the source of the 1950 data in Table 2.1 and all the data in Table 2.2. A comparison with the pre-war growth rates illustrates the extent of the post-war acceleration. For a 16-nation sample (our cases minus Greece, Ireland, New Zealand, Portugal and Spain), average growth of per capita income of 3.8 per cent per annum between 1950 and 1973 contrasts with figures of 0.9 per cent for the period 1820 to 1870, 1.4 per cent between 1870 and 1913 and 1.2 per cent between 1913 and 1950 (Maddison, 1991, 49). These figures suggest that there was a greater quantum of economic development in these countries in the four post-war decades than in the entire 130 years preceding them.

Table 2.2   Levels and growth rates of real GDP per capita in constant dollars (expressed in international prices, base 1985), 1960–early 1990s

Country	1960	1974	Early 1990s	Growth rate: 1960–early 1990s
Australia	7782	11391	14458	1.9
Canada	7258	12225	16362	2.5
Ireland	3311	5711	9637	3.3
New Zealand	7960	11088	11363	1.1
UK	5823	9411	12724	2.4
USA	9895	14078	17945	1.9
Denmark	6760	10428	14091	2.3
Finland	5291	9614	12000	2.6
Norway	5610	9461	15518	3.2
Sweden	7592	11697	13986	1.9
Austria	5143	8974	12955	2.9
Belgium	5495	9871	13484	2.8
France	5823	10510	13918	2.7
Germany	6570	10211	14709	2.5
Italy	4564	8669	12721	3.2
Netherlands	6077	10375	13281	2.4
Greece	2093	4967	6790	3.7
Portugal	1869	4645	7470	4.3
Spain	3123	7291	9802	3.6
Switzerland	9409	14091	15887	1.6
Japan	2954	8295	15105	5.1
Mean	5733	9667	13057	2.8
Correlation with 1960		0.96	0.76	−0.88
Coefficient of variation	38.65	26.26	21.50	

Source and notes: Data for 1960 and 1974 from Summers and Heston (1991). The data-point for the early 1990s is 1992 and is from an upate of the Summers and Heston dataset (Penn World Tables Mark 5.6). Growth rates are average year-to-year percentage changes as calculated by the author.

Looking at the figures in Table 2.2, it is possible to discern patterns related to families of nations. In 1960, the four English-speaking nations of European settlement, Australia, Canada, New Zealand and the USA, were all amongst the richest countries in the OECD. This represented the remains of an older historical pattern where Britain, the country of the original industrial revolution, had exported her wealth through trade to nations, substantially of British settler stock, which demanded the products of her factories and/or supplied them with raw materials. This pattern is even more pronounced in the data for 1937 and 1950 contained in Table 2.1. At the opposite extreme from the overseas English-speaking nations in 1950, there was a clearly identifiable grouping of poor Southern European nations which, together with Japan and Ireland, had the lowest per capita incomes in the group. This contrast of the rich English-speaking nations with average per capita incomes of over US$6500 in 1950 and the poor Southern European ones with average per capita incomes of around US$1500 dramatically illustrates the huge divergence of starting-points for economic modernization in the early post-war period.

After 1960, the English-speaking family of nations ceased to have such a distinct identity as previously. This was because all these nations manifested rates of economic growth below the OECD mean, with New Zealand experiencing the poorest growth performance in the OECD. On the other hand, Southern Europe maintained its profile as a low-income area, despite growth rates that very substantially exceeded the OECD average. That the high-income nations of 1960 grew less rapidly than the norm and that the low-income nations grew much more rapidly shows that catch-up was now occurring on a major scale, as demonstrated by the very strong negative correlation of –0.88 between 1960 GDP per capita and subsequent per capita growth. Interestingly, this catch-up trajectory did not make very much difference to the per capita income league table, even over a period of more than three decades. Only three countries changed position very markedly between 1960 and 1992. New Zealand dropped from the top to the bottom third of the distribution. Japan, the country with much the best post-war record of economic growth, made the reverse transition and Norway, reaping the fruits of the discovery of North Sea oil, moved from twelfth to fourth in the rank order.

Catch-up was also accompanied by a considerable degree of convergence. Over the post-war period, the countries became more tightly bunched in terms of relative income levels, as shown by the continuous decline in the coefficient of variation from the 1950 column in Table 2.1 through to the early 1990s column in Table 2.2. A simple way of understanding what this means is in terms of changes in the relative dispersion of values. In 1950, the average per capita GDP of the top third of the distribution was approximately 3.25 times that of the bottom third; in 1992, it was only around 1.5 times greater. The story for productivity is similar to that for GDP per capita, although the initial dispersion of values in 1950 was marginally greater and the final dispersion slightly smaller. Over the post-war period as a whole, and very much in line with the predictions of modernization theory, the countries of Western capitalism became far more alike in terms of both income and productivity.

The idea that policy outcomes are likely to be influenced by levels of and changes in economic development is one which has commonly been discussed in the comparative literature. Wagner's law that the demand for public goods is 'income-elastic', that is, that such demands increase as individuals and nations become more affluent, has already been mentioned and has been an important focus of debate and further elaboration (Musgrave 1969; Gemmell, 1993). As with every hypothesis in the area, this one is not uncontested. A plausible counter-argument suggests that countries experiencing rapid economic growth will, all else being equal, experience proportionately lower spending increases, because in high-growth economies a given level of demand for services can be met with a lower share of national income (Wildavsky, 1975). Although strictly speaking Wagner's law relates only to the impact of economic growth on public expenditure development, a relationship of a similar kind in respect of levels of expenditure has also frequently been hypothesized, that is, that more affluent countries will experience a greater demand for public goods than poorer ones.

Despite the frequency with which such views have been advanced, there seems to be little evidence of a direct link between affluence and public expenditure, at least as manifested within the grouping of advanced industrial states (see Castles, 1982). A possible reason for this failure to discern what is often presented as an obvious connection between spending and resource availability may lie in the fact that the relationship between affluence and state intervention has been a historically contingent one. The societies which first became affluent in the latter part of the nineteenth century generally tended not to become welfare state innovators because they did not have resort to the standard repertoire of interventionist responses which has become commonplace in the twentieth century. Instead, they were frequently pioneers of voluntary (trade union and friendly society) and market initiatives to protect against the risks of sickness, unemployment and old age, and these private responses were, to some extent, institutionalized as lasting preferences of political élites. For nations becoming affluent in the twentieth century, statist responses may well have been more natural, but evidence of a link between economic development and public spending may well be masked by the fact that the rich 'liberal' states of the late nineteenth century remained in the vanguard of Western affluence throughout the post-war era. This is a possibility explored in some detail in the later chapters on public expenditure development.

The potential impacts of greater affluence and higher rates of economic growth are not, of course, restricted to the public expenditure arena. Because increased income gives a greater command of resources, it provides individuals and societies with the potential to satisfy needs and/or fulfil preferences to a greater degree than previously. This applies to all the policy areas discussed in later chapters. Higher incomes make it possible for individuals to satisfy demands for owner-occupied housing, and this may lead to a change in the way housing policies are framed. Moreover, income elasticity applies to demands other than those for public goods, with greater preferences for leisure at higher income levels an obvious candidate to account for male labour force decline in recent decades. It also seems very probable that higher levels of family income, either as a consequence of increased real wages and/or greater female labour force participation, have served to empower women in decisions concerning the fundamentals of family life: decisions to have children and decisions to terminate unsatisfactory marriages. Later analysis will demonstrate that the policy consequences of economic modernization are often far less direct than is implied by these hypotheses. Nevertheless, the sheer magnitude of post-war economic change makes an assessment of its influence a priority in most areas of policy development.

TRADE AMONGST NATIONS

International trade has not featured conspicuously in modernization theory's account of the genesis of a modern public policy. In a way this is strange, since the theory of comparative advantage, which economists see as providing the rationale for trade amongst nations, rests on precisely the same kind of logic of increasing differentiation and specialization that sociologists see as impelling the modernization process more generally. That trade growth has not been centrally located as an aspect of modernization does not mean that international trade has been ignored by theorists of policy development. On the contrary, in the 1970s and mid-1980s, it featured as a significant factor in accounts which contested the primacy of socio-economic forces in policy determination, whilst, more recently, it has been identified as a factor inducing nations to modify their public policies in such a way as to maximize economic competitiveness. In this latter context, increases in international trade and in international capital movements have been seen as twin forces promoting a globalization of the economy which markedly constrains the policy-making autonomy of the nation-state.

Both kinds of theoretical account point to the way in which international trade has impinged on post-war domestic politics, but, that apart, their stories are very different. During the 1970s, and until the mid-1980s, the emphasis was on political responses to economic vulnerability. Like contemporary globalization theory, this argument began from the idea that countries which traded extensively in international markets were not masters in their own house. However, rather than seeing the natural response of governments as accommodation to the demands of the market, the earlier view was that vulnerable economic actors would fight back. They would use political channels – in particular, trade unions and parties – to press governments for compensation for those who lost their jobs or who worked in industries made progressively less viable by international competition. Governments and business would also see it as in their interests to protect the domestic economy. Governments would provide retraining programmes designed to give workers the skills required for export competitiveness, and big business would actively collaborate in a process that made for a satisfied workforce and facilitated access to overseas markets. In short, countries substantially exposed to international trade would experience a greater expansion of the public economy than those which did not and this would come about not through the operation of market forces, but as a consequence of purposive political action (Cameron, 1978; Katzenstein, 1985).

The story from the mid-1980s onwards does not necessarily deny this prior account of the impact of trade, but notes its historical contingency. Where once the growth of international trade may have promoted a consensual relationship between labour and business, new conditions, including the growth of manufacturing in developing nations, the emergence of new technologies and a reduction in the cost of international transactions, have tended to split this alliance apart (see Gourevitch, 1986; Frieden and Rogowski, 1996; Rodrik, 1997). Rather than high labour costs being the price that business was ready to pay for domestic stabilization, as had been the case in the early post-war decades, cost minimization has now become the objective of a ruthless campaign of rationalization to be effected through downsizing in the private sector and cut-backs and privatization in the public sector. With the argument that resistance to these pressures can only bring about a decline in national economic competitiveness, the labour movement has been forced on to the defensive and governments of all political complexions find themselves in a position where, as Margaret Thatcher once put it, 'there is no alternative'.

In Table 2.3, we provide figures for imports plus exports as a percentage of GDP, which is the standard measure of exposure to international trade used in the comparative public policy literature. These data demonstrate clearly that international trade has increased massively in the period under review, a finding seemingly compatible with the notion that trade is an integral aspect of economic modernization. However, there is little else to support such a conclusion. Evidence from another source (Maddison, 1991, 326–7) suggests that, for many of these nations, post-war trade expansion was only a matter of returning to a pre-World War I situation, which had been undermined by inter-war protectionism.

Moreover, the data in Table 2.3 demonstrate no obvious signs of correspondence with the pattern of economic development shown in Table 2.2. Most conspicuously, affluent nations, like the USA and Australia, and more recently Japan, have been amongst the OECD nations least involved in international trade. Finally, there has been absolutely no tendency for the degree of trade exposure of these nations to become more similar over time or to manifest any catch-up tendency of the kind that would follow if it were really true that the growth of international trade has been part of a coherent process of socio-economic modernization.

Indeed, precisely contrary to such expectations, it was in two of the earlier period's most trade-exposed nations, Belgium and Ireland, that trade increased most rapidly thereafter. The fact that these two countries started out in the vanguard of trade development, and yet increased their relative trade exposure with passing decades, points up the major source of difference between nations in respect of participation in international trade; namely, that large-scale exposure to trade is substantially a function of a small population size and, hence, of a restricted domestic market. This inverse relationship between market size and trade development is a well-known phenomenon, also accounting for the USA's and Japan's low degrees of trade exposure, and explicable in terms of the far greater need of smaller nations to extend their potential markets by means of export specialization (Dahl and Tufte, 1973, 130). The countries which diverge most from this inverse pattern – Australia and New Zealand – are nations in which tariffs have been used historically to foster domestic manufacturing. Because our families of nations are relatively heterogeneous in terms of population size, international trade is not an area in which such commonalities are readily observed.

Apart from the massive overall increase in post-war trade, the other major point to note in Table 2.3 is the unevenness of that development. Of the 16.4 percentage points average increase in trade exposure between 1960 and 1993, all but 1.6 percentage points of the increase occurred before 1974. This is a pattern of development which does not fit very well with either of the contending theories linking trade patterns to expenditure development.

Table 2.3 Levels and changes in international trade (imports plus exports of goods and services as a percentage of GDP), 1960–early 1990s

Country	1960	1974	Early 1990s	Change: 1960–early 1990s
Australia	30.6	31.9	38.9	8.3
Canada	35.6	49.8	59.8	24.2
Ireland	66.5	96.1	122.7	56.2
New Zealand	46.2	55.5	59.8	13.6
UK	43.2	61.0	52.2	9.0
USA	9.6	17.3	21.9	12.3
Denmark	65.6	66.5	61.6	−4.0
Finland	45.7	58.7	60.8	15.1
Norway	76.9	86.9	70.3	−6.6
Sweden	46.0	64.4	61.8	15.8
Austria	49.3	66.4	73.4	24.1
Belgium	77.7	122.0	132.8	55.1
France	30.1	42.4	41.8	14.9
Germany	29.9	45.3	43.8	10.7
Italy	26.5	44.5	43.0	16.5
Netherlands	90.9	102.2	95.3	4.4
Greece	21.8	35.1	44.0	22.2
Portugal	36.1	60.5	60.4	24.3
Spain	16.2	33.6	39.4	23.2
Switzerland	58.9	67.0	68.0	9.1
Japan	20.9	27.9	16.7	−4.2
Mean	44.0	58.8	60.4	16.4
Correlation with 1960		0.93	0.83	0.10
Coefficient of variation	49.9	44.38	47.15	

Source and notes: Data from OECD, *Historical Statistics*, Paris, 1966. The data-point for the early 1990s is 1993. The figure reported in the final column is the percentage point change over the entire period.

Theories which see trade as the key to expansion of the public economy need to explain why the public economy went on expanding after 1974, even though trade did not. Theories which imply that recent globalization trends have been fuelled by dramatic increases in world trade since the early 1970s (see Milner and Keohane, 1996) need to explain why such increases are not apparent in the standard OECD dataset which is the basis for the figures in Table 2.3. Nor, in the absence of major overall increases in trade, can postulated globalization trends be attributed to changes in the pattern of variation amongst countries. After 1974, there is almost no change in the ordering of countries on the trade league-table, with a correlation between 1974 and 1993 international trade levels of no less than 0.95. Under these circumstances, any evidence that may be forthcoming of a negative relationship between trade exposure and public expenditure development should probably be interpreted as much in terms of changing policy responses as of changing economic realities.

OCCUPATIONAL STRUCTURE

At the same time as the Western economies were growing at an unprecedented rate and trading a vastly increased national product to a degree unmatched since before World War I, their occupational structures were undergoing a complex process of transformation. This is indicated by the figures in Table 2.4, which show levels and changes in agricultural, manufacturing and services employment as percentages of civilian employment in the OECD nations. This transformation in the occupational sphere was scarcely on a lesser scale than growth in the economy, once we take into account the fact that the measuring rod for income is unbounded (in principle, real GDP per capita can grow indefinitely), whilst there is a limit to the possible decline in agricultural employment (to 0 per cent) or increase in services employment (to 100 per cent). Over the period as a whole, agricultural employment went down by more than two thirds and manufacturing employment by more than a quarter. Services employment, on the other hand, increased by over 50 per cent, so that in 1993 two out of every three workers in the OECD were employed in this sector and there was no country which had less than 50 per cent of its workforce in services production. Occupational changes in both agriculture and services were continuing processes, whilst the decline in manufacturing employment occurred only after 1974. Given that the rate of productivity increase in manufacturing is markedly higher than in services (Baumol, 1967), the relatively high level of employment in manufacturing in the early post-war decades can be seen as the key to the sustained economic growth of that period. By the same token, it was clearly not coincidental that the shift out of manufacturing from the mid-1970s onwards has been associated with a marked decline in economic growth.

Table 2.4 Levels and changes in the structure of employment, 1960–early 1990s

Country	AG 1960	AG 1974	AG 1993	AG 1960–93	MAN 1960	MAN 1974	MAN 1993	MAN 1960–93	SER 1960	SER 1974	SER 1993	SER 1960–93
Australia	11.0	6.9	5.3	−5.7	30.7	25.1	13.2	−17.5	50.1	58.0	71.0	20.9
Canada	13.2	6.3	4.3	−8.9	24.6	21.7	14.3	−10.3	54.1	63.2	73.5	19.4
Ireland	37.3	22.8	12.7	−24.6	17.2	21.7	17.7	0.5	39.0	44.6	59.7	20.7
New Zealand	14.6	10.9	10.6	−4.0	26.4	25.7	15.1	−11.3	46.7	52.9	66.0	19.3
UK	4.7	2.8	2.2	−2.5	38.4	34.6	20.2	−18.2	47.6	55.2	71.6	24.0
USA	8.5	4.2	2.7	−5.8	26.5	24.2	16.0	−10.5	56.2	63.3	73.2	17.0
Denmark	18.2	9.6	5.2	−13.0	25.1	21.4	21.0	−4.1	44.9	58.1	68.5	23.6
Finland	35.2	16.3	8.6	−26.6	27.9	29.0	23.1	−4.8	32.2	47.7	64.4	32.2
Norway	21.6	10.6	5.6	−16.0	25.6	23.7	14.4	−11.2	42.8	55.1	71.3	28.5
Sweden	15.7	6.7	3.4	−12.3	31.5	28.3	17.2	−14.3	44.0	56.3	71.1	27.1
Austria	22.6	11.4	7.0	−15.6	31.3	32.4	24.0	−7.3	37.1	46.3	57.9	20.8
Belgium	8.7	3.8	2.6	−6.1	30.6	31.2	21.6	−9.0	46.3	55.2	67.9	21.6
France	22.5	10.6	5.1	−17.4	27.3	28.3	19.1	−8.2	39.9	50.0	67.2	27.3
Germany	14.0	7.0	3.5	−10.5	34.3	35.8	27.1	−7.2	39.0	46.3	57.9	18.9
Italy	32.6	17.5	7.5	−25.1	24.2	28.0	22.9	−1.3	33.5	43.2	59.6	26.1
Netherlands	9.8	5.7	3.9	−5.9	29.7	25.7	16.4	−13.3	49.7	58.4	71.5	21.8
Greece	57.1	36.0	21.3	−35.8	11.6	18.5	15.6	4.0	25.5	36.2	54.5	29.0
Portugal	43.9	34.9	11.3	−32.6	22.6	24.9	20.6	−2.0	24.8	31.3	55.7	30.9
Spain	38.7	23.2	10.1	−28.6	23.0	26.3	17.4	−5.6	31.0	39.6	59.2	28.2
Switzerland	14.5	7.5	4.3	−10.2	37.6	35.0	23.6	−14.0	39.1	48.2	66.8	27.7
Japan	30.2	12.9	5.9	−24.3	21.3	27.2	23.7	2.4	41.3	50.1	59.8	18.5
Mean	22.6	12.7	6.8	−15.8	27.0	27.2	19.2	−7.8	41.2	50.4	65.2	24.0
Correlation with 1960		0.96	0.88	−0.98		0.84	0.33	−0.8		0.96	0.86	−0.7
Coefficient of variation	61.04	73.95	65.9		23.26	16.86	20.33		20.72	16.79	9.6	

Source and notes: AG = Agricultural employment; MAN = Manufacturing employment; SER = Services employment. All measured as percentages of civilian employment. 1960–93 values are percentage point changes between 1960 and 1993. From OECD (1996a).

The families of nations apparent *circa* 1960 are rather similar to those which we saw in the context of economic development. Poor Southern Europe is also agricultural Southern Europe, with Greece, Portugal and Spain having the highest proportions of the population working on the land, the lowest in services and amongst the lowest in manufacturing. The English-speaking group is not as tightly bunched in respect of agriculture or manufacturing, but is very clearly defined in respect of services. In 1960, the USA, Canada, Australia, the United Kingdom and New Zealand featured amongst the six countries with the highest levels of services employment. Much in line with the thrust of the hypotheses of modernization theory, the countries which had been first made rich by industrialization were the first to become fully fledged service economies.

Just as in the case of economic development, the enormous changes taking place in the agricultural and service sectors over the period did little to change countries' positions relative to each other, although, once more, there was a dilution of the distinctiveness of the English-speaking group. In the case of agriculture, this was because agricultural employment in New Zealand declined more slowly than in most other countries. In the case of services, it was because a Scandinavian grouping of Norway, Sweden and Denmark joined the English-speaking nations in the services vanguard. The coherence of the Southern European family also declined somewhat – Spain is no longer amongst the more agricultural nations and Portugal has a major manufacturing sector – but in respect of the leading services sector of the modern economy, these countries, together with Greece, remained amongst the OECD's most conspicuous laggards.

The area where massive change did occur was in manufacturing, where a correlation of only 0.33 between 1960 and 1993 employment levels suggests a world of work transformed almost beyond recognition. From early in the nineteenth century until well after World War II, a group of continental and Northwest European nations had constituted the engine-room of the emergent industrial society built on the basis of factory production, with the final climax of European industrialization taking place in the 1950s and 1960s (Ambrosius and Hubbard, 1989, 183–92). Now things were beginning to change, with a move southwards in Europe as well as the beginnings of a shift towards Asia–Pacific. In this process of transformation, many countries moved from the top to the bottom of the distribution and vice versa. Britain, once the 'workshop of the world', was, perhaps, the most notable instance of decline, but other countries making a downward shift of roughly comparable dimensions included Sweden and the Netherlands. The country which most radically improved its position was Japan, followed by Italy and Portugal. In the European heartland, only Austria, Germany and Switzerland stand out against this trend, being amongst the leading nations of manufacturing employment throughout the period. The possibility of a family-type affinity between the German-speaking nations was noted in passing in Chapter 1, and it may well be significant that research identifying such a pattern of historical and cultural likeness focuses primarily on aspects of labour market behaviour (von Rhein-Kress, 1993; Schmidt, 1993).

The summary statistics in Table 2.4 illustrate beautifully the difference between catch-up and convergence as defined here. Agricultural employment manifests an almost perfect catch-up trajectory, meaning that the countries of high agricultural employment in 1960 consistently displayed a greater decrease in such employment than the countries with lower levels. This catch-up led to a narrowing of the absolute gap in values between countries from over 50 percentage points (Greece and the UK) to less than 20 (these same countries). However, in the sense used here, the picture for the OECD as a whole is one of minor divergence rather than convergence, since the positions of the countries relative to the mean had actually widened marginally. Manufacturing is also an instance of marked catch-up conjoined with only a marginal diminution in the relative dispersion of cases. At the other end of the spectrum, the degree of catch-up in respect of services employment was less pronounced, but convergence was very considerable indeed, with an already quite moderate coefficient of variation in 1960 halved by 1993.

Whether we should be more impressed by the continuing divergence of the agricultural and manufacturing remnants in advanced societies or the clear evidence of convergence in the widely dominant services sector depends on the focus of interest. Whilst the pattern of transformation revealed by Table 2.4 is quite compatible with a modernization interpretation, the salience of these trajectories of change to policy development clearly depends on the kinds of mechanisms by which occupational factors are linked to outcomes. One set of linkages is around the labour market. Clearly, it makes sense to think of the occupational composition of employment as being related to the size of the labour force and to the availability of work. Hypotheses linking the size of the male labour force to the dominance of manufacturing, and the growth of unemployment since the 1970s to the decline in manufacturing (Rowthorn and Glyn, 1990) seem obvious enough. If demonstrated, we might expect to locate trajectories of labour market development reflecting the continuing cross-national diversity of the manufacturing sector. On the other hand, post-war growth of the female labour force seems likely to be associated with the emergence of the services sector as the primary source of employment for women. This latter effect is also potentially influential with respect to outcomes in the personal sphere, where changes in the prevailing mode of work organization may be a source of changed attitudes to family roles and responsibilities (see Goode, 1963, 58–9). In these instances, the presumption must be of convergent patterns of development. Lastly, it seems possible that changes in the employment structure may also be associated with housing preferences, with the initial influx of labour into the new and overcrowded manufacturing centres being gradually reversed as industrialism, in turn, produced a view of the home 'as a sanctuary to escape from the workplace' and a consequent demand for private home ownership in the suburbs (see Duncan, 1981).

Linkages between occupational structure and outcomes will be examined in later chapters on the labour market and the role of policy in the realm of the personal. Occupational structure does not, however, feature in our later statistical analysis of the determinants of public spending and taxing and the rise of the welfare state. To argue that changes in the occupational structure influence patterns of public spending is to reverse the true order of causality. It is the increased spending of the state, particularly in the areas of education, health and welfare, which has been one of the most potent forces contributing to the growth of the services sector in certain countries. Hence, it is not the fact that the Scandinavian countries have become a part of the services employment vanguard that has made them into advanced welfare states. Rather it is the fact that these countries have vastly expanded public sector welfare employment which has made them exemplars of what can properly be described as the (social) services society.

URBANIZATION

There can be no doubt that urbanization, the shift of population from the countryside to the towns, is a phenomenon which has been closely linked to the process of industrialization. In Europe during the nineteenth century, population increase combined with enhanced agricultural productivity led to a mass migration from the countryside to the new centres of factory production (Stearns, 1967). However, other factors have also been important, including the role of urban settlements as a focus for trade, commerce, banking and public administration. These other factors sometimes predate and often cross-cut the patterns of settlement produced by industrialization, so that cross-national variation in levels of urban density cannot always be easily understood in terms of a unidimensional thrust to modernity. As Table 2.5 shows, the original centres of European industrialization, the United Kingdom and Belgium,

Table 2.5   Levels of and change in the percentage of the population living in urban areas, 1960–early 1990s

Country	1960	Mid–1970s	Early 1990s	Change: 1960–early 1990s
Australia	80.6	85.9	85.5	4.9
Canada	68.9	75.6	77.1	8.2
Ireland	45.8	53.6	57.1	11.2
New Zealand	76.0	82.8	84.0	8.0
UK	85.7	88.7	89.1	3.4
USA	70.0	73.7	75.0	5.0
Denmark	73.7	81.8	87.0	13.3
Finland	38.1	58.3	59.7	21.6
Norway	49.9	68.2	75.0	25.1
Sweden	72.6	82.7	84.0	11.4
Austria	49.9	53.2	58.4	8.4
Belgium	92.5	94.5	96.9	4.5
France	62.4	73.0	74.3	11.9
Germany	77.4	80.1	86.3	8.9
Italy	59.4	65.6	68.9	9.6
Netherlands	85.0	88.4	88.5	3.5
Greece	42.9	55.3	62.5	19.6
Portugal	22.1	27.7	33.6	11.5
Spain	56.6	69.6	78.4	21.8
Switzerland	51.0	55.8	59.9	8.9
Japan	62.5	75.7	77.0	14.5
Mean	63.0	71.0	74.2	11.2
Correlation with 1960		0.96	0.94	−0.62
Coefficient of variation	28.35	22.51	19.94	

Source and notes: Data are from United Nations, *World Urbanization Prospects*, New York, 1991. No standard definition of urbanization is offered in this source which reports data collected according to national definitions. The data-point for the early 1990s is 1990. The figure reported in the final column is the percentage point change over the entire period.

remained the OECD's most urban nations throughout the second half of the twentieth century. Germany, which industrialized somewhat later, but very rapidly, also features in the leading group. On the other hand, there are obvious exceptions: the Netherlands, highly urbanized through trade and commerce long before the advent of factory production, and Australia and New Zealand, countries in which port cities were the locus of initial settlement and subsidized thereafter by the surplus produced by the export of primary produce.

There are no obvious families of nations here or, indeed, at the other, rural, end of the spectrum. Portugal and Greece are amongst the six nations with less than 50 per cent of the population living in towns in 1960, but the other nations are Finland, Ireland, Norway and Austria, suggesting a phenomenon of the European peripheries rather than of industrial backwaters. According to the data, Switzerland and Austria remained relatively rural throughout the post-war decades, despite being, as we saw in the previous section, amongst the countries with the largest manufacturing base. Spain, Italy and France, the urban civilizations of the European Enlightenment, cluster together just below the mean of the 1960 distribution.

In terms of the absolute quantum of change taking place over the period, the figures shown in Table 2.5 suggest a transformation of lesser proportions than in respect of either economic development or occupational structure, with an average increase in urbanization over the period as a whole of less than 20 per cent. This was not because urbanization lagged behind, but because in many countries it was largely complete, with the initial European influx into the towns having taken place between 1870 and 1910 (Flora, 1986, xiii), a process of uneven development characterizing the inter-war period and a strong convergent trend emerging in the immediate post-war years (Ambrosius and Hubbard, 1989, 37–41).

However, much depends on measurement. Urbanization figures represent thresholds (that is, numbers living in areas of a certain minimum population density), so it is perfectly possible for urban density to increase without any apparent increase in measured levels of urbanization; in particular, as a consequence of people moving from small to larger towns. This, certainly, was an important phenomenon of the post-war years in many countries. In 1950, only seven European countries had more than a quarter of their population living in large towns; by 1980, only Ireland, of the countries featuring in this study, had not achieved such a level of urban concentration (Ambrosius and Hubbard, 1989, 40). Taking the figures in Table 2.5 at face value, what we can say is that, by the end of the period, with the exception of Portugal, the urbanization process was more or less complete, with well over a majority of the population living in towns. Whilst this ascendancy of the urban way of life did not much alter the rank order of these nations over time or lead to catch-up of major proportions, a decline of around 30 per cent in the coefficient of variation over the period suggests that, in these threshold terms at least, the countries were becoming considerably more alike (cf. Kaelble, 1989, 60–62).

Urbanization is a standard sociological variable often linked with aspects of policy development and the rise of the interventionist state. Indeed, an increase in urban density was prominent amongst the forces Alfred Wagner saw as driving the growth of government: urban life gave rise to new social problems and heightened social tensions, and would result in an increased intensity of public activity (Wildavsky, 1985, 234). Examples familiar to Wagner would have been the growth of a medical inspectorate to enforce standards of public hygiene and the creation of an urban police force to provide public order. Urbanization was also the fillip for the emergence of city government as a provider of such collective goods as pavements, clean water, sewerage, elementary education and the like (De Swaan, 1988, 126–7). Over the past century, the urban services role has expanded further to take in new functions, including gas and electricity generation, public transport, town planning, slum clearance and pollution control. Only in very recent times, with the emergence in certain countries of an ideology of privatization and contracting-out of service provision, has the notion of urban life as a locus of public activity been radically challenged.

As mentioned previously, the factors encouraging urban concentration have also impacted on housing preferences. The conditions of a rural and agricultural society were conducive to peasant home ownership, if often of a very basic kind, whilst the shift into towns attendant on industrialization was associated with the provision of rental housing to an urban proletariat for whom ownership was not a material possibility. Today, the shift to the suburbs, with a lower urban density, once again encourages private ownership, although, in this instance, it is not easy to disentangle the causality. Finally, it should be noted that the move from countryside to town involves not only a change of location and of living conditions, but also a change of social horizons. Sociologists see urban lifestyles as conducive to more cosmopolitan attitudes and a greater tolerance of diversity. For this reason, urbanization frequently features as a variable in studies of the determinants of behaviour relating to various aspects of family life, such as the choice of marriage partner, fertility and divorce.

In later chapters, we examine the association between urbanization and a variety of policy outcomes. However, there have to be real doubts about the adequacy of the cross-national data available for this purpose. Part of the problem is the already mentioned fact that urbanization data only refer to a threshold of population density. Even more serious is the fact that, unlike all the other factors reviewed in this chapter, there is no generally accepted definition of urbanization that can be used as a comparable measuring rod for cross-national research. This is not a difficulty for sociological research in individual nations over time, since the definition of rural and urban areas is generally unchanging within each nation, but it raises serious questions concerning the validity of comparisons between countries. For instance, are Austria and Switzerland really as rural as they appear from Table 2.5, given that both countries are in the forefront of manufacturing employment? Or why did Portugal, much the most rural of these nations in 1960 according to the data in Table 2.5, experience such a relatively low rate of urbanization over the following years, especially since it simultaneously experienced a flight from agriculture on an enormous scale (see Table 2.4)? Because of these problems of definition, any conclusions we may come to concerning the impact of urbanization or its absence will necessarily be more tentative than the other findings of this study.

AGEING OF THE POPULATION

In some influential accounts of post-war welfare state development, ageing of the population has been seen as the crucial link between economic modernization and increased levels of public expenditure. At its simplest, the argument is one about responses to societal change. The twin processes of industrialization and urbanization are seen as creating new needs and new problems to which governments are forced to respond through ameliorative programmes. How to cope with the income support and health needs of the old in a society in which kinship ties have been sundered by the processes of modernization is not necessarily the first such set of problems to emerge, but, as modernization leads to population ageing via a reduced birth rate and greater longevity, the problems mount and become a significant call on the public purse. Expenditure on the aged becomes the major component of the welfare state and the welfare state becomes the biggest component of public expenditure as a whole.

This is one of the few propositions of the comparative public policy literature that has become an orthodoxy of real-world policy advice. The impact of an ageing society is today one of the foremost concerns of policy analysts working in international economic agencies such as the World Bank and the OECD, who consistently warn governments that, in the absence of expenditure reforms, the effect of demographic development on pension spending in coming decades will be the accumulation of public debt at an unsustainable level (see World Bank, 1994; OECD, 1996e).

The classic scholarly statement of this argument is to be found in the work of Harold Wilensky, one of the earliest scholars to employ statistical analysis of cross-national variation as a means of understanding the causes of welfare state development. 'As economic level climbs,' he argues, 'the percentage of the aged climbs, which shapes spending directly; with economic growth the percentage of the aged goes up, which makes for an early start and swift spread of social security programs . . . which, in turn, is expressed in big spending' (Wilensky, 1975, 27). Wilensky's interpretation of his research findings is that 'if there is one source of welfare spending that is most powerful – a single proximate cause – it is the proportion of old people in the population' (Wilensky, 1975, 47). In his view, this implies that nations, irrespective of their types of economy and of the ideological complexions of their governments, will become more alike in welfare spending terms as their populations age. This convergence argument is not, however, a feature of all theories highlighting the crucial impact of population ageing. Some researchers have suggested that, in addition to a direct demographic effect of the kind adduced by Wilensky, there is also likely to be an interest group impact as the old mobilize to achieve favourable outcomes for their section of the community, suggesting that the impact of demographic ageing will be greater in countries where a pluralistic form of politics confers on such groups the right to articulate their demands (see Pampel and Williamson, 1989).

Wilensky's research was based on an analysis of social welfare spending levels in more than 60 countries using data for the mid-1960s. The analysis here is of a more homogeneous group of 21 advanced democracies over the period 1960 to the early 1990s. Age effects are measured identically as the proportion of the population aged 65 years and over. Despite differences in country numbers and time-periods, there is much in Table 2.6 that appears broadly compatible with Wilensky's account. Certainly, the aged population has been growing right across the OECD, with an average change over the period as a whole of nearly 50 per cent compared with 1960. Moreover, convergence is quite clearly the name of the game, with a decline in the coefficient of variation between 1960 and the early 1990s of quite similar proportions to that manifested by services employment (see Table 2.4 above). In age structure terms, the OECD countries are now very alike, with Ireland, the bottom country in the distribution, less than 20 per cent below the mean, and Sweden, the top country, less than 25 per cent above it.

Comparative public policy

Table 2.6 Levels of and change in the percentage of the population aged 65 and over, 1960–early 1990s

Country	1960	1974	Early 1990s	Change: 1960–early 1990s
Australia	8.2	8.6	11.7	3.5
Canada	7.6	8.4	11.8	4.2
Ireland	11.1	10.9	11.4	0.3
New Zealand	8.7	8.6	11.6	2.9
UK	11.7	13.7	15.8	4.1
USA	9.2	10.3	12.7	3.5
Denmark	10.6	13.1	15.5	4.9
Finland	7.5	8.4	13.8	6.3
Norway	11.1	13.5	16.1	5.0
Sweden	11.8	14.8	17.6	5.8
Austria	12.2	14.8	15.2	3.0
Belgium	12.0	14.8	15.3	3.3
France	11.6	13.3	14.6	3.0
Germany	10.2	14.1	15.0	4.8
Italy	9.2	12.0	14.6	5.4
Netherlands	8.6	10.7	13.0	4.4
Greece	8.1	12.0	14.8	6.7
Portugal	8.1	10.7	14.2	6.1
Spain	8.1	10.3	14.4	6.3
Switzerland	10.7	12.7	15.0	4.3
Japan	5.7	7.7	13.4	7.7
Mean	9.6	11.6	14.2	4.6
Correlation with 1960		0.88	0.55	−0.56
Coefficient of variation	19.07	22.51	11.67	

Source and notes: Data for 1960 and 1974 from OECD (1993a). Data for the early 1990s from OECD, *Labour Force Statistics 1973–1993*, Paris, 1995. The data-point for the early 1990s is 1993. The figure reported in the final column is the percentage point change over the entire period.

Not all the summary statistics in Table 2.6 are this supportive of Wilensky's argument. If population ageing reflects fundamental processes of socio-economic modernization, it is, perhaps, surprising that the correlation between the proportion of the aged in 1960 and in the early 1990s is as low as 0.55. Admittedly, the lack of correspondence between the two time-points owes much to two cases – Ireland dropping 14 places in the distribution and Greece rising by nine places – but, even when these cases are excluded, it appears that cross-national patterns of population ageing are less stable than is true of most other socio-economic factors. It is also, perhaps, a little surprising that there was relatively little catch-up during the period. This is not, however, because catch-up is a necessary corollary of convergence in the sense in which we use the term here, but because real GDP, the factor seen by Wilensky as the driving force of the demographic transformation, was manifesting such a strong catch-up tendency over precisely this time-period (see Table 2.2).

Where Wilensky's story does seem to come seriously unstuck is not in regard to the potential implications of ageing for the development of the welfare state, but rather in regard to the linkage with the core processes of socio-economic modernization. This can be most easily seen by focusing on the families of nations which are apparent in the distributions of countries shown in Table 2.6. Throughout the period, the picture is essentially the same. Families do not cluster very tightly, but they do cluster. At the top of each distribution are the countries of continental Western Europe plus all of Scandinavia bar Finland. At the bottom of each distribution, we find the countries of Southern Europe plus the overseas English-speaking nations. It is the position of this latter grouping which is anomalous in terms of a link with the core processes of socio-economic modernization. As we have seen, the English-speaking family of nations stands out in economic development terms in the early post-war period. Thereafter, the relative affluence of these countries declines, but it is replaced by vanguard status in terms of services employment. However, neither of these marks of modernity translates through to the age structure. For the overseas English-speaking nations, at least, modernity is associated with an age structure quite the reverse of that suggested by theory.

Rather than population ageing being associated with economic affluence or services employment, the closest connection seems to be with a production structure dominated by industry and manufacturing. Belgium, Germany and the United Kingdom are amongst the European nations in which industry has been entrenched for the longest period of time and which, at the 1970s peak of the manufacturing boom, employed the largest proportion of their work forces in this sector (Therborn, 1995, 69). Sweden and Austria were somewhat later industrializers, but amongst the leading manufacturing nations in 1974 (see Table 2.4). These five nations were in the vanguard of population ageing at this date and remained so in the early 1990s, despite major declines in manufacturing employment in some of them. These links may well not be fortuitous. As Chapter 7 shows, there is a moderately strong inverse relationship between manufacturing employment and fertility. With a lag of some decades, low fertility inevitably produces an ageing population.

This identification of what appears to be a major discontinuity in the postulated sequence of societal transformation leading from economic development through population ageing to an expanded reach of the state represents an important step in our analysis. Earlier, we noted a lack of correspondence between patterns of economic development and of international trade, but that could scarcely serve as a major challenge to a modernization theory in which trade plays no specific role. The disjuncture between the age structure of the population and other aspects of socio-economic modernization has a much greater theoretical significance. It provides the first really strong evidence we have encountered which challenges the notion of a singular trajectory of post-war societal change. This is a point to which we shall return in the final section of the next chapter, where we more systematically examine the relationships between the main factors constituting the post-war transformation.

THE RELIGIOUS FACTOR

The final topic to be discussed in this chapter is the potential impact of religious belief on public policy outcomes, with the guiding hypothesis being that outcomes shaped by Catholic beliefs and doctrines may, in certain respects, be quite different from outcomes influenced by Protestant beliefs and doctrines. An analysis which focuses on the potential of such cultural differences to impact on policy would not be seen as the most obvious approach from a modernization theory point of view, since, in terms of that theory, the crucial aspect of post-war cultural modernization has been the decline in religiosity amongst the adherents of all religious denominations.

We choose to focus on differences between religious denominations for a number of reasons. A major consideration is that the theorists of modernization have not explicitly addressed the policy implications of increasing secularization, except in so far as they have suggested that family and societal issues may be the subject of fewer cultural sanctions as religiosity declines. A more mundane consideration is that the attitudinal data required to map post-war secularization patterns in these 21 countries are not available, with the most complete available dataset providing measures of religious versus secular values for only about three quarters of the countries featuring in this study and only for a period commencing in the early 1980s (see Ester, Halman and de Moor, 1993). Interestingly, too, attitudinal data for a much larger number of countries, although once again not including all of our full group of 21, suggest that the historical divide between Catholic and Protestant societies is amongst the most important factors in mapping cross-national cultural differences (Inglehart, 1997). Most compellingly, our focus on religious beliefs is determined by the fact that the specific hypotheses in the comparative literature linking religion and policy outcomes have actually been focused around type of faith rather than degree of faith, so it seems only sensible to discuss these.

The potential relevance of the religious divide to contemporary policy development is wide-ranging. In terms of the differential emergence of statist attitudes, it has been suggested that 'the fusion of secular and religious powers' (Flora, 1986, xviii) brought about by the Reformation rendered the Northern, Lutheran countries less suspicious of the extension of public power. Moreover, since the late nineteenth century, the Roman Catholic Church has been active in propagating a social policy doctrine which favours a particular kind of response to the needs produced by industrialization. Reinforcing the original thrust of the cultural divide, this doctrine argues for the 'subsidiarity' of social policy and preaches the virtues of the state using income transfers to provide male family heads with a 'just wage' adequate to support a family. On the one hand, a social policy informed by such principles leads to a bias against direct service provision by the state and, on the other, it has major implications for the role of women in the labour market (see van Kersbergen, 1995).

Finally, since religion defines both the cultural appropriateness of beliefs and behaviour, religious differences are clearly relevant to policies concerning education and personal conduct. Traditionally, the Catholic Church has pursued a policy of teaching the faithful in church schools, while many Protestant denominations have been willing to entrust their children's education to the state. In the nineteenth century this meant that the introduction of compulsory primary education occurred later in Catholic than in Protestant Europe (see data in Flora, 1983). In the twentieth century, the public expenditure implications of this suspicion of state intervention in education depended on whether the Church sought to foster a private alternative to state education (see Heidenheimer, Heclo and Adams, 1990, 26–7) or whether, as in the Netherlands (Therborn, 1989), or more recently in Australia (Anderson, 1991), it succeeded in obtaining public subsidies for Catholic education. In the arena of codes of personal conduct, the emphasis of the Protestant Churches on individual salvation may be argued to have resulted in a greater emphasis on individual rights in the areas of marriage, the family and gender than in countries where religious beliefs and doctrines focus more strongly on the sanctity of traditional family ties (Castles, 1994a).

Reflecting on these hypotheses, the implications are not necessarily so very different from those suggested by the adherents of modernization theory, with the very big caveat that secularization is here restricted to, or is seen as moving at a far greater pace in, the nations where Protestantism has been strongest. Such a conclusion is, perhaps, less surprising when one considers that the Reformation must itself be regarded as Christendom's first and most fundamental act of secularization. A statist public policy, public education and family and gender policies respecting individual rights only become possible when the power spiritual gives way to the power temporal as the basis of earthly law, and conscience supersedes the Church as the arbiter of personal morality.

Such potentialities were for the long rather than the short term. For centuries after the Reformation, there was little change in the legal rules regulating family life, and the main difference between Catholic and Protestant worlds was the concession in the latter that divorce might be a possibility *in extremis* (Phillips, 1988). But the changed ethos did mean that Protestant societies have been open to the forces of social change in ways that were not possible where Catholic beliefs were more dominant. Catholics have not been free to modify tenets of personal morality, because morality remains the province of the Church and because Catholic schools reinforce the doctrines of the Church. By the same token, when Catholic nations were confronted by the emergent needs of an industrial society, they had to develop responses compatible with traditional beliefs in the role of the family and the notion of a 'just wage'. In this sense, continuing religious differences in the post-war era may be seen as a kind of filter for modernity, allowing some nations to move farther and faster than others in transforming policy outcomes in many areas.

Capturing this cultural division empirically involves certain problems. First, there are two countries in our sample which do not easily fit. They are Greece, where the faith is Orthodox rather than Roman Catholic, and Japan, where Christian denominations of any kind are in a very small minority. Greece presents the lesser difficulty of the two. Classification of the Orthodox faith on the same basis as Western Catholicism in the last two columns of Table 2.7 rests on the fact that, like its Roman cousins, Greece was largely untouched by the Reformation and that the Orthodox Church continues strongly to emphasize traditional family values. Essentially, then, Orthodoxy is more like Roman Catholicism than

Protestantism in regard to those aspects of the religious divide that have been hypothesized as significant for public policy development. The classification of Japan is much more difficult, given that the country's traditional religious values are clearly not inimical to statism, but are no less clearly familial in orientation. The ultimate designation of Japan as non-Catholic for the purposes of this analysis, while obviously correct in literal terms, can be regarded as, to some degree, arbitrary. Nevertheless, however debatable, a choice had to be made since the alternative was to exclude Japan from much of the subsequent analysis.

The second problem is a matter of how we capture religious influence on policy-making. A standard response has been to look at the way in which the Churches have organized themselves in politics, focusing on the link between policy outcomes and the strength of the Catholic or Christian Democratic parties that have been an important new feature of post-war politics in a number of continental European countries (Wilensky, 1981; Huber, Ragin and Stephens, 1993; van Kersbergen, 1995). The trouble with this approach is that it implies that the Churches have no influence on policy in many of the countries in which they have had the most devout adherents and the most organizational clout; for instance, in Ireland, where Catholic principles relating to family life, education and the role of the state are built into the Constitution (Higgins, 1981), and in Spain, where church organizations, such as Catholic Action and Opus Dei, had a major influence in a number of important ministries during the Franco years (Gunther, 1980).

The solution we adopt here is to use a variety of measures of religious influence. In the first column of Table 2.7, we report a measure of the average level of cabinet incumbency of Christian Democratic parties over the entire period from 1950 to the early 1990s. All incumbency measures used in this study are relatively long-term and cumulative, based on the assumption that the policy impact of incumbency results from an accumulation of effects over many years, rather than simply reflecting the short-term fortunes of a party over a particular electoral period. Measures used to explore partisan impacts on levels of policy development commence in 1950 and terminate at or prior to the time-point at which the dependent variable is measured. Typical periods are 1950–59, 1950–73 and 1950–93. In the case of change over the entire period, the starting date is 1960 and the termination date a point in the early 1990s. In the second column of Table 2.7, we report data on the percentage of the population baptized into the Roman Catholic or Orthodox faiths. This makes it possible to assess the impact of the religious divide as articulated through popular adherence and via the influence of the organs of the Church. In the final column a dummy variable, 'Catholic cultural

Table 2.7 Indicators of religious differences in the advanced nations in the post-war era

Country	Christian Democratic incumbency 1950–early 1990s	Catholicism	Catholic cultural impact
Australia	0	29.6	0
Canada	0	46.6	0
Ireland	0	95.3	1
New Zealand	0	14.0	0
UK	0	13.0	0
USA	0	26.0	0
Denmark	1	0.6	0
Finland	0	0.1	0
Norway	5	0.3	0
Sweden	1	1.4	0
Austria	36	88.8	1
Belgium	53	90.0	1
France	8	76.4	1
Germany	53	43.8	1
Italy	70	83.2	1
Netherlands	47	42.6	1
Greece	0	96.7	1
Portugal	0	94.1	1
Spain	3	97.0	1
Switzerland	32	52.8	0
Japan	0	0.6	0
Mean	14.7	47.3	
Coefficient of variation	156.56	80.69	

Sources and notes: 1950–early 1990s Christian Democratic incumbency measures the average percentage of cabinet seats held by such parties over the years 1950–94 and is calculated from the dataset in Woldendorp, Keman and Budge 1993 and 1998. Catholicism measures the percentage of the population baptized into a non-Protestant Christian faith. Data from Barrett (1982). Catholic cultural impact is a dummy variable indicating countries in which at least 75 per cent of the population are baptized into a non-Protestant Christian faith or in which Christian Democratic parties have held more than 40 per cent of cabinet seats over of the post-was era as a whole.

impact', seeks to combine both political and popular impacts in one very simple measure that locates the countries where policy outcomes could be effected by either form of religious influence. The definition of this variable is to be found in the notes to Table 2.7.

In family of nations terms, the story of the religious divide amongst the advanced nations is quite easy to tell. Essentially, continental Western Europe and Southern Europe contain nations which either have a substantial majority Catholic adherence or are divided roughly equally between the Catholic and Protestant denominations. In Germany and the Netherlands, both of which fall into the divided category, Christian Democracy has been the dominant partisan force in post-war politics. Switzerland, which is also religiously divided, is different. That country's permanent coalition arrangements have meant that a Christian party has had permanent executive representation throughout the period, but, by same token, the party's influence has always been quite circumscribed (see Lehmbruch, 1993).

The big difference between the cabinet incumbency measure and the others is that, whereas the former locates a potential religious impact only amongst a group of continental Western European nations, the other measures point to a no lesser potential in Southern Europe and Ireland. On the other side of the cultural divide are the Scandinavian countries, with a strong nominal attachment to the Lutheran Church, and the English-speaking countries, where Protestant Churches of various kind dominate, but Catholics sometimes constitute a sizeable minority. There are only two exceptions to this story: Ireland, which on this count is part of continental Europe, and, to a lesser extent, Canada, where the French influence in Quebec makes for a population divided equally between the major Christian denominations.

An adequate time-series for baptisms is not available and our Catholicism measure is for the early 1980s. Catholic cultural impact is also operationalized in such a way as to be invariant across the whole post-war period. However, although Table 2.7 only provides a cumulated measure of Christian Democratic strength over the entire post-war period, our dataset makes it possible to calculate measures for different time-periods. A correlation of 0.98 between average incumbency in 1950–59 and in 1960–74, and an only marginally weaker one of 0.93 between incumbency in 1950–59 and in 1974–93, suggests little change in this dimension of religious difference. Table 2.7 also shows that both the Christian Democratic incumbency and Catholicism measures are characterized by very high coefficients of variation. Thus, in the case of religious differences, and in very real contrast to most of the variables surveyed in this chapter, nations cluster at the extremes of the distribution. Theories premised on socio-economic modernization generally suggest that national policy profiles will become more alike because the factors shaping them are becoming more alike. Such an account is obviously persuasive if the forces pushing policy development are factors such as economic affluence, occupational change and population ageing. It is likely to fit the facts far less well if religiously shaped cultural differences prove to be a significant part of the policy equation.

CONCLUSION

The discussion of religious differences concludes this chapter on the nature of the post-war economic and social transformation. The object has been to draw attention to cross-national differences and to note potential implications for public policy development. The account we have given has underlined strong connections between various aspects of the modernization process, but has also noted major discontinuities which suggest that national experiences of post-war socio-economic development may have been rather more diverse than is sometimes supposed. A more systematic analysis of the linkages between different aspects of the post-war experience is clearly required to take us any further. However, socio-economic factors are not the only variables that need to be included in such an analysis. Chapter 3 discusses the political dimensions of post-war transformation and then proceeds to examine how aspects of the post-war transformation fit together.

3. Institutions and ideology

INTRODUCTION

At this roughly half way stage in our review of the major factors which have been identified as significant for post-war public policy development, we shift our attention from economic and social to political aspects of post-war change. In this chapter, we look at two aspects of political life potentially of great consequence for the nature of policy outcomes. The first is the character of the institutional framework through which political demands and interests are expressed. The second relates to the character of the demands themselves and, in particular, to the balance of power between contending ideological viewpoints. The standard strategies by which scholars in this field have sought to provide evidence that politics matters have involved either showing how certain types of institutions condition the capacity of the political system to translate demands into outcomes or demonstrating that, where parties or groups with a particular ideological leaning are strong, policies of a particular kind are likely to be adopted. Such theories suggest, for instance, that it is likely to make a difference to the outcomes of policy whether countries have federal or unitary systems of government or whether they usually have right- or left-wing governments in office.

The degree to which accounts of modern policy development resting on the impact of politics are compatible with accounts stressing the importance of socio-economic factors depends on whether the arguments are framed in such a way as to exclude alternative perspectives. If, for instance, it is implied that the only thing that makes a difference to pensions systems in capitalist and communist nations is the age structure of society, then political choice becomes largely irrelevant. Equally, if the development of an advanced welfare state is seen simply as a matter of the choices of the political party in office, then the changing character of social needs may be beside the point. Neither viewpoint recommends itself as particularly sensible when taken to these extremes. Clearly, social needs do shape the character of political demands, but the extent and urgency with which such demands become policy is likely to be a function of the institutional and ideological prisms through which they are refracted. In the previous chapter, we examined theories premised on the assumption that socio-economic factors shape modern policy development. Here, we examine theories which suggest that politics is no less important.

This chapter has one further task. Having discussed the main economic, social and political dimensions of the post-war transformation, we need to establish the links between these factors. Modernization theory tells us that there is essentially one big picture, but, in the previous chapter, we noted that at least some of the connecting links were rather weaker than implied in that account. In the final section of this chapter, we use the simple statistical technique of correlation analysis to establish just how strong and just how weak these connections are and how politics fits into the picture. Our guiding problematic is that with which we began Chapter 2: can the history of the post-war era be written in terms of progressive steps along a defined path of economic and political modernization, or are there many routes to and through modernity?

DEMOCRATIZATION

Not all theorists of modernization have seen politics as irrelevant. For some sociologists working in this tradition, the process by which states have come to grant a voice to their citizenry, the process of democratization, has been regarded as an integral aspect of the transition to modernity. The same forces of industrialization and urbanization that create new needs and problems simultaneously lead to pressures for the institutionalization of political democracy and for the development of a competitive party system as means by which popular demands can be translated into policy. In this account, democratization becomes the vital transmission mechanism of socio-economically generated needs. Flora and Heidenheimer (1981, 47), for instance, suggest that the rise of mass democracy in Europe favoured the development of welfare states, because political élites had to confront a 'more organized working class and greater competition for the votes of economically disadvantaged groups'. This is a story which explicitly concedes that politics may make a real difference, since electoral competition for the votes of such disadvantaged groups is not inevitable or, at least, may be very much more delayed in some countries than in others.

Political scientists, of course, take even less convincing that democratic participation makes a difference, although they are not always certain whether that influence is for the good or the bad. Half a century ago,

V.O. Key (1949, 308) argued that what prevented the emergence of programmes for the poor in the USA's southern states was a one-party politics which provided 'no institutionalized mechanism for the expression of lower-bracket viewpoints'. Today, the President of the American Political Science Association notes that 'the overall weight of the evidence strongly supports the view that who votes and how people vote matter a great deal' and that 'any other conclusion would be extremely damaging for the very concept of representative democracy' (Lijphart, 1997, 5). The notion that democratization leads to a public policy incorporating the interests of all citizens is indicative of an optimism and a belief in progress common to both modernization theory and the theory of representative democracy. However, the linkage between democracy and policy outcomes is not always presented by political commentators in so benign a light. Since the mid-1970s, democratic institutions have, on occasions, been portrayed as leading to a crisis of ungovernability, in which politicians progressively promise more than they can deliver and deliver more than they can pay for, and in which policy effectiveness declines along with faith in the capacity of democratic governments to deliver (Crozier, Huntington and Watanuki, 1975; King, 1975; Brittan, 1977). What the optimistic and the pessimistic accounts have in common is, of course, the hypothesis that democratic government is, for good or ill, big government and it is this hypothesis that we seek to test in later chapters.

There is no lack of possible measures of democratization (Lane and Ersson, 1990, 130–33). Not all, however, are suitable for our purpose. Most of the democratization research in the quantitative political economy tradition has been in areas where it has been appropriate to utilize wide samples of nations at quite disparate levels of economic and political development. Important areas for such research have included the relationships between economic development and democracy (Lipset, 1959; Burkhart and Lewis-Beck, 1994) and between inequality and democracy (Simpson, 1990; Castles, 1997a). The democratization measures used in this kind of work have generally been based on the presence or absence of democratic rights and institutions and are not suitable for differentiating amongst nations which, since the mid-1970s, have, in formal terms at least, all been fully fledged democracies. What we therefore require is a democratization measure which can identify gradations in the extent of democratic participation. In Table 3.1, we use electoral turnout for this purpose. This measure has the threefold advantage of directly measuring participation in elections, of dramatically capturing major departures from democratic conditions (no elections, no turnout) and of distinguishing mature democracies in terms of their differing potential for popular voice to influence policy development.

Comparative public policy

Table 3.1   Levels of and change in electoral turnout as a percentage of the electorate, 1960–early 1990s

Country	1960	1974	Early 1990s	Change: 1960–early 1990s
Australia	95.5	95.4	95.3	−0.2
Canada	80.6	77.2	69.6	−11.0
Ireland	71.3	76.6	68.5	−2.8
New Zealand	93.4	89.1	83.3	−10.1
UK	78.7	72.2	77.8	−0.9
USA	61.6	57.1	55.3	−6.3
Denmark	83.7	87.7	83.0	−0.7
Finland	75.0	81.4	68.4	−6.6
Norway	78.3	80.2	75.8	−2.5
Sweden	77.4	90.8	86.7	9.3
Austria	97.2	94.1	86.3	−10.9
Belgium	93.6	91.5	92.7	−0.9
France	77.0	81.2	69.3	−7.7
Germany	87.8	91.1	77.8	−10.0
Italy	93.7	93.1	87.3	−6.4
Netherlands	95.6	83.5	78.8	−16.8
Greece	75.5	0	83.2	7.7
Portugal	0	0	62.0	62.0
Spain	0	0	76.4	76.4
Switzerland	34.3	56.8	46.0	11.7
Japan	77.0	71.8	73.3	−3.7
Mean	72.7	70.0	76.0	3.3
Correlation with 1960		0.82	0.59	−0.91
Coefficient of variation	38.49	44.54	15.84	

Sources and notes: Turnout is defined as total vote as a percentage of the electorate. Dates are for the last election in the 1950s, the election before 1974 and the election immediately after 1990. For the two initial dates, the source is Mackie and Rose (1990); for the last date, the data sources are the election updates published regularly in the *European Journal of Political Research*. Where free elections were not held, as in Portugal and Spain immediately preceding 1974, and in Greece between 1967 and 1974, a figure of zero is given. In the case of Switzerland, where women were not given the vote until 1971, the level of turnout for the last election in the 1950s reported in Mackie and Rose is halved. The figure reported in the final column is the percentage point change over the entire period.

Before turning to the data in Table 3.1, it is important to note that an analysis which focuses exclusively on the years from 1960 onwards cannot possibly capture the distinctiveness of the post-war period as the era of democracy triumphant. That is because World War II itself served as a major watershed between a period in which a country's democratic credentials were largely a matter of domestic concern and one in which the international community employed sanctions to guarantee the adoption of democratic institutions in certain countries, and in which, democratic practice became almost mandatory for nations wishing to be regarded as properly civilized. Before the war, Austria, Germany, Italy, Japan, Portugal and Spain had authoritarian governments. In the decade following the war, the victorious Allies imposed democratic constitutions on all the defeated Axis powers. Before the war, women had played no role in politics in Belgium, France, Italy, Japan, Portugal, Spain and Switzerland. Irrespective of whether they had been winners or losers, all those countries which had participated in a war frequently billed by the victors as a 'struggle for democracy' now felt constrained to demonstrate their own democratic credentials and introduce universal suffrage. The countries that remained as autocracies into the post-war period were Portugal and Spain, and the only non-autocratic country to hold out against the immediate introduction of female suffrage was Switzerland. What these countries had in common was that they had been amongst the non-combatants of World War II, demonstrating very clearly the role of the war as a midwife of social and political change.

This general post-war acceptance of democratic institutions must be borne in mind in interpreting the data in Table 3.1, which reports electoral turnout for periods starting with the last election in the 1950s in each of our 21 countries. An initial impression of continuing dissimilarity, based on the relatively high coefficients of variation reported for 1960 and 1974, is largely due to the absence of democratic elections in Portugal and Spain prior to the mid-1970s and in Greece between 1967 and 1974. However, calculating coefficients of variation for these years excluding these countries suggests a degree of similarity amongst the remaining countries as great as for any of the other variables examined in the previous chapter over the same period. Some of the other figures of Table 3.1 are also deceptive for much the same reason. The modest average increase in turnout of 3.3 per cent over the period as a whole disguises the fact that, without the massive increases in democratic participation experienced by Portugal and Spain, there would actually have been a decline of comparable dimensions. Similar reversals apply to the correlations with the 1960 level of turnout. Without Portugal and Spain, the ordering of countries in the early 1990s distribution was very similar to that of 1960. Most of the catch-up effect disappears as well, with the correlation between the 1960 level and subsequent change going down from –0.91 to –0.57.

There are two obvious families of nations stories in what we have said so far. The first is about the English-speaking alliance of nations that imposed democratic solutions on much of continental Western Europe by its victory in World War II. The second is of continuing democratic weakness and instability in Southern Europe in the early post-war decades and of a successful transition to democracy in the decades there-after. Given the role of war in the first story, it is not self-evident that the forces bringing about this clean sweep for democracy were exclusively socio-economic in character. Nevertheless, this account of democratic progress to the mid-1970s could quite possibly be seen as conforming with the broad sweep of modernization theory in that all these nations could now be regarded as having moved beyond an institutional thresh-old of political modernity, allowing for the free expression of political ideas and interests.

However, this interpretation ignores the fact that the countries of Southern Europe have not been the only laggards in terms of electoral turnout. Looking down the columns of Table 3.1, we see that other countries with conspicuously low levels of turnout have been Switzerland and the USA and that, unlike Greece and Spain, although not Portugal, these countries have been laggards throughout the period. Not only have Switzerland and the USA been amongst the richest coun-tries in the OECD throughout the post-war period; they have also been amongst the nations with the longest continuous records of liberal democratic government. However, in both cases it was a democracy that was incomplete. In the USA, that was because voter registration proce-dures effectively excluded large sections of the poor and, in particular, poor blacks. In Switzerland, it was initially because women were not granted the right to vote in federal elections. The persistently low vote in Swiss federal elections since the early 1970s, when universal suffrage was first introduced, reflects a variety of factors including the role of direct democracy, the salience of state (canton) level politics, declining party differences on the bourgeois side of politics and the lack of any direct connection between parliamentary voting and the composition of the federal executive.

In terms of the modernization thesis, this grouping of very poor and very rich nations at the tail of the distribution is quite anomalous. Nor is it the only anomaly shown up in Table 3.1. Australia, Belgium and Italy have no obvious credentials to be the post-war era's exemplars of democratic participation, but over the three decades from 1960 to 1990 that is exactly what they were. Both anomalies are only comprehensible in terms of political choices about the nature and forms of political representation. In the long-term liberal democracies, the choice was to restrict those permitted into the charmed circle of political representation. In Australia, Belgium and Italy, it was to encourage the widest possible degree of participation by means of laws and practices making voting effectively compulsory. Clearly, then, even amongst systems which have all moved beyond a basic threshold of democratization, institutional choices continue to affect the potential for popular participation. The question for this study is whether they also influence the character of the policy outcomes resulting from that participation. Findings showing that the extent of democratization impacted on the reach of the state only up to the mid-1970s might be regarded as confirming a modernization interpretation. On the other hand, findings indicating the continued impact of democratization throughout the post-war period would argue for the importance of institutional choice.

CLASS POLITICS

The view that political differences between countries structure the character of those countries' public policy outcomes brings us to a real point of departure with modernization theory. Such differences may be ideological as well as institutional. In the next three sections, we examine post-war trends in the strength of class and party ideologies, before briefly discussing a variety of institutional differences between these countries, which have been argued to be relevant to the character of post-war policy development. Except where politics is seen as a kind of conveyor-belt of societal needs, the notion that ideologies and institutions may have a major influence on policy outcomes challenges modernization theory fundamentally by implying that the modern expansion of the role of the state may owe much to factors other than socio-economic transformation.

Various responses to this challenge have been forthcoming. One is to argue that only the broad parameters of policy are determined by the modernization process and that, within those parameters, outcomes may be a function of many forces, including ideological and institutional differences. On such a basis, it is possible for analysts working within the modernization paradigm to suggest that the strong impetus to welfare state development arising from the emergence of mass democracy may be complemented by 'great variations . . . result[ing] from differences in the party system, above all the strength and coherence of the working class movement, as well as from differences in the development of state bureaucracies' (Flora and Alber, 1981, 47). But the normal response of those most concerned to demonstrate how modernization has impacted on policy outcomes has been to suggest that, however important political differences may once have been, they have become progressively less relevant as countries approach full modernity. In the 1960s, in an era when Otto Kirchheimer (1964, 287) could note that 'diminished social polarisation and diminished political polarisation are going hand in hand' and Daniel Bell (1960) could write of an 'end of ideology' in the West, this view became virtually an orthodoxy in political science as well as in sociology.

There are at least three possible implications of this thesis of lessened ideological salience: that differences have become less important, that they have a lessened relevance for policy, and/or that countries have become more alike in their array of political views. If a lessening of ideological differences is taken to mean that there has been a decrease in the intensity of class conflict, there is clearly some genuine support for the thesis both in terms of the declining significance of anti-system parties in the early post-war years and in a trend towards declining industrial conflict already noticeable by the early 1960s (Ross and Hartman, 1960). However, if the argument is that there has been a tendency for parties to become more alike in their views, the proposition is far more debatable. Early data refer to no more than ten countries and indicate a decline in polarization to quite minimal levels between the 1950s and 1970s (Thomas, 1979). However, later data, based on larger numbers of countries, point to very appreciable differences (Castles and Mair, 1984; Laver and Hunt, 1992; Huber and Inglehart, 1995). A study examining changes in polarization between 1983 and 1994 suggests that the distance between the most left-located and the most right-located parties has, if anything, increased in recent years, although with a marginal tendency for the difference between the two biggest parties in the system to diminish somewhat (see Mair and Castles, 1997). The second implication, that parties will impact on policy less as time goes on, is tested in the research reported in later chapters of this book. It is the third possible implication of a lessening of cross-national differences which is the main focus of attention in the following sections on the post-war transformation of class and party politics.

The case that class politics in contradistinction to party politics is an important influence on the policy development of the modern state is a difficult one to make. Its intellectual genesis is in Marxist thought, yet, in at least one essential, it seems to contradict the fundamental tenets of Marxist theory. Marxism posits class conflict as the central fact of capitalist development, and sees such conflict as the engine which terminates bourgeois rule, replacing it initially by a proletarian state and then by a classless and stateless society. The trouble is that present societies are unequivocally capitalist societies in which, according to the Marxist orthodoxy, working class action can do nothing to forestall the increasing misery of the proletariat. The only way around this impasse is to assume some degree of relative autonomy of the state, which can be the more readily intellectually defended when it is seen as a temporary aberration from the logic of class rule and ultimately unavailing against the fullest development of a capitalist society in which the state is the mere executive of the bourgeoisie.

The stories told in this genre are therefore tragic rather than celebratory. Piven and Cloward (1972) argue that, whilst poor people's revolts, such as the riots of blacks in the northern cities of the USA in the mid-1960s, can succeed in the short term, the reforms the state concedes as the price of social peace tend to be wound back once turmoil gives way to apathy. O'Connor (1973) outlines a self-defeating process by which the state makes welfare concessions to enhance its legitimacy, but is forced to 'counterattack' before 'fiscal crisis' threatens the viability of the capital accumulation process on which the capitalist order rests. Gough (1979, 70–71) argues that the establishment of the British welfare state reflected the collective mobilization resulting from the wartime experience and the increased radicalism of the industrial working class, but sees such victories as intrinsically precarious because they are the reversible outcomes of strategic concessions made only under threat. He would, almost certainly, have seen the victory of Margaret Thatcher in the year that his book was published as a nice irony, illustrating precisely the point he was making.

The only indicators of the strength of class mobilization in capitalist societies that are readily available on a cross-national basis and which are separate from considerations of party relate to the size, activity and organizational characteristics of the trade union movement (see Cameron, 1984). The measure shown in Table 3.2 is trade union membership as a percentage of wage and salary earners or, as it is often called, 'union density'. This variable may be taken as indicating the nominal allegiance of workers in the modern sectors of the economy to an ideology of collective solidarity broadly associated with labour movement goals. There are ways in which Table 3.2 conceals as much as it reveals. Although the means for the three time-periods suggest an apparent stability, the real picture is of increasing union density in many OECD countries during the course of the 1970s and a decline of comparable proportions in the following decade. Western (1995, 196) has attributed the decline of union density in the later period to 'the decentralization of collective bargaining institutions and the electoral failure of labour parties', although, as we shall see in the next section, there are question marks concerning the reality of the electoral failure of the Left in these

Table 3.2 Levels and change in trade union membership as a percentage of wage and salary earners, 1960–early 1990s

Country	1960	1974	Early 1990s	Change: 1960–early 1990s
Australia	61.0	50.2	40.4	−20.6
Canada	31.0	31.0	35.8	4.8
Ireland	50.0	53.1	49.7	−0.3
New Zealand	54.0	45.0	44.8	−9.2
UK	45.0	44.8	39.1	−5.9
USA	31.0	23.2	15.6	−15.4
Denmark	69.0	60.0	71.4	2.4
Finland	33.0	51.4	72.0	39.0
Norway	62.0	51.4	56.0	−6.0
Sweden	73.0	67.7	82.5	9.5
Austria	72.0	62.2	46.2	−25.8
Belgium	58.0	45.5	51.2	−6.8
France	17.0	22.3	9.8	−7.2
Germany	39.0	33.0	32.9	−6.1
Italy	61.0	36.3	38.8	−22.2
Netherlands	44.0	38.0	25.5	−18.5
Greece	–	0	34.1	–
Portugal	0	0	31.8	31.8
Spain	0	0	11.0	11.0
Switzerland	36.0	30.1	26.6	−9.4
Japan	11.0	35.1	25.4	14.4
Mean	42.3	37.2	40.0	−2.0
Correlation with 1960		0.88	0.69	−0.53
Coefficient of variation	53.27	53.04	48.30	

Sources and notes: Most of the 1960 data are from Stephens (1979). Data for 1974 and the early 1990s (data point is 1990) are from OECD (1994), *Employment Outlook*, Paris. Under the Greek, Portuguese and Spanish juntas, free trade union organization is regarded as being in abeyance and is scored as zero. The figure reported in the final column is the percentage point change over the entire period.

years. The apparent stability of union membership also conceals that quite major changes were taking place in the relative positions of various countries. Most spectacular was Finland's shift from fifteenth to second place in the distribution, but there were also other changes of considerable substance, including the emergence of a substantial union movement in Portugal after the revolution of 1974 and the decline of the once powerful Austrian movement. As these examples demonstrate, there was no common trajectory of change during this period. Countries such as Finland, Japan, Portugal and Sweden manifested marked increases in union membership, whilst Australia, Austria, Italy, the Netherlands and the USA experienced membership decline in excess of 30 per cent.

This brings us to a point which does emerge very clearly from the data in Table 3.2: the absence of any trend towards greater similarity amongst these nations with the passing of time. The coefficient of variation starts out high and it remains high. The extent of the initial variation is influenced by the absence of free trade unions in Southern Europe, but, even when these countries are excluded from the analysis, the pattern is not one of marked similarity. Moreover, excluding these same countries from the 1990s analysis actually suggests that underlying cross-national variation has been increasing rather than decreasing in recent decades. This is not a story readily compatible with the notion of a lessening of ideological differences in the post-war era.

The family of nations patterns evident in the data in Table 3.2 are no more supportive of an account based on hypotheses derived from modernization theory. Admittedly, Southern Europe starts out at the bottom of the distribution. However, judging from Greece and Portugal's growing trade union membership after the fall of their respective juntas, this has to be regarded as a direct consequence of the institutional suppression of free trade unions rather than as a reflection of these countries' levels of socio-economic development. Looking at the top half of the distribution reveals still fewer signs of a modernization effect. The persistent weakness of trade unionism in the USA and Canada suggests that neither affluence nor services sector development have much to do with class mobilization. Moreover, the perhaps more obvious possibility of a direct link between trade union strength and manufacturing employment is contradicted by the middling mobilization of countries such as Germany, Switzerland and the United Kingdom.

Looking down the first column of Table 3.2 reveals that the group of countries which stand out is the Scandinavian family of nations minus Finland. This final exception does not last long. By 1974, Finland is already in the top third of the distribution and, by the 1990s, the four Scandinavian nations are quite unequivocally the four vanguard nations of trade unionism. This pattern, with Scandinavia in the lead and countries like the USA and Japan bringing up the rear, is quite unlike the patterns displayed by variables more obviously associated with modernization and is one which we shall encounter in quite similar forms when we examine post-war distributions of Left and Right party strength. This is not to say that the post-war history of union mobilization has been simply a matter of the fortunes of the political Left writ large. In fact, there is clear evidence that patterns of union growth and decline have been strongly influenced by institutional features specific to the task of union recruitment in different countries (Wallerstein, 1989; Rothstein, 1992). It does suggest, however, that cross-national changes in the strength of the trade union movement over this period may well have been part of a broader set of ideological trends cross-cutting the trajectory of post-war socio-economic development.

LEFT INCUMBENCY

The most important of those trends has been the post-war emergence in many nations of Social Democratic or Labour parties as equal, or even as the dominant, contestants in the 'democratic class struggle' (Korpi, 1983). With the exception of Scandinavia, this was not an immediate development, but required a learning process by which the experience of successive defeats led parties to adopt a more inclusive and compromising stance in the hope of obtaining office (see Urwin, 1981, 240–45). To Marxist critics, this embrace of moderation demonstrated precisely why the capture of the bourgeois state was futile: in order to win control of the state, it was necessary to become a bourgeois party in all but name. From more sympathetic commentators, however, it called forth a theoretical response justifying the new emphasis on the capture of state power as a means of achieving real gains for the working class and the poor.

This kind of argument for office-seeking by democratic socialists was not new. It dated back to Bernstein's *Evolutionary Socialism* (1909) and found its clear post-war expression as a set of doctrines for practical reform politics in Crosland's *The Future of Socialism* (1963). However, from the 1970s onwards, these ideas moved out of the realm of political justification and were transformed into a set of hypotheses concerning the determinants of policy outcomes in democratic capitalist societies. These hypotheses can be seen as constituting a 'social democratic model' of the advanced capitalist state, which departs from the assumptions of the class politics approach outlined in the previous section in two significant ways:

First, this model asserts that partisan control of the executive branch of government, rather than sheer electoral support or extraparliamentary forms of political power, is the primary means by which class forces are politically translated into policy outcomes. And second, the social democratic model assumes substantial independence of the political and economic arenas, in the sense that in spite of the privileged position of private employers and investors in the capitalist political economy, it is deemed possible for the subordinate class to peacefully conquer the state and to exploit such conquest to intervene in class conflict on the side of labor. (Shalev, 1983, 319)

Early comparative research supporting such an account of the workings of the modern capitalist state included Stephens's (1979) demonstration that welfare spending in advanced nations was in large part a function of socialist rule, and the seminal findings of Hibbs (1977), which purported to demonstrate that Social Democratic governments had achieved lower levels of unemployment than their bourgeois competitors, even if at some cost in higher levels of inflation (cf. Payne, 1979). Two decades of continuing research on the effects of Left partisanship on policy outcomes have produced a huge amount of work exploring almost every possible intricacy of a theme which has remained the crucial benchmark for the proposition that 'politics matters' (for a recent review of this literature, see Schmidt, 1996a).

The most theoretically developed version of the social democratic model has been associated with work emerging from the Swedish Institute of Social Research, which has argued that social democratic rule represents a mobilization of the 'power resources' of the labour movement with the goal of extending citizenship rights from the legal and political spheres to the domain of social rights (Korpi, 1978; Esping-Andersen and Korpi, 1984; Korpi, 1989). Such a mobilization is seen as having taken place to its fullest extent in the nations of Scandinavia, where it is regarded as the dynamic underlying the establishment of welfare societies in which economic and social inequalities have been markedly reduced and of labour markets in which full employment and gender equality have been the guiding principles. Hence cross-national research in this tradition has been premised on the view that countries in which partisan control of government by the Left has been strong are likely to have very different policy outcomes from countries in which this is not the case.

The measure of Left incumbency used in Table 3.3 is the percentage of cabinet seats held by parties aligned with the Socialist International or holding similar views. As in the case of Christian Democratic incumbency, the measure used seeks to assess the cumulative impact of party over longish periods rather than being based on the manifestly improbable premise that a party newly in office can transform policy outcomes overnight. Table 3.3 reveals a picture which neatly divides the post-war

Table 3.3   Average percentage of left cabinet seats for various periods between 1950 and the early 1990s

Country	1950–59	1960–73	1974–early 1990s	1950–early 1990s
Australia	0	8	65	33
Canada	0	0	0	0
Ireland	10	2	15	11
New Zealand	21	14	39	27
UK	18	41	25	28
USA	0	0	0	0
Denmark	59	61	40	51
Finland	30	33	36	34
Norway	100	54	73	74
Sweden	84	100	57	77
Austria	41	49	78	61
Belgium	23	33	26	28
France	13	0	46	24
Germany	13	33	31	24
Italy	0	12	19	13
Netherlands	31	5	21	18
Greece	0	0	46	22
Portugal	0	0	21	10
Spain	0	0	55	26
Switzerland	6	29	29	24
Japan	0	0	1	1
Mean	21.4	22.6	34.4	30.0
Correlation with 1960		0.83	0.55	0.88
Coefficient of variation	133.30	119.54	65.72	78.18

Sources and notes: The Left is defined as Social Democratic (membership of the Socialist International) and other leftist parties. The data are from Schmidt (1996b). Greece, Portugal and Spain are regarded as having exclusively non-Left government during the periods of their respective juntas. The data-point for the early 1990s is 1994. The use of the time-periods is illustrative only. In the statistical analysis of later chapters, average Left cabinet seats are generally calculated for periods starting in 1950 and culminating with the time-point under analysis (i.e. the assumption is that the impact of parties is cumulative over longish time-periods).

era into two halves. Before the 1970s, there were really only four countries in which Left parties had succeeded in challenging their bourgeois opponents as the natural parties of government. They were Austria, Denmark, Norway and Sweden. From the 1970s, the number of countries in which the Left had a major governmental role doubled, with Australia, France, Greece and Spain being added to the group. In each of these countries, accession to power represented a historical turn in the fortunes of the political Left and it is these quite dramatic changes which explain why the correlation between Left incumbency in the early and late post-war periods is of only moderate proportions.

The post-war expansion of Left power was not, however, only a matter of a transformed status in just a few places. The Left was acquiring a foothold in office in many countries in which it had hitherto had no success. In 1950–59, there were eight countries in which the Left was excluded from office for the entire period. In 1960–73, there were still seven. However, in the 1970s and 1980s, the only countries without any experience of democratic socialist government at a national level were the USA and Canada, with the latter country only being a partial exception to the general trend since it experienced substantial periods of socialist rule at the provincial level. The fact that in recent decades democratic socialist parties have become normal parties of government in most Western nations is difficult to reconcile with arguments that the Left is in a process of decline because of a diminishing constituency of working class support (Przeworski, 1985; Przeworski and Sprague, 1986) and/or the failure of the Keynesian approach to come to grips with the new realities of a globalized capitalist economy (Scharpf, 1991, Western, 1995).

The final column of the table provides a picture of Left strength over the post-war period as a whole. In a manner similar to the cross-national distribution of union density, the main contrast here is between the strength of the Left in the Scandinavian family of nations and its weakness in North America and Japan. However, the extent of difference in respect of Left incumbency is appreciably greater than in the case of trade unions and, indeed, greater than in respect of any of the other dimensions of post-war transformation discussed in this chapter. Nor, to any significant degree, is this because of the inclusion of Southern Europe in the analysis. Recalculating the coefficients of variation in Table 3.3 excluding these nations suggests marginally greater similarity in the first two periods, but marginally greater dissimilarity from the mid-1970s onwards. Overall, the trend of Left incumbency in the post-war era simply reinforces the story told by changing patterns of working class mobilization that countries have not become so alike that differences between them have ceased to be relevant for public policy development.

RIGHT INCUMBENCY

The class politics hypothesis has in common with the social democratic model the notion that the formative actor in post-war politics has been the labour movement, acting as the fighting arm or political representative of the industrial working class. This is a natural enough idea, since the working class was the legitimate offspring of the industrialization process, and the labour movement, as the newest kid on the political block, might seem the obvious source for novel initiatives concerning the role of the state. It is, however, possible to reverse these arguments and to see the crucial political factor shaping post-war policy transformation as the capacity of the political Right to resist the forces of change set in motion by processes of modernization and put on the political agenda by interests newly represented in the democratic arena.

This formulation of the policy dynamic of advanced nations was initially advanced in the context of research I undertook on the welfare state achievements of the Scandinavian nations (Castles, 1978). It has subsequently found some favour as an explanation of more general cross-national differences in a number of areas, including broad measures of the reach of the state (Castles, 1982; Hicks and Swank, 1984), issues relating to economic and sexual equality (van Arnhem and Schotsman, 1982; Norris, 1987), foreign development aid (Imbeau, 1988) and a variety of aspects of educational policy (Castles, 1989; Castles and Marceau, 1989). The findings of this body of research suggest that the state will be less interventionist, will spend less on most aspects of the welfare state and will be less active in promoting social and gender equality in countries where the political Right has been the dominant political force during the post-war era. Research on macro-economic policy has suggested more conditional findings (see Alvarez, Garrett and Lange, 1991). Both Right and Left may preside over favourable outcomes under certain circumstances. Where unions are weak, the Right can utilize a low-wage strategy to boost employment and economic growth without risking high inflation. Where the Left rules in conjunction with a union movement which adopts the corporatist strategy of trading off wage restraint for social wage gains, similar outcomes may be forthcoming. In this account, the ideological preferences of both Right and Left matter, but what matters most is the configuration of class and party politics as a whole.

The argument for the negative impact of the Right in respect of public expenditure and equality starts out in a way quite compatible with the modernization thesis by implying that, for most groups, the industrialization process has led to emergence of needs that can only readily be catered for through collective action organized by the state. The question, then, is why some countries have experienced a much greater expansion of the role of the state than others. The key to an answer lies in the fact that not all interests are equally served by an extension of the role of the state. In all societies, there is likely to be a social stratum that is privileged by the present distribution of resources between classes. This stratum is likely to be the core of the political Right: those who, in passive mode, seek to frustrate threats to the *status quo* or who, in the active mode of today's radical Right, seek to create an economic environment which favours those who compete most effectively, that is, generally, those already holding the greatest economic power. So the question now becomes: why has this stratum been more successful in shaping policy outcomes in some nations than in others? The answer I gave to this question in my work on welfare state development in Scandinavia was that the 'political influence' of this stratum depended 'on the historical and structural forces which have shaped the party system' and that 'to the degree that such forces have led to a large and united party of the Right, which can act as a political instrumentality of the privileged stratum, there will be a strong impediment to welfare' (Castles, 1978, 75).

What, in effect, this hypothethis argued was that the impact of ideologies and class conflict in modern societies was not just a function of the size of the contending classes created by industrialization, but also depended on historical and institutional factors which shaped the democratic expression of class interests. Thus, to give the example that was foremost in my mind in formulating this hypothesis, there was likely to be a major difference between the impact of the political Right in Scandinavia and in the English-speaking countries because, in the former, proportional representation allowed historical cleavages to fragment the 'bourgeois' interest into competing parties, whilst, in the latter, first-past-the-post electoral systems strongly discouraged party splintering. Consequently, in Scandinavia it was relatively easy for a growing political labour movement to exploit differences between the parties of the Right, whereas, in the English-speaking countries, the Right stood united against change (cf. Esping-Andersen, 1985).

The identification of the major party of the Right is not always straightforward. Whereas democratic socialist parties have generally worn their ideology on their sleeves by announcing their membership of the Socialist International, the same has not been true on the other side of politics. The problem of identification has been most acute where the space on the right of the political spectrum has been occupied by both secular and Christian Democratic parties of the centre right. In these circumstances, the solution adopted in my previous research, and embodied in the figures in Table 3.4, has been to count a secular party of the Right

Table 3.4 Average percentage of cabinet seats for the major party of the Right for various periods between 1950 and the early 1990s

Country	1950–59	1960–73	1974–early 1990s	1950–early 1990s
Australia	100	92	38	67
Canada	25	24	47	35
Ireland	24	4	29	20
New Zealand	79	79	61	73
UK	82	59	74	72
USA	69	43	70	62
Denmark	13	9	21	16
Finland	1	5	13	8
Norway	0	16	19	11
Sweden	0	0	12	7
Austria	53	51	17	36
Belgium	24	10	19	18
France	20	57	20	32
Germany	70	51	46	53
Italy	79	75	63	70
Netherlands	3	18	21	22
Greece	70	71	56	64
Portugal	100	100	61	83
Spain	100	100	10	71
Switzerland	36	29	29	32
Japan	95	100	96	97
Mean	49.67	47.3	39.1	45.1
Correlation with 1960		0.92	0.66	0.95
Coefficient of variation	74.59	73.89	62.89	61.62

Sources and notes: The major party of the Right is defined according to criteria to be found in Castles (1982). The data are from Schmidt (1996b). Greece, Portugal and Spain are regarded as having been ruled exclusively by rightist governments during the periods of their respective juntas. The data-point for the early 1990s is 1994. The use of the time-periods is illustrative only. In the statistical analysis of later chapters, average cabinet seats for the major parties of the Right are generally calculated for periods starting in 1950 and culminating with the time-point under analysis (i.e. the assumption is that the impact of parties is cumulative over longish time-periods).

as the major party of the Right where it has been able consistently to command 10 per cent of the vote, but, in the absence of such a party, to count the Christian Democratic party as the major party of the Right. According to this criterion, the German and Italian Christian Democratic parties are counted as parties of the Right, but not the Christian parties in Belgium and the Netherlands. This operational definition has been criticized (Schmidt, 1986, 1996a), but may be defended on the ground of the *prima facie* absurdity of the alternative implication, that Germany and Italy have been without major parties of the Right throughout the post-war era.

The post-war fortunes of the political Right as shown in Table 3.4 have been relatively unchanging. As between 1950–59 and 1960–73, there were no major changes in the extent of Right incumbency. In the post-1974 period, there was an average decline in Right incumbency of around 8 percentage points. However, this was almost entirely accounted for by change in just three countries, Spain, Australia and Austria, a trio which in the 1980s became the somewhat unlikely vanguard of contemporary democratic socialism. Otherwise, there was relatively little movement in the positions of countries over time and only a quite marginal diminution in the extent of their variation. The story is one of nations which started out by being rather dissimilar and which stayed that way.

This impression of major cross-national difference and a lack of widespread change is reinforced by the family of nations patterns revealed by Table 3.4. With only a few exceptions, family groupings are clustered in much the same way over the entire period. The grouping that has much the lowest level of Right incumbency is the Scandinavian family. It is followed by the other small European nations and then by France and Germany. The countries in the bottom half of the distribution consist of Southern Europe minus Spain in the most recent period, but plus Italy throughout, the English-speaking nations minus Ireland and Canada, and Japan. The gulf between the groupings at the extremes is huge, with the Right in Scandinavia struggling to average 10 per cent of cabinet seats over the post-war period as a whole and only managing to achieve around 16 per cent in recent decades, whilst the English-speaking nations averaged over 55 per cent for the entire period and around 53 per cent in recent decades. These patterns can no more be interpreted as indicating the development of post-war ideological similarity amongst these nations than those observed earlier in respect of class politics and Left incumbency.

INSTITUTIONS, CONSTITUTIONS AND TREATIES

Politics is not just about conflicting demands and opposed ideologies; it is also about the institutional arrangements that societies devise to process demands and to manage conflicts. Such arrangements vary considerably in their degree of formality. They may simply be accustomed ways of tackling problems or they may involve procedures required to enact legislation or to change it as stipulated by constitutional documents or by treaty obligations. Whether formal or otherwise, institutions provide the basic ground rules of politics. They say who may enter the contest, how long it will last and how many hurdles must be surmounted before the winning-post is reached. Since these ground rules also shape the administrative and fiscal capacities of the state, they say much about how effective governments are likely to be in pursuing their objectives (Skocpol, 1985; March and Olsen, 1989; Steinmo, Thelen and Longstreth, 1992; Weaver and Rockman, 1993). We have already seen examples of such institutional rules in action in our earlier discussion. Voter registration procedures and compulsory voting arrangements condition levels of democratic participation; different types of electoral system hinder or encourage party fragmentation. Our purpose in this section is to outline some of the major institutional differences amongst the nations of advanced capitalism which have been considered particularly important as determinants of post-war public policy development.

The variables measuring these differences are to be found in Table 3.5. Corporatism, the variable in the first column of the table, is a concept which has been used extensively in the modern political economy literature to denote the institutionalization of class conflict in modern societies. The implication here is that differences in the extent of class mobilization of the kind discussed in an earlier section of this chapter may matter less for successful macro-economic policy outcomes than whether unions and business have a set of rules in place to regulate their conflicts. The variables in the second and third columns of the table seek to capture the argument that some types of constitutional structures make economic and social reform more difficult than do others. The political institution which has been most commonly identified as having such an impact is federalism, and the presence or absence of a federal structure is reported in the second column. However, federalism is not the only constitutional provision that makes reform more difficult to achieve, and the constitutional structure variable in the third column attempts to quantify the number of such impediments in each country. Finally, in the fourth column, we focus on a development which has some claim to be regarded as the most significant institutional innovation of the post-war

Table 3.5 Institutional variables

Country	Corporatism	Federalism	Constitutional structure	European Community: Year joined
Australia	−1.02	1	4	Never
Canada	−1.33	1	4	Never
Ireland	−0.53	0	0	1973
New Zealand	−1.10	0	0	Never
UK	−0.86	0	2	1973
USA	−1.34	1	7	Never
Denmark	0.51	0	0	1973
Finland	0.42	0	1	1995
Norway	1.53	0	1	Never
Sweden	1.40	0	0	1995
Austria	1.60	1	2	1995
Belgium[1]	0.29	0	1	1957
France	−0.72	0	2	1957
Germany	0.48	1	4	1957
Italy	−0.85	0	1	1957
Netherlands	1.00	0	1	1957
Greece[2]	−0.90	0	2	1986
Portugal[2]	0.51	0	0	1986
Spain[2]	−0.12	0	1	1986
Switzerland	0.57	1	6	Never
Japan	0.05	0	2	Never

Sources and notes: The corporatism scores are from Crepaz (1992) and are based on averaging and standardizing the many corporatism scales in the literature. Data for the Southern European countries supplied by Hans Keman of the Free University of Amsterdam.

Federalism is a dummy variable with federal states = 1, others = 0.1.

[1] Belgium became a federal state in 1993. However, since the most recent dependent variable in this study is for 1995, a time-point at which the change is most unlikely to have had an effect, we continue to score Belgium as a unitary state for the entirety of this study.

Constitutional structure is an additive index designed to capture constitutional impediments to policy change. Constitutional features covered include whether a country is a federation, whether it is bicameral, whether it is presidential, whether it has single-member constituencies and whether it has a referendum procedure. The source is Huber, Ragin and Stephens (1993) as modified by Schmidt (1996a).

[2] For the periods during which these nations were under dictatorial rule, the constitutional structure variable is set at zero (see discussion in text above).

European Community is a dummy variable which designates whether countries were EC members at the various time-points used for analysis in this study.

era in the OECD area. This was the establishment and further elaboration, initially by the Treaty of Rome in 1957 and subsequently by later agreements between the member states, of the European Community (now European Union), which by the late 1990s contained no less than 14 of the 21 nations under examination in this study. The issue here, as earlier in respect of the supposed development of globalizing trends in world trade, is whether the emergence of a transnational institution of this kind has led to a commensurate decline in policy autonomy at a national level.

Corporatism

The concept of corporatism has been both influential and contested in the comparative public policy literature. On the one hand, the notion that the emergence and institutionalization of consensual relations among labour, management and government in certain countries during the post-war era has been a key to superior outcomes in the areas of unemployment, inflation and economic growth has been a frequent theme of comparative economic policy analysis (see Schmitter, 1974; Lehmbruch, 1977; Schmidt, 1982; Crouch, 1985; Bruno and Sachs, 1985; Crepaz, 1992; Keman, 1993). On the other hand, the precise designation of which countries have corporatist institutions has differed from author to author, with the consequence that findings have been neither cumulative nor consistent (Therborn, 1987). One obvious reason for this disagreement amongst authorities concerning relative degrees of corporatism has been that relationships between actors in the labour market have not only differed as between countries, but also over time within countries. Ideally, what is required is a time-series tapping changes in labour market relationships. For union participation in economic decision-making since 1970, that is now becoming available (Compston, 1994, 1995a, 1995b), but only for about half the countries and part of the time-period covered by this study. Under these circumstances, the only particular virtue of the corporatism measure reported in Table 3.5 is that it represents an attempt to get away from the idiosyncrasies of particular definitions by averaging a large number of the scales available in the literature.

The essential basis of the corporatist argument as applied in the macro-economic policy area has been that, where unions have been ready to adopt a more 'encompassing' stance by sacrificing short-term gains to a longer-term public interest (see Olson, 1982), it has been possible to transform industrial relations into a positive-sum game, with returns to business in terms of a stable climate of economic expectations, to labour in terms of lower unemployment and social wage gains and to government in terms of favourable macro-economic outcomes. There is also, however, a broader conception which sees corporatism as a coalition of social interests built on the long-term hegemony of the labour movement which creates the basis for an emergent societal collectivism. The Scandinavian countries are most often described in these terms and both the comprehensiveness of their egalitarian welfare state policies and the collectivist flavour of their housing and urban policies have been attributed to a corporatist hegemony of this kind (Kemeny, 1992). Both a willingness to sacrifice short-term economic gains and a wider societal collectivism may also be involved in the generation of favourable environmental outcomes, which recent research has shown to be strongly associated with corporatist institutions (Crepaz, 1995; Jahn, 1997).

Looking at the figures in the first column of Table 3.5 in family of nations terms shows a pattern of differences among countries which has strong affinities with the ideological factors discussed earlier. The English-speaking nations, with long traditions of adversarial industrial relations, all score low on corporatism, whilst the countries scoring high are a mixture of Scandinavian and smaller European nations. The Scandinavian countries have been generally recognized as exemplars of consensual industrial bargaining as well as of societal collectivism, whilst the smaller European states are countries in which peaceful labour market relations are an aspect of a broad social consensus, owing much less to labour movement ideology, which is sometimes described as 'consociationalism' (Lijphart, 1968). The closest resemblance in family of nations terms is not, as one might imagine, between corporatism and the class mobilization, but between corporatism and Left incumbency. This would scarcely surprise Marxist critics, who see tripartite bargaining between unions, business and the government not as a way of realizing working class interests, but as a means of taming them. Whether, however, the institutionalization of class conflict should be seen as a precondition for continuing electoral support for the Left (the sell-out argument) or whether a left-wing government provides the unions with the guarantees needed to take a long-term encompassing perspective (the 'power resources' argument) remains essentially a matter of interpretation.

Finally, it is important to note one crucial difference between corporatism as measured here and the other political variables discussed in this study. This is Japan's middling corporatism score, which contrasts markedly with its extreme position with respect to both measures of party ideology and, to a somewhat lesser extent, that for class mobilization. This point has to be highlighted, since the concept's ability to account for favourable labour market outcomes rests largely on Japan's outstanding macro-economic performance, and Japan's positioning on corporatism scales is probably more contested than that of any other country in our sample. There can be no doubt whatsoever that labour relations in Japan are consensual, and have become more so as the post-war period has progressed, but whether this is a function of the incorporation of the labour movement into the economic decision-making process or of freezing it out altogether is a matter of very considerable debate (cf. Pempel and Tsunekawa 1979).

Constitutional impediments to change

In a recent paper on the link between federalism and social policy out-comes, Pierson (1995) suggests that what he calls 'new institutionalist' arguments are relatively new in the comparative public policy field. At least in regard to the potential impacts of federalism itself this is not true. Although Wilensky's main focus was on explaining differences in welfare spending amongst countries at quite disparate economic levels, he argued that, amongst the rich countries, centralization of government was an important factor contributing to higher spending and greater equality (Wilensky, 1975, 52–3). In a similar vein, Cameron (1978, 1253), whose main contribution was to discuss the role of an open economy in promot-ing public spending, suggested that federalism 'dampen[s] the degree of expansion of the public economy'. Moreover, early work in the 'politics matters' tradition demonstrated that federal institutions led to lower wel-fare spending and higher levels of infant mortality than unitary institutions and that these effects were actually greater than those associ-ated with partisan incumbency (Castles and McKinlay, 1979). In fact, one might point to the federalism/social policy linkage as one of the very few areas of unanimity in the literature, with writers from all the main com-peting explanatory paradigms arguing that federal institutions are inimical to high levels of social spending (see also Gordon, 1988, 23).

There are at least three obvious mechanisms which make federalism potentially inhospitable to social reform on a major scale. First, the exis-tence of a division of powers between central and state governments rests on constitutional stipulations which make it very difficult to amend the fun-damental rules of the political game. Second, federalism implies a proliferation of political levers for opposing change, including second chambers representing the states, state legislatures and state and federal judiciaries. Finally, where the states have the responsibility for policy-making, provision is likely to be patchy – good in some jurisdictions, but less good elsewhere – with this lack of national uniformity tending to lead to lower overall spending than in unitary nations. These arguments are essentially negative: federalism undercuts the potential for groups to mobi-lize for extensive change. In his recent contribution to this literature, Pierson

(1995, 453–4) suggests a more positive twist to the story: the fragmenting effect of federal institutions prevents the formation of class alliances of the kind associated with welfare reform, whilst the territorial bias of these institutions simultaneously creates the basis for regional coalitions of interests.

Federalism is not the only constitutional lever available to those opposing change and, arguably, wherever power is divided between institutions, there will be a proliferation of veto points that can be used by those seeking to frustrate the wishes of the majority. Thus, to give two examples from the recent literature, the fact that the spending initiatives of Swiss governments may be challenged by citizen plebiscites (Immergut, 1992) and that the US Congressional committee system separates the responsibility for taxing and spending decisions (Steinmo, 1995) have been variously identified as important determinants of the low levels of public expenditure in these nations. The third column of Table 3.5 presents an index of institutional veto points which is drawn from the work of Huber, Ragin and Stephens (1993) as amended by Schmidt (1996b). These impediments include the existence of federal institutions and their strength, whether there is a presidential form of government, whether elections have a territorial bias, whether the legislature is bicameral and, if so, how strong the second chamber is and whether there are provisions for popular referenda. In each case, the index scores positively the presence of institutions to which citizens and organized interest groups can appeal in order to prevent change: state governments, the president, constituencies, the upper house and the people.

In relation to the data in the second and third columns of Table 3.5, we wish to make only three very brief points. First, and for obvious reasons, there are very strong affinities between the federalism and constitutional structure variables. In substantive terms, the only major difference is that Austria is a federal state, but is scored as having fewer veto points than the other federal nations. Austrian federalism has often been considered almost exclusively administrative in character, and the nuance provided by the constitutional structure index is almost certainly an appropriate one. Second, federalism offers an interesting family of nations story, with two distinct clusters apparent in the data – the overseas English-speaking countries and the German-speaking nations. In both cases, the adoption of federal institutions reflects the creation of nations out of previously sovereign states: the settler colonies of the British Empire and the principalities of Germanic Europe. Third, it is necessary to emphasize that neither of these variables measuring constitutional impediments to change will necessarily function particularly well for the earlier periods of this analysis. The reason is that the authoritarian regimes of Southern Europe prior to the mid-1970s did not require constitutional provisions to inhibit change precisely because conservative authoritarianism was itself the ultimate defence against democracy's potential for radical reform.

The European Community

The inclusion of the European Community (EC) as a final institutional
variable in this study is less because of clear predictions in the comparative literature of the likely policy impacts of this post-war innovation in
European political institution-building than because of developments,
such as the emergence of an integrated market and steps towards monetary union, which make it quite clear that the Community has such a
potential (see Wallace and Wallace, 1996). Such arguments rest on the
view that the Community has progressively acquired characteristics
making it into what Sbragia (1992) calls a 'quasi-federal', and what
Leibfried and Pierson (1995) describe as a 'multi-tiered', political system.
Various implications in respect of both social and labour market policy
follow from this view. First is the implication that, as the new European
political entity has acquired greater decision-making authority, so the
nation-states constituting it have begun to lose their policy autonomy.
This development is almost certainly less pronounced in the area of social
policy than of labour market policy, since, in the former, the focus
has been on minimum social protection rather than on new social policy
initiatives, which are reserved for the nation-states making up the
Community, whereas a fundamental rationale of the treaties has been
progressively to remove all market distortions. However, even minimum
conditions may matter when countries falling below the minima have
treaty obligations to rectify the situation. Moreover, the removal of
market distortions itself has direct and indirect social policy impacts,
including stipulations concerning health and safety standards, the porta-
bility of social policy protections and the removal of national public
service monopolies in the area of service provision.

Second is the implication that, as the Community has acquired more
authority in these areas, policies have become more standardized. Instead
of many national policies, a genuinely European social policy and a genuinely European labour market policy are in the process of emerging.
These implications are neutral or benign, but a third possible implication
is that the Community has created the conditions for undermining the
existing social and labour market protections of European nation-states.
Factors contributing to such a development may include the proliferation
of veto points in an institutional structure, which has some claim to be
far more complex than any national federation, and the essentially negative basis for integration given by the rationale of creating a single
European market (see discussion in Leibfried and Pierson, 1995). These
latter tendencies are exemplified by the strong emphasis on market-
conforming deregulatory policies which has accompanied intensified

moves towards stronger economic integration from the early 1990s onwards (Streck and Schmitter, 1991). They are also evident in pressures to cut national social policy budgets in order to meet the maximum budget deficit criterion for accession to the single currency.

These implications suggest that we should be looking for trends towards greater standardization and/or deterioration in the social and labour market protections of countries belonging to the EC. It is quite possible, however, that the data at our disposal are too crude for the purpose. Partly that is because much of the real activism in building the institutions of a single market has taken place only in the last 15 years or so, whilst the deregulatory zeal of the Community has been an even more recent phenomenon. Hence, an analysis based on an early 1990s data point and a measure of change from 1960 to the early 1990s is unlikely to capture the policy consequences of either of these developments. No less problematical is the fact that the composition of the EC has itself changed radically over its four-decade history, and this shows up in its social expenditure profile. The five nations featuring in this study which signed the Treaty of Rome (Belgium, France, Germany, Italy and the Netherlands) were all European social expenditure leaders (see Table 4.1 below). In 1973, they were joined by one welfare state leader, Denmark, and two welfare state laggards, Ireland and the United Kingdom. In 1986, the admission of the three Southern European nations meant that the Community now contained a very mixed profile of high- and low-expenditure states. Only with the last wave of entrants in 1995 did the tide once again turn with the accession of Austria, Finland and Sweden, all of them in the post-1960 vanguard of OECD welfare state development. These changes in the composition of membership obviously make it difficult to be sure that any observed change in EC member nations' social expenditure performance is a function of the altered policy dynamics created by the emergence of the Community as a separate political institution.

A FRACTURED MODERNITY

In Chapters 2 and 3, we have reviewed the major factors identified by the comparative literature as significant in shaping the trajectory of post-war public policy outcomes, and this has involved providing an account of the changing character of the main economic, social and political parameters of post-war development in the OECD nations. Partly because it has been amongst the most influential of the theoretical frameworks in the literature, and partly because it provides an account which purports to show the interconnections between different factors, we have framed our discussion as a kind of loosely knit commentary on modernization theory. The final task for this chapter is to focus more squarely on the patterns of association manifested by the variables featuring in our discussion. At every point we have seen that the trajectory of policy change has been attributed to the major economic, social and political transformation of the post-war era. What we seek to establish here is whether that means that policy-makers in different nations progressively find themselves in a world in which their decisions are shaped by the same range of closely interlinked socio-economic considerations or whether the post-war context of policy-making manifests a more substantial diversity resting on the variety of routes to and through modernity.

The main basis for our analysis in this section is the set of correlation matrices which appears in Appendix 3.1. Rather than describing the degree of association between variables at different points of time, as did the correlations reported in previous tables, the figures reported here indicate the degree of association between the main factors discussed in Chapters 2 and 3. With only minor exceptions, the data from which these correlations are calculated are the measures contained in Tables 2.2 to 2.7 and 3.1 to 3.5 above. A few variables are omitted to avoid duplication. On these grounds Catholicism stands as the only measure of religious division, and constitutional structure as the only indicator of institutional impediments to change. The only other difference between the data here and those in the tables in the text is that the Left and Right incumbency measures in Appendix 3.1(d) are for the 1960–93 period rather than the 1950–94 period reported in the final columns of Tables 3.3 and 3.4. Useful benchmarks to keep in mind for those unaccustomed to interpreting such statistics are that correlations greater than + or – 0.50 indicate that two variables share 25 per cent or more of the same variation and that correlations greater than + or – 0.70 indicate a shared variation of 50 per cent or more. Correlations at or above + or – 0.40 may be regarded as statistically significant. It may also be useful to know that variables within each matrix are arranged in descending level of association with GDP. This has been done in order to provide a simple way of seeing which variables are most closely associated with the most commonly used measure of socio-economic modernization.

A first point to make is that there are only a few instances of very high (more than +/– 0.70) correlations in the matrices making up Appendix 3.1. Those that there are relate almost exclusively to relationships amongst the core socio-economic variables. In 1960 and 1974, there was a strong clustering of GDP, urbanization and agricultural and services employment. By the early 1990s, this clustering had diminished and the only association of this magnitude was the negative correlation between GDP per capita and agricultural employment. For change between 1960 and the early 1990s, there was a strong association between GDP and the various measures of occupational structure, but the earlier link with urbanization was somewhat less pronounced. With the exception of these socio-economic linkages, the only other associations of comparable magnitude were between electoral turnout and union density in both 1960 and 1974. This latter linkage is an artefact of the decision to code both variables with zero values under circumstances of authoritarian rule, although there is clearly a substantive rationale for a coding that is based on seeing authoritarianism as the antithesis of both democracy and free trade unionism. After the mid-1970s and the democratization of Southern Europe, this relationship is much diminished. The general picture of only a moderate degree of interconnection between most of the factors featuring in this study is to be welcomed on technical statistical grounds. On the one hand, it means that the variables located as the main determinants of policy development are likely to capture substantially different portions of the policy variation amongst these nations. On the other, it means that high levels of intercorrelation amongst variables are less likely to undermine the validity of our later statistical analysis.

The strong linkages around GDP per capita, employment structure and urbanization are exactly the kinds of associations that would be hypothesized on the basis of modernization theory. Countries that are rich are likely to be urban and will tend to have experienced a shift away from agriculture and, more recently, towards services. This clustering of characteristics is clearly indicative of a developmental trend in which these variables have been closely interlinked, but its implications for the present degree of similarity of these nations is more open to question. Establishing trends, even as strong as some of those shown here, is not the same thing as demonstrating that countries that are high on one measure will invariably be high on associated measures. For instance, were we to take GDP, urbanization, services and agricultural employment as measures of socio-economic development, and argue that to be fully modern a country must fall in the top third of the distribution for the first three variables and in the bottom third for the last one, only one country, Australia, would qualify as fully modern in 1960, and none in the early 1990s. Were we to reverse these criteria as a means of categorizing nations which were wholly non-modern, only Greece, Ireland and Portugal would meet the criteria in 1960 and only Greece and Portugal in the early 1990s. Between these extremes of full socio-economic modernization and its absence are to be found virtually all the countries in this study, characterized by diverse combinations of high, medium and low values on different measures of modernization. Moreover, judging by the general decline in the level of association between these variables over time, the likelihood of any given nation exhibiting all the features of socio-economic modernity or non-modernity simultaneously has been decreasing rather than increasing over time.

Protagonists of modernization theory would argue, with some considerable justification, that this was a somewhat peculiar way of assessing whether countries were really modern. Criteria resting on positions in a cross-national distribution imply a relativity quite foreign to the notion of modernization, which is generally seen as involving an absolute measure of the progress of nations. Modernity is achieved by attaining certain levels of development, not by being more developed than other nations. Seeing things in this light wholly modifies the conclusions we may draw about nations' progress towards modernity over the course of the post-war era. For instance, taking as our measure of modernity the level of GDP per capita and services employment achieved in 1960 by the USA, which, at the time, was the OECD's most advanced nation according to both criteria, only Greece, Ireland, Portugal and Spain of the countries analysed here would not have been fully modern by the early 1990s. Seen in this way, the processes of socio-economic development examined in Chapter 2 have created a group of nations virtually all of which share the same characteristics of modernity.

One way of recognizing the simultaneous validity of both these perspectives is to think in terms of threshold values of the kind that we earlier suggested might characterize the democratization process. The argument might then be that certain facets of socio-economic development had a more or less common trajectory until they reached certain critical values, beyond which point change in any one factor had a diminishing or negligible impact on the other factors with which it had formerly been associated. Such an interpretation would be compatible with the observed post-war pattern of a continuing, but declining association between core socio-economic variables. It would also be compatible with the view that diminishing differences between nations in respect of individual components of modernization (namely, the declining coefficients of variation of most of the variables examined in Chapter 2) do not necessarily lead to greater national uniformity, but rather may result in continuing national diversity based on differences in the ways in which specific trajectories of socio-economic development have combined to produce distinctive routes to modernity.

The clustering of nations in terms of modernization is not merely a matter of riches, occupational structure and urbanization. Two other variables in Appendix 3.1 are consistently associated with these socio-economic measures, although to a somewhat lesser degree. First, there is some coincidence between the religious division amongst these countries and measures of socio-economic modernity, with Protestant nations being significantly richer and having significantly higher levels of services employment than Catholic nations. Second, and much more surprisingly, constitutional structure is consistently positively associated with high levels of GDP per capita, a finding which might well be of interest to 'new institutionalists' seeking to provide an account of the factors promoting economic development, were it not for the fact that Appendix 3.1(d) shows a negative, if insignificant, relationship between constitutional structure and post-war economic growth.

In reality, it would seem that both the Catholic and the constitutional linkages are the legacies of historical contingencies long predating the post-war period. Certainly, the Catholic nations of Western Europe were those in which industrial development was slowest to take off in the nineteenth century, and arguably that was a function of the ways in which capitalist enterprise was encouraged by Protestant attitudes to worldly endeavour in earlier centuries (Weber, 1968). The positive correlation between economic growth and Catholicism in Appendix 3.1(d) suggests some minor catch-up by these nations in the post-war era, but the persisting negative relationships between socio-economic indicators and Catholicism shown in Appendix 3.1(c) indicate that these countries still lag behind in modernization terms. What makes for the strong association between constitutional structure and economic development is that the English-speaking settler states, which had found it natural to create new nations via the federation of existing colonies, had been made rich in the nineteenth century by their trading relationships with Britain and by a ratio of land to labour far more favourable than any which existed in the Old World. As trading patterns have changed, as the new nations have grown in population and as capital has become relatively more important as a source of the wealth of nations, these advantages have waned and these countries' head-starts in economic modernity have disappeared.

If the clustering of variables around socio-economic modernization is, in some respects, wider than we might expect, in other ways it is much narrower. This is true of manufacturing employment, where the association with these variables is strong in 1960, but declines to almost nothing by the early 1990s. It is also true of the size of the aged population, which is very modestly associated with these variables in 1960, but not at all in 1974 or in the early 1990s. These two findings would seem to contradict two central tenets of the modernization thesis: that it is industrial manufacturing which has been the engine of socio-economic modernization, and that the way in which modernization most directly impacts on public expenditure development is through a changing demographic structure. However, the first contradiction is more apparent than real. Looking at Appendix 3.1(d), we can see that the strong association between GDP and services and the progressively weaker one between GDP and manufacturing that are manifested in Appendix 3.1(a), (b) and (c) are almost exactly reversed for change between 1960 and the early 1990s. This is compatible with an interpretation in which manufacturing remains the key to growth (exemplified by the post-war economic miracles of Germany and Japan), but in which countries shift to services employment as they become richer, with some consequent slowdown in their rate of economic growth.

The second contradiction is more fundamental. It may well be, as comparative public policy research inspired by modernization theory has insisted, that the age structure of the population is pivotal to the growth of the welfare state, but, at least in terms of levels of development, the connections between demography and other indicators of socio-economic modernity are negligible. In terms of change over time, there are some quite modest positive relationships between population ageing, economic growth and growth in the services sector. However, they are hardly of a magnitude likely to lead to a greater correspondence between these diverse components of socio-economic development in the near future. Thus, if population ageing is seen as an aspect of socio-economic modernity, it would appear to be a modernity so deeply fractured that the linkages between its separate elements are scarcely discernible at any time during the post-war era.

It is only possible to interpret this finding in a manner broadly compatible with the thrust of the modernization thesis by, once again, thinking about the developmental sequence in terms of threshold effects. Clearly, as nations industrialize, urbanize and become more affluent, their populations grow older, but, beyond a certain point, changes in these variables are only weakly interconnected. It can be argued that for all but the very poorest countries in the group of nations treated here, this threshold had already been reached quite early in the post-war period. While some modestly significant relationships between these variables are noticeable in Appendix 3.1(d), they are, in fact, all dependent on the inclusion of the Southern European nations in the sample. Although the age structures of the countries featuring in this study did become more similar between 1960 and the early 1990s (see coefficients of variation in Table 2.6), there is nothing in any of the correlation matrices in Appendix 3.1 to suggest that this was a result of socio-economic modernization. The most recent forecasts of the likely pattern of the future ageing of the population suggest that, in coming decades, there will be a marked increase in the percentage of the population of 65 years and over right across the OECD. However, it is estimated that, by the year 2030, the 21 countries under analysis here will not be any more similar than they are now, with an estimated coefficient of variation for that date of 12.39 (calculated from OECD, 1996e) compared with the figure of 11.67 for the early 1990s appearing in Table 2.6.

The notion of a fractured modernity, emerging as nations progressively surmount the various thresholds of socio-economic modernization, is reinforced when we examine the patterns of association manifested by the political variables in Appendix 3.1. Here, as might be expected, we once again encounter a distinct clustering of variables, although somewhat less pronounced than in the case of the core socio-economic factors. The Right and Left are negatively related at around the 0.60 level throughout, union density and Left incumbency are positively related at around the same magnitude in the earlier periods, but much less strongly in the 1990s, and the unions and the Right are modestly and negatively associated throughout. As noted previously, despite the fact that corporatism has been conceptualized as a measure of the institutionalization of class conflict, it is most closely associated with Left incumbency, with a strong positive relationship in the earlier periods declining to a barely significant one in the early 1990s.

It is not, however, this clustering of political variables which so decisively fragments modernity, but rather the fact that this cluster of variables is, with only a very few exceptions, wholly unconnected with the core measures of socio-economic modernization. In the earlier periods, union density was very modestly negatively linked to agricultural and services employment, while, in 1974, the Right appeared to be more at home in countries with high levels of agricultural employment than in those in which services were dominant. In respect of change over the period as a whole, unions grew significantly more in countries which were becoming richer, more urbanized, and in which manufacturing and services were expanding at the expense of agriculture. As the unions developed in directions partially shaped by their socio-economic environment, they became less strongly linked with both Left incumbency and corporatism. However, when all these exceptions are fully itemized, what remains is an extraordinary picture in which there is almost no sign that partisan incumbency reflected the massive economic change of the period or its repercussions on social structure. It would thus appear that the 'politics matters' theorists are quite correct in seeing the political dimension as cutting directly across most aspects of socio-economic development and as having the potential to shape public policy outcomes in directions quite other than those reflecting that development.

Given that the stuff of politics is conflict concerning issues of contemporary economic and social relevance, the fact that patterns of partisan incumbency and the institutionalization of class conflict manifest no obvious connections with core socio-economic processes requires some explanation. The answer lies in distinguishing between the content and the structure of partisan politics. The content is contemporary debate on socio-economic issues, and the state of that debate determines the relative state of the parties. But how many parties there are, and the normal parameters within which their strength can vary, is a consequence of the institutional structuring of the party system, and this has very little to do with issues of contemporary socio-economic relevance. As Stein Rokkan (Lipset and Rokkan, 1967; Rokkan, 1970) so brilliantly documented, the emergent party systems of the Western democracies were an expression of historical cleavages pertaining to cultural, territorial, industrial and class conflicts over successive centuries. For much of this century, these divisions were 'frozen' through the institutionalization of party systems that occurred contemporaneously with the advent of mass democracy, with the choice of electoral system and the huge advantages accruing to incumbent parties being the key factors locking in the democratization settlement. In the political realm, democratization was the decisive threshold of modernity, but, for most of the nations we are discussing, it is a modernity which is now many decades old.

Thus, a major reason why modernity is fractured is that it contains echoes of its own past. In the last few decades, there has been some evidence of an 'unfreezing' of party systems (Daalder and Mair, 1983; Bartolini and Mair, 1990), but, if our earlier analysis of changing patterns of Left and Right incumbency is correct, the impact on the balance of partisan strength was scarcely visible prior to the mid-1970s, and has been more pronounced in respect of Left than of Right incumbency since that time. More fundamental changes may be taking place in the 1990s, as countries such as Italy, Japan and New Zealand remodel the electoral rules which are the key to party-system transformation, but a discussion of the policy impact of these changes will have to wait for some later account of patterns of public policy development in the post-post-war era.

To complete our analysis of Appendix 3.1, we finally examine how the European Community and international trade variables are linked with the other factors analysed in this study. What both variables have in common is that they may be seen as influences potentially impinging on and restricting the policy-making autonomy of nation-states. In the case of the European Community, any influence manifested is likely to be in directions quite different from those implied by other variables, with which it seems only marginally connected. In the whole of Appendix 3.1, there are only three linkages of even marginal significance: positively with Catholicism and negatively with GDP in the early 1990s, and positively between original Community membership and growth in international trade over the whole period. The first two linkages seem unlikely to have survived the accession of Finland and Sweden to Community membership in 1995.

Patterns of international trade have much closer links with other variables. However, in a manner which is a mirror image of the way in which constitutional structure featured as part of a syndrome of socio-economic factors, patterns of trade appear here as part of the politics cluster of variables. In both 1960 and 1974, trade is positively associated with Left incumbency, corporatism and union strength. In these years, it is still more strongly negatively associated with Right incumbency and, unlike the other linkages, this one remains significant into the early 1990s. These are relationships which have been discussed extensively in the comparative policy literature. Cameron's (1978) account of the way in which trade dependence leads to greater state intervention sees labour movement strength as the vital factor mediating between exposure to an open economy and the adoption of socially protective policy initiatives. On the other hand, Castles (1982, 77–83) has suggested that the greater association with Right incumbency is compatible with a historical account resting on the way in which trade exposure fostered political conflicts between landed and urban élites in the smaller nations of Western Europe in the latter part of the nineteenth century. This conflict splintered the political Right and became institutionalized in the newly democratic party systems which emerged in these countries with the adoption of mass suffrage early in the twentieth century. In other words, international trade was one of the factors which etched the templates of partisan cleavage in these countries, with implications for the post-war patterns of public policy that can only be assessed on the basis of our subsequent analysis.

Four main points emerge from the account of the post-war transformation presented in these chapters. Each highlights ways in which the modernization process has failed to deliver uniformity amongst nations, producing a fractured modernity in which continuing economic, social and political diversity promises a comparable diversity of national policy outcomes. The first point is that, despite the clear evidence of clustering amongst core socio-economic factors and of a general tendency towards greater similarity in respect of each of them, individual nations have continued to be characterized by quite different combinations of attributes as they have moved beyond diverse thresholds of modernity. The second point is that this diversity of national experience goes along with clear evidence, provided by the frequency with which families of nations were apparent in our data, of commonalities amongst groups of nations and differences between these groupings. These differences can be seen as a manifestation of the fracture lines existing between alternative routes to and through modernity. The third point is that there is a major disjuncture between the age structure of the population and other aspects of socio-economic development which is likely to matter hugely from a public policy viewpoint if that factor turns out to be as crucial for public expenditure development as is generally thought. The final point is that the most radical fractures of all are constituted by partisan differences, which, unlike socio-economic factors, show few signs of a convergent tendency, and which, as institutionalized outgrowths of historical cleavages, appear largely unconnected to the main socio-economic cleavages of the post-war era. Such a highly schematic representation of the character of post-war transformation leaves many, many questions unanswered, but that is as must be expected of an account which seeks to cram the experience of 21 countries over five decades into just two chapters. From a comparative public policy viewpoint, the really big question that remains is how the transformation we have sketched has impacted on post-war policy outcomes. It is that question which preoccupies us in the remainder of this volume.

APPENDIX 3.1 CORRELATION MATRICES

(a) 1960

	GDP	Agr.	Ser.	Man.	Con.	Urb.	Cath.	Uns.	Turn.	Age	Rgt	Left	Trade	Crp.	EC
GDP	1.00														
Agriculture	-0.81	1.00													
Services	0.74	-0.87	1.00												
Manufacturing	0.63	-0.79	0.41	1.00											
Constitution	0.58	-0.38	0.39	0.33	1.00										
Urbanization	0.53	-0.80	0.76	0.49	0.15	1.00									
Catholicism	-0.50	0.48	-0.51	-0.34	-0.06	-0.31	1.00								
Unions	0.40	-0.45	0.36	0.29	-0.17	0.39	-0.26	1.00							
Turnout	0.29	-0.43	0.48	0.16	-0.04	0.56	-0.32	0.72	1.00						
Age	0.27	-0.38	0.14	0.46	-0.09	0.23	0.12	0.56	0.22	1.00					
Right	-0.26	0.21	-0.23	-0.12	0.20	-0.05	0.25	-0.39	-0.32	-0.43	1.00				
Left	0.18	-0.23	0.15	0.21	-0.41	0.08	-0.49	0.60	0.28	0.50	-0.66	1.00			
Trade	0.11	-0.31	0.21	0.25	-0.38	0.19	-0.12	0.51	0.29	0.45	-0.68	0.58	1.00		
Corporatism	-0.09	-0.02	-0.23	0.28	-0.32	-0.18	-0.13	0.26	-0.04	0.35	-0.46	0.70	0.57	1.00	
EC 1960	-0.01	-0.21	0.03	0.20	-0.04	0.40	0.30	0.04	0.34	0.22	-0.16	-0.11	0.18	0.04	1.00

(b) 1974

	GDP	Agr.	Ser.	Con.	Turn.	Urb.	Cath.	Uns.	Man.	Rgt	Left	Trade	EC	Crp.	Age
GDP	1.00														
Agriculture	-0.84	1.00													
Services	0.79	-0.87	1.00												
Constitution	0.61	-0.38	0.32	1.00											
Turnout	0.53	-0.75	0.64	-0.01	1.00										
Urbanization	0.53	-0.77	0.75	0.07	0.57	1.00									
Catholicism	-0.52	0.55	-0.63	-0.06	-0.45	-0.46	1.00								
Unions	0.36	-0.59	0.54	-0.22	0.85	0.40	-0.53	1.00							
Manufacturing	0.35	-0.50	0.02	0.28	0.33	0.18	-0.05	0.20	1.00						
Right	-0.32	0.40	-0.45	0.13	-0.45	-0.20	0.25	-0.56	0.01	1.00					
Left	0.22	-0.38	0.30	-0.35	0.42	0.24	-0.49	0.70	0.16	-0.60	1.00				
Trade	-0.09	-0.17	0.11	-0.45	0.31	0.08	0.11	0.43	0.10	-0.65	0.42	1.00			
EC 1974	-0.09	-0.24	0.09	-0.23	0.38	0.37	0.18	0.18	0.20	-0.26	0.00	0.42	1.00		
Corporatism	-0.06	-0.06	-0.11	-0.32	0.14	-0.15	-0.13	0.37	0.27	-0.43	0.70	0.51	-0.05	1.00	
Age	0.02	-0.19	-0.05	-0.11	0.17	0.09	0.20	0.25	0.41	-0.36	0.59	0.41	0.42	0.50	1.00

(c) Early 1990s

	GDP	Agr.	Ser.	Con.	Cath.	EC	Urb.	Trade	Turn.	Left	Corp.	Man.	Age	Uns.	Rgt
GDP	1.00														
Agriculture	-0.83	1.00													
Services	0.69	-0.69	1.00												
Constitution	0.61	-0.35	0.27	1.00											
Catholicism	-0.55	0.48	-0.59	-0.06	1.00										
EC 1990s	-0.52	0.24	-0.37	-0.37	0.54	1.00									
Urbanization	0.47	0.47	0.58	0.05	-0.42	0.04	1.00								
Trade	-0.19	0.01	0.08	-0.39	0.30	0.25	0.03	1.00							
Turnout	-0.17	0.04	-0.03	-0.04	0.00	0.17	0.52	0.15	1.00						
Left	-0.16	0.14	-0.07	-0.26	0.04	-0.15	0.03	0.03	0.46	1.00					
Corporatism	0.04	-0.20	-0.09	-0.32	-0.13	-0.10	-0.10	0.34	0.07	0.47	1.00				
Manufacturing	0.04	-0.20	-0.48	0.03	0.10	0.20	-0.17	-0.00	-0.13	-0.14	0.36	1.00			
Age	0.02	-0.21	-0.04	-0.20	-0.09	0.16	0.10	0.00	0.16	0.43	0.61	0.38	1.00		
Unions	-0.02	-0.04	0.17	-0.49	-0.44	-0.23	0.09	0.38	0.39	0.31	0.43	0.04	0.34	1.00	
Right	0.02	0.09	-0.16	0.26	-0.13	-0.04	-0.07	-0.51	-0.15	-0.60	-0.54	0.06	-0.30	-0.36	1.00

(d) Change: 1990–early 1990s

	GDP	Agr.	Man.	Age	Urb.	Uns.	Rgt.	Turn.	Cath.	Con.	Left	Ser.	Corp.	Trade	EC
GDP	1.00														
Agriculture	-0.75	1.00													
Manufacturing	0.73	-0.84	1.00												
Age	0.47	-0.48	0.32	1.00											
Urbanization	0.44	-0.70	0.49	0.51	1.00										
Unions	0.42	-0.60	0.41	0.55	0.56	1.00									
Right	0.39	-0.19	0.26	0.31	-0.15	-0.01	1.00								
Turnout	0.39	-0.51	0.19	0.38	0.37	0.48	0.19	1.00							
Catholicism	0.35	-0.44	0.41	-0.22	-0.05	-0.16	0.08	0.39	1.00						
Constitition	-0.31	0.36	-0.32	-0.10	-0.33	-0.34	0.20	-0.20	-0.06	1.00					
Left	-0.30	0.11	-0.34	0.02	0.28	-0.11	-0.52	0.00	-0.24	-0.30	1.00				
Services	0.21	-0.59	0.16	0.46	0.63	0.53	-0.23	0.51	0.15	-0.35	0.33	1.00			
Corporatism	0.12	-0.06	-0.06	0.22	0.27	0.14	-0.54	0.09	-0.13	-0.32	0.64	0.30	1.00		
Trade	0.11	-0.18	0.24	-0.48	-0.18	0.09	-0.21	0.15	0.70	-0.18	-0.19	-0.05	-0.17	1.00	
EC 1960	-0.02	0.17	0.00	-0.13	-0.32	-0.36	-0.12	-0.29	0.30	-0.04	-0.15	-0.11	0.04	0.14	1.00

4. The causes of big government

INTRODUCTION

In this chapter, we begin our task of trying to make sense of the forces impacting on public policy development in the post-war era by looking at the big aggregates of expenditure and taxation which define the reach of the modern state. Although this focus on aggregates conveys little information about the specific character of public programmes and their particular outcomes, it speaks to a question of abiding political significance: namely, does the modern state do too much or too little for its citizens? On the one side are arrayed those who argue that the growth of the state stifles individual initiative and economic incentive; on the other are those who see state programmes as means of helping the weak and of redressing the harmful effects of an untrammelled pursuit of economic self-interest.

These arguments are ultimately normative and cannot be decided by resort to analysis of the kind to be found in the pages of this book. However, the appeal and intellectual coherence of normative positions often rests on an understanding of the causes and consequences of human action, and these are matters which are properly addressed by systematic analysis. For instance, it may well make a difference to our view of the role of big government if we see it as a response to the ageing of the population. Partly, that is because such a finding implies that increases in state expenditure have been directed to meeting genuine need, and partly, it is because it suggests that, however much we may be anxious about a 'big brother' state, slash and burn campaigns against public spending are likely to have horrendous consequences for a major section of the population. But systematic analysis is not on one side or the other. If this example suggests a soft liberal realism concerning the present size of the state, others may indicate viable strategies for curbing big government. Analysis which demonstrated that constitutional arrangements such as federalism and strong bicameralism were effective in dampening public expenditure growth would equally provide the basis for a reform agenda for those with a normative preference for small government (cf. Brennan and Buchanan, 1980, 173–81).

Understanding the causes and consequences of big government cannot tell us what we should believe about the role of the state in modern society, but it can tell us a great deal about the kinds of policies which are likely to be realistic in the future and about the options we have for reshaping that future.

Apart from speaking to normative concerns, analysis of the reach of the state has the more obvious pay-off that it speaks directly to the theories of public expenditure development discussed in the last two chapters. Not all of these theories address the reach of the state as such, with the majority most immediately concerned to account for the ameliorative functions of modern government, but all have major implications for the size of government. If the welfare functions of the state have grown on the scale suggested in most accounts, then the size of government as measured by its overall expenditures and by its tax take is likely to be associated with the factors determining the size of the welfare state. It should be noted, too, that our findings concerning the forces influential in shaping the reach of the modern state are not merely of scientific interest, but also have important implications for the ways in which we view our own societies. Were we to discover, for instance, that politics really doesn't matter – that how you vote and whether you vote makes no difference to government expenditure programmes – then some quite serious thought would be required about what it means to say that these societies are democratic.

The three kinds of policy outcomes discussed in this chapter are total government outlays, total government receipts and civilian public consumption expenditure. Only the latter requires more specific comment at this stage. Government consumption expenditure for civilian purposes consists of the goods and services purchased by government for its own use other than those utilized for defence purposes. As we shall note subsequently, defence expenditures were of declining salience throughout the post-war period. Civilian public consumption expenditures include aspects of the welfare state, in particular, education, social services and, in most countries, a substantial part of the health sector, as well as public administration, infrastructure and other government services. The reason for isolating this category of expenditure as particularly significant is that it gives us real purchase on the notion of the state and its extent. Total expenditure and total taxes do not provide such effective measures, because so much of what governments spend and tax is returned to citizens as transfers, which become part of individual incomes to be spent as the individual chooses. But civilian public consumption expenditure measures how much the government spends and how many people it employs for its own purposes. It is, thus, a direct measure of the resources at the command of the state and one directly related to the traditional socialist goal of enhancing the public sphere at the expense of the private. If we are interested in how the line between public and private choice has been redrawn in the post-war era, the expansion of civilian public consumption is an important key to understanding.

This chapter and those that follow have a standard logic of presentation, even though practical considerations prevent an altogether standard format. Each chapter consists of three major sections, each of which examines a different policy outcome. In respect of each outcome, the initial step is to look at data for the 21 countries in much the same manner as in previous chapters, noting indications of increasing similarity amongst nations and signs of grouping into families of nations. The next logical step of discussing the relevant hypotheses is where format to some degree departs from logic. With regard to the growth of big government and the welfare state, most of the pertinent hypotheses have already been examined at some length in Chapters 2 and 3, so that, for the most part, all that is required is some summary and highlighting of previous discussion. Moreover, broadly speaking, the hypotheses in these areas have quite similar implications for the aggregated measures of big government and the more specific programmes and clusters of programmes making them up, so that it is possible to provide a consolidated set of hypotheses at the beginning of this chapter which apply across all expenditure areas. Apart from this consolidated presentation, the only additional hypotheses pertain to the welfare state sectors, where factors relating to the coverage and clientele of different programmes require specific discussion. In the later chapters on the labour market and policy in the personal sphere, relevant hypotheses will be discussed in each of the separate sections on particular policy outcomes.

The third stage of our inquiry in each section involves looking at findings, starting with figures showing the strength of the relationships between the hypothesized explanatory variables and each of the policy outcomes examined. Looking at these relationships is a preliminary to using statistical techniques to discover which of the many alternative hypotheses best fit the data. The resulting statistical models are reported in appendices to each chapter, whilst the results are presented verbally in the text, with a focus on demonstrating the real difference made by the various explanatory factors which feature in these models. Finally, we seek to analyse the findings for all three time-periods and for change in such a way as to provide a coherent account of the forces impacting on policy change in the post-war period. The nature of the broader patterns, which link findings on policy development in one area to those in another, is the subject matter of the concluding chapter.

THE TOTAL OUTLAYS OF GOVERNMENT

Data

The first topic on which we focus is total government expenditure or outlays. Table 4.1 shows that, in the three and a half decades between 1960
and 1995, OECD average total public spending levels as a percentage of
GDP increased by 75 per cent. Whereas in 1960 the biggest spender in
these terms was Austria, with an expenditure level of just over 35 per cent
of GDP, by 1995 no less than eight of our 21 countries were spending
over 50 per cent of GDP and only four countries – Australia, Japan,
Switzerland and the USA – were spending less than 40 per cent. If big
government was now the rule, the pace of change had been very different
in different countries. Seven countries – Denmark, Finland, Greece,
Japan, Portugal, Sweden and Switzerland – had experienced growth of
government in excess of 100 per cent, whilst, at the other end of the distribution, in the USA, outlays had grown by only 22 per cent and, in the
United Kingdom, by only 35 per cent. Measuring national trajectories of
public expenditure growth in terms of their changing share in GDP over
the entire period, the three Scandinavian countries – Denmark, Sweden
and Finland – each with more than 30 percentage points growth, clearly
set the trend, whilst the English-speaking nations – in particular, the
USA, Britain, Ireland and Australia – were at the rear. OECD data are
not available for New Zealand for either total outlays or the receipts of
government, but data from other sources suggest that public expenditure
in the early 1990s was below 40 per cent of GDP and had grown more
slowly than in most other OECD countries since the 1950s (see Gould,
1982, 201; Rudd, 1992, 44).

   The Scandinavian expenditure explosion and English-speaking expenditure containment changed the families of nations patterns over time. In
1960, big government was a largely continental Western European phenomenon, with Austria, France, Belgium, the Netherlands and Germany
in the vanguard and Southern Europe, Switzerland and Japan in the rearguard. By the end of the period, the larger countries of continental
Western Europe feature in the middle of the distribution with
Scandinavia and some of the smaller continental Western European
nations at the top and Switzerland and Japan continuing to bring up the
rear along with the overseas English-speaking nations. These substantial
changes were not a function of catch-up, with the initial values scarcely
related to the subsequent trajectory of change. However, there was a
modest shift towards greater similarity between these nations, all of
which seems to have occurred after the mid-1970s. Public expenditure

Table 4.1   Levels and change in total outlays of government as a percentage of GDP, 1960–95

Country	1960	1974	1995	Change: 1960–95
Australia	21.2	31.6	37.1	15.9
Canada	28.6	36.8	46.2	17.6
Ireland	28.0	43.0	42.0	14.0
New Zealand	–	–	–	–
UK	32.2	44.8	43.4	11.2
USA	27.2	32.1	33.3	6.1
Denmark	24.8	45.9	62.4	37.6
Finland	26.6	32.0	57.6	31.0
Norway	29.9	44.6	47.4	17.5
Sweden	31.0	48.1	66.2	35.2
Austria	35.7	41.9	52.8	17.1
Belgium	34.6	45.6	54.9	20.3
France	34.6	39.3	53.7	19.1
Germany	32.4	44.6	49.5	17.1
Italy	30.1	37.9	51.9	21.8
Netherlands	33.7	47.9	50.9	17.2
Greece	17.4	25.0	46.0	28.6
Portugal	17.0	24.7	43.1	26.1
Spain	–	23.1	44.3	–
Switzerland	17.2	25.5	36.9	19.7
Japan	17.5	24.5	35.6	18.1
Mean	27.4	36.9	47.8	20.6
Correlation with 1960		0.85	0.51	–0.23
Coefficient of variation	23.51	23.99	18.43	

Sources and notes: Data for 1960 and 1974 from OECD, *Historical Statistics*, Paris, various years. Data for 1995 from OECD (1996b). The data for Greece and Switzerland are for current disbursements rather than total outlays and, hence, somewhat underestimate spending for those countries. The figure reported in the final column is the percentage point change over the entire period. Where data are missing and there are available data for a year within +/– 2 years of the data-point, those data are given. – indicates the absence of any adjacent data-point.

growth cannot be seen as a phenomenon peculiar to any particular period, with the two decades following the first oil shock manifesting outlays growth on almost the same scale as during the 'Golden Age' of economic growth. Only the United Kingdom and Ireland managed to cut back total expenditure in absolute terms during this latter period, and then only to a minimal degree.

Although the main focus of the analysis here is on indicators of the size of government measured in terms of percentages of national product, it is of some interest to inquire into the composition of government expenditure as well as its extent. Table 4.1.1, which provides data on defence expenditure and total welfare spending as percentages of total government outlays, tells us something of the changing functions of the state in the post-war period. Whereas, in earlier centuries, the primary role of government was generally seen as the defence of the national territory, by 1960, defence spending at 14 per cent of outlays was somewhat less than a third of aggregate public spending on social security, health and education combined. Three and a half decades later, the defence function was down to around 5 per cent and spending on the welfare state took up almost two thirds of public expenditures. That defence spending went down by 9 percentage points and welfare expenditure went up by exactly the same percentage over the period might be regarded as contemporary evidence for the very ancient proposition that there is a trade-off between the external defence and domestic policy functions of the state, that is, that more guns mean less butter (see Keman, 1982). However, calculations of the correlations between the defence and welfare components of outlays in 1960, in the early 1990s and for change over time reveal quite negligible relationships in all instances.

The lack of connection between the trajectories of change in these components of public expenditure is also evident when we look at the relationships between the 1960 and early 1990s values of each separate variable. Defence spending went down everywhere, but, as indicated by the correlation of 0.91, the league table of big and small spenders was substantially untouched with the passing of time. These figures may be interpreted in terms of a general secular decline in the defence function in these nations as the risk of a large-scale European war diminished, with the big spenders in both periods being those countries with superpower status – that is, the USA, Britain and France – and those involved in colonial or local conflicts – that is, Portugal in 1960 and Greece throughout. In sharp contrast, there appears to be absolutely no connection between welfare spending as a percentage of total outlays in 1960 and in the early 1990s. Nor are there any obvious patterns in spending measured in this way at either date. In both periods, there were very high spenders and

Table 4.1.1 Defence expenditure and welfare state expenditure as shares of total outlays in 1960 and the early 1990s

Country	1960 defence expenditure	1960 welfare state expenditure	Early 1990s defence expenditure	Early 1990s welfare state expenditure
Australia	12.3	54.5	5.9	60.8
Canada	15.0	56.2	4.1	66.9
Ireland	5.0	44.3	3.1	63.4
New Zealand	–	–	–	–
UK	20.2	45.5	8.3	58.9
USA	32.7	47.5	14.1	73.1
Denmark	10.9	58.5	3.2	53.7
Finland	6.4	52.5	3.6	68.6
Norway	10.7	52.7	6.5	75.4
Sweden	12.9	54.3	3.8	60.0
Austria	3.4	54.6	1.7	63.1
Belgium	9.8	56.3	3.3	67.3
France	18.5	55.5	6.3	68.3
Germany	12.3	57.5	4.2	53.2
Italy	11.0	56.5	4.0	59.7
Netherlands	12.2	49.3	4.5	77.7
Greece	28.2	52.9	12.0	48.9
Portugal	24.7	–	6.5	49.9
Spain	–	–	3.8	65.3
Switzerland	14.5	67.4	4.6	77.1
Japan	6.3	60.7	2.8	62.0
Mean	14.0	54.3	5.3	63.7
Correlation with 1960			0.91	0.00
Coefficient of variation	55.50	10.12	57.82	13.27

Sources and notes: Data for outlays from OECD, *Historical Statistics*, Paris (various dates). Data for defence expenditure from SIPRI (various dates). Data for welfare state expenditures are the sum of social security transfers, public health and education spending to be found in Tables 5.1, 5.2 and 5.3 in the next chapter. The data-point for the early 1990s is 1993. – indicates the absence of any adjacent data-point.

very low spenders in GDP terms amongst those countries whose government sectors were dominated by the welfare state, and a similar picture is observable at the other end of the distribution. There is, however, some pattern with respect to change, in that the countries in which the relative share of welfare state functions was increasing most turn out to be those in which the total outlays of government were increasing least (correlation = –0.52). This is indicative of an expenditure cut-back profile in which the nations most committed to restraining the growth of public spending paradoxically adopted a course which made what expenditure there was more welfare-statist in character than before. The country exemplifying this tendency was the USA, which had little choice but to trade off butter for guns in the Reagan era, given that it simultaneously manifested the highest level of defence spending and the fourth highest level of welfare statism amongst this group of countries, with only around 13 per cent of outlays utilized for other purposes.

Hypotheses

As we have already noted, the major hypotheses which seek to account for the phenomenon of big government measured in aggregate expenditure terms are also likely to be applicable to the major spending programmes and clusters of spending programmes from which that aggregate is derived. In the early 1990s, health and education were each averaging around 6 per cent of national resources across the OECD. At the same time, the two umbrella programmes, social security transfers and civilian public consumption expenditure, were each using up around a sixth of national income, whilst, as shown by Table 4.1.1, the aggregation of welfare state programmes, including social security transfers and much of civilian public consumption expenditure, made up no less than two-thirds of total government spending. Government is big in the OECD countries because these programmes and metaprogrammes are big.

It should, of course, also be the case that hypotheses accounting for outlays should give a no less adequate account of the receipts from which that expenditure is financed. Given that, over the medium to long run, governments seek to balance their budgets, producing neither persistent surpluses nor persistent deficits, the expectation must be that countries with high expenditure levels will have similarly high tax levels and that low expenditure will be matched by low taxation. It would, indeed, be strange if the two sides of the budget ledger were so out of kilter as to give rise to wholly different accounts of the genesis of big government.

However, the in-principle identity of government outlays and receipts does not mean that we should expect precisely similar results from the two analyses. There are at least three reasons why not. The first is that, despite their best intentions, governments do allow deficits and surpluses to last for considerable periods. In 1960, the average discrepancy between total outlays and total receipts was 2.4 per cent of GDP, with a somewhat greater number of surpluses than deficits, leading to an average OECD surplus of 0.57 per cent of GDP. In the mid-1990s, reflecting the far less propitious economic climate, the average discrepancy was 4.4 per cent of GDP, with only Norway in surplus, and an average deficit of –4.1 per cent of GDP (all figures calculated from the data in Tables 4.1 and 4.2). In both periods, these discrepancies were equivalent to around 10 per cent of expenditures and revenues and were of a sufficient magnitude to suggest the possibility that the factors influencing the two kinds of aggregates may not always have been identical.

A second reason, according to an influential critique of the contemporary functioning of democratic systems, is that governments are forced to move towards deficit financing in order to cope with the 'rising expectations trap which electoral competition has created' (Dunleavy and O'Leary, 1987, 101). This argument, which is part and parcel of a democratic 'ungovernability' thesis variously advanced on both Left and Right, has sometimes been allied with the proposition that there is a distinct political business cycle based on the systematic proclivity of democratic politicians to increase fiscal stimulus via public spending in election years, leaving tax collections to catch up later (Buchanan and Wagner, 1977; cf. Hibbs, 1987). A final reason for possible differences between findings concerning outlays and findings concerning receipts is that different hypotheses rest on diverse causal mechanisms, some of which impact more directly on the expenditure side of the equation and some on the revenue side. A possible implication is that such factors will show up more strongly on one side of the budget ledger than the other.

There is, of course, still less reason to assume that the analysis of total outlays and of the separate programmes and metaprogrammes making up that total will produce identical results. As we have already noted, a preference for high levels of public consumption expenditure can be seen as representing the quintessence of a statist approach to social intervention. By contrast to income transfers, which make up the remaining bulk of public expenditure, public consumption involves direct provision of services and an enhanced reach of the state through public employment. This is a strategy which has been traditionally favoured by trade unions and Left parties and, hence, we would expect measures of class politics and Left incumbency to be particularly strongly associated with cross-national differences in public consumption expenditure.

Most of the hypotheses examined here are drawn from the account in the two previous chapters. The figure in parentheses accompanying each hypothesis indicates the table in the text which provides data relevant to a given hypothesis. It should be noted that no hypotheses are presented which link changes in the occupational structure to either aggregate or specific programme spending, since, as noted previously, the growth of government has itself been one of the factors implicated in the transformation of the occupational structure in recent decades. Because they have been discussed previously, the hypotheses listed below are presented in summary fashion. In concluding the section, some attention is given to two other factors, not previously mentioned, which must also be seen as potentially involved in the growth of big government in the post-war era.

The hypotheses derived from our earlier discussion are as follows:

- Because the tasks of post-war reconstruction were greater where wartime experience was most severe, the reach of government and the size of the welfare state are likely to have been greater where the impact of the war was greater (2.1). Clearly, this hypothesis is likely to apply most strongly in the immediate post-war years.
- In order to compensate or make up for wartime experience, the reach of government and the size of the welfare state is likely to have been greater where 1937–50 economic growth rates were lower (2.1).
- By an extension of Wagner's law, government expenditures, taxes, public consumption and welfare are likely to be have been greater in countries which had greater levels of GDP per capita (2.2).
- By a further extension of the same argument, the reach of government and the size of the welfare state are likely to have been greater where productivity levels were greater (data calculated from same source as 2.2).
- Given the possibility that the effects of GDP per capita and productivity may be masked by the fact that early affluence was associated with private or market responses to need, it may be that these relationships take a curvilinear rather than a linear form; that is, the relationship between the variables may only be positive up to a point and thereafter become negative. This possibility is tested with models including measures of both income and income squared. A significant and positive income term together with a significant and negative squared term can be interpreted as evidence of curvilinearity (data calculated from same source as 2.2).
- Since international trade creates labour market vulnerability and hence additional needs for social protection, greater levels of trade are likely to have been associated with greater levels of public expenditure, taxes, public consumption and welfare (2.3) or, alternatively,
- Because, in recent decades, increasing international trade has constrained the autonomy of domestic economic policy-makers, greater levels of trade since the mid-1970s are likely to have been associated with lesser levels of outlays, taxes, consumption and welfare (2.3).

- Since urbanization leads to greater needs for government support and intervention, it is likely to have resulted in an extension of the reach of the state in terms of expenditure, taxes, consumption and welfare programmes (2.5).
- Because population ageing results in higher levels of need in respect of pensions, health care and aged services, countries with a larger proportion of old people are likely to have had higher levels of government expenditure and taxes (2.6). However, given that income transfers to the old constitute so large a proportion of the budget in most OECD countries (around a sixth of total outlays in 1990 according to OECD, 1996d), it is possible that this effect has been greater in respect of total outlays, receipts and transfers than in respect of public consumption expenditure. Moreover, since the elderly are substantial users of health resources and virtual non-users of education resources, we would expect a positive link with the first programme and the absence of any link with the second.
- The expenditure argument from the nature of Catholic social policy preferences is that where Catholicism is dominant there is likely to be an emphasis on social security transfers rather than direct provision of welfare services. The implication is that all the variables to be found in Table 2.7 will be associated with higher social security transfer and with lower public consumption expenditure, and that none will be significantly associated with either the total outlays or the total receipts of government. In addition, the traditional Catholic insistence on the provision of church schooling might suggest lower educational expenditures in countries in which the Church was influential.
- Because democratic participation provides a necessary conveyor-belt for the articulation of emergent socio-economic needs, turnout is likely to have been most strongly positively associated with measures of the reach of government and the welfare state in the earlier period, when the contrast between countries having authoritarian and democratic governments was at its greatest (3.1), or, alternatively,
- Because high levels of democratic participation make it easier for citizens to obtain satisfaction of their demands (or, in another formulation, because modern democracy leads to unwarranted popular expectations and hence to ungovernability), higher levels of turnout are likely to have been associated with a greater reach of government and with higher expenditures on welfare throughout the post-war period (3.1).
- Because trade union membership represents popular mobilization for the achievement of working class goals, greater levels of union density are likely to have been associated with an extended reach of government and with bigger welfare state programmes (3.2).

- Since a Left government has the power to implement policies which serve the needs of its working class constituency of support, greater Left incumbency is likely to have led to big government across the board (3.3). Moreover, as noted above, both union density and Left incumbency are likely to have been particularly strongly associated with public consumption spending and therefore, arguably, with the programmes constituting that spending.
- Because Right governments seek to minimize redistribution, countries which have experienced higher levels of Right incumbency are likely to have been ones in which expenditures, taxes, consumption and welfare have been significantly smaller. Since a primary influence here is likely to have been tax aversion on the part of right-wing voters, we might expect this factor to have impacted most directly on the taxation side of the budget (3.4).
- Since the institutionalization of class conflict may be seen as creating a social partnership between business and labour, allowing the simultaneous achievement of economic stability and social wage goals, corporatism is likely to have been associated with higher levels of public expenditures, taxes, consumption and welfare state spending (3.5).
- Since constitutional structures involving a proliferation of institutional veto points make major reform programmes more difficult to achieve, it is likely that countries with federal structures or other constitutional impediments to change will have experienced lower levels of aggregate spending, taxes, public consumption and welfare spending than countries without such veto points (3.5).
- Because the European Community is an emergent 'multi-tiered' constitutional structure limiting the policy autonomy of member states, it is likely to be a factor leading to a reduced reach of government and a declining welfare state in expenditure terms as the economic integration of the Community increases (3.5).
- Since the overall trajectory of policy development amongst the OECD countries has been from historically conditioned diversity to a common state of socio-economic modernity, the dominant pattern of policy change will betray strong catch-up tendencies (a measure of catch-up in terms of the correlation between 1960 values and subsequent change over time is to be found in each of the basic data tables in Chapters 4 to 7).

Only two general points concerning these hypotheses are required. The first is that wherever a hypothesis has been formulated in terms of increasing needs or of redistributive goals, there is some *a priori* possibility that the impact will be experienced more directly on the expenditure than the receipts side of the budget. Forces pushing for the budget to increase in expenditure terms – labour market vulnerability, urbanization, the ageing of the population, popular democratic demands, class politics and Left incumbency – are exactly the kinds of factors which have been implicated by critics as leading to higher budget deficits. The second point to note is that, with the exceptions of the last two hypotheses concerning the impact of EC institutions and of catch-up, all these propositions have been formulated in terms of levels of government activity. However, with only the further exception of the two wartime experience variables, all of them can also sensibly be reformulated in terms of change over time. Thus change in an independent variable may be related to change in the dependent variables, as in the hypothesis that an increasingly elderly population is likely to lead to increasing expenditure on health and social security transfers, or an invariant independent variable may be related to change in the dependent variables, as in the hypothesis that, in federal nations, the reach of the state and welfare spending are likely to grow more slowly than in unitary nations. Findings concerning both levels and changes are reported in the next section.

There are two further hypotheses that have not been raised in the context of our previous discussion. Both involve factors which are likely to impact most immediately on the revenues or receipts of governments. The first concerns the likely influence of inflation on revenue growth. The argument is that inflation results in a process of 'bracket creep' or 'fiscal drag', which moves tax-payers into higher tax brackets and leads to an increase in the government's total tax take and an incentive to use this windfall gain to finance higher levels of expenditure (Larkey, Stolp and Winer 1981; Rose, 1984, 114–15). Only where the government is willing to forgo this painless source of additional revenue extraction via the self-denying ordinance of bracket indexation will such a result not follow. This argument suggests that:

- since inflation automatically produces higher revenue levels, high levels of post-war inflation are likely to have been associated with increasing levels of total receipts, outlays, public consumption and welfare spending (data on inflation from OECD, 1996a).

The second factor is the extent and growth of home ownership, which is a topic investigated in its own right in Chapter 7. It has been argued that home ownership involves a trade-off with government expenditure on welfare because individuals generally find it extremely onerous to save sufficient from their incomes to finance owner-occupation whilst simultaneously making the necessary tax contributions to finance a generous welfare state. Hence, in societies where home ownership is a cultural norm or where the government encourages a shift to owner-occupation, as for instance in Thatcher's Britain, the likely consequence will be a high degree of tax aversion and the emergence of a large electoral constituency resisting the expansion of the welfare state (see Kemeny, 1980 and 1981). This argument implies that:

- since home ownership is conducive to tax aversion, countries with higher levels of owner-occupied housing are likely to have been characterized by lower levels of revenues, outlays, public consumption and welfare state development (data to be found in Table 7.1 below).

It is perhaps testimony to the significance of the topic of the causes of big government that so many hypotheses of so diverse a character have been developed to account for the phenomenon. The remainder of this chapter seeks to establish which of them best account for levels and changes in the size of government during the post-war era.

Findings

The initial findings of this study are presented in Figure 4.1, which provides graphic representations of the strengths of all the relationships designated in the hypotheses above in terms of the size of the correlations between total outlays and measures for each of the variables specified in those hypotheses. The first general point to note is that, taking + or – 0.40 as the threshold of statistical significance, there are very many significant relationships for each time-point and for change over time. This makes it clear just why there are so many theories about the causes of big government: it is simply because it is relatively easy to point to empirical evidence supporting so many of them. On the other hand, such a plethora of relationships suggests the need to go beyond simple associations in order to sort out which set of factors best fits the evidence available. In this study, going beyond simple associations takes three forms. First, in the appendices to each chapter, we report statistical models which maximize the level of explained variation produced by a set of independent variables all of which are themselves statistically significant. Second, because it is abundantly clear that this technique cannot produce wholly reliable results under circumstances where there are too many theories and too few cases, we seek to interrogate these findings by asking how far they make sense in terms of our wider understanding of policy development in this and other areas. Finally, our concluding chapter builds on that analysis by locating common patterns across time and across adjacent policy areas. In this way, we hope to generate an account of post-war policy development which is convincing in its broad outline if not always in its minute detail.

Looking initially at Figure 4.1(a), we note that the two variables most significantly related to outlays in 1960 were the age structure of the population and electoral turnout, and that a wide range of hypotheses, pointing to the influence of factors such as urbanization, home ownership, class politics and partisan control, are supported by this initial reading of the data. The factors substantially unconnected to outcomes are those relating to wartime experience, affluence, institutions and, Christian Democratic incumbency apart, the religious divide. Virtually all the associations reported in the figure have the sign predicted by the relevant hypothesis, with the only point of special interest being that the original membership of the European Community was associated with significantly higher outlays than the OECD average. This can scarcely be seen as a causal consequence of membership and must be regarded as a family likeness of the countries originally signing the Treaty of Rome.

A best-fit linear modelling points to the relevance of population ageing, turnout and EC membership as factors strongly associated with big government in the early post-war period. However, as reported in Appendix 4.1, the strongest model is one which includes a curvilinear specification of GDP per capita together with the measure of Catholic cultural impact. Trying to interpret these results in real terms, we can calculate what the coefficients reported in the appendix mean in terms of differences in outlays between a country at the mean for a given variable and for others at the extremes of the distribution (for a reminder about how such calculations are made, see the methodology appendix to Chapter 1). In this instance, the curvilinear specification implies that the net effect of GDP per capita will be that countries at average income levels will have higher outlays than countries at the extremes, the estimated figures being 12.9 per cent of GDP less spending for the bottom country in the distribution and 5.0 per cent less spending for the country at the top. Countries which were characterized by Catholic cultural impact are estimated to spend 6.1 percentage points of GDP more than countries which were not.

In 1974, the variables most strongly associated with outlays had not changed markedly, although Christian Democratic incumbency had drifted down in significance and Left incumbency and trade exposure were more strongly associated with outlays than previously. Figure 4.1(b) shows that, in general, the strength of many of the relationships had increased, with the links with turnout and class politics now particularly strong. Again, with the exception of EC membership, all the more substantial relationships are in the predicted direction. Age structure, although its degree of association with outlays was no less than in 1960, was now seemingly less important than a number of political factors. This is reflected in the 1974 model reported in

(a) 1960

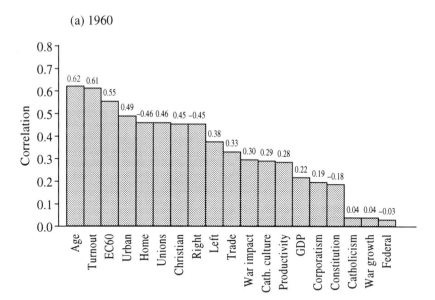

(b) 1974

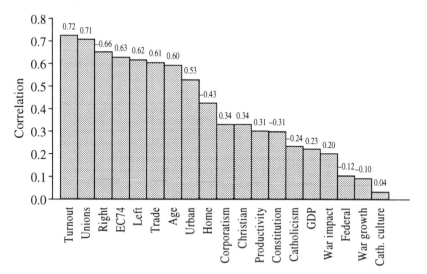

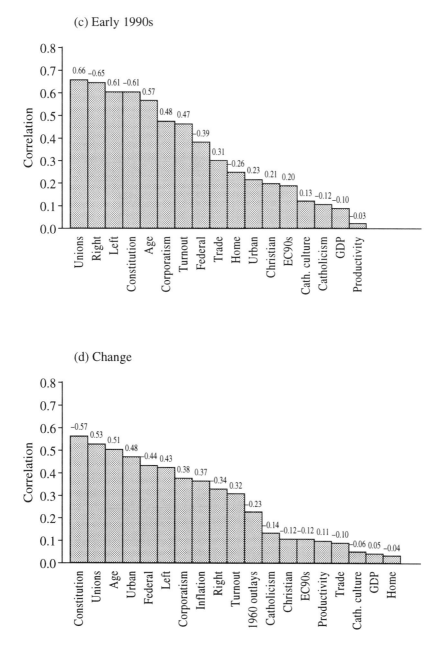

Figure 4.1 Bivariate tests: total outlays of government (1960, 1974 and early 1990s and change over time)

Appendix 4.1, in which Left incumbency and EC membership are the most significant factors, with electoral turnout of somewhat lesser importance. Although a curvilinear model for 1974 can be generated from the data, it provides a markedly less successful account than the linear model presented in Appendix 4.1. Contrasting the average OECD nation with those with the lowest values on the respective independent variables, we estimate that Left incumbency made a difference to spending of 3.6 per cent of GDP and electoral turnout of 5.7 per cent. The latter figure needs evaluating in light of the strong skew in turnout in the early 1970s. What the model is telling us is that absence of turnout made a major difference in the size of government for the countries of Southern Europe, but a relatively minor difference for most of the others. In the somewhat enlarged European Community of 1974, membership made a difference of no less than 9.1 percentage points.

According to the findings for the mid-1990s presented in Figure 4.1(c), there had been no further increases in the levels of association between ideological factors and outcomes over a period of two decades. Since, however, other previously important variables had declined in importance, ideology was now clearly the dominant influence. The decline in the significance of age structure was marginal. That of electoral turnout was far more substantial, although it is of interest that this factor remained significantly associated with outcomes in a period in which the democratic credentials of all the OECD nations were impeccable. Other major differences between the mid-1970s and the mid-1990s findings are that outlays were now very significantly lower in countries in which constitutional structures manifested multiple veto points to change and that EC membership was now only negligibly associated with outcomes. Less dramatic changes included the reduced significance of international trade, home ownership and urbanization.

The model reported in the appendix includes a number of surprises. Although the correlation for trade in Figure 4.1(c) remained positive, this term becomes a significant negative predictor of outcomes in the successful model, suggesting effects compatible with the globalization thesis. Interestingly, the strong positive effect of Left incumbency reported for 1974 has, by the mid-1990s, become a still stronger negative Right incumbency effect. Apart from these factors, the best-fitting model also contains terms for electoral turnout and constitutional structure. In a world of almost universally big government, where average outlays were now only a shade below 50 per cent, the positive influence of turnout at 6.5 percentage points was counterbalanced by the negative impact of trade exposure at 5.3 points and Right incumbency at 9.5 points. Of course, there is no such thing as an average constitutional structure, but taking the arithmetic mean for this measure of 1.95 implies that this factor also had a negative impact of 3.9 points. For countries like the USA and Switzerland, however, with extreme values on this variable, this is a factor which has a huge real effect on estimated outcomes.

Our final task is to examine the factors associated with change in outlays over time. It is important to emphasize that, here and throughout the book, the majority of findings relating to change over time involve reporting associations between variables measuring differences between 1960 and early 1990s values. This applies to the change measures for all the dependent policy variables in the analysis and most of the variables measuring economic and social factors. There are three categories of exceptions. The first relates to variables which are unchanging over time, as in the case of the dummy variables measuring war impact, Catholic cultural impact and constitutional structure. Another consists of the measures of party incumbency which are averaged over the period from 1960 to the early 1990s, that is, we wish to look at policy change in relation to party control over the period in question. Finally, in accordance with standard practice in the economics discipline, we measure change in real GDP per capita and per worker in terms of growth rates rather than of absolute differences. It should be noted that, because growth rates are measured relative to initial values, there is an inherent tendency for growth to be fastest in nations coming off a lower base.

Turning now to the findings reported in Figure 4.1(d), we observe rather fewer significant associations than previously. The findings here show that outlays had been growing conspicuously more slowly in countries where there were federal institutions and/or wider constitutional impediments to change and that they had grown more strongly in nations where union density was rising, where ageing and urbanization were occurring on a major scale and where the Left had a good record of office-holding. Although change in trade exposure was not significantly associated with change in outlays, the relationship between these variables was by now a marginally negative one. In the change model in Appendix 4.1, an ageing population and the size of the Right turn out to be the most important explanatory factors conditioning the overall growth in public spending in the post-war period, with inflation a somewhat weaker influence. In substantive terms, age structure makes the biggest difference, contributing 13.7 percentage points to the outlays growth of the average OECD country. Inflation increases spending levels by 4.5 points, whilst Right incumbency reduces them by 7.7 points.

Analysis

Basing our interpretation on the findings reported in Appendix 4.1, what emerges is the variety of factors significantly related to the development of big government during the post-war era. At the beginning of the period, the best account is provided by a curvilinear specification of income per capita and by Catholic cultural impact. By the end of the period, politics had become crucial in many guises, through partisanship, constitutional structure and electoral turnout, but economic and social factors have a continuing relevance. The negative impact of international trade suggests the possibility of developments consonant with the globalization hypothesis, whilst population ageing is revealed as hugely important in determining the growth trajectory of outlays over time. The variety of the findings here strongly supports the view that only an interdisciplinary and wide-ranging approach can fully make sense of post-war public policy development.

Four issues arising from the findings require some further attention. First, the findings relating to electoral turnout look as if they might assist us in answering the question of whether links between democratization and public policy development are threshold effects, indicative of the absence of democratic institutions in Southern Europe, or whether they demonstrate the more direct policy impact of the institutions determining electoral participation levels. On the face of it, the persistence of the turnout term in the mid-1990s model lends support to the latter interpretation. However, since the turnout term in this model is only of marginal statistical significance and disappears from the equation if any one of a number of countries is excluded from the sample, it seems sensible to defer firm conclusions until we have results for other categories of spending. Scepticism about an interpretation going beyond a threshold effect is reinforced by further analysis of the 1974 model, which shows that the significant turnout term in that model is wholly dependent on the inclusion of the Southern European countries.

The second point that requires some discussion is why membership of the European Community should feature in the linear best-fit equations for both 1960 and 1974. As we have said, it is clear that membership is not of itself the cause of high spending, and it is interesting to seek to identify the characteristics the countries have in common which lead to such a relatively strong degree of association. An obvious clue is that the EC term disappears in the successful curvilinear model for 1960, which also contains a term for Catholic cultural impact. All the original EC members were strongly Catholic in social policy orientation and, in 1960, several among them (France, Germany and the Netherlands) were in a group of countries clustering somewhat above the OECD mean for real GDP per capita. What had changed by 1974 was that three more nations – Denmark, Ireland and the United Kingdom – had joined the EC, all of them with public expenditure levels above the OECD mean and two of them – Britain and Denmark – also in the moderately affluent group. In contrast, the three non-EC big spenders (Austria, Sweden and Norway) were all distinguished by strong Left incumbency. Under these circumstances, the 1974 model simply identifies big spending as a function of Left partisanship or EC membership or both in combination (Denmark and to a lesser extent Belgium, Germany and the United Kingdom).

There is no reason to suppose that for the original EC members the sources of big government have been transformed with the passing of time. All these nations are now relatively affluent, although not super-rich, and their political life continues to reflect Catholic social values, with Christian Democratic parties dominant in four of them for almost the entire post-war period. The translation into policy preferences of Catholic social values in moderately affluent nations seems to be a key to early welfare state innovation, leading to distinctively higher outlays in the early post-war period despite the supposed aversion to public consumption spending and public expenditure on education built into those preferences. What changes as the post-war period progresses is not so much these countries' public spending behaviour, but the extent to which that behaviour translates into differences between these nations and others, with class ideology and constitutional structure now becoming crucially significant factors conditioning the development of the interventionist state.

The third issue which requires some attention is the apparent emergence of a further constraint on spending arising from the openness of the economy, or at least from the change in policy responses to the economic vulnerability such openness implies. A possible interpretation of this finding is that governments in countries that rely heavily on international trade no longer feel that they have the autonomy to use government spending to redress the problems arising from economic openness. Probably the fairest judgement of the case for the impact of globalization implied by this finding is that it is suggestive rather than proven. The difficulty is that this result is wholly dependent on one case – that of Ireland. Without Ireland in the analysis, the trade term is wholly insignificant, although still negative, and one can devise a wholly robust model with greater explanatory power based exclusively on the negative impact of the Right and of constitutional structure. That the Irish case should be crucial is hardly surprising, since it is the country which, along with Belgium, has experienced the largest growth in international trade in the OECD over the post-war period. However, quite unlike Belgium, Ireland is one of the very few nations to experience an actual decline in outlays in the two decades following the crisis of the 1970s. So Ireland can easily be represented as the exemplar story for the globalization thesis, with high unemployment, inflation and budget deficits in the 1970s and early 1980s serving as potent warnings to a nation seeking to expand its international trade of the need to follow the path of economic rectitude. But comparative research should not reach its conclusions on the basis of single extreme cases and it seems preferable to await more evidence before making any strong case for reduced domestic policy autonomy. If the globalization thesis is correct, that evidence should be forthcoming in the very near future, as countries exposed to high levels of trade openness are forced to cut back their public spending along the lines of Ireland in the late 1980s and early 1990s.

Finally, it is worth inquiring why it is, when constitutional structure is crucial to the 1995 model and has the strongest relationship with change in Figure 4.1(d), that inflation replaces this variable in the change model. Almost certainly the answer to this question lies in a misspecification of the change model. Many studies have suggested that inflation is itself a policy outcome strongly related to institutional factors, with most focusing on inverse relationships between inflation and various aspects of decentralized policy-making, including central bank independence and federal arrangements (see Brennan and Buchanan, 1980; Alesina, 1989; Busch, 1993). In our dataset, the average rate of inflation over the period 1960 to 1993 is correlated with federalism at -0.47 and with constitutional structure at -0.45. Moreover, it is possible to elaborate a version of the change model in which constitutional structure is a significant negative predictor of outcomes, although the overall explanatory power of the model is somewhat reduced.

A possible interpretation of these relationships is that constitutional impediments, by making it more difficult to enact expensive reform programmes, restrain the inflationary tendencies that may result from low productivity growth in the expanding state services sector and from excessive fiscal stimulus and deficit financing more generally. In so far as it is effects of this kind which are being picked up in the analysis, the change model is misspecified and the real causal sequence is one in which constitutional impediments lead to reduced outlays which in turn produce lower inflation. An important clue to the true character of the relationships here will be provided by our analysis of change in the total receipts of government in the next section. If inflation were to prove a major factor driving the tax take of government via bracket creep, it would suggest that the result here is a genuine one, with the expansion of outlays driven by the availability of additional taxation revenue. If, on the other hand, constitutional structure were to feature as a major impediment to the growth of the receipts of government, then the safest conclusion would almost certainly be that this factor is a major brake on the growth of government as well.

THE TOTAL RECEIPTS OF GOVERNMENT

Data

The total receipts of government consist largely of direct and indirect taxes plus social security contributions paid by employers and employees. As we have already noted, there is an in-principle identity between total receipts and total expenditures, so we should be more surprised to encounter major discrepancies between data and findings concerning these alternative measures of big government than the reverse. In fact, however, there are sufficient differences between the aggregates in each period to warrant comment and to suggest the possibility of discrepant findings.

Counting a major difference between outlays and receipts as one where the resulting surplus or deficit exceeds 10 per cent of receipts, there are six differences of such a magnitude in both 1960 and 1974 and no less than ten in the mid-1990s. In 1960, four of the discrepancies were surpluses and only two were deficits. The Belgian deficit at 5.2 per cent of GDP was in a league of its own. By the mid-1990s, all the countries in which the budget was seriously out of kilter were in deficit, including Austria, Finland, France, Greece, Italy, Japan, Portugal, Spain, Sweden and the United Kingdom. The only consistent family of nations pattern here is that of the Southern European nations, each of which had a deficit of over 5 per cent of GDP by the early 1990s.

Looking now to receipts (Table 4.2) rather than the differences between receipts and outlays, we discover patterns quite similar to those discussed in the previous section. The big tax state, like the big spending state, started out as a continental Western European phenomenon and moved northward to Scandinavia. If anything, because the Scandinavian countries tended to be deficit-averse to a greater extent than the countries in the continental Western European grouping, the shift northward started earlier and was more decisive. Already in 1960, Norway and Sweden were in the big tax state league and, by the mid-1990s, the four Scandinavian nations were the four largest tax states in the OECD. Between 1960 and 1974, growth in receipts more or less kept pace with the expansion of outlays, increasing by roughly 33 per cent from 27.4 to 36.1 per cent of GDP. Thereafter, revenue growth was appreciably slower than expenditure growth, leading to the high level of deficits we have already noted as typical of the 1990s. Despite the slowdown in the expansion of total receipts of government, the tax state in 1995 was 60 per cent bigger than it had been in 1960. Over the period as a whole, there was little indication of catch-up and absolutely none of convergence, although there was a slight increase in the extent of cross-national differ-

Table 4.2　Levels and change in total receipts of government as a percentage of GDP, 1960–95

Country	1960	1974	1995	Change: 1960–95
Australia	24.4	28.5	34.7	10.3
Canada	25.7	37.2	42.1	16.4
Ireland	24.8	35.2	39.7	14.9
New Zealand	–	–	–	–
UK	29.9	39.6	37.6	7.7
USA	26.3	30.3	31.3	5.0
Denmark	27.3	48.4	60.6	33.3
Finland	29.7	35.7	52.1	22.4
Norway	33.1	48.5	50.5	17.4
Sweden	32.1	48.8	58.2	26.1
Austria	34.4	42.5	46.7	12.3
Belgium	29.4	42.5	50.5	21.1
France	34.9	38.4	48.8	13.9
Germany	35.0	42.8	45.9	10.9
Italy	28.8	30.6	44.7	15.9
Netherlands	33.9	47.0	47.6	13.7
Greece	21.1	27.0	36.8	15.7
Portugal	17.6	23.0	38.0	20.4
Spain	18.1	22.8	38.1	20.0
Switzerland	23.3	29.7	36.7	13.4
Japan	18.8	24.5	31.7	12.9
Mean	27.4	36.1	43.6	16.2
Correlation with 1960		0.84	0.63	–0.07
Coefficient of variation	20.66	24.25	19.04	

Sources and notes: Data for 1960 and 1974 from OECD, *Historical Statistics*, Paris, various years. Data for 1995 from OECD (1996b). The figure reported in the final column is the percentage point change over the entire period. Where data are missing and there are available data for a year within +/– 2 years of the data-point, those data are given. – indicates the absence of any adjacent data-point.

ence before 1974 which was matched by a more or less equivalent decrease thereafter. That these countries were no more similar in 1995 than in 1960, despite the massive growth in revenues which took place in the interim, does not seem readily compatible with theories which suggest that the forces pushing the growth of the state or, more recently, constraining its development have markedly reduced the scope for differences amongst nations.

Finally, while space considerations prevent us from analysing cross-national differences in the incidence of different types of taxes, it is at least worth mentioning research findings which suggest even more distinct groupings of nations in this respect. A study which examines different varieties of tax mix in the 1960s and 1980s identifies four distinct clusters of countries rather similar to our four families of nations (Peters, 1991, 61–8). In 1965, it was possible to locate an English-speaking grouping minus Ireland and plus Switzerland and Japan, which had a higher than average reliance on property, corporation and income taxes. At the same time, a Scandinavian grouping was characterized by high personal income taxes, employers' social security contributions and consumption taxes, a combination which the study attributes to the strong influence of Left incumbency in these nations (Peters, 1991, 65). Many of the continental Western European countries, including Germany, Belgium and the Netherlands, but also Spain, belonged to a cluster which relied on broad-based taxation, using a wide variety of tax instruments, but only using them in moderation. Finally, there was a 'Latin Cluster', including France, Greece, Ireland, Italy and Spain, which relied substantially on indirect taxes. These groupings still existed in the latter part of the 1980s, although the differences between them had diminished somewhat as France joined the continental Western European grouping and as most nations shifted towards the more broadly based tax systems required to finance big government in the closing decades of the Twentieth Century.

Findings

Since, with a somewhat varying emphasis, all the hypotheses which apply to total outlays also apply to total receipts, we may move directly from data to findings. Focusing first on Figure 4.2(a), we note a still wider range of significant relationships than in the case of 1960 outlays (Figure 4.1 (a)). No less than 13 variables are correlated with receipts at a level of + or – 0.40 or greater and all the relationships are in the directions suggested by the hypotheses discussed previously. Turnout and age structure are the variables with the strongest correlations, as they were also in respect of outlays, but the relationships with home ownership, union

(a) 1960

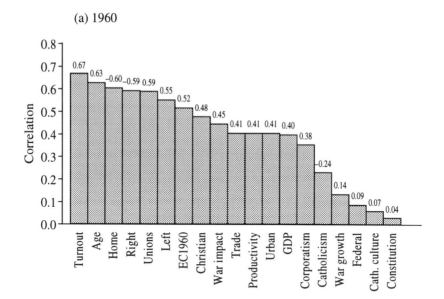

(b) 1974

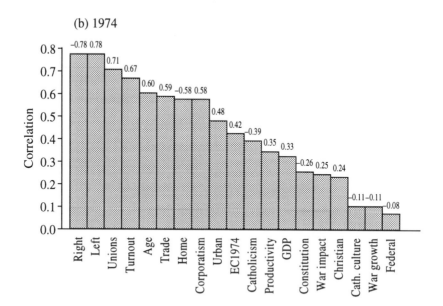

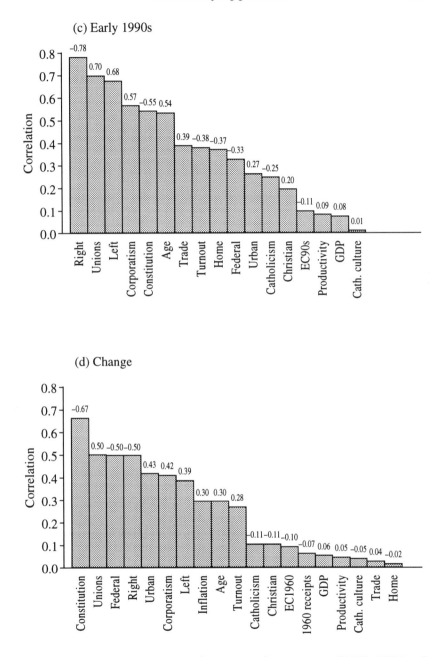

Figure 4.2 Bivariate tests: total receipts of government (1960, 1974 and early 1990s and change over time)

density and Right and Left incumbency are stronger than in the case of outlays, whilst those with the European Community and urbanization are weaker. Factors which are significant in the case of receipts but not outlays include the level of economic development, both as measured by real GDP per worker and per capita, and war impact.

The 1960 receipts model reported in Appendix 4.2 involves, like its 1960 outlays counterpart, a curvilinear specification of real GDP per capita. In addition, it identifies wartime experience and the age structure of the population as factors with a positive effect on government receipts. The net effect of the curvilinear specification is that a country with the mean level of real GDP per capita gathered an estimated 6.8 percentage points of GDP more in revenues than the poorest country and an estimated 1.3 percentage points more than the richest. The latter figure does not sound particularly dramatic, but the point at which the negative impact of high income levels kicks in is well above the average level of real GDP per capita, so that the estimated gap in receipts between a country like Denmark, which was only just in the top third of the income distribution, and the USA, which was at the top, would be much greater. The average difference made by wartime experience was around 2.7 percentage points of GDP and around twice that contrasting the estimated outcomes in defeated and neutral nations. Finally, age structure has a substantial real effect, with the estimated difference between a country at the bottom of the age distribution and at the mean of around 5.2 percentage points of GDP.

Just as in the case of outlays, the 1960s and early 1970s were a period in which the association between receipts and political variables strengthened considerably. By 1974, as Figure 4.2(b) shows, Left and Right incumbency, with correlations of identical strength but opposite signs, manifest much the strongest relationships with the size of the tax state, followed by union density, turnout and the age structure of the population. Among the interesting changes between the first and second periods are the increasing positive significance of international trade and corporatism and the declining association with levels of economic development. Turning to Appendix 4.2, the best-fitting model is again one with a curvilinear specification of income and a significant term for age structure. However, just as in the case of outlays, party politics had become important by the 1970s, although, in the case of receipts, the crucial factor appears to have been the negative influence of Right incumbency rather than the positive impact of Left government. The net effect of the curvilinear specification is that the estimated value of receipts for a country with the mean level of GDP per capita in 1974 is 6.0 percentage points higher than for both the poorest and the richest countries. The estimated effect of age is identical to that in the 1960 model at 5.2 percentage points of GDP, while the negative influence of the Right is very substantial, implying that receipts were an estimated 6.8 percentage points of GDP lower in a country experiencing the average level of Right incumbency over the early post-war period as compared to a country, like Sweden, experiencing none.

Figure 4.2(c) tells a story in which politics has become still more influential. In the early 1990s, the Right is the factor most strongly associated with receipts, followed by union density, Left incumbency and corporatism. As in the case of outlays in the same period, constitutional structure has come from nowhere to be a major influence, and the only other factor of significance is the age structure of the population. Again, as in the case of outlays, trade has ceased to be significant, but the correlation remains positive. Looking at Appendix 4.2, we can see that there are strong similarities and some differences between the models for receipts and outlays *circa* the mid-1990s. In both, the Right is a dominant influence and in both, international trade and constitutional structure have a clear restraining effect on the size of government. However, in the case of receipts, there is no apparent turnout effect, and age structure features as it did in both the 1960 and 1974 receipts models. The estimates derived from the 1990s model imply that an average level of Right incumbency reduced revenue by 9.3 percentage points, average trade exposure by 3.5 percentage points and a standard constitutional structure by 3.2 points. Countries with an average age structure gathered an estimated 3.4 percentage points more revenue.

Figure 4.2(d) shows constitutional structure to be far and away the factor most strongly correlated with change in receipts over the entire period. Other significant factors are Right incumbency, union density and corporatism, urbanization and federalism. Neither change in the age structure nor inflation over the period as a whole, both of them factors which featured in the change model for outlays, are significantly correlated with change in the receipts of government. However, demographic change does feature in the successful model in Appendix 4.2, as do Right incumbency and constitutional structure. Both age structure and Right incumbency have a lesser real impact on receipts than on outlays, the estimated difference made by the former going down from 13.7 to 7.1 percentage points and by the latter from 7.7 to 4.8 points. Calculating the real impact of constitutional structure on the basis of the estimated difference between a country with no constitutional impediments to change and one with the arithmetic mean for this variable implies a reduction in receipts of 2.9 percentage points of GDP. This may seem quite negligible in the context of the massive increases in the size of the tax state in this period, but, for the countries at the extremes of the distribution, it makes a difference to the total receipts of government of no less than 10.4 percentage points of GDP.

Analysis

Not surprisingly, the overall story of the post-war development of the tax
state conveyed by a joint reading of Figure 4.2 and Appendix 4.2 has many
of the same features as our earlier account of the growth of big government in expenditure terms. One constant is the early curvilinear
relationship with real GDP per capita, which persists somewhat longer in
the case of receipts than of outlays. Another is that partisan politics starts
being important from the 1970s and becomes more so with the passing of
time, while the negative influence of constitutional structure has become
clearly evident by the early 1990s. By the end of the period it would also
appear that international trade is a restraining influence on the receipts of
government. The story for change over time also has strong similarities.
Common parameters are the negative influence of the Right and the positive impact of population ageing. However, in contradistinction to our
previous findings for outlays, constitutional structure now shows up as
strongly in the change model as in the model for the early 1990s. This is,
however, consistent with our earlier speculation that the outlays model was
misspecified by the inclusion of inflation, and that constitutional structure
serves uniformly as a restraint on the growth of expenditures and revenues.

If this is accepted, then the 'big picture' story of big government in the
latter half of the twentieth century seems reasonably straight forward:
government started out big in the early post-war period in the moderately
rich continental Western European nations variously identified by their
Catholicism, their wartime experience and their ageing population, and it
grew most thereafter in countries where parties of the Right were weak,
where population ageing was continuing and where constitutional
arrangements provided few veto points for those opposed to change.

The one way in which the outlays and receipts models systematically
differ is that, while electoral turnout is a factor consistently making for
higher aggregate spending levels, it is age structure which performs this
role in the revenue models. This is a somewhat surprising result, not
because we lack theoretical models accounting for the way in which
democratic participation translates into expenditure demands, but rather
because we normally conceptualize the influence of age structure as also
being about claims for higher levels of public spending. Indeed, as we
noted earlier in elaborating our hypotheses, there is some *a priori* reason
to assume that variables such as age structure, which measure the extent
of needs, are just those that one might expect to be most closely associated with variation on the expenditure side of the budget ledger.

It is arguable, however, that precisely because the needs of the aged
constitute the single largest claim on the public purse, and because the

fulfilment of that claim is largely non-discretionary and predictable, age structure has, for much of the post-war period, served as the bottom line for government revenue extraction. Given demographic projections and the nature of accumulated pension entitlements, governments know all too well the size of the burden on government revenues imposed by population ageing, and that is, of course, just the reason why organizations such as the OECD and the World Bank have presented a 'greying' population as the most imminent threat to public solvency and the continued viability of the welfare state. When one also takes into account that pension programmes are the social insurance schemes most widely financed on a contributory basis, linking revenue extraction to the extent of entitlements, the close identity of age structure and government revenues becomes more comprehensible. Clearly, were we to regard the positive effect of turnout on outlays in the 1990s as substantive finding, this difference in the way in which popular demands and demographic needs impact on the two sides of the budget ledger could be regarded as a factor contributing to the widening budget deficits of recent decades.

At first glance the fact that a negative relationship between the size of government and international trade is evident in the 1990s receipts of government model as well as in the 1990s outlays of government model seems to add force to an interpretation pointing to the inhibiting effect of an increasingly globalized economy on the size of government. However, this finding, together with the positive term for age structure, is once again purely a consequence of the inclusion of the Irish case. As previously in the case of outlays, excluding Ireland from the analysis produces a robust model based exclusively on the combined negative influences of Right incumbency and constitutional structure, and this model has a superior explanatory power to that reported in Appendix 4.2. Overall, the most sensible conclusion concerning the 1990s findings for both outlays and receipts is that the negative effects of rightist government and constitutional structure are demonstrated beyond all reasonable doubt, but leave room for legitimate speculation as to possiible impacts by other factors. Given the undoubted significance of population ageing on the trajectory of post-war change in respect of both aggregates, and the complete absence of any sign that changing patterns of international trade impact on either, it is arguable that the balance of the evidence still favours an interpretation which sees the positive influence of age structure as a more relevant factor than the negative impact of international trade.

CIVILIAN PUBLIC CONSUMPTION EXPENDITURE

Data

In the introduction to this chapter, we noted that, unlike transfers expenditure, civilian public consumption expenditure was a direct measure of the resources at the command of the state and, as such, possibly the best available indicator of the extent to which the line between public and private choice has been redrawn in the post-war era. According to Kohl (1981, 313–4), the distinction between transfers and public consumption expenditures represents two distinct approaches to public policy. The transfers approach involves a redistribution of cash income amongst members of a society, with choices concerning final consumption made on the basis of individual preferences. This market conforming model is contrasted with a more collective approach favouring 'the public provision of services whereby collective choice more directly shapes the structure of supply and mode of control' (Kohl, 1981, 314). Kohl, using public expenditure data for 1950 and 1975, and contrasting 14 of the countries under analysis here, sees continental Western Europe as the epitome of the transfers approach and Scandinavia as the exemplar of the statist public consumption approach.

Looking at the figures in Table 4.3 does not reveal a picture nearly as clear-cut as that suggested by Kohl. Partly, that is because he measures expenditures as percentages of government outlays rather than as percentages of GDP as here; partly it is due to the fact that our sample of countries is substantially larger than his, including both Southern Europe and a wider range of non-European OECD members. More or less in line with Kohl's analysis, the four Scandinavian countries always feature in the top half of the OECD distribution, and Sweden and Denmark are invariably at or near the top. However, the continental Western European countries tend to have quite divergent profiles, with Austria and Germany having no less a claim than Norway and Finland to count amongst the expenditure leaders, whilst the Netherlands and, to a somewhat lesser extent, Belgium, consistently feature as public consumption laggards. For the first half of the post-war era, the Southern European family of nations, together with Japan and Switzerland, made up the tail of the OECD distribution, but this altered after the mid-1970s, with Spain and Portugal moving ahead of several of the continental Western European countries.

Nor is there any greater sign of coherence in the English-speaking grouping. These countries featured right across the distribution. The United Kingdom, like Austria and Germany, had as much right to the title of 'big spender' as the lesser members of the Scandinavian family, whilst Australia and New Zealand were always towards the middle of the

Table 4.3 Levels and change in civilian public consumption expenditure as a percentage of GDP, 1960–93

Country	1960	1974	1993	Change: 1960–93
Australia	8.5	12.7	16.0	7.5
Canada	9.1	16.2	19.8	10.7
Ireland	10.4	14.6	14.7	4.3
New Zealand	8.4	13.0	14.1	5.7
UK	9.9	15.4	18.4	8.5
USA	7.9	11.9	12.4	4.5
Denmark	10.6	21.0	24.3	13.7
Finland	10.2	13.8	17.0	6.8
Norway	9.7	15.2	19.0	9.3
Sweden	12.1	20.0	25.5	13.4
Austria	11.8	14.8	18.3	6.5
Belgium	9.0	11.9	13.5	4.5
France	7.8	11.7	15.9	8.1
Germany	10.7	17.7	17.6	6.9
Italy	8.7	11.0	15.6	6.9
Netherlands	8.2	12.5	12.3	4.1
Greece	6.8	9.5	13.6	6.8
Portugal	5.6	5.7	14.4	8.8
Spain	6.2	8.2	15.8	9.6
Switzerland	6.3	9.6	12.6	6.3
Japan	6.9	8.2	8.6	1.7
Mean	8.8	13.1	16.2	7.4
Correlation with 1960		0.89	0.70	0.32
Coefficient of variation	20.75	29.31	24.35	

Sources and notes: Civilian public consumption expenditure = government final consumption expenditure as a percentage of GDP; from OECD, *Historical Statistics*, Paris, various years minus military expenditure as a percentage of GDP from SIPRI, *Yearbook*, Stockholm, various years. The figure reported in the final column is the percentage point change over the entire period.

distribution, and the USA was somewhat closer to the bottom. Moreover, whilst these countries stayed roughly in the same positions in the distribution over the whole period, Ireland and Canada shifted their positions quite markedly, the former going down from fifth in 1960 to thirteenth in 1993 and the later going up from ninth to third over the same time-period. Of these divergent trajectories of change, the Canadian one was the more remarkable, with a growth of more than 10 percentage points of GDP in just over three decades. This put Canada next in the growth league after Sweden and Denmark and ahead of Spain, Norway and Portugal. The bottom of the change distribution is a no less mixed bag, with Belgium, the Netherlands and Japan featuring alongside the English-speaking trio of New Zealand, the USA and Ireland. Thus, contrary to the implications of Kohl's analysis, it would appear that families of nations patterns are actually rather less distinct in respect of civilian public consumption than are total outlays or receipts of government.

The average level of public consumption expenditure in the OECD countries almost doubled over the period as a whole. The bulk of this increase took place in the years between 1960 and 1974, with the average rate of change in the earlier period being nearly twice that occurring over the next two decades. Our earlier analyses of outlays and receipts showed few signs of catch-up as big government expanded in the post-war era. Although not quite statistically significant, the trend for public consumption expenditure was actually in the other direction. With the exception of Spain and Portugal, where catch-up clearly did take place to some extent, the statist forms of service provision expanded most strongly where such provision was already best established in 1960. This tendency was accompanied by an increasing dissimilarity amongst these nations, as shown by a substantial increase in the coefficient of variation between 1960 and 1974, which was only partially reversed in subsequent decades. Of all the tax and expenditure outcomes discussed in this volume, civilian public consumption expenditure provides the only instance where countries were less alike in the early 1990s than they had been at the beginning of the period. Thus the story of the changing line between the public and private spheres in the post-war era has two dimensions: within a general tendency for the public sphere to expand, the contrast between the more and the less statist countries actually increased with the passing of time. The peculiarities of that story stand out nowhere more clearly than in the contrast between Canada and the USA, countries often seen as the twin exemplars of a non-statist market approach to public policy, which by the early 1990s were at opposite ends of the public consumption spectrum.

Findings

An immediate contrast between the findings reported in Figure 4.3 and earlier figures is that there are far fewer significant relationships between the independent variables and public consumption expenditure than was the case for either total outlays or total receipts. Four factors are consistently related to outcomes irrespective of period: the three main measures capturing the ideological dimension of post-war political differences between nations – union density and Left and Right incumbency – together with the age structure of the population. In both 1960 and 1974, electoral turnout was also significantly related to expenditures, but had declined in importance by the early 1990s. All the variables mentioned are related to outcomes in the manner predicted by our hypotheses. In 1974, but at no other time-point, Catholicism was negatively related to outcomes, a finding which is in conformity with the hypothesis that the Catholic Church has favoured transfers at the expense of a more directly statist approach. Finally, Left incumbency is the only variable which is significantly associated with change in civilian public consumption expenditure over time.

Turning to the results reported in Appendix 4.3, we note that, in general, the level of explained variation provided by the models is lower than in the case of either outlays or receipts. There is, moreover, a marked decline in our capacity to understand what is driving public consumption in the latest period and in respect of change over time. Despite the relative weakness of the models in Appendix 4.3, they do have one wholly consistent feature in common: the main factor associated with public consumption expenditure turns out to be Left incumbency. For an average OECD nation, this factor made a difference in expenditure of just under 0.7 of a percentage point of GDP in 1960, 1.6 percentage points in 1974 and 3.5 percentage points in 1993. For change over time, Left incumbency made a difference of 2.5 percentage points. However, this is another instance where the real impact of a variable cannot be conveyed by averages alone. Looking to the extremes, with the USA and Canada at the bottom of the distribution throughout and Norway at the top in 1960 and Sweden thereafter, the differences made by Left incumbency are 3.2 percentage points in 1960, 7.0 in 1974, 9.6 in 1993 and 6.3 for change over time. Although Figure 4.3 shows that union density, Right incumbency and demographic structure are all significantly associated with levels of expenditure throughout the period, none of these factors features in any of the relevant expenditure models.

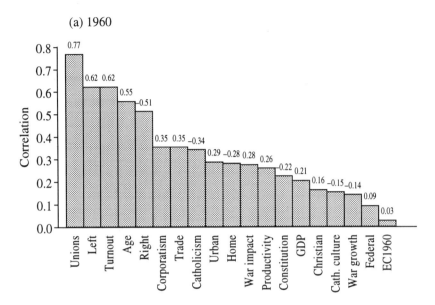

(a) 1960

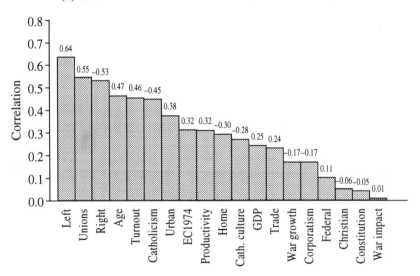

(b) 1974

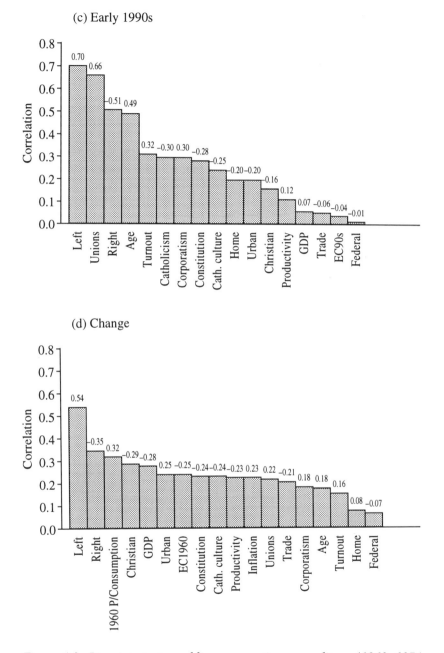

Figure 4.3 Bivariate tests: public consumption expenditure (1960, 1974 and early 1990s and change over time)

In both the 1960 and 1974 models, electoral turnout is the only factor other than Left incumbency which is associated with public consumption expenditure, making a difference of 2.3 percentage points of GDP in the former year and 3.7 in the latter. Although these figures appear to suggest a bigger impact than Left incumbency, it must once again be remembered that the average OECD country had a level of electoral turnout of around 70 per cent in both of these years and that these figures capture the estimated difference that turnout makes between such a country and one of the Southern European autocracies. Re-estimating these models without Southern Europe makes it clear that in both periods the electoral turnout variable is only relevant as a factor explaining the differential public consumption levels of dictatorships and democracies. This differential, however, has a genuine theoretical significance in providing us with some leverage on the probable threshold value of public consumption expenditure in a democratic state.

In 1993, the only factor that was associated with outcomes was Left incumbency, whilst, for the change model, in addition to the impact of Left incumbency, inflation made a difference of around 1.5 percentage points of GDP. However, given the inverse relationship between service provision and productivity growth (Baumol, 1967; Esping-Andersen, 1990), and, assuming comparable wage developments in public and private sectors, it seems quite possible that the model here reverses the real order of causality, with public consumption growth contributing to wage inflation and helping to account for the seemingly no less spurious relationship between inflation and outlays located in Appendix 4.1.

Analysis

Only three points will be discussed here. The first is a question of why the curvilinear specifications of income that were strongly apparent in the case of receipts and somewhat less so in the case of outlays do not show up with regard to civilian consumption expenditure. The second relates to the relative weakness of the public consumption findings presented in Appendix 4.3 and how that weakness may best be accounted for, and the third to the reasons why political variables and, in particular, Left incumbency, feature so prominently in our findings. This last point leads us into some general discussion of the likely future development of state provision of services in an era when the realities of big government are increasingly challenged by the rhetoric of small government and the sovereignty of the market. These remarks serve as the conclusion to this chapter, but the role of Left incumbency is taken up again at the end of the next chapter, where we seek to provide a reconciliation of our findings concerning the determinants of public consumption expenditure and those influencing health and education spending which, in most countries, constitute its main components.

The first point can be dealt with very briefly. There is little difference between civilian public consumption expenditure and the big aggregates of spending and taxation in respect of the low spending at both extremes of the distribution of real GDP per capita. However, consumption expenditure is unlike these aggregates in that there is, in addition, a group of moderately affluent countries which are also low spenders. These turn out to be a sub-set of Kohl's continental Western European nations, and precisely the Catholic, EC nations – Belgium, France, Italy and the Netherlands – which were earlier identified as big spenders in outlays terms. Obviously, when we come to discuss the other main sub-category of public expenditure, social security transfers, we would strongly expect extremely high spending amongst these nations and a curvilinear specification of early expenditure development.

The two models which are particularly weak are those which seek to account for the level of public consumption expenditure in the early 1990s and for change over time. In both cases, that weakness is attributable to a single aberrant case. Canada is a country with no socialist presence at the federal level of government but it has, nevertheless, manifested massive public consumption growth in an era when the engine of growth for this kind of public spending has been Left incumbency. Excluding Canada, the correlation between Left incumbency and civilian public consumption in the early 1990s is no less than 0.81, and a very much stronger model can be elaborated in which Left incumbency has much the greatest influence, but in which EC membership also has a significant positive effect (see note to the early 1990s equation in Appendix 4.3). This latter finding appears to contradict the notion that the preferred Western European mode of policy delivery is via transfers rather that state services provision. However, given that, by 1993, EC membership takes in roughly half our sample of countries, all the finding really means is that, leaving Canada aside, continental Europe finds itself broadly in the middle of a distribution with leftist Scandinavia at the top and the largely non-leftist countries outside Europe plus Switzerland towards the bottom.

Re-estimating the change model without Canada also produces a more satisfactory result. By a whisker, the terms of the model remain the same. However, harking back to our doubts about whether the model including inflation is correctly specified, it is worth noting that a model constituted by Left incumbency plus change in electoral turnout fits only marginally less well (see note to the final equation in Appendix 4.3). This latter model intuitively seems more sensible, accounting for the otherwise unexplained catch-up of the Southern European nations in terms of the massive increase in democratic participation these countries experienced after the mid-1970s. Between 1974 and 1993, the countries which led the way in expanding the reach of the state were not the heartlands of Scandinavian social democracy, but the countries of the Iberian Peninsula freed of decades of autocratic rule.

Turning from the picture revealed by the recognition of Canada's aberrant status to the question of why that country's public consumption expenditure expanded in the way it did, probably the best answer is that Canada's performance is much less anomalous than it appears on the surface. The crucial point to emphasize is that Canada's lack of socialist government is only at the federal level. At the provincial level, where the bulk of public consumption expenditure takes place (Cameron, 1986, 36), overtly leftist parties – initially the Co-operative Commonwealth Federation (CCF) and later the New Democratic Party (NDP) – have formed governments in Saskatchewan, British Columbia, Manitoba and Ontario at various times. The NDP was consciously formed as an instrument of the working class movement and, apart from its provincial successes, has succeeded in obtaining up to 20 per cent of seats in the federal lower house as well as having a pivotal role in supporting a Liberal minority government in the early 1970s (Jackson, Jackson and Baxter-Moore, 1986).

So, in terms of the 'power resources' model discussed in Chapter 3, it would seem that leftist governments have been in a position to influence provincial spending decisions, and it is a widely accepted view that CCF and NDP health initiatives in Saskatchewan provided the basis for subsequent federal schemes in this field (see Kudrle and Marmor, 1981, 112; Weller and Manga, 1983, 227; Tuohy, 1992, 111). From a class politics viewpoint, it might also be argued that the Canadian Left was in a position to use its parliamentary presence at both federal and provincial levels as a political lever for progressive reform, although a sceptic might well note that Canadian public sector transformation has been largely in the mainstream areas of health and education rather than in the area of social service provision typical of social democratic Scandinavia (see O'Connor, 1989). Nevertheless, it seems clear that measuring the influence of the Left in terms of federal incumbency does not do justice to the Canadian situation, wrongly making it appear identical to that of the USA, where socialist ideas failed to be institutionalized through the party system (Lipset, 1976). Seeing Canada as a country in which the major party of the Right has not been particularly successful during the post-war era (Table 3.4 above), and in which the Left has pushed for reform from the provincial periphery, makes that country's trajectory of public consumption development considerably less anomalous than suggested by our statistical findings.

CONCLUSION

There is a significant contrast between our findings concerning the deter-minants of outlays and receipts of government on the one hand and of public consumption spending on the other. In the case of the broader aggregates of taxing and spending, our findings suggest the relevance of a mixture of economic, social and political influences, whereas in the case of public consumption only politics seems to matter. Since the measures of total spending and taxing are effectively the sum of consumption expenditure plus transfers, it follows that transfers spending must be shaped by a much wider range of influences than is public consumption expenditure. The models of social security transfers spending elaborated in the next chapter bear this out, pointing to economic resources, citizen needs and cultural preferences as factors which are variously associated with post-war spending levels.

These differences in causal configuration reflect the diverse character of these forms of state intervention. While service provision can prop-erly be regarded as more statist than transfers, there is a sense in which it is an optional activity of government in a way in which transfers are not. Transfers – or, at least, those transfers which cannot be provided on the basis of actuarially sound insurance principles – involve shifts of resources from one individual to another which would be unlikely to occur as a result of self-interested behaviour. Hence, redistribution from those with adequate resources to those who are without can only take place via the mechanisms of private charity or public largesse. The implication is that, if transfers are to occur on any large scale, it must be through the instrumentality of the state. In contrast, although, services can be supplied to citizens without charge by the state, it is also often quite possible to provide them through the market and, in the absence of state intervention, it is almost certain that they would be provided on such a basis.

Paradoxically, this means that the public provision of services involves choice in a more fundamental way than does the provision of transfers. Of course, in any given society, there is likely to be some democratic con-sensus on a range of essential services to be provided by the state. This may well vary from society to society, although in Western industrialized nations it is likely to include some minimal level of access to emergency health care and some degree of compulsory schooling for the young, aspects of welfare state provision that will be discussed in the next chap-ter. However, above and beyond a threshold level of provision premised on full democratic participation, levels of public consumption are likely to be determined less by the extent of need and the availability of resources than by popular views as to the kinds of service provision mechanisms that are considered appropriate. Thus, what matters most for the role of government as service provider is whether there is a strong body of organized opinion which favours public provision either because collectivism is seen as intrinsically desirable or because it is regarded as the only way of guaranteeing equality of access for the broad mass of citizens. In the period under analysis here, large bodies of organized opinion which have held views of this kind have tended to describe themselves as parties of the Left. It is, therefore, scarcely surprising that state provision has been strongest where this partisan tendency has been most dominant. Because the distribution of ideological preferences has differed widely amongst nations and because that diversity has persisted throughout the post-war era, so too has the cross-national distribution of service provision by the state.

The optional character of public consumption expenditure has become a more and more prominent issue over the past decade as proposals for privatization and greater freedom of choice for the individual have been advocated by those who favour a greater role for the market. Mechanisms for achieving this end, such as voucher schemes, are particularly interesting because they involve transforming public services into tied transfers to individuals, whose freedom to choose is constrained to a limited range of alternatives in a particular policy sphere. Given the wider range of options for service provision currently discussed by politicians and policy-makers, at least three possible trajectories of future development can be visualized. The most commonly discussed in recent times has been the globalization scenario, leading to a convergent trend towards market solutions premised on the greater economic efficiency of the market under circumstances of enhanced international competition. The findings reported here only offer limited support for this scenario, with some precarious evidence of a negative relationship between trade exposure and both outlays and receipts, but little sign of emergent similarity amongst OECD nations in respect of either receipts or civilian public consumption over the period as a whole. A second scenario suggests the possibility of still greater dissimilarity amongst nations as some countries opt for the new range of private and semi-private modes of service provision, whilst others continue to pursue a progressively statist path. Given the slight reversal of dissimilarity amongst these nations after the mid-1970s and the coincident decline in the rate of growth of public consumption expenditure in virtually all of them, the evidence in support of this scenario is no stronger than for the first.

On the whole, the scenario that seems most consistent with the evidence presented here and with the general tenor of current political developments in Western nations is of a stationary or, perhaps, a somewhat declining level of provision combined with persisting differences among countries largely dependent on their diverse partisan complexion of government. Supporting the notion of a stationary level of provision is the evidence from the public consumption models for the earlier periods that democratic participation underpins the demand for a base level of state service provision. The argument for some degree of decline, or perhaps of a translation of public consumption expenditures into tied transfers, lies in the potency of the present rhetoric of small government, which has led countries such as the USA and Britain to test the limits of what are the minimum levels of provision compatible with democratic governance. That cross-national difference is likely to persist at least at the present level is suggested by the fact that, even though Leftist governments in countries with large welfare states have been far from immune from calls for a more market approach, their efforts at reform have been more than matched by rightist governments in countries with smaller welfare states (see Cooper, Kornberg and Mishler, 1988; Castles, 1992). Obviously, a belief that this is the most probable scenario influences our broader view of the likely future development of the bigger aggregates of public spending and public revenues. However, the wider applicability of such an analysis depends also on the forces driving transfer expenditures and on the dynamics of particular programmes. These are the subject of our next chapter.

APPENDIX 4.1 OUTLAYS OF GOVERNMENT MODELS

1960	Coefficient	Standard error	t-value
Intercept	–4.9		
1960 real GDP per capita	0.01	0.002	6.083
1960 real GDP per capita squared	–0.0000007566	0.0000001414	5.351
Catholic cultural impact	6.122	1.916	3.195

Adj. R^2 = 0.703

Sources and notes: 1960 Real GDP per capita from Table 2.2; 1960 Real GDP per capita squared calculated from Table 2.2; Catholic cultural impact from Table 2.7. 19 cases in regression.

1974	Coefficient	Standard error	t-value
Intercept	24.03		
1974 electoral turnout	0.082	0.034	2.412
1950–73 Left cabinet seats	0.164	0.036	4.502
1974 European Community	9.11	1.937	4.704

Adj. R^2 = 0.819

Sources and notes: 1974 electoral turnout from Table 3.1; 1950–73 Left cabinet seats calculated from the same source as Table 3.3; 1974 European Community is a dummy variable denoting EC membership *circa* 1974 (see Table 3.5). 20 cases in regression.

1995	Coefficient	Standard error	t-value
Intercept	54.786		
Early 1990s international trade	−0.124	0.049	2.531
Early 1990s electoral turnout	0.205	0.096	2.137
1950–early 1990s Right			
cabinet seats	−0.248	0.049	5.094
Constitutional structure	−2.028	0.638	3.178

Adj. R^2 = 0.734

Sources and notes: Early 1990s (1993) international trade from Table 2.3; early 1990s electoral turnout from Table 3.1; 1950–early 1990s (1994) Right cabinet seats from Table 3.4; constitutional structure from Table 3.5. 20 cases in regression.

1960–95 change	Coefficient	Standard error	t-value
Intercept	6.238		
1960–early 1990s change in			
aged population	3.176	0.708	4.486
1960–early 1990s Right cabinet			
seats	−0.214	0.045	4.758
1960–early 1990s average change			
in consumer price index	1.31	0.47	2.786

Adj. R^2 = 0.671

Sources and notes: 1960–early 1990s (1993) change in aged population from Table 2.6; 1960–early 1990s (1994) Right cabinet seats calculated from the same source as Table 3.4; 1960–early 1990s (1993) average change in consumer price index from OECD, *Historical Statistics*, Paris, 1995. 19 cases in regression.

APPENDIX 4.2 RECEIPTS OF GOVERNMENT MODELS

1960	Coefficient	Standard error	t-value
Intercept	−2.943		
War impact	1.769	0.652	2.712
1960 real GDP per capita	0.005	0.002	3.078
1960 real GDP per capita squared	−0.0000003669	0.0000001385	2.649
1960 aged population	1.33	0.388	3.426

Adj. R^2 = 0.78

Sources and notes: War impact from Table 2.1; 1960 real GDP per capita from Table 2.2; 1960 real GDP per capita squared calculated from Table 2.2; 1960 aged population from Table 2.6. 20 cases in regression.

1974	Coefficient	Standard error	t-value
Intercept	−6.039		
1974 real GDP per capita	0.007	0.002	3.948
1974 real GDP per capita squared	−0.0000003736	0.00000009679	3.86
1974 aged population	1.331	0.368	3.615
1950–73 Right cabinet seats	−0.141	0.026	5.509

Adj. R^2 = 0.842

Sources and notes: 1974 real GDP per capita from Table 2.2; 1974 real GDP per capita squared calculated from Table 2.2; 1974 aged population from Table 2.6; 1950–73 Right cabinet seats calculated from the same source as Table 3.4. 20 cases in regression.

1995	Coefficient	Standard error	t-value
Intercept	44.995		
Early 1990s international trade	−0.081	0.039	2.047
Early 1990s aged population	1.222	0.563	2.169
1950–early 1990s Right cabinet			
seats	−0.242	0.039	6.164
Constitutional structure	−1.647	0.469	3.509

Adj. R^2 = 0.826

Sources and notes: Early 1990s (1993) international trade from Table 2.3; early 1990s aged population from Table 2.6; 1950–early 1990s (1994) Right cabinet seats from Table 3.4; constitutional structure from Table 3.5. cases in regression.

1960–95	Coefficient	Standard error	t-value
Intercept	17.07		
1960–early 1990s change in			
aged population	1.679	0.596	2.818
1960–early 1990s Right cabinet			
seats	−0.135	0.039	3.44
Constitutional structure	−1.482	0.48	3.087

Adj. R^2 = 0.647

Sources and notes: 1960–early 1990s (1993) change in aged population from Table 2.6; 1960–early 1990s (1994) Right cabinet seats calculated from the same source as Table 3.4; constitutional structure from Table 3.5. 20 cases in regression.

APPENDIX 4.3 CIVILIAN PUBLIC CONSUMPTION EXPENDITURE MODELS

1960	Coefficient	Standard error	t-value
Intercept	5.823		
1960 electoral turnout	0.032	0.01	3.162
1950–59 Left cabinet seats	0.031	0.01	3.177

Adj. R^2 = 0.563

Sources and notes: 1960 electoral turnout from Table 3.1; 1950–59 Left cabinet seats from Table 3.3. 21 cases in regression.

1974	Coefficient	Standard error	t-value
Intercept	7.762		
1974 electoral turnout	0.053	0.019	2.73
1950–73 Left cabinet seats	0.075	0.023	3.281

Adj. R^2 = 0.594

Sources and notes: 1974 electoral turnout from Table 3.1; 1950–73 Left cabinet seats from Table 3.3. 21 cases in regression.

1993*	Coefficient	Standard error	t-value
Intercept	12.682		
1950–early 1990s Left cabinet seats	0.126	0.03	4.234

Adj. R^2 = 0.458

Sources and notes: 1950–early 1990s (1993) Left cabinet seats calculated from the same source as Table 3.3. 21 cases in regression. *Re-estimating this model excluding Canada produces the following result: 1993 civilian public consumption expenditure = 9.826 + 0.168 (0.024) Left cabinet seats + 2.337 (1.011) early 1990s EC membership (figures in parentheses are standard errors). Adj. R^2 = 0.709. For discussion of the re-estimated model, see text.

1960–93*	Coefficient	Standard error	t-value
Intercept	1.718		
1960–early 1990s Left cabinet seats	0.085	0.025	3.345
1960–early 1990s average change in consumer price index	0.455	0.217	2.095

Adj. R^2 = 0.371

Sources and notes: 1960–early 1990s (1993) Left cabinet seats calculated from the same source as Table 3.3; 1960–early 1990s (1993) average change in consumer price index from OECD, *Historical Statistics*, Paris, 1995. 21 cases in regression. *Re-estimating this model without Canada, and leaving out the inflation term because of suspected endogeneity, produces the following result: 1960–93 change in civilian public consumption expenditure = 3.866 + 0.046 (0.019) change in electoral turnout + 0.101(0.022) 1960–early 1990s (1993) Left cabinet seats (figures in parentheses are standard errors). Adj. R^2 = 0.563. For discussion of the re-estimated model, see text.

5. The welfare state

INTRODUCTION

The English historian Asa Briggs (1961, 228) once defined the welfare state as 'a state in which organized power is deliberately used (through politics and administration) in an effort to modify the play of market forces'. According to Briggs, for a nation to qualify as a fully fledged welfare state, it must undertake three kinds of activity: it must provide individuals and families with income guarantees that obviate poverty on any major scale, it must remove the causes of insecurity by ensuring that individuals and families have sufficient resources to meet social contingencies, such as sickness, old age and unemployment, and, finally, it must offer all citizens access 'to a certain agreed range of social services' (ibid.) In this chapter, we examine the development of the welfare state in the post-war era by means of an analysis of public spending on social security transfers, health and education. Transfers, which provide social assistance to the poor and income maintenance to those falling into an ever wider range of risk categories, have been the mechanism of the poverty alleviation and risk reduction functions of the modern state. Access to high-grade health and education services has progressively become regarded as a social right of citizenship.

The welfare state as defined here is clearly a post-war creation. Although individual programmes had, in some instances, been in existence for quite long periods, only in a few instances was their pre-war coverage sufficient to qualify by modern standards. Nor, prior to World War II, was there a comprehensive approach to welfare intervention involving a co-ordinated effort to undertake all three types of activity simultaneously. The nearest to an exception was probably New Zealand, whose Social Security Act of 1938 was hailed by the International Labour Organization as 'determin[ing] the practical meaning of social security, and ... deeply influenc[ing] the course of legislation in other countries' (ILO, 1949). The more conventional candidate for the honour of being the first welfare state is Britain, with the formative moment seen as the passing of the National Health Act of 1948. Whilst that claim may be justified in the sense that Britain's range of social insurance coverage and provision was probably the most comprehensive of any country at the time, Britain's pioneering role was short-lived, with a substantial number of European nations revealed as bigger spenders on social security by the early 1950s (see ILO, 1958).

In the very broadest terms, the sequence by which modern states became involved in welfare state provision was initially education, then social security and lastly health. Compulsory primary education was introduced in Prussia as early as 1763 and most European countries had followed suit by the end of the Nineteenth Century (Heidenheimer, 1997, 59). The general tendency has been towards a decline in private educational provision across all sectors, so that, today, in the majority of OECD countries, fewer than 10 per cent of the population attend private schools (OECD, 1989). The minority of countries in which there is a substantial private sector, Australia, Belgium, France, the Netherlands and Spain, are nations in which the Catholic Church has maintained its own schools, although, in many cases, largely supported from the public budget. There are only a very few nations in which less than 90 per cent of school funding is met from the public purse. At the tertiary level, the average figure for the OECD nations for which we have data is around 84 per cent, with the countries with the largest private sectors being the USA and Japan (OECD, 1996g).

Contributory social insurance was a German innovation of the 1880s, generally seen as an initiative by Bismarck to build support for the authoritarian regime amongst the increasingly politically aware industrial working class (De Swaan, 1988, 187–92). Whilst much of continental Europe followed the German lead in creating contributory systems, starting in the 1890s the nations of the English-speaking world and Scandinavia developed an alternative model based initially on flat-rate, means-tested provision, but later moving towards universal citizen benefits (Overbye, 1994). By the 1950s, social security schemes covering old age, disability, sickness and unemployment were general throughout Western Europe and the Antipodes, with only the countries of Southern Europe and North America lagging behind. Whereas initial schemes were focused on providing basic income support for workers and those in poverty, a feature of development since the 1960s has been the provision of earnings-related benefits (Gordon, 1988), which, although expensive and one of the main factors driving the growth of public expenditure, has been seen by some commentators as the necessary price paid for obtaining middle class political support for the welfare state (Esping-Andersen, 1985).

Public intervention in health started out at the municipal level, with city governments the prime movers in the growth of public hygiene and the provision of hospital beds for the indigent poor. Early health insurance schemes often built on pre-existing provision by trade unions and friendly societies, and coverage was generally restricted to industrial workers and those below certain stipulated income levels. While the earliest state schemes of public health insurance were contemporaneous with other types of social insurance, there was a stronger emphasis on voluntarism, with many countries only moving to mass compulsory coverage after World War II (Fulcher, 1974). The public share in total expenditure on health has grown appreciably over the course of the post-war era as the coverage of public schemes has increased, but a substantial private sector remains in a number of countries, including Australia, Austria, Portugal, Switzerland and, most conspicuously, the USA. In 1960, the average public share in OECD countries was around 60 per cent; by the early 1990s, it was close to 75 per cent (OECD, 1993).

Before turning to individual welfare state programmes, it is worth noting that of the three aspects of the welfare state discussed here, social security has been the area of overwhelmingly the greatest attention in the comparative public policy literature. This has not been a matter of the availability of comparative data, which are no less adequate for education and health than for social security. More compelling has been the fact that social security has been seen as the most redistributive form of state spending, so that accounting for its development has been regarded as directly relevant to questions concerning the ameliorative role of the modern state and the extent to which politics has shaped that role. Whilst such a rationale may account for the original focus on social security spending, it does not justify the continued, disproportionate emphasis on just this one measure of state activity. In fact, the original rationale has become increasingly questionable as the post-war development of earnings-related social security schemes has made transfers less exclusively a mechanism for income redistribution and the relief of poverty. The premise of this book is that all major arenas of state activity are worthy of comparative analysis in their own right and that the wider the focus of research, the greater the potential for locating patterns of similarity and difference across policy areas. We simply cannot assume that all programmes will have similar antecedents. As we have already established, there are significant differences in the range of factors influencing the aggregates of spending and taxing which define the reach of the modern state. Between the expenditure programmes of the welfare state, with diverse goals and very different clienteles, the differences are likely to be at least as great.

SOCIAL SECURITY TRANSFERS

Much the most influential analysis of social security outcomes in the past decade has been Gøsta Esping-Andersen's *The Three Worlds of Welfare Capitalism* (1990). The book has been extremely well received, in part because of its readiness to move beyond the simplicities of measuring policy outcomes exclusively in expenditure terms, but also because of its clear identification of the clustering of welfare state outcomes in distinct groupings of nations. The move beyond expenditure measures to a more nuanced account of outcomes in terms of such dimensions as benefit replacement rates, coverage rates, the basis of entitlements and the occupational segregation of social insurance schemes obviously represents an important advance. Expenditure data are, however, likely to remain the basis for most comparative research in this area. The new measures require a heavy investment in time and resources and there is often a substantial lag in their publication. In contrast, expenditure data are routinely available, usually with a lag of only one or two years.

While the greater richness of the new measures makes their lack of availability a matter of regret, for most routine research the loss may be relatively minor. Partly that is because the new measures are effectively disaggregations of broader expenditure outcomes, so that conclusions arrived at by the two different methods may not be hugely different. This is amply demonstrated in the analysis which follows. In addition, the more ready availability of routine spending data may make up for some of their other deficiencies, allowing us to replicate findings in a way that is often difficult with more multidimensional data. In this context, it is of interest to note that Esping-Andersen's findings were based on data for 1980, and that we do not know whether they remained accurate at the time he wrote, much less now – almost two decades later.

Esping-Andersen's three worlds of welfare capitalism have close affinities with three of our four families of nations. First, there is a liberal world in which the replacement rates of benefits tend to be low, means-testing is prevalent and private coverage has a major role. This is the world of the 'residual' welfare state, inhabited largely by the English-speaking nations, but with Japan and Switzerland closely aligned in terms of adherence to liberal principles of provision. Second, there is a 'corporatist' or 'conservative' world, based on contributory financing, the maintenance of occupational status distinctions and an étatist emphasis on the privileged welfare status of public employees. This world coincides substantially with the core countries of continental Western Europe, where social policy has been substantially shaped by corporatist and Catholic traditions. Finally, there is the social democratic world, premised on universal provision and a high degree of benefit equality, which seeks to avoid 'a dualism between state and market [and] between working class and middle class ... [and to] provide an equality of the highest standards, not an equality of minimal needs as ... pursued elsewhere' (Esping-Andersen, 1990, 27). This model of egalitarian social policy typifies the Scandinavian nations in which the power resources of the labour movement have been strongest, but is one to which some of the smaller continental European nations, such as Belgium and the Netherlands, have approximated in recent years. Whilst Esping-Andersen does not discuss the countries of Southern Europe in his 1990 study, the corporatist and étatist traditions of these nations make it clear that they most resemble their 'conservative' cousins of continental Western Europe (see Esping-Andersen, 1993; cf. Castles, 1995).

Data

Looking at the data on social security spending provided in Table 5.1 shows that it is possible to identify outcome clusters rather similar to those located by Esping-Andersen. Moreover, the routine availability of spending data provides a sense of the dynamics of policy development that is missing when information is available for only a single time-point. In the early post-war period, there were not really three worlds of welfare at all, but only two: the 'conservative' world and the rest, with the six continental European countries clustered together right at the top of the social security league table. Only after 1960 did the expenditure levels of the Scandinavian countries begin to outpace those of the English-speaking nations. By 1974, Denmark, Norway and Sweden, but not Finland, had caught up with the rear of the European group, but were still spending appreciably less than countries such as Belgium, the Netherlands, Austria and Germany. It is only in the most recent period that one can argue that Scandinavia has become the area with consistently the highest levels of social security spending. Even so, most of the continental Western European nations remained big spenders into the 1990s, with only Germany, the country with much the weakest post-war record of transfers growth, failing to keep up with other nations in this cluster. Throughout the whole period, the English-speaking nations, Southern Europe, Japan and Switzerland consistently feature towards the bottom of the distribution. The only really major exception is Spain, whose spending profile was becoming more akin to that of the 'conservative' continental European nations by the end of the period.

Turning now to the summary statistics at the bottom of Table 5.1, the first thing to strike one is the huge increase in expenditure over the period

Table 5.1 Levels of and change in social security transfers as a percentage of GDP, 1960–93

Country	1960	1974	1993	Change 1960–93
Australia	5.5	7.0	11.3	5.8
Canada	7.9	9.2	16.1	8.2
Ireland	5.5	11.4	15.3	9.8
New Zealand	–	–	–	–
UK	6.8	9.2	14.6	7.8
USA	5.0	9.5	13.2	8.2
Denmark	7.4	12.0	20.5	13.1
Finland	5.1	7.6	25.4	20.3
Norway	7.6	13.3	20.5	12.9
Sweden	8.0	14.3	25.2	17.2
Austria	12.9	15.5	21.4	8.5
Belgium	11.3	18.0	24.5	13.2
France	13.5	15.5	23.6	10.1
Germany	12.0	14.6	15.8	3.8
Italy	9.8	13.7	19.3	9.5
Netherlands	10.4	20.7	26.9	16.5
Greece	5.3	7.1	15.9	10.6
Portugal	3.0	5.3	12.4	9.4
Spain	2.3	9.5	18.6	16.3
Switzerland	5.7	10.6	17.5	11.8
Japan	3.8	6.2	12.1	8.3
Mean	7.4	11.5	18.5	11.1
Correlation with 1960		0.82	0.54	–0.16
Coefficient of variation	43.98	35.96	26.20	

Sources and notes: Data from OECD, *Historical Statistics*, Paris, various years. Data for the Netherlands in 1960 from Professor Hans Keman of the Free University of Amsterdam. The figure reported in the final column is the percentage point change over the entire period. Where data are missing and there are available data for a year within +/– 2 years of the data-point, those data are given. – indicates the absence of any adjacent data-point.

as a whole. Between 1960 and the early 1990s, the average social security spending of the OECD countries grew by more than 10 per cent of GDP or by around 150 per cent compared to its initial level. Of the spending categories examined in this book, only public health manifests an expansionary trend of comparable dimensions. However, the trajectory of social security development is unlike that of all the other programmes of government spending surveyed here in being substantially stronger in the second half of the period than in the first, almost certainly to some degree reflecting the massive increase in OECD unemployment levels since the mid-1970s. Also, in sharp contrast to the trend of taxing and spending aggregates analysed so far, the social security profiles of OECD nations became appreciably more alike across both sub-periods. However, this consistent pattern of convergence started from a baseline of cross-national diversity well in excess of that characterizing the aggregates previously discussed and, even by the early 1990s, social security was the area of spending in which variation was greatest, if only by a smallish margin. Thus, at the beginning of the period when there were really only two worlds of welfare in social security terms, they were, indeed, worlds apart; today, although the differences in spending patterns between families of nations are somewhat smaller, the diversity that remains is no less significant than in most other areas of state activity.

Hypotheses

Because the welfare state provides income maintenance payments and services to particular categories of individuals, it is necessarily the case that increases in the proportion of the population eligible to receive benefits or services in a given country will translate into increased spending in that country. By the same token, if benefits increase or services become more costly, these changes will also translate into additional expenditure. However, what shows up as a significant relationship for individual nations across time will not necessarily be apparent in cross-national comparisons of public spending levels and changes. That is because different countries do not offer identical services to their citizens and do not treat income maintenance needs in the same manner. A country can seek to ensure its aged population a quality of life comparable to that of the working population, in which case an ageing population is likely to imply a substantially increasing bill for pension transfers. Alternatively, a country can seek to provide a minimum income to the aged, and further restrict benefit access to those without other means of support, in which case the increase in pension costs is likely to be much smaller. Similar considerations apply to service provision, where standards can vary from de luxe to a basic minimum. These considerations suggest that international comparisons of welfare state expenditures should be looking for relationships between policy outputs and changing levels of eligibility, coverage rates and standards of service. They also suggest that we should not be too surprised when seemingly obvious relationships do not show up or appear only for certain periods.

In the case of social security transfers, the most obvious category of need is the aged and the presumed impact of population ageing is so great that it has been regarded as a factor likely to influence the overall parameters of taxing and spending. In the previous chapter, we found considerable evidence that this was, indeed, the case. For the group of countries we are examining here, the minimum level of spending on old-age cash benefits in the early 1990s was Australia's 3.2 per cent of GDP in 1992, whilst the maximum in that same year was Italy's 10.6 per cent of GDP (OECD, 1996d). Age pensions dwarf other programmes, such as child benefits, sickness compensation, disability support and single-parent pensions. The only programme to rival age pensions in terms of the size of its clientele, if not its claims on national product, is unemployment compensation. In 1993, the country with the lowest level of unemployment was Japan, with 2.5 per cent of its labour force seeking work, whilst the country with the highest level was Spain, with 22.4 per cent (OECD, 1996a; for further data on unemployment, see Table 6.3 below). In the same year, the country with the lowest expenditure on unemployment benefits was the USA with 0.58 per cent of GDP, whilst Denmark was the OECD's biggest spender with 5.5 per cent of GDP (OECD, 1996d). Around the early 1990s, OECD countries were on average spending more than 8 per cent of GDP on age pensions and only around 2 per cent of GDP on unemployment benefits (OECD, 1996d). Since the mid-1970s, the rate of growth of unemployment has much exceeded that of population ageing, with the OECD average rate of unemployment increasing from 2.9 to 9.8 per cent between 1974 and 1993 (OECD, 1996a) and the size of the aged population going up from 11.6 to 14.2 per cent over the same period (see Table 2.7 above). It seems an almost self-evident hypothesis that the growth of unemployment is likely to have been a factor leading to higher transfers spending in individual nations, although it may well be that the relative lack of generosity to the unemployed compared to the aged masks that relationship in cross-national comparison.

Findings

Figure 5.1 shows the strength of the relationships between social security transfers and the standard set of variables examined in the previous chapter plus unemployment. As was also true of both outlays and receipts, class politics and ideology are less strongly associated with outcomes at the beginning of the period than are measures relating to various aspects of the modernization process such as democratization and population ageing. Where transfers differ from outlays and receipts is that EC membership and Christian Democratic cabinet incumbency are the strongest factors of all. These findings fit with our prior theoretical understandings: with Kohl's view of transfers as the characteristic mode of social policy provision in the countries of continental Europe, with Esping-Andersen's identification of a distinctive 'conservative' world of welfare capitalism and with Van Kersbergen's notion of a 'social' form of capitalism based on a Christian Democratic political hegemony.

As in the case of the 1960 outlays and receipts models, the best-fit model for social security expenditure identifies a strong curvilinear relationship between real GDP per capita and spending. In addition, Appendix 5.1 locates war impact, age structure and Catholic cultural impact as significant factors influencing outcomes. The estimated difference in spending between the poorest nation and one at an average level of affluence is 5.8 percentage points of GDP. In this instance, the curvilinear relationship does not lead to an estimated value for the richest nation lower than for one with an average level of GDP per capita, but it does compress the estimated difference between them to 2.2 per cent of GDP. War impact has a modest estimated effect, with the difference between victorious and defeated nations being approximately 2.2 percentage points of GDP, whilst the estimated influence of age structure is of comparable dimensions, working out at around 2.1 percentage points of GDP for the typical OECD nation. Finally, the countries of Catholic cultural impact have an estimated level of social security spending 3.4 percentage points higher than countries in which other religious beliefs are dominant.

Looking at the correlations for 1974 in Figure 5.1(b) suggests only minor changes. Christian Democratic incumbency, age structure, home ownership and EC membership remain amongst the most influential factors, war impact and union density are no longer associated with outcomes, and both trade exposure and real GDP per worker come into the picture for the first time. A major difference in contrast to the big aggregates of spending and taxing in this same period is that the negative association with Right incumbency is not nearly as strong and the positive association with the Left is not significant at all. Again, a model based on a curvilinear relationship between real GDP per capita and social security outputs provides a better fit than a wholly linear specification. Four terms, real GDP per capita, its square, age structure and Catholic cultural impact are the same as in the 1960 model, whilst war impact drops out to be replaced by Right incumbency. The net effect of real GDP is almost exactly the same as a decade and a half previously, with the poorest nation estimated to spend 7.7 per cent of GDP less than an average nation and the richest nation estimated to spend only 2.0 per cent of GDP more. Age structure increased spending for the average nation by 1.4 per cent of GDP and Catholic cultural impact by 5.8 per cent. The negative impact of Right incumbency reduced spending by 2.2 percentage points of GDP.

By the early 1990s, patterns of social security spending had changed quite radically. Figure 5.1(c) shows that the influence of the religious factor had declined appreciably. Christian Democratic incumbency was only marginally below the level of significance, but the other measures were now clearly unrelated to outcomes. EC membership has also faded from the picture. On the other hand, ideological differences have now become very important, with Right incumbency much the strongest factor associated with outcomes, and with the Left and corporatism more important than either age structure or trade openness. Finally, and by now, familiarly, constitutional structure emerges as a negative influence on spending. Federalism itself, although not quite significant, is also clearly negatively related to outcomes. Although there remains a significant curvilinear relationship between real GDP per capita and spending, it is much weaker than previously and does not figure in the best-fit model appearing in Appendix 5.1. This model is dominated by the negative impact of the Right, which makes an estimated difference to spending of around 6.2 percentage for the average OECD nation. Federalism reduces spending by a further 4.0 percentage points, whilst Christian Democratic incumbency raises it by 1.3 percentage points. In reality, however, there is no such thing as a typical country in terms of Christian Democracy and the impact of this variable is best gauged in terms of its estimated influence on countries like Belgium, Germany and the Netherlands, where a post-war level of Christian Democratic incumbency of around 50 per cent translates into a level of social security spending 4.4 percentage points of GDP higher than in countries where such parties had no presence in government at all. Finally, for the average OECD nation, international trade reduces expenditure by around 2.5 percentage points.

(a) 1960

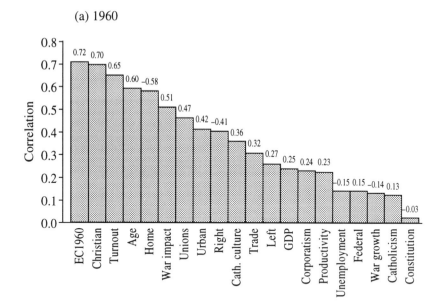

(b) 1974

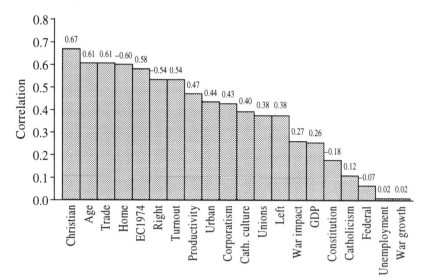

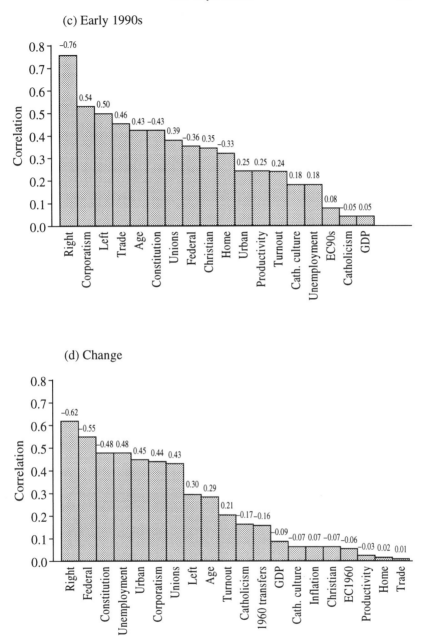

Figure 5.1 Bivariate tests: social security transfers (1960, 1974 and early 1990s and change over time)

Figure 5.1(d) presents correlations relating to change in social security spending between 1960 and the early 1990s. The picture is largely dominated by politics, with Right incumbency again much the strongest factor, but with federalism and constitutional structure now both negatively and significantly associated with outcomes. Interestingly, despite the strong negative correlation with Right incumbency, there is no sign of a comparable positive relationship with the Left. Although the religious factor featured in some form in each of three models for expenditure levels, it appears to have no influence on change. On the contrary, the correlations for all three measures are marginally negative, implying that the strong religious influence on policy outcomes so evident in the early post-war period was not further augmented in subsequent decades. Finally, we turn to relationships between spending and measures of citizen need. The findings here are mixed. Despite the lack of any earlier indication of a connection between levels of unemployment and of spending, unemployment growth has the expected positive relationship with change in transfers spending. However, quite surprisingly, given the major role of pensions in the overall transfers budget, the correlation between change in the age structure and in spending is insignificant.

The successful model in Appendix 5.1 again points to the major importance of Right incumbency as a factor shaping outcomes over three decades, making a difference of 4.9 percentage points to spending growth over this period. Having controlled for the impact of the Right, age structure re-enters the picture, with an estimated effect for the average OECD country of 4.1 percentage points of expenditure. The role of institutional structures in constraining public spending is again demonstrated, with federal nations experiencing 2.8 percentage points, less growth than unitary ones. For the first time in the analysis in this book, we also encounter a significant catch-up term, with growth in spending being reduced by 0.329 per cent of GDP for every percentage point of spending in 1960. Overall, catch-up makes an average difference of 1.7 percentage points of GDP. Given that the countries of continental Western Europe were much the biggest spenders at the beginning of the period, this term captures these nations' declining social security leadership.

Analysis

The findings reported in Appendix 5.1 suggest that social security development in the early post-war decades reflected four kinds of factors: citizen needs, cultural patterns, the availability of economic resources and, towards the end of the period, ideological partisanship. By the end of the period, partisan politics and constitutional impediments to change are the dominant influences on spending and there are also signs of an emergent constraint on social security development imposed by responses to economic vulnerability. The presence of the negative international trade term is solely dependent on the Irish case and, as previously in the case of the aggregates of spending and revenues, the finding must be interpreted with considerable caution.

The evidence that transfers were, at least in part, a direct response to need is not just a matter of the presence of the age structure term in the 1960 and 1974 models, but is also manifest in the positive effect of the war impact variable in the 1960 model, which is explicable in terms of the additional burden of disability and survivors' benefits resulting from the wartime experience. That all explicit need terms disappear from the scene by the 1990s does not mean that transfers spending had ceased to be a response to such imperatives. Rather the story is one of the needs of particular categories of beneficiary being obscured by the ever widening aggregate of transfers claimants and by the huge variation in system generosity. That need remained a crucial factor impelling the growth of the welfare state is strongly suggested by the coefficient for change in the age structure, which tells us that, for every additional 1 per cent of the population aged 65 years and over, OECD countries increased their spending by roughly an additional 1 per cent of GDP. Given that around half the OECD nations under analysis here face increases in the aged population in excess of 10 percentage points over the next 50 years (see OECD, 1994, 112–13), this finding underlines just how difficult it is going to be to cut back on the overall size of the transfers budget in coming decades.

The presence of the Catholic cultural impact term in the models for the two earlier periods and its replacement by Christian Democratic incumbency in the early 1990s model provides strong confirmation for the broad thrust of an argument much rehearsed in the literature in recent years. Here, shown up in different ways in different periods, is Esping-Andersen's 'conservative' world of welfare capitalism with the formative influence of Catholic social policy clearly apparent. What is interesting, however, is the form the influence takes and the implications this has for the borders of this conservative world. Paradoxically, it is in the earlier decades, when Catholic Southern Europe had low levels of transfers and Christian Democratic Western Europe extremely high levels, that the more inclusive definition of Catholic influence was most closely associated with outcomes, and it is more recently, when the Christian Democratic nations have lost their leadership and those of Southern Europe have moved up in the distribution, that the less inclusive measure of Christian partisan affiliation is the one that counts. The best way to understand this paradox is to think what the terms measuring the religious factor are doing in the different models. In the earlier period, the

Catholic cultural impact term is capturing the fact that, when we take account of the influence of real GDP, some of the poorer Catholic nations are spending rather more than we would otherwise expect. More recently, when the social security leadership of the Scandinavian and Benelux countries is accounted for by the weakness of the political Right, the Christian Democratic term is identifying a characteristic of a group of nations that come in the second rank. The former part of the story implies that the boundaries of the 'conservative' world should include Catholic Southern Europe (cf. Castles, 1995), whilst the latter part suggests that, with the passing of time, this world has become both more homogeneous and less distinctive in its spending patterns.

There is a strong link between Catholic social policy and the availability of resources to fund the welfare state. The conservative world of welfare is one in which benefits are funded on the basis of social insurance contributions, implying that as national income increases so too will the receipts of government. In addition, there is an inherent transparency in the contributory funding nexus which implies that contributions are likely to be raised as entitlements proliferate. In both the 1960s and 1970s, the Catholic countries which were in the vanguard of social security spending were also the countries in which social security contributions as a percentage of GDP were highest (see OECD, 1996f). Thus it is the funding mechanism particular to the conservative world of welfare capitalism that explains why the pattern of association between real GDP and transfers continues to show up longer on the receipts side of the budget ledger than on the outlays side.

The contributory funding mechanism is also the key to understanding both the curvilinear relationship between real GDP and spending and the way in which religious differences have impacted on that relationship. Observation of the scatterplots for the relationship between real GDP per capita and transfers spending show that, until the point at which the slowdown in Germany's transfer spending is translated into a major drop in its position in the distribution towards the end of the period, all the countries defined by the Catholic cultural impact term were on the upward slope of the curve, that is, they spent a greater proportion of national income on transfers as the size of national income increased. Indeed, for this small sub-sample of ten nations, national wealth seems to be almost the only thing that matters, with extraordinarily strong correlations between real GDP per capita and a variety of spending and taxing measures throughout the period. These include transfers (1960: 0.89; 1974: 0.90; 1993: 0.66), social security contributions as a percentage of GDP (no data for 1960; 1974: 0.88; 1993: 0.66), total receipts (1960: 0.94; 1974: 0.79; 1995: 0.92) and total outlays (1960: 0.92; 1974: 0.73; 1995:

0.81). There are no comparable relationships for Protestant countries, which are to be found on both the upward and downward slopes of the real GDP per capita curve. Whilst some of these latter countries, particularly those of Scandinavia, have become progressively more generous in their transfers spending, others have tended to rely on means-testing as the allocative mechanism for income maintenance spending, with the clear implication that, to the extent that poverty was alleviated by growing income levels, *transfers would decline*. Thus the fact that the Catholic countries, and they alone, consistently respond to the greater availability of economic resources by increased spending and taxing reveals a further aspect of this grouping's very distinctive political economy.

Just as in the case of outlays and receipts, partisan control of government emerges as an influence on transfers from the mid-1970s onwards and becomes much the most influential term in the models for both the early 1990s and change over time. Moreover, as was also true of the big aggregates, politics has an institutional dimension as well as a partisan one, although on this occasion manifested through the negative impact of federalism rather than the constraining influence of constitutional structure as a whole. Possibly the most interesting feature of the partisanship story is the contrasting importance of Right incumbency in the case of transfers and Left incumbency in the case of civilian public consumption. Again the explanation is connected to the role of Catholicism as a factor facilitating transfers expenditure. Whereas the salience of Left incumbency in respect of public consumption reflects the exceptional growth of such expenditures in Scandinavia, what the Right variable is picking up is the fact that non-Right parties both in Scandinavia (that is, Social Democrats) and in continental Western Europe (that is, Christian Democrats) were at the forefront of the postwar expansion of social security. That the Right incumbency measure generally features in the models accounting for the big aggregates of spending and taxing is simply a function of the fact that when civilian consumption and transfers are conflated, what is common to the countries in which growth was greatest is that it took place most spectacularly where the Right was weakest.

The final point that should be noted is that the patterns of association revealed in the case of transfers translate through to both outlays and receipts far more readily than do the patterns of association related to civilian public consumption. The obvious explanation, that transfers have a greater weight in total expenditure than does consumption expenditure, turns out only to be true for the early 1990s. The real reason is that cross-national variation in transfers spending has been greater throughout than variation in public consumption spending (see coefficients of variation in

Tables 4.3 and 5.1), with the difference at its greatest at the beginning of
the period. Because this has been so, the countries at the extreme ends of
the transfers distribution have tended to shape aggregate patterns of
spending and taxing to a far greater degree than have the countries at the
extremes of the public consumption distribution. This may not be the
case for much longer, given that the degree of variation in the two
metaprogrammes of public spending is now quite similar.

PUBLIC HEALTH EXPENDITURE

In most OECD countries, health care now constitutes the single largest
industry and, in all these countries bar the USA, it is an industry very
largely financed from the public purse. A typology of public health systems based on criteria relevant to funding differences is provided by
Gordon (1988, 204–5). It includes four types in descending order of
reliance on insurance principles: national health services, national health
insurance systems, mixed systems and traditional systems of sickness
insurance. At one extreme are schemes like the British National Health
Service funded exclusively from general taxation, and at the other are
schemes adhering to the original Bismarckian model of benefit exclusively on the basis of contribution. In most OECD countries, spending
falls disproportionately under the public consumption heading, but there
is a minority of countries, most of them in the traditional sickness insurance and mixed categories, in which transfers are much more prominent.
These latter include Australia, Belgium, France, the Netherlands,
Switzerland and the USA (see OECD, 1996h; cf. OECD, 1996i).

The size of the health sector and the steep trajectory of health care
costs over recent decades has made the issue of controlling the level of
the public health budget a matter of serious public policy concern and an
important focus for the professional activity of a vastly expanded health
care bureaucracy. OECD research on the determinants of total health
expenditure suggests that GDP per capita accounted for as much as 95
per cent of cross-national variation in health spending per capita in both
1980 and 1990 (OECD, 1993, 14–15). However, we cannot extrapolate
from total spending to public spending. In fact, the association between
these two categories is surprisingly weak, with correlations of only 0.35 in
1960, 0.61 in 1974 and 0.58 in the early 1990s (calculated from OECD,
1993). Arguably, the inclusion of the USA, with much the highest level of
total spending but only a relatively modest public sector, masks the
strength and convergent character of the relationship in the remaining
countries, but even dropping this case only improves the correlations to

0.55, 0.74 and 0.84 respectively. Hence, it is only for the most recent period that we have any reason to assume that findings concerning the determinants of these different categories of health spending are likely to demonstrate any major affinities.

Nevertheless, the role of the public sector has been central to the debate on cost containment. A generic argument favouring market solutions over interventionist ones has pointed to the supposed efficiency gains resulting from competition, whilst a concern with a balanced budget has led some to emphasize the dangers of public over-involvement in an area in which costs are often seen as out of control (Friedman and Friedman, 1980). Countering such views, it has been argued that uncertainty about health risks makes insurance-based provision inevitable (Arrow, 1963), that the lack of adequate medical knowledge on the part of consumers destroys the basis of informed choice on which competitive markets operate, and that private practice leads to strong incentives to utilize new, expensive, and sometimes unproven technologies (see Sax, 1990).

Under these circumstances, it has been suggested that centralized control of health spending may actually serve to inhibit the inherent tendency of the market to oversupply medical services. OECD research (1987) has lent some support to this latter view by demonstrating that the percentage of GDP spent on health is not merely a positive function of GDP per capita, but also a negative function of the public sector share of health expenditure. Case-study comparisons of the US and Canadian health care systems before and after the latter moved over to a fully fledged public system in 1968 have also been used to argue for similar conclusions (Detsky, Stacey and Bombadier, 1983; Newhouse, Anderson and Roos, 1988). In seeking to establish the factors associated with levels and change in post-war public health expenditure, we shall be particularly concerned to establish whether the early emergence of a strong public health sector has been associated with an increasing or decreasing trend in public spending on health.

Data

An examination of the data in Table 5.2 reveals much less evidence of a clustering of outcomes along family of nations lines than was typical of the measures of public spending previously examined. The closest approaches to definable clusters are in 1974, when three of the four Scandinavian countries were near the top of the distribution and Greece, Portugal and Spain were all close to the bottom, and in 1993, when all three Southern European countries were to be found in the

Table 5.2 Levels of and change in public health expenditure as a percentage of GDP, 1960–93

Country	1960	1973	1993	Change: 1960–93
Australia	2.5	4.2	5.7	3.2
Canada	2.4	5.2	7.2	4.8
Ireland	3.0	6.0	5.1	2.1
New Zealand	3.3	4.0	5.8	2.6
UK	3.3	4.7	5.8	2.5
USA	1.3	3.3	5.8	4.5
Denmark	3.2	5.8	5.6	2.4
Finland	2.3	4.4	6.9	4.6
Norway	2.8	5.8	6.8	4.0
Sweden	3.4	6.9	6.2	2.8
Austria	2.9	3.6	6.1	3.2
Belgium	2.5	3.9	7.4	4.9
France	2.5	4.7	7.3	4.8
Germany	3.1	5.9	6.4	3.3
Italy	3.2	5.8	6.3	3.1
Netherlands	1.3	5.4	6.8	5.5
Greece	1.9	2.4	3.5	1.6
Portugal	–	2.5	4.1	–
Spain	0.9	3.2	5.7	4.8
Switzerland	2.5	4.2	5.8	3.3
Japan	1.3	3.7	5.3	4.0
Mean	2.4	4.6	6.0	3.6
Correlation with 1960		0.66	0.02	–0.65
Coefficient of variation	31.52	24.65	16.16	

Sources and notes: Data for 1960 and 1974 from OECD (1994). Data for 1993 from OECD (1996d). The figure reported in the final column is the percentage point change over the entire period. Where data are missing and there are available data for a year within +/– 2 years of the data-point, that data is given. – indicates the absence of any adjacent data-point.

bottom third of the distribution. Otherwise, the picture is very mixed indeed. At the beginning of the period, the big spenders included two English-speaking, two Scandinavian and two German-speaking nations and the low spenders were Spain, the Netherlands and the USA. By the end of the period, a number of the continental Western European countries, Belgium, France, Italy and the Netherlands, all featured in the top third of the distribution along with Canada and two of the Scandinavian nations. At the bottom of the distribution, apart from the countries of Southern Europe, were to be found Ireland, Japan, Australia and Denmark.

The statistics in Table 5.2 show that the public health sector was simultaneously one of the fastest growing areas of public expenditure development in the post-war era and one of the most convergent. Between 1960 and 1993, average OECD expenditure increased by exactly 150 per cent, with the pace of change appreciably greater in the earlier period than the later one. Indeed, after the mid-1970s, a number of countries, including Sweden, Ireland and Denmark, the three expenditure leaders of the time, actually succeeded in cutting back spending as a proportion of GDP, a finding which seems to fit with the notion that public systems have some genuine cost-cutting capacity. At the same time as the OECD countries were increasing their spending, they were also becoming substantially more alike in how much they spent. In 1960, of 20 countries for which we have data, 13 spent 25 per cent or more above or below the mean level of spending of 2.4 per cent of GDP. In 1993, only Greece and Portugal spent 25 per cent or more below the OECD mean of 6 per cent of GDP and no countries spent 25 per cent or more above the mean.

As the moderately strong negative correlation between the 1960 level of spending and subsequent change in expenditure shows, part of what was taking place was a process of catch-up. However, this was not just a matter of closing the gap between leaders and the led, but of countries substantially changing their positions in the rank order. Thus, of the six leading nations in 1960, none was in the top third of the distribution in 1993 and their average spending level was actually marginally below the 1993 OECD mean, again suggesting that the popular image of a public sector caught up in runaway cost spiral is very far from accurate. The country that stands out as the greatest exception to the convergence and catch-up trends noted here is Greece, which started out in 1960 as one of a number of OECD public health spending laggards and ended the period as conspicuously the lowest spender of all.

Hypotheses

In addition to the variables listed in Chapter 4, we examine the relationships between public health expenditure and two other factors that seem
likely to have influenced post-war spending patterns. The first is the
extent of public coverage against medical care costs (for data, see OECD,
1993), with the self-evident hypothesis being that public health spending
as a percentage of GDP will be higher where the eligibility for benefits
under a public scheme is higher. Indeed, it might be argued that such a
proposition is almost tautological and that what is really required is an
explanation of why eligibility was higher in some countries than in others
in the first place. It is, however, virtually impossible to make sense of
public health spending trends without a term for the extent of coverage.
This is particularly true at the beginning of the period when coverage
rates varied appreciably, with countries which had pioneered national systems of health care, like Britain and New Zealand, catering for the health
needs of the entire population, whilst the call on the public purse in other
countries was obviously far less.

The best way to depict the process by which coverage has been
extended in OECD countries during the course of the post-war era is in
terms of a ratchet effect, with massive, legislated, once-off hikes in eligibility levels effectively making the trajectory of change into a one-way
street. Politics certainly mattered in this process, with the introduction of
national schemes of health care often a major victory for parties of the
Left, but, with the temporary exception of Australia in the late 1970s
(Najman and Western, 1984), parties of the Right have not been game to
reverse reforms which have been almost universally electorally popular.
Thus a fundamental reason for the convergence of public health spending
levels over time has been the simple fact of the democratic irreversibility
of public health care reform. Once high levels of coverage became a general phenomenon – and already by the early 1970s eligibility ratios were
over 90 per cent in 17 of the 21 OECD countries – the few remaining differences are likely to have become less consequential.

Another reason for paying attention to the extent of public coverage is
that it gives us some leverage on the argument about whether public
sector control promotes or constrains public expenditure growth. In our
analysis of change in public health spending, we examine the possible
impact on expenditure growth of initial coverage levels. A positive and
significant association would, of course, be proof positive of the con-
tention that public ownership encouraged public profligacy. A negative
association, however significant, would need to be interpreted more care-
fully, since it is probable that countries with initially high levels of

coverage were also the big public health spenders of the early post-war period. A negative association under these circumstances would be indicative of a catch-up phenomenon and a demonstration of the capacity of the countries with longest experience of centralized public control to pursue policies enabling them to stay at or close to OECD public expenditure norms.

The second variable additional to those discussed in Chapter 4 is a measure of inputs into health care. There has been a long-term debate on the contribution to the costs of health care of technological innovations in medical practice (see Fuchs, 1990), but technology take-up is by no means the only source of cross-national variation in the quantity and quality of the inputs supplied. Others include major differences in the costs of essentially similar services (OECD, 1987, 74) and quite astonishing variations in hospital admissions rates for different conditions – why, for instance, are there 557 hysterectomies per 100 000 of the population in the USA and only 90 per 100 000 in the Japan, and why 340 appendectomies in Australia and only 74 in Switzerland (see McPherson, 1990)? There are also considerable cross-national variations in doctors' income levels, with clear evidence that the more nationalized systems of health care tend to be characterized by lower remuneration levels (OECD, 1987, 76).

Since hospital treatment brings the patient to the high-technology interface and involves substantially higher costs than out-patient treatment even where the use of high-tech medicine is minimal, the measure we use here to assess the relationship of inputs to expenditure is per capita use of in-patient care or average bed-days per person (OECD, 1993). Although there has been a general downward trend in this measure over recent decades, as governments have sought to find ways of countering burgeoning health costs, the cross-national diversity in hospital use remains extraordinary (with Norway's average of 5 bed-days per annum contrasting with Portugal's and Spain's 1.1 per annum). We would clearly expect that countries with higher levels of usage would, all other things being equal, experience higher public health costs.

Findings

Figure 5.2 shows correlations between levels and change in public health expenditure and measures of the variables hypothesized to be associated with such outcomes. In 1960, much the strongest relationship was with the extent of public coverage, but bed-days were also significantly and positively related to expenditure. Fitting with the notion that the forces of the Left have often been the engine of public health care reform, both union density and Left incumbency were positively and significantly

(a) 1960

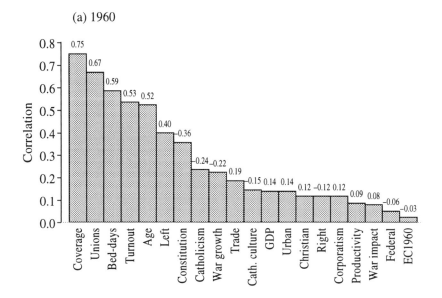

(b) 1974

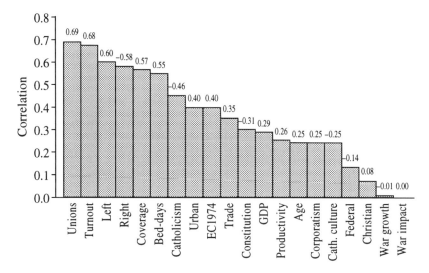

(c) Early 1990s

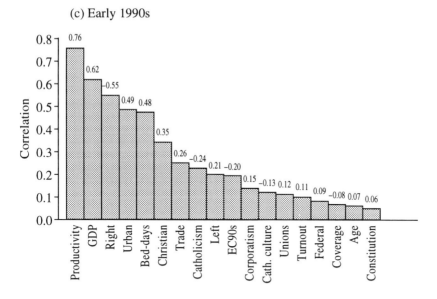

(d) Change

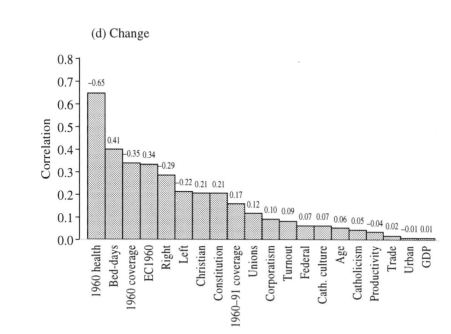

Figure 5.2 Bivariate tests: public health expenditure (1960, 1974 and early 1990s and change over time)

associated with spending and, in line with the democratic irreversibility thesis, electoral turnout was also a positive factor. Age structure of the population is the only socio-economic variable significantly associated with expenditure in 1960. In contrast to OECD findings for total health expenditure, there was absolutely no relationship between the measures of national income per capita or per worker and the level of public health spending at this date.

The 1960 model in Appendix 5.2 contains terms for public coverage, age structure, electoral turnout and international trade in descending order of statistical significance. Average coverage increased spending by 1.14 percentage points, age structure by 0.67 of a point and turnout by 0.87 of a point. An average degree of trade exposure decreased spending by 0.38 of a point. The figure for coverage suggests a rather strong effect, with high levels of eligibility for medical care benefits making a substantial difference to spending, but this is one of the occasions when this measure is quite deceptive. Coverage has a highly skewed distribution, with Portugal and the USA at the bottom of the distribution roughly 50 percentage points below the mean and the countries with complete coverage only 28 percentage points above the mean. Thus, while coverage laggards spent around 1 per cent of GDP less than the mean, coverage leaders spent only 0.5 of a per cent more.

Figure 5.2(b) indicates that, by the mid-1970s, public coverage, although still significant, was ceasing to be a major influence differentiating cross-national expenditure levels, with a correlation now only marginally stronger than that for bed-days. In 1974, the really strong factors were union density and turnout, with both Left incumbency and Right incumbency in the moderate range. Perhaps reflecting an aversion to public consumption spending, which had been the prevalent mode of expanding coverage in the early days of public health system development, Catholicism also turns out to be negatively and significantly associated with spending levels. Neither real GDP per capita nor per worker are significant predictors of outcomes, but in the former case this was only because of the anomalously low public expenditure of the USA. Appendix 5.2 identifies only two significant terms in a 1974 model with a somewhat lesser degree of explanatory power than that for the earlier period. They are electoral turnout and Left incumbency, making estimated differences of 1.33 and 0.34 percentage points of GDP respectively.

By the early 1990s, the world of public health spending appears almost wholly changed. Figure 5.2(c) shows that public health expenditure now reflects the same forces that had long dominated total expenditure levels, with productivity much the strongest influence on outcomes, followed by real GDP per capita. Only three other factors are significantly correlated with spending levels: urbanization and bed-days positively and Right incumbency negatively. Where once political factors had been crucial in determining the share and spending level of the public sector, the main factor now was the availability of economic resources. Where once the Left had been the mobilizing force for public sector expansion, the only remaining partisan influence was now the financial parsimony of the Right. The 1993 model in Appendix 5.2 demonstrates the hugely significant impact of productivity, which makes a difference to spending levels for the average OECD country of around 2.2 percentage points of GDP. A wholly unexpected finding on the basis of the results in Figure 5.2(c) is the negative influence of constitutional structure. For countries whose scores on this measure are only the standard distance apart, this factor reduces expenditure by 0.5 of a percentage point of GDP, but for countries at the extremes of the distribution, like Switzerland and the USA, the effect is very considerable. Figure 5.2 shows bed-days to be the only factor consistently associated with spending at all times. Now, for the first time, our measure of health care inputs features in the best-fit model, making a positive difference of 0.29 of a percentage point of GDP for the average OECD nation.

Figure 5.2(d) suggests a picture dominated by catch-up. Only two variables are significantly associated with change in health expenditures, the initial level of spending and change in bed-days per capita and, of these, the negative influence of initial level far outweighs the positive influence of health care inputs. For what is the only occasion in this study, outcomes appear completely unrelated to any of the major facets of the socio-economic and political transformation of the post-war era. Catch-up is the only intelligible theme of the change model in Appendix 5.2. For every 1 per cent of GDP spent in 1960, the subsequent rate of expenditure growth was lower by 0.97 per cent of GDP. As a result, by the early 1990s, the countries which had been expenditure leaders at the beginning of period were spending an amount which was almost precisely what they would have been spending if they had not been leaders in the first place. The only other term in the model is inflation. However, the negative relationship, implying that higher inflation reduced expenditure by 0.69 per cent of GDP for the average OECD country, defies the received wisdom that inflationary tendencies tend to increase service sector costs relative to those of the economy as a whole.

Analysis

A possible way of looking at changes in the factors impinging on public health expenditure is to see them as a kind of mirror image of those encountered in the area of social security transfers. Transfers started out by being influenced by citizen need and resource availability and ended up being hugely influenced by partisan politics. In contrast, in the health care arena, politics was initially the dominant factor, but was replaced in the 1990s by considerations of the availability of resources and the control of health care inputs. The reversal is made complete by the fact that trade exposure restrains health spending at the beginning rather than at the end of the period, a finding which is, however, wholly dependent on the Netherlands' initially weak expenditure development.

The dominance of politics in 1960 is actually greater than it appears in the model in Appendix 5.2. Although further analysis demonstrates that electoral turnout only accounts for the weak expenditure development of the countries of Southern Europe, there are good reasons for thinking that the strongest term in the model, the extent of public coverage, directly reflects the impact of Left partisan politics in the early post-war period. In 1960, in the only five countries in which eligibility for medical care benefits under a public scheme exceeded 90 per cent of population – Britain, Denmark, New Zealand, Norway and Sweden – that scheme had been introduced by a Labour or Social Democratic government. The situation is simply more explicit in 1974, with turnout again accounting for the low spending of the Southern European nations, and Left incumbency now showing up as a factor in its own right as coverage rates ceased to be so diverse.

By the 1990s, the only sign of a political influence is the negative impact of constitutional structure. This is an interesting finding, since the influence of institutions on the development of public health care systems has been a matter of some debate, with Gray (1991) using the Australian and Canadian cases to argue that federal institutions have been no bar to the emergence of comprehensive public systems, and Immergut (1992) suggesting that the continuing privatized character of Swiss health care has been a direct outcome of the referendum procedure which is an integral aspect of Swiss federalism. The evidence here suggests that institutions matter and made a very considerable difference for the small number of countries with many veto points to change.

For most countries, however, what mattered most by the 1990s was the way in which growing prosperity was being transformed into burgeoning health care demands, with only modest signs that the trend might be partially contained by bureaucratic efforts to cut back on health service inputs. That resource availability now showed up as the primary determinant of public as well as total spending was, of course, a consequence of the diminished difference in these categories over time. Paradoxically, this is a story that can also be told as a victory of politics over economics, for the forces pushing countries to raise eligibility levels until the public sphere subsumed the private one were clearly political. Partisan politics only ceased to matter in the health arena because the demands of radical reformers that all citizens should have access to a high standard of medical care regardless of their means had now been satisfied in nearly all advanced countries.

That leaves the question of whether the process by which health spending became a part of the public domain was itself a source of increasing public expenditure. We know, of course, that initially the countries which had higher levels of public coverage also had higher levels of public expenditure, but that such a relationship no longer existed by the early 1990s (see Figure 5.2(c)). We also know that the countries which had the highest initial levels of public health spending were those which subsequently experienced the least growth in public spending. A possible interpretation of these findings is that the initially higher levels of public spending in countries with higher coverage largely reflected the fact that the proportion of the total health budget financed by the public purse was greater in these countries than in those in which initial coverage rates were lower, the clear implication being that, as these latter countries subsequently extended their coverage rates, their expenditure levels would catch up with those of the early leaders. This would suggest that the long-run expenditure impact of increased public coverage was likely to be negligible, with any apparent early overspending disappearing as all countries moved towards universal coverage (cf. Pfaff, 1990).

If this interpretation is correct, the major anomaly in our findings is the absence of significant correlations between change in public health spending and the initial level of coverage or the change in coverage. However, this is simply a result of a single case which fails to conform with otherwise clear patterns in the data. Excluding Greece, both coverage terms become highly significant in precisely the manner predicted by the catch-up thesis, as with a high level of initial coverage associated with a marked reduction in expenditure growth (–0.67) and growth in coverage associated with an increase in expenditure of somewhat lesser proportions (0.55). Nevertheless, the strongest correlation remains that with the initial level of expenditure (–0.79), and catch-up continues to be the dominant term in the best-fit model excluding the Greek case (see notes to change equation in Appendix 5.2). In this model, the aberrant term for inflation disappears, to be replaced by Right incumbency. This finding is far more in line with expectations, suggesting that it was the countries with the strongest and most unified parties of the Right which most successfully resisted the siren calls of socialized medicine. Otherwise, this respecification of the change model simply reaffirms the appropriateness of seeing the post-war transformation of the public health sector as a catch-up process which is now almost complete. In the early post-war years, the health policy arena had been the scene of some of the most significant skirmishes in the long-drawn-out battle to build the welfare state; it has now become the habitat of a cost-conscious bureaucracy dedicated to the task of containing the ever rising tide of demand for new and improved services.

PUBLIC EDUCATION EXPENDITURE

Although education is generally regarded as a part of the welfare state, it has rarely featured in comparative public policy analysis broadly focusing on that area. The reason is that, while education, like health, is a major state-provided service, it has often been seen as serving purposes quite different from those of other aspects of the welfare state. Thus, according to Harold Wilensky (1975, 3–6), 'education is special' because, unlike a nation's 'health and welfare effort', it is 'a contribution to equality of opportunity' rather than to 'absolute equality'. This particular contrast now seems somewhat overdrawn, given that much of the recent expansion of welfare effort has involved the growth of earnings-related benefits aimed at winning the support of the middle classes, and that there is now a general recognition of the fact that the benefits of public health spending, like those of education, often flow disproportionately to the better-off (Le Grand, 1982).

However, it is certainly true that education differs in important ways from other areas of state intervention in the welfare arena. In particular, education is as much about services to the economy, society and the state as it is about services to the individual. Modern economies require an educated work force if they are to be productive, and modern democratic institutions require an educated populace if they are to maintain their legitimacy and vitality. Modern nation-states must train administrative personnel if they are to rule effectively and must inculcate loyalty in their citizens if that rule is not to be questioned. These latter reasons explain why countries got into the business of education from the late eighteenth century onwards and all of them explain why they stay in it. While education, in common with other aspects of public consumption expenditure, may be optional in the sense that it is possible to organize supply through the market, these imperatives make it extremely unlikely that the state will relinquish its core role in educational provision. Certainly it is true that education has, in recent times, been one of the areas in which governments have sought to make savings through privatization and user charges. However, it is notable that this policy thrust has been almost exclusively in the realm of higher education and élite secondary education, where costs are particularly high and the private benefits to individuals are quite unequivocal. For the state to abandon its control of mass education would be not only to reverse the tide of post-war public intervention, but also to relinquish its key roles in the areas of human capital development and political socialization.

The fact that education is, in important respects, different is not, however, a reason for neglecting its study. Indeed, a premise of the approach taken here is the need to focus our analysis more broadly than hitherto, with a particular emphasis on areas where at present we have the least understanding. In any case, the fact that there are significant differences in function between different aspects of the welfare state does not settle the question of whether the factors determining the role of the state in different areas must, therefore, also be different. In his 1975 study, Wilensky (1975, 6–7) argued that the sources of educational and welfare spending were different on the strength of a –0.41 correlation between the two. Our own data for 1993 show significant and positive correlations of 0.45 between educational spending and social spending and of 0.62 between educational spending and health spending. Neither demonstrated differences nor similarities of this order tell us a great deal about the influences shaping public spending on education in the post-war period. For that, what is required is a full-scale comparative analysis along the lines of those already undertaken in this volume.

Even when it is conceded that it might be desirable to study cross-national differences in educational policy in their own right, there may remain doubts about the usefulness of focusing on educational spending as the preferred dependent variable. This is a point recently argued by Arnold Heidenheimer, the one conspicuous exception to the rule that comparative public policy specialists have neglected educational outcomes. Heidenheimer (1996, 13–25) suggests that our data on educational spending may be less satisfactory than corresponding datasets for health and social security. His most important reason is that figures for educational spending are substantially influenced by the diversity of educational systems, with his main example being the way in which the apprenticeship-based 'dual systems' of secondary education in the German-speaking countries lead to a systematic underestimation of educational spending in those countries. The point is extremely well taken, but is scarcely unique to education. Because similar policy objectives can, almost invariably, be achieved by alternative means, and because some of those means do not always feature in the national accounts, it will invariably be the case that cross-national spending figures for public programmes will only be broadly indicative of differences in the degree of national commitment to particular policy goals. This is just as true of social security as it is of education, with cross-national relativities in spending equally distorted by the insistence of many countries on mandating employers to pay benefits rather than counting them as a part of public expenditure (see Castles, 1994b). Such difficulties do not mean that we should give up the attempt to compare spending levels, but rather that we should constantly remind ourselves that policy outputs are not the same thing as policy outcomes and that, having established the determinants of the former, there is a further task of locating the sources of cross-national diversity in respect of the latter.

Data

Turning to the data in Table 5.3, it is easy to see why anyone writing about educational expenditure in the earlier decades of the post-war period might be inclined to argue that education was quite different from other aspects of welfare state spending. In 1960, three of the five countries at the top of the educational expenditure distribution – the USA, Canada and Japan – were nations which featured conspicuously as laggards in our previous accounts of aggregate and welfare state spending. By 1974, although Japan had dropped out of the leading group, the English-speaking nations were still more prominent in the top half of the distribution. However, the fact that the countries that spent large amounts on education were not always the same ones that spent large amounts in other areas does not mean that the overall pattern of spending was completely at odds with others we have encountered. Just as in other policy areas, the Scandinavian countries were always near the top of the distribution and the countries of Southern Europe were firmly ensconced at the bottom. In fact, the salient difference between education and other spending areas in these decades was simply a reversal in position between the English-speaking countries and a number of the countries of continental Western Europe, with the German-speaking nations prominent amongst them. By 1993, this reversal was no longer so clear-cut: the Scandinavian countries plus a few of the English-speaking group remained the biggest spenders, Southern Europe, Japan and Germany brought up the rear and, in between, there was a mix of continental Western European and English-speaking nations. As we have already noted, there are statistically significant correlations between this distribution and those for both social security and health expenditure at the same date.

Table 5.3 Levels of and change in public education expenditure as a percentage of GDP, 1960–93

Country	1960	1974	1993	Change: 1960–93
Australia	3.6	6.4	5.5	1.9
Canada	5.8	7.6	7.6	1.8
Ireland	3.9	5.9	6.2	2.3
New Zealand	3.8	5.6	7.3	3.5
UK	4.5	6.2	5.2	0.7
USA	6.6	6.3	5.3	–1.3
Denmark	3.9	7.1	7.4	3.5
Finland	6.6	6.1	7.2	0.6
Norway	5.4	7.0	8.4	3.0
Sweden	5.4	7.5	8.3	2.9
Austria	3.7	5.3	5.8	2.1
Belgium	5.7	5.1	5.1	–0.6
France	3.2	4.7	5.8	2.6
Germany	3.5	4.5	4.1	0.6
Italy	4.0	5.2	5.4	1.4
Netherlands	4.9	7.9	5.9	1.0
Greece	2.0	1.6	3.1	1.1
Portugal	2.2	2.1	5.0	2.8
Spain	1.5	1.7	4.6	3.1
Switzerland	3.4	4.8	5.2	1.8
Japan	5.5	5.1	4.7	–0.8
Mean	4.2	5.3	5.9	1.7
Correlation with 1960		0.75	0.51	–0.52
Coefficient of variation	33.62	33.32	23.60	

Sources and notes: Data from UNESCO, *Statistical Yearbook*, Paris, various years. The figure reported in the final column is the percentage point change over the entire period.

The statistical summary in Table 5.3 demonstrates a very real difference between education and other welfare state programmes. Where other programmes were more than doubling in size over these decades, educational spending as a percentage of GDP increased by only 40 per cent, with around a third of the countries experiencing zero or negative growth after 1974. The contrast with health is very clear. In 1960, health spending in the OECD was around 60 per cent of that on education; by the early 1990s, the resource demands of the two programmes were almost exactly the same. The story here is one of the differential maturity and differing client base of the programmes. Already before World War II, compulsory state schooling at primary level existed in virtually all these countries and post-war expansion has been largely a matter of increasing coverage at secondary and tertiary levels. In contrast, the role of the state as a provider of comprehensive health services has been essentially a post-war phenomenon. Moreover, since the early 1960s, decreasing fertility rates have simultaneously implied a declining youthful population and a growing aged one, the former constituting the clientele for schools and universities and the latter for hospital beds and pensions. Despite the relatively low rate of change in the area of educational spending, countries have become appreciably more similar over time and there has been a moderate degree of catch-up. Interestingly, the latter has owed as much to the decline in relative expenditure levels of countries such as Japan and the USA as to the expansion of spending in the countries of Southern Europe after the fall of their respective dictatorships. It is worth noting that, without Southern Europe in the sample, there would have been markedly greater similarity throughout, but that there would also have been a slight tendency towards increased divergence in spending levels since the mid-1970s.

Hypotheses

As in the case of health expenditure, a salient difference between national systems of education is the extent of coverage they provide. However, in this instance, coverage is not a matter of eligibility. All Western systems of education insist on universal and compulsory coverage at the primary level, although, in some nations, other organizations than the state are licensed as providers, and all public education systems offer access to free or highly subsidized secondary and tertiary level education under certain conditions. The conditions, however, differ very widely. In the early post-war period, the basic distinction was between systems of secondary education along American lines, where there was little differentiation of students on academic grounds and where the majority of children stayed on until high school graduation, and more élitist European systems, where a strong distinction was made between vocational training for the majority and academic education for the élite. Arguably, Heidenheimer's caveat about the comparability of education systems in the German-speaking countries simply highlights the end-point of the élitist spectrum, where apprenticeships are used to take those pursuing the vocational route out of the education system altogether. The basic thrust of change in the post-war period has been to increase years of schooling in all countries and to soften, but not wholly remove, the early meritocratic selection of the European systems. Countries adhering to or adopting something akin to the American model in the early post-war decades included the English-speaking nations of overseas settlement plus Japan, whose education system was remodelled by the US Occupation, and this seems clearly relevant to these countries' relatively high spending levels in this period.

Prior to World War II, tertiary education was to varying degrees an élitist institution in all countries. The overall effect of post-war educational expansion was partly to shift the distinction between élitist and non-élitist systems from the secondary to the tertiary level and partly to modify its contours. In 1960, the countries with the highest tertiary enrolment ratios (for definition, see notes to the 1960 model in Appendix 5.3) were the USA, Canada and New Zealand. These same countries remained at or near the top of the distribution three decades latter, with ratios of 74.1, 102.9 and 57.5 respectively (data from UNESCO, *Statistical Yearbook*). The European educational systems which had moved farthest from their élitist origins were those of the Scandinavian countries, which had consciously embraced a philosophy of comprehensive education 'as a means of overcoming class barriers to educational opportunities' (Heidenheimer, Heclo and Adams, 1990, 43). These organizational and attitudinal changes, which also reflected changing attitudes to gender equality which were particularly pronounced in Scandinavia, carried over to the tertiary sphere and made countries like Finland and Norway second only to the North American nations as countries of mass higher education by the early 1990s.

In the analysis that follows, we include terms both for the combined percentage of primary and secondary enrolments and for tertiary enrolments. The UNESCO data we use make it impossible to disaggregate enrolments at primary and secondary levels, but since primary enrolments were virtually universal throughout, the variation of the combined measure is effectively that of the secondary sector. Since differences in school enrolment levels were no longer pronounced by the mid-1970s, and since higher education is, in any case, markedly more expensive than school education, it seems probable that the tertiary enrolments variable is likely to be the more influential of the two.

Findings

Figure 5.3 provides correlations between public education spending and the standard measures elaborated to test the hypotheses advanced in Chapter 4. It also provides correlations for primary plus secondary and tertiary enrolments. In 1960, the enrolment measures vie with Catholicism and Catholic cultural impact as the variables most strongly associated with outcomes. In line with the argument that the Catholic Church has sought to minimize the influence of state education, both of these latter relationships are negative. There are also some modest correlations between political and economic variables and outcomes. All are in the expected directions, with Right incumbency negatively associated with spending levels, and turnout, per capita GDP and productivity positively associated. The best-fit model in Appendix 5.3 contains three terms, Catholicism, Right incumbency and tertiary enrolments, all with quite similar degrees of significance and real impact. For the average OECD country spending 4.2 per cent of GDP on education in 1960, tertiary enrolments increased expenditure by an estimated 0.65 per cent of GDP, while Catholicism and Right incumbency reduced it by an estimated 0.66 and 0.69 per cent respectively.

Not for the first time, the mid-1970s turns out to be the period with the largest number of significant correlations, some of them very strong indeed. Turnout and union density are prominent because these variables pick up on the dramatic gulf between Southern European spending levels and those in the remainder of the OECD at this time. Catholicism and Catholic cultural impact are still prominent, as are both Right incumbency and the various measures of national product. As expected, school enrolments have ceased to be a source of differentiation by the mid-1970s and, perhaps surprisingly, the positive association with tertiary enrolment is quite modest. There are also modestly significant associations with both the degree of urbanization and of Left incumbency. Despite these changes, Appendix 5.3 shows that the best-fit model for 1974 is the same as for 1960, with the single addition of a term for electoral turnout. For the average OECD country, turnout made a difference of 1.89 per cent of GDP in spending terms. However, since most of these countries were clustered quite closely around the mean, the real effect of this variable is largely to account for the low spending of the Southern European countries. Controlling for the effect of turnout, the real impacts of the other variables in the model are hardly changed since 1960. The positive effect of tertiary enrolments declines slightly to 0.51 per cent, the negative influence of Catholicism remains virtually the same at 0.67 per cent, whilst the negative impact of the Right increases marginally to 0.78 per cent.

In part, Figure 5.3(c) tells a story familiar from our earlier findings – other than those for the health sector – of ideological differences triumphant, with union density and Right and Left incumbency all moderately strongly associated with outcomes by the early 1990s. Where the story departs from the familiar pattern is in the continuing negative influence of the measures of Catholic influence and the resulting negative relationship with European Community membership. Tertiary enrolment remains modestly associated with spending, but neither per capita GDP nor productivity are now significant variables. The early 1990s model in Appendix 5.3 again contains the same common core of factors present since 1960. However, in the manner common to outlays, receipts and health spending, the positive impact of electoral turnout in 1974 is replaced by the negative influence of constitutional structure two decades later. All four variables are of comparable significance and have remarkably similar estimated effects. For the average OECD country, tertiary enrolments increase spending by 0.73 per cent of GDP, whilst both Catholicism and Right incumbency each reduce it by 0.71 per cent. For countries a standard score apart in terms of the constitutional structure measure, this variable makes an estimated difference of 0.56 per cent of GDP, whilst for countries as radically different as Denmark and the USA, it makes a difference of almost exactly 2 per cent of GDP.

The most immediately striking feature of Figure 5.3(d) is that, as previously in the case of health, the factor most strongly associated with expenditure change is catch-up. Only three other variables are significantly associated with outcomes: constitutional structure negatively, change in school enrolments positively and Left incumbency also positively. Despite this lack of obvious relationships, once we control for the effect of catch-up in the change model in Appendix 5.3, precisely the same set of factors emerge that have been influential throughout. Thus education spending grew least in Catholic countries and in ones in which the Right had a major presence in government, and grew most in those countries which had most expanded their level of tertiary enrolments. In addition, spending increased weakly, if at all, in the countries in which constitutional structures contained a substantial number of veto points for those opposed to welfare expansion. The effect of catch-up was very substantial indeed, with a reduction in expenditure growth of 1 per cent of GDP for each percentage point of GDP that expenditure was higher in 1960, making a difference of 2.8 per cent of GDP for

(a) 1960

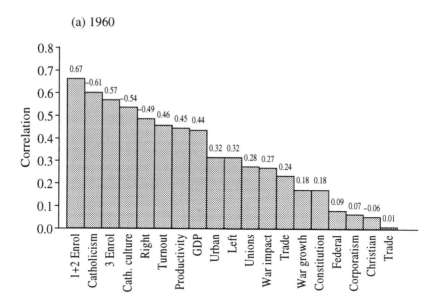

(b) 1974

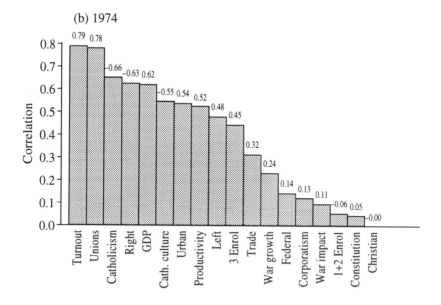

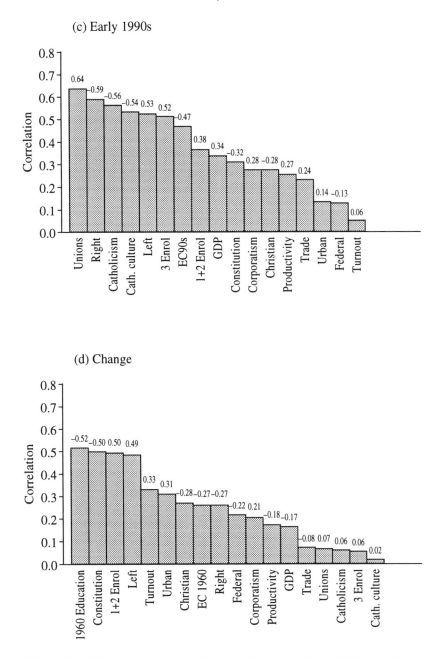

Figure 5.3 Bivariate tests: public education expenditure (1960, 1974 and early 1990s and change over time)

the average OECD country. Other effects were of a similar magnitude to those suggested in previous models. Catholicism reduced average expenditure growth by 0.80 per cent, and Right incumbency by 0.70 per cent, while expansion in tertiary enrolments increased it by 0.57 per cent. The constitutional structure effect was moderate at 0.46 per cent of GDP for countries only the standard score apart, but very substantial indeed for countries at the extremes.

Analysis

The astounding consistency of the models accounting for levels and change in educational spending over more than three decades leaves only a few questions unanswered. There should be no surprise in discovering that Catholicism and Right incumbency are negative parameters of spending. Both have long historical antecedents. To the Church, the emergence of education under the control of a secular power has always been deeply suspect. That the Church has consistently attempted to establish its own schools for the faithful and has been most successful in those countries with substantial Catholic populations is sufficient explanation for the Catholicism finding. The implication is not necessarily that there is less educational spending in these countries, but that there is less public spending by the state.

A quite similar story can be told of the Right, with the rise of mass education frequently viewed as a challenge to the authority of traditional rule and with some preference for educating the sons of the ruling élite in institutions where they would be socialized into leadership roles and less likely to be infected by the egalitarian spirit of the times. Private schools for the well-off are the equivalent of confessional schools for the faithful: ways of protecting the young from the contagion of the masses. Indeed, given that the Church has been assiduous in seeking subsidies from the state to run its own school system and that Conservative governments have often found ways of underwriting private élite education, perhaps the only surprise is that these defections from state-provided education continue throughout the post-war period to show up in lower public spending totals.

The third consistent element in the educational spending story does, perhaps, require some further discussion. Differences in educational enrolments do, clearly, owe much to differences in the structures of educational systems, with the elitism of the European systems historically reflecting the rigidity of class barriers in these countries and the primary function of secondary schooling as a stepping-stone to employment in the government bureaucracy (see Heidenheimer, 1981; Archer, 1979).

However, examining the relationships between the independent variables in Figure 5.3, it is also apparent that levels of tertiary enrolments are, to some extent, influenced by the availability of economic resources, with correlations between enrolment and productivity of 0.70 in 1960, 0.59 in 1974 and 0.59 in the early 1990s. Whilst educational spending continues to be shaped by cultural and political factors in a way that public health spending is not, it is interesting to note that, via the impact of enrolments, spending in the educational sector reflected resource constraints from a much earlier date than is true of the public health sector. This difference presumably stems from the differential maturity of the two areas, with resources only kicking in as a crucial limiting factor on the extent of public spending in a given area once the structural parameters of cross-national difference have been fully established.

Two final points are worth brief mention. It will have been noted that the catch-up coefficients for health and education have an almost identical value of close to –1.00, indicating that the countries which had the highest and lowest levels of spending in the early post-war years were no longer in any way distinctive by the early 1990s. This strongly suggests that, in both areas, programme maturation had been fully achieved by the end of the period under analysis here. Seen in this light, the post-1974 slowdown in welfare state expansion may have less to do with cost cut-backs under circumstances of financial exigency and more to do with the fulfilled potential of at least some its major programmes.

It also seems worthwhile checking out Heidenheimer's argument that the German-speaking countries are too different to be compared. Excluding Austria, Germany and Switzerland from the equations in Appendix 5.3 produces models of comparable or slightly superior explanatory power in all cases. Moreover, except that tertiary enrolments cease to be significant in the 1974 model and constitutional structure in the change model, the terms included are otherwise identical. At a minimum, this seems to suggest that these countries' expenditure patterns are not so aberrant that their inclusion distorts our understanding of the trajectory of post-war expenditure development. With this potential caveat to the validity of our findings removed, there seems to be a strong case for arguing that, in respect of the factors shaping spending outcomes, and with the obvious exception of the negative influence of Catholicism, education is not really so very different from the rest of the welfare state after all.

CONCLUSION

A number of the issues raised in the analytical sections of Chapters 4 and 5 will be examined further when we discuss the broader patterns of post-war public policy development in Chapter 8. However, having now completed our analysis of expenditure variation, it is important to tie up a couple of loose ends. Whereas most previous comparative research in the public expenditure area has had a narrow focus on particular categories of spending, this study has ranged more widely, focusing successively on the determinants of spending aggregates and of the metaprogrammes and programmes constituting them. However, the moment one juxtaposes accounts of the factors operating at these different levels, the question of the compatibility of findings at different levels becomes a litmus-test of the validity of the entire analysis. In most respects, the analysis here passes the test in the sense that the sets of variables encountered in modelling outcomes at higher levels of aggregation have generally been replicated at lower levels and vice versa.

In only two instances do there appear to be major discrepancies. Both relate to a disjunction between the public consumption metaprogramme and the health and education programmes of which it is largely constituted. First, there is no sign that the very strong catch-up effects located in respect of both health and education programmes are replicated at the level of the wider aggregate of civilian public consumption expenditure. Second, at the programme level, the only evidence for Left incumbency effects are a moderate impact in the 1974 health model and an imputed indirect effect on early levels of health spending via coverage rates, but, at the meta-programme level, Left incumbency is the dominant theme of all the models accounting for levels and changes in public consumption expenditure.

One key to these discrepancies lies in the fact that choices of health sector funding mechanisms are politically structured. Whilst, as previously noted, in most OECD countries health spending falls substantially under the public consumption heading, there is a minority of nations in which transfers spending has a more significant role. Looking at the final column of Table 5.2, it is apparent that certain countries of this latter type – including Belgium, France, the Netherlands, Switzerland and the USA – were prominent amongst the countries in which health sector funding expanded most rapidly after 1960. This was anything but fortuitous. These were countries in which the Left had been historically weak and/or in which Catholic social policy had favoured transfers as a means of enhancing the family's role as the main provider of welfare. In contrast, the nations which had established major public health programmes relatively early on (countries like Britain, Denmark, New Zealand and

Sweden) had done so by direct funding of goods and services, a choice obviously in tune with the ideological preferences of the Labour and Social Democratic parties in office when these programmes were adopted. Thus, an important factor contributing to the discrepancy between findings at the programme and metaprogramme levels was the fact that the countries most active in expanding health spending after 1960 were precisely those which were most reluctant to enhance the reach of the state in the process.

But this is only part of the story. While one group of countries consciously sought to expand their welfare effort without boosting direct state intervention, another group took the opposite tack of developing a whole new range of state services, all of them falling under the public consumption heading. These include services to the aged (residential care, rehabilitation, home help, and so on), services to families (in particular, day care and personal services) and services to employment (active labour market policies, including employment services, subsidized employment and labour market training). Services to families and to the aged promote the personal autonomy of working and older women (Anttonen and Sipilä, 1996) and can be seen as representing a new stage of welfare state development designed to cope with the emergent problems of a post-industrial society in which high levels of female labour force participation have largely replaced unpaid caring work. Services to employment are a novel response to the growing potential for structural unemployment after the end of the 'Golden Age' of economic growth. Because state services are relatively new, systematic data collection has only just begun and information on the expenditure of the majority of OECD countries is only available from 1980 to the present (OECD, 1996d).

Looking at levels of total spending on services to the aged, to families and to employment in the early 1990s reveals a distribution far more skewed than any we have previously encountered. The four Scandinavian countries are the four biggest spenders, with Sweden at 8.9 per cent of GDP, Denmark at 6.2 per cent, Norway at 5.7 per cent and Finland at 4.7 per cent. For these countries, provision of state services is as significant or nearly as significant as the provision of health or education services. Nowhere else is this even faintly true. After the Scandinavian countries, there is a substantial gap in the distribution to Germany at 2.7 per cent of GDP and the Netherlands at 2.3 per cent and, at the bottom of the distribution, we find countries such as Japan, the USA, Spain and New Zealand all spending less than 1 per cent of GDP on such services. Given the countries at the top and the bottom of this distribution, the best-fit equation for total state services not surprisingly locates Left incumbency and trade union density as the only two significant influences on outcomes, a result which is precisely what might be expected on the basis of the 'power resources' model, which sees the main factor determining the size of the welfare state as the degree of mobilization of the working class movement (Korpi, 1978 and 1989).[1]

Clearly, this resolves the problem of reconciling our findings at different levels of aggregation. Strong catch-up effects in education and in health spending did not flow through to public consumption for at least two reasons. First, it was precisely those countries which least relied on public consumption as a mechanism of health funding that did much of the catching up after 1960. Thus, at the beginning of the period under examination here, the correlation between the level of health spending and of public consumption spending was as high as 0.72, whereas, by the early 1990s, it was only 0.23. Second, in just a few countries, there was major public consumption item that did not exist elsewhere. The Scandinavian countries started out as relatively high spenders on health and education. With the emergent emphasis on the provision of state services, they were increasingly in a league of their own as big public consumption spenders. Hence the modest, although not significant, positive correlation between 1960 levels of public consumption spending and subsequent expenditure change shown in Table 4.3. Moreover, because the Scandinavian countries simultaneously constituted the vanguard of post-war democratic socialism, this category of spending turns out to be more closely associated with measures of Left partisan incumbency than with any other factor analysed in this study.

The resolution of these discrepancies brings us to the end of our analysis of post-war public expenditure development. However, the discussion here does raise at least one other issue of interest. Because post-war socialist hegemony has been an almost exclusively Scandinavian phenomenon, there has to be a real question as to whether the undoubtedly greater reach of the state manifested by these countries has been more a consequence of the distinctive cultural and historical characteristics defining this particular family of nations or of their uniqueness in putting socialist principles into public policy practice. This is not a question which can be resolved in this book, but it does raise an important methodological issue which will be discussed in our final chapter.

NOTE

1. 1992/93 state services = $-1.022 + 0.068$ (0.016) 1950–early 1990s (1993) Left cabinet seats + 0.042 (0.016) early 1990s (1990) trade union density (figures in parentheses are standard errors). Adj. $R^2 = 0.821$. Data missing for Austria, Canada and Greece.

APPENDIX 5.1 SOCIAL SECURITY TRANSFERS MODELS

1960	Coefficient	Standard error	t-value
Intercept	−10.088		
War impact	1.118	0.315	3.544
1960 real GDP per capita	0.003	0.001	3.33
1960 real GDP per capita squared	−0.0000001711	0.00000006668	2.566
1960 aged population	0.541	0.204	2.658
Catholic cultural impact	3.356	0.759	4.42

Adj. R^2 = 0.85

Sources and notes: War impact from Table 2.1; 1960 real GDP per capita from Table 2.2; 1960 real GDP per capita squared calculated from Table 2.2; 1960 aged population from Table 2.6; Catholic cultural impact from Table 2.7. 20 cases in regression.

1974	Coefficient	Standard error	t-value
Intercept	−14.369		
1974 real GDP per capita	0.004	0.001	4.69
1974 real GDP per capita squared	−0.0000001588	0.00000004207	3.775
1974 aged population	0.359	0.175	2.055
Catholic cultural impact	5.85	0.912	6.414
1950–73 right cabinet seats	−0.045	0.011	3.969

Adj. R^2 = 0.866

Sources and notes: 1974 real GDP per capita from Table 2.2; 1974 real GDP per capita squared calculated from Table 2.2; 1974 aged population from Table 2.6; Catholic cultural impact from Table 2.7; 1950–73 (1993) Right cabinet seats calculated from the same source as Table 3.4. 20 cases in regression.

1993	Coefficient	Standard error	t-value
Intercept	28.803		
Early 1990s international trade	−0.057	0.022	2.638
1950–early 1990s right cabinet seats	−0.162	0.021	7.697
1950–early 1990s Christian Democratic cabinet seats	0.088	0.021	4.211
Federalism	−4.029	1.001	4.026

Adj. R^2 = 0.838

Sources and notes: Early 1990s (1993) international trade from Table 2.3; 1950–early 1990s (1993) Right cabinet seats calculated from the same source as Table 3.4; 1950–early 1990s (1993) Christian Democratic cabinet seats calculated from data in Woldendorp, Keman and Budge (1993 and 1998); federalism from Table 3.5. 20 cases in regression.

1960–93 Change	Coefficient	Standard error	t-value
Intercept	15.387		
1960 social security transfers	−0.329	0.144	2.288
1960–early 1990s aged population	0.976	0.297	3.288
1960–early 1990s right cabinet seats	−0.133	0.018	7.272
Federalism	−2.839	0.948	2.994

Adj. R^2 = 0.808

Sources and notes: 1960 social security transfers from Table 5.1; 1960–early 1990s (1993) aged population from Table 2.6; 1960–early 1990s (1993) Right cabinet seats calculated from the same source as Table 3.4; Federalism from Table 3.5. 20 cases in regression

APPENDIX 5.2 PUBLIC HEALTH EXPENDITURE MODELS

1960	Coefficient	Standard error	t-value
Intercept	−1.222		
1960 International trade	−0.11	0.005	2.446
1960 Aged population	0.17	0.055	3.105
1960 Electoral turnout	0.012	0.004	2.975
1960 Public coverage	0.021	0.004	4.703

Adj R^2 = 0.745

Sources and notes: 1960 international trade from Table 2.3; 1960 aged population from Table 2.6; 1960 electoral turnout from Table 3.1; 1960 public coverage against medical care costs (i.e. percentage of population eligible for medical care benefits under a public scheme) from OECD, (1993). 20 cases in regression.

1974	Coefficient	Standard error	t-value
Intercept	2.895		
1974 Electoral turnout	0.019	0.006	3.117
1950–73 Left cabinet seats	0.016	0.007	2.258

Adj. R^2 = 0.537

Sources and notes: 1974 electoral turnout from Table 3.1; 1950–73 Left cabinet seats calculated from the same source as Table 3.3. 21 cases in regression.

1993	Coefficient	Standard error	t-Value
Intercept	−0.406		
Early 1990s real GDP per worker	0.0001991	0.00002366	8.413
Constitutional structure	−0.25	0.058	4.312
Early 1990s bed-days per patient	0.197	0.087	2.261

Adj. $R^2 = 0.828$

Sources and notes: Early 1990s (1990) real GDP per worker from the same source as Table 2.2; constitutional structure from Table 3.5; early 1990s bed-days per patient from OECD, (1993). 21 cases in regression.

1960–93[*] change	Coefficient	Standard error	t-value
Intercept	7.335		
1960 public health expenditure	−0.974	0.246	3.964
1960–early 1990s average change in consumer price index	−0.202	0.089	2.261

Adj. $R^2 = 0.498$

Sources and notes: 1960 public health expenditure from Table 5.2; 1960–early 1990s (1993) average change in consumer price index from OECD, *Historical Statistics*, Paris, 1995. 20 cases in regression.[*] Re-estimating this model for a sample excluding Greece produces the following result: 1960–93 change in public health expenditure = 7.035 − 1.146 (0.191) 1960 public health expenditure − 0.012 (0.006) 1960–early 1990s (1993) Right cabinet seats (figures in parentheses are standard errors). Adj. $R^2 = 0.672$. For discussion of the re-estimated model, see text.

APPENDIX 5.3 PUBLIC EDUCATION EXPENDITURE MODELS

1960	Coefficient	Standard error	t-Value
Intercept	4.621		
Catholicism	−0.014	0.006	2.42
1950–59 Right cabinet seats	−0.014	0.006	2.54
1960 Tertiary enrolment ratio	0.102	0.035	2.872

Adj. $R^2 = 0.596$

Sources and notes: Catholicism is from Table 2.7; 1950–59 Right cabinet seats is from Table 3.4; 1960 tertiary enrolment ratio is the number of students in tertiary education in a given country in 1960 expressed as a percentage of the age group, 20–24 (the data are from UNESCO, *Statistical Yearbook*, Paris, various years). 21 cases in regression.

1974	Coefficient	Standard error	t-value
Intercept	4.072		
Catholicism	−0.014	0.005	2.667
1974 electoral turnout	0.027	0.007	3.995
1950–73 Right cabinet seats	−0.016	0.005	3.007
1974 Tertiary enrolment ratio	0.041	0.02	2.05

Adj. $R^2 = 0.82$

Sources and notes: Catholicism from Table 2.7; 1974 electoral turnout from Table 3.1; 1950–73 Right cabinet seats calculated from the same source as Table 3.4; 1974 tertiary enrolment ratio defined as in and from the source cited above. 21 cases in regression.

1993	Coefficient	Standard error	t-Value
Intercept	6.381		
Catholicism	−0.015	0.004	3.524
1950–93 Right cabinet seats	−0.018	0.006	3.053
Constitutional structure	−0.289	0.085	3.412
Early 1990s tertiary enrolment ratio	0.034	0.01	3.519

Adj. R^2 = 0.757

Sources and notes: Catholicism from Table 2.7; 1950–early 1990s (1993) Right cabinet seats calculated from the same source as Table 3.4; constitutional structure from Table 3.5; 1993 tertiary enrolment ratio defined as in and from the source cited above. 21 cases in regression.

1960–1993	Coefficient	Standard error	t-Value
Intercept	6.638		
1960 public education expenditure	−1.006	0.167	6.03
Catholicism	−0.017	0.005	3.082
1960–early 1990s Right cabinet seats	−0.019	0.007	2.705
Constitutional structure	−0.238	0.088	2.696
1960–early 1990s change in tertiary enrolment ratio	0.038	0.013	2.975

Adj. R^2 = 0.724

Sources and notes: 1960 public education expenditure from Table 5.3; Catholicism from Table 2.7; 1960–early 1990s (1993) Right cabinet seats calculated from the same source as Table 3.4; Constitutional structure from Table 3.5; 1960–early 1990s (1993) change in tertiary enrolment calculated (1993 value minus 1960 value) from the source cited above. 21 cases in regression.

6. The state and the labour market

INTRODUCTION

At this half-way point in our analysis, we shift the focus of our attention from the factors determining the size of government funding programmes to the forces impacting on labour markets and choices in the personal sphere. In this chapter, we explore the sources of cross-national variation in male and female labour force participation and in unemployment during the post-war period. In the next, we examine cross-national differences in the extent of home ownership, fertility and marital break-up. This change in focus allows us to assess what is undoubtedly one of the crucial aspects of post-war policy development: the extent to which the growth of government has transformed the context of individual and collective decision-making in both the economic and the domestic arenas. When government was relatively small, it was possible to think in terms of the state, the economy and the family as separate spheres, which, whilst intersecting at significant points, nevertheless had a life and logic of their own. Commentators now suggest that both the intended and unintended effects of post-war public policy development have reshaped the parameters of choice by individuals in labour markets and in households. The role of public spending, taxing and regulation is so great that there are no areas in which the influence of government is not felt. As a consequence, it can be argued, there is no longer any clear dividing line between state and society in the modern world.

In many ways, it is this widening of the sphere of government to encompass other arenas of economic and social behaviour which has made the role of post-war public policy so controversial. The critics of big government and the welfare state rarely articulate their views as criticisms of the goals of poverty amelioration and better health and education as such, and often they make only a tokenistic challenge to the proposition that state intervention is, at least, a partially effective means of securing these goals. Instead, most of their ire is directed toward the effects that the pursuit of such goals has had on the wider

economy and society. The view of the critics is that big government and
the welfare state have destroyed the structure of incentives that underpinned an efficiently functioning labour market and have created a
degree of welfare dependency which has rendered traditional moral
values redundant. Seen in this light, the broad thrust of public policy
development in the post-war era has been to weaken the will to work
and to undermine the economic rationale of family life; the indictment
is that the growth of big government is responsible both for mass
unemployment and for burgeoning marital break-up.

As we shall note at various points in the coming chapters, these critics
are often far from the mark in their specific diagnoses of the problems
which assail contemporary societies, but they are undoubtedly correct in
their general perception that the growth of government has had a major
influence on behaviour in the wider economy and society. The aim of this
chapter and the next is to use the same comparative methods as were used
to explore the factors associated with the growth of government to determine the extent and character of that influence. Clearly, if the intention
were merely to demonstrate that post-war policy transformation has also
transformed the lives of individuals on a massive scale, this could be
more simply accomplished by showing how the welfare state programmes
we have already examined served to ameliorate poverty, reduce economic
inequality, improve life expectancy and health status and broaden the
scope of educational opportunity. Whilst there are critics – this time as
much on the Left and as on the Right – who are ready to point to failures
in welfare programmes to achieve their goals, there would probably be
few unwilling to concede the major changes in the living conditions of
the disadvantaged wrought by five decades of post-war welfare development. Our goal, however, is different. We want to demonstrate how
far-reaching is the influence of the modern state, whilst simultaneously
offering a realistic appraisal of the nature of its influence. The labour
market and household, once seen as distinct spheres of individual and
familial choice, and now supposedly distorted by the growth of big government, are ideal arenas in which to map the outer limits of
contemporary public policy.

Before turning to our analysis of these arenas, it is important to note
that the shift in focus from government programmes to individual
choices has methodological implications. Where the focus of interest is
on national programmes of expenditure and taxation, the only feasible
strategies for establishing the antecedents of policy involve comparisons
of entire programmes either across time or across space. This is not the
case when the focus of interest is on the forces shaping individual
choices and behaviour. Where that is so, the standard strategy in both

economics and demography – the two disciplines most concerned with the choices we are examining here – is to use large-scale sample surveys to determine the population characteristics associated with particular outcomes. This procedure allows us to match up variation in the factors impinging on individuals with the behaviours they exhibit. Its drawback is that it does not provide analytical purchase in the one area in which this study most requires it; that is, in respect of the effects of institutional structures and policy programmes on the kinds of choices made by different national communities.

Because we wish to understand how states and their actions shape behaviour in both labour markets and the personal arena, we are constrained to adopt a cross-national approach even though our focus of interest is on the character of choices made by individuals. We should be aware, however, that what we study under such circumstances are not choices as such, but their aggregate outcomes. This means that we should be doubly wary in our causal attributions, for linkages established at the aggregate level do not necessarily hold at the individual level. For instance, to establish that fertility rates are higher in richer countries does not establish that affluent individuals in any of those countries have higher fertility rates than those who are poorer. In what follows, it is crucial to remember that, despite major linguistic difficulties in constantly maintaining distinctions between levels of analysis, the conclusions we arrive at here apply only to aggregates and not to individuals.

MALE LABOUR FORCE PARTICIPATION

Our concern in the first two sections of this chapter is with the factors which have influenced cross-national variation in the supply of labour during the post-war period. In this section, we examine patterns of male labour force participation and in the next we discuss female labour supply patterns. Although, as throughout this book, the main focus of analysis is on cross-national variation, the big story of the post-war era is of two long-term developmental trends: a large-scale decline in the proportion of males seeking gainful employment and a still greater increase in the proportion of females entering the labour market. Although these trends have been universal amongst the OECD nations in the third of a century for which we present data here, they have proceeded at markedly different rates in different countries. Hence it is possible to use the natural experiment of cross-national variation to gain some leverage on the factors associated with decreasing labour supply amongst males and increasing labour supply amongst females.

In shifting our attention from the realm of public expenditure to that of labour supply, we are, of course, moving into a disciplinary area largely claimed by the economics profession. This, it could be argued, requires us to make a shift from the highly empiricist approach we have so far employed to one informed by findings based on the more deductive theoretical framework of the economics discipline. In principle, this might be conceded, if work in labour economics had arrived at a body of conclusions which could readily be applied to understanding the sources of cross-national variation in male and female labour supply. Unfortunately, this is not the case. The fundamental insight from economic theory is that aggregate labour supply is a function of a trade-off between income and leisure involving offsetting income and substitution effects. However, several decades of theoretical elaboration and modelling of male labour supply have not produced evidence of decisive effects which would warrant predictions concerning the probable impacts of cross-national differences in income levels (Pencavel, 1986). Whilst there are somewhat stronger theoretical grounds for assuming that women's participation will increase at higher income levels, an overview of the literature points out that 'it is the variability, rather than the uniformity, of the estimates that is noteworthy' (Killingsworth and Heckman, 1986).

Quite apart from the limited assistance economic theory gives us in understanding the character of cross-national differences in labour supply, it should also be noted that the economics discipline has a quite different research agenda from that which informs this study. Labour economics seeks to locate the factors associated with change in labour supply across time in particular countries, and, not infrequently, researchers appear to start from the implicit assumption that individuals in different nations behave in quite similar ways because they come to the labour market with similar preferences and are constrained by similar sets of institutions. But that is not, in fact, the case. As we shall see, cultural preferences differ, and so too do institutional contexts. The result is different outcomes, with male labour force patterns diverging over the post-war period and female outcomes, although converging somewhat, still differing very markedly. Such cross-national variation allows us to test the extent to which differences in levels and changes in labour supply have been associated with aspects of the post-war economic, social and political transformation and with the policy developments to which they have given rise. Some of the factors discussed here will be quite familiar to those working in the labour economics tradition; others will be less so, because they identify the sources of institutional, cultural and policy distinctiveness which often make national economies perform in rather different ways.

Data

Table 6.1 presents information on levels and changes in post-war male labour supply. The male participation rate is defined as the percentage of the adult male population between the ages of 15 and 64 who are in employment or who are seeking employment at a given time. For those unfamiliar with the concept of labour supply, it is important to stress that this figure includes both the employed and the unemployed, that is, it includes all those with an active commitment to be employed. The participation rate should be contrasted with the inactivity rate, which consists of those who are not actively seeking employment at a particular time. The inactive population is likely to include a number who would like to find work, but who have given up seeking it for the present. These individuals, who would prefer to be employed but who no longer make the effort to seek work, are frequently described as 'discouraged workers'. In a few countries, conspicuously those of Southern Europe, inactivity is an official category only, with large numbers so classified highly active in the so-called 'black economy'.

The post-war decline in male labour force participation can be seen as a continuation of a much longer trend in the diminution of male working hours in the countries of advanced capitalism. At one end of the age distribution, initial changes took the form of legislation preventing or limiting child labour and enacting increased years of compulsory schooling. At the other end of the age distribution, the emergence of social security pension schemes facilitated earlier retirement, whilst, for those who remained a part of the active population, hours of work decreased as a consequence of labour movement struggles to limit the length of the working day and to increase annual leave entitlements. Nevertheless, as Table 6.1 shows, there was substantial cross-national uniformity in the proportion of the male labour force who were economically active in the early post-war period. Leaving aside as outliers Portugal and Switzerland – where figures over 100 per cent are probably only the most extreme result of the fact that participation as measured here takes no account of the fact that some workers of 65 years and older remain in the labour force – the percentage of those employed or seeking work was everywhere in a narrow band between 100 per cent and 90 per cent of the adult male population.

As shown by the summary statistics in Table 6.1, three sorts of change were taking place in the decades following 1960. The first, of course, was a universal fall in the male participation rate, which went down from a mean of 95.2 per cent of the adult population in 1960 to 80.8 per cent in 1993. The extent of this change varied from country to country, with very sharp

Table 6.1 Levels of and change in the male labour force as a percentage of the male population aged 15–64, 1960–93

Country	1960	1974	1993	Change 1960–93
Australia	97.2	99.1	85.0	−12.2
Canada	91.1	86.5	78.3	−12.8
Ireland	99.0	91.1	83.0	−16.0
New Zealand	93.8	89.2	83.3	−10.5
UK	99.1	91.8	84.0	−15.1
USA	90.5	85.4	84.9	−5.6
Denmark	99.5	89.9	86.9	−12.6
Finland	91.4	80.4	77.6	−13.8
Norway	92.2	86.7	82.0	−10.2
Sweden	98.5	88.5	79.4	−19.1
Austria	92.0	85.9	80.6	−11.4
Belgium	85.5	83.1	72.8	−12.7
France	94.6	85.1	74.5	−20.1
Germany	94.4	88.5	77.8	−16.6
Italy	95.3	84.7	74.8	−20.5
Netherlands	97.8	84.2	78.6	−19.2
Greece	91.8	82.5	73.7	−18.1
Portugal	104.4	96.1	82.5	−21.9
Spain	99.5	90.8	74.5	−25.0
Switzerland	100.4	100.2	92.5	−7.9
Japan	92.2	89.9	90.2	−2.0
Mean	95.2	88.2	80.8	14.4
Correlation with 1960		0.74	0.36	−0.44
Coefficient of variation	4.64	5.23	6.69	

Sources and notes: Data from OECD, *Historical Statistics,* Paris, various years. The figure reported in the final column is the percentage point change over the entire period.

falls in Southern Europe and France, and with a much more muted trend in Japan, the USA and Switzerland. Interestingly, the rate of decline was, if anything, slightly greater in the 14 years between 1960 and 1974 than in the two decades which followed, casting some doubts on theories which identify the post-oil shock fall in economic growth rates as the ultimate cause of the male labour force decline. The second change involved some degree of increase in cross-national variation with the passing of time. Whereas in 1960 most countries varied within a range of 10 percentage points, by the early 1990s that range was closer to 16 points. Finally, the correlation between 1960 and 1993 values is surprisingly low at 0.36, indicative of a distribution which had changed its character quite markedly.

Possible clues as to the nature of that change are forthcoming if we look at the emerging family of nations patterns in the data. In 1960, such patterns are difficult to discern, with conspicuously high values appearing in each of the groupings. However, by 1974 a slight tendency is emerging for the continental Western European grouping to display somewhat lower average values than any of the other groupings. Two decades later, the distinctiveness of this family and, arguably, also of the Southern European group, as countries of low male participation, has become more pronounced. Leaving aside Canada and Finland, all the countries of Scandinavia and the English-speaking world, together with Switzerland and Japan, have activity rates over 79 per cent. Excluding only Austria and Portugal, none of the countries of continental Western or Southern Europe had levels this high. The countries featuring as having the lowest levels of male labour supply are precisely those that might be expected on the basis of Esping-Andersen's (1990) proposition that the main mechanism of male labour force withdrawal since the 1970s has been the way in which 'conservative' welfare states have sought to contain labour market stress by buying the elderly poor out of unemployment queues.

Hypotheses

In order to establish whether the growth of big government and the welfare state has impacted on the character of labour supply in the post-war era, we seek to discover whether there is any association between participation rates and the degree of state intervention. The measures of state activity used here are total outlays of government (Table 4.1), civilian public consumption expenditure (Table 4.4) and social security transfers (Table 5.1). As we shall see, social security development has featured as a prominent explanation of the decline in male labour force participation over recent decades. In addition to the role of government, a number of the aspects of the post-war transformation discussed in Chapters 2 and 3 may also be relevant in explaining cross-national differences in levels and changes in labour force participation. It is not our intention to revisit these in detail, but only to mention some of the more obvious kinds of linkages, which may be discussed more fully to the degree that they prove to yield significant findings.

Wartime experience as measured by the war impact variable may well be relevant to male labour supply in the decades immediately following World War II, since it seems reasonable to suppose that invalidity and disability resulting from wartime service would have been a direct function of the extent of military involvement. However, there is no reason to believe that income growth during the wartime period will influence personal choices a decade down the track, so neither here nor subsequently in Chapters 6 and 7 do we use our alternative measure of wartime experience. Income measures might be expected to be positively related to participation rates in so far as they stand as proxies for wage levels. It is quite possible, however, that such effects might be counterbalanced by increased preferences for both learning and leisure, also resulting from increasing income levels. Arguably, exposure to international trade increases the vulnerability of labour markets, which suggests that economic openness could well lead to increased unemployment and some flow on into increased inactivity rates. Change in the occupational structure may also be relevant. One of the earliest cross-national studies in the field argues that a strong positive link between agricultural employment and male participation demonstrates how socio-economic modernization impinges on the workings of modern economies (Pampel and Weiss, 1983). It is also possible that cultural values reflecting religious beliefs may have some impact. Catholic social policy has been built around the notion of the 'just wage', seen as the basis on which a male breadwinner could support a family. At first glance, this notion might be argued to be conducive to policy action to promote higher levels of male participation. However, it is quite possible that, under circumstances of labour market crisis, the reverse may be the case. A social policy doctrine resting on the just wage gives reasons to use income transfers to provide high levels of income support where the market cannot. In other words, such values may lead governments to seek to buy workers out of the labour market.

Turning to politics, it is far from obvious that measures of the extent of class conflict and its institutionalization will have strong implications for male participation. It might be argued that strong trade unions with predominantly male membership and/or corporatist systems based on tripartite bargaining between established labour market groups would have some tendency to favour male interests over female interests. Although we test for this possibility, it is not at all clear whether such a bias would translate into campaigns to preserve male jobs or into support for favourable conditions for early labour market withdrawal. Quite probably the answer will be both, with counterbalancing effects obscuring any clear findings. It is still less apparent why democratization, ideological partisanship, federalism or constitutional structure should have any direct influence on male labour supply and we do not include terms for these variables in our subsequent analysis. Having said that, it is also important to remember that a number of these political variables have proved extremely important in accounting for various aspects of the development of big government and the welfare state, and that a demonstration of the impact of policy factors on labour market outcomes would necessarily imply a considerable degree of indirect influence. Finally, given arguments that moves towards European integration have fostered market-conforming deregulatory policies of a kind that might affect labour market performance (see Streek and Schmitter, 1991), we include EC membership as one of the variables in the analysis.

Apart from seeking to identify the role of state activity and of aspects of the post-war transformation, we also focus on a variety of accounts more specifically designed to account for post-war changes in male labour supply. These accounts fall into two main categories: explanations based on the impact of labour market stress and explanations based on life-cycle choices. The former suggest that decisions to leave the labour market are frequently involuntary and a function of growing unemployment, whilst the latter account for the choices of labour market participants in terms of the factors impinging on particular age cohorts within the population.

Unemployment may lead to a decline in participation for a variety of reasons (see Hamermesh and Rees, 1988). Employers may use inducements, such as occupational pension benefits, to persuade older workers to leave the labour force. Alternatively, unemployed workers may become discouraged and cease to seek employment. The effects of labour market stress are likely to be particularly pronounced amongst older workers who have progressively outdated skills and diminished physical capacities and who have, hence, a reduced capacity to retain or regain employment. Where a source of income support is available, this choice may eventually become a decision to take early retirement. From this perspective, early retirement may be seen as a matter of going before one is pushed or as a strategy designed to cope when one has been pushed. This account appears to fit well with recent labour market trends within the OECD. Whilst declining male labour force participation has been a continuous feature of post-war development, the decline in participation amongst older men has accelerated over the past two decades of mounting unemployment.

Essentially, life-cycle accounts point to institutional factors encouraging particular age-defined groups of workers to remain within or to leave the labour force. That male labour force participation is in some part a function of events impinging on different age groups can be readily demonstrated by the differentials in the average OECD inactivity rates for males in the age groups 15–24, 25–54 and 55 64 for the period 1980–91, which were 31.6, 5.6 and 39.6 per cent respectively (calculated from OECD, 1994). Almost 95 per cent of prime aged males were in the job market in the 1980s despite changing patterns of participation and labour market trauma. In contrast, only about 70 per cent of younger males were active and only around 60 per cent of mature aged men. The key to lower participation rates amongst the young is, of course, education beyond the minimum age of labour market participation. Many studies suggest investment in human capital through educational qualifications leads to higher subsequent levels of participation (see Pencavel, 1986), but given a definition of participation based on the activity rates of those in the age group 15–64, we would expect a negative correlation between educational enrolment past the age of 15 and the extent of male labour force participation. For mature aged workers what matter are the institutional arrangements which provide workers with income streams permitting them to leave the labour force prior to the date of statutory retirement. In both the labour force withdrawal of the young and the old, the handiwork of big government is readily apparent: life-cycle accounts of labour supply are telling us that two of the most significant changes in post-war labour markets are the growth of public education and the growth of public spending on income transfers.

A large number of studies have investigated the possibility that early retirement is largely a function of the attractiveness of the benefit packages available to workers in older age cohorts. Work in the labour economics tradition on the impact of the American social security system has shown that both eligibility for benefits and the size of benefits at the time of eligibility are inducements to labour force withdrawal (Boskin, 1977; Boskin and Hurd, 1978). Research in the same tradition on the impact of private pensions appears to be less clear-cut (Lazear, 1986, 329). Comparative studies by Esping-Andersen and Sonnenberger (1989), von Rhein-Kress (1993) and Schmidt (1993) all support the view that the characteristic response of many European nations to the economic crises of the 1970s and early 1980s was to use their existing social security arrangements to promote early retirement in the hope of reducing levels of unemployment. Earlier cross-national research using econometric methods to establish the determinants of male labour force participation, although arguing that socio-economic modernization has been much the strongest factor influencing outcomes, also points to a negative relationship between male labour supply and social security expenditure as a percentage of GDP (Pampel and Weiss, 1983).

The small number of comparative studies in this area have tended to restrict their focus to the role of state benefits and have not considered a variety of alternative institutional mechanisms facilitating early labour force withdrawal. However, income streams available to the old in some countries by virtue of social security entitlements may in other countries be available by virtue of private savings, private insurance or through equivalent benefits stemming from property ownership. This latter possibility, that widespread home ownership may be, in part, a functional alternative to pension entitlements, has recently been explored in work by Castles (1997b) on the determinants of early retirement in Australia, which suggests that, for any given level of income, individuals will be able to retire earlier if they are the owners of residential property free of mortgage obligations. In what follows, we seek to establish whether a model taking account of the positive impact of home ownership on early labour force withdrawal provides a more adequate explanation than an account resting on social security entitlements alone.

Finally, we examine two other possible factors impacting on male labour supply: the burden of dependency and the availability of part-time employment. As the recent literature on population ageing suggests (World Bank, 1994; OECD, 1996e), we may expect that in future years the active population will be required to support an increasingly aged population, implying that more labour time will have to come from a smaller pool of workers if existing living standards are to be maintained. If the logic of this argument is accepted, it seems worth investigating the possibility that labour supply will be higher in nations where the dependency ratio – the aged plus the young as a percentage of the total population – is greatest. Another possibility is that labour supply – again of both men and women – will be influenced by opportunities to obtain part-time employment, which vary very considerably amongst OECD nations. Since part-time employment is a step into the labour market for women and often also for young men and may serve as a means of delaying exit for men, it seems reasonable to argue that labour force participation for both sexes will be higher where the share of part-time employment as a percentage of total employment is greatest. Cross-national data for the share of part-time employment are only available from 1973 onwards (see OECD, 1996c), and so this hypothesis can only be tested for the 1974 and early 1990s cross-sections.

Findings

Turning to our findings for 1960 as shown in Figure 6.1(a), we note that there are only two correlations which meet our rule-of-thumb test for significance of + or – 0.40. These are war impact and home ownership, both

(a) 1960

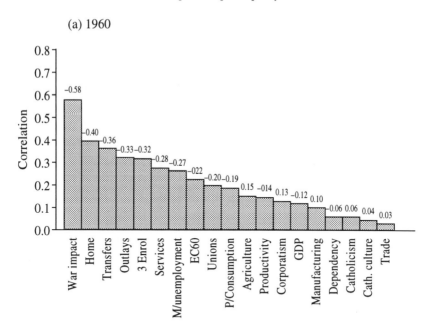

(b) 1974

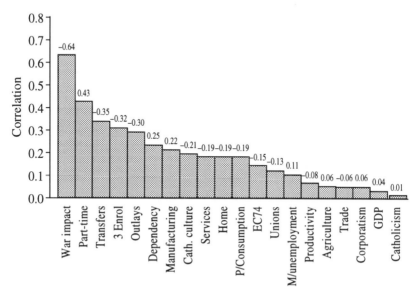

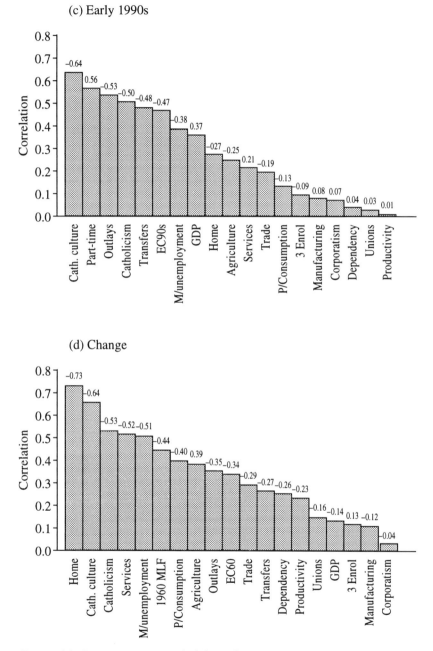

Figure 6.1 Bivariate tests: male labour force participation (1960, 1974 and early 1990s and change over time)

of which have negative signs, indicating that high values are associated with lower levels of male labour supply. Apart from these correlations, there are three others which exceed the + or − 0.30 mark. They relate to social security expenditure, tertiary educational enrolments and total outlays of government. Again, all have the negative signs which indicate that they are associated with lower levels of participation. The sign for male unemployment is also negative, but the degree of association is weak. Unfortunately, data on part-time employment are unavailable for 1960. Given the modesty of these correlations, one might expect some difficulty in generating a model with some reasonable capacity to account for early post-war male labour supply. In fact, the model which appears in Appendix 6.1 is quite respectable, accounting for just over 60 per cent of the variation in levels of labour supply. Surprisingly, war impact, the strongest factor in Figure 6.1(a), does not feature in the successful model, with the explanatory power stemming equally from the negative effects of social security spending and home ownership. In respect of social security, the estimated difference in the participation rate of the lowest-spending country and an average spending country is of the order of 5.9 percentage points; for home ownership, the corresponding figure is 6.3 percentage points.

Figure 6.1(b) shows no increase in significant correlations. War impact is, if anything, slightly more influential in 1974 than previously, and part-time employment now has its predicted positive influence on participation, but otherwise no factors stand out as being particularly strongly associated with outcomes. The correlations for social security expenditure, tertiary enrolments and outlays all have negative signs and remain in the + or − 0.30 band. The association with home ownership, whilst remaining negatively signed, now appears extremely weak; the association with male unemployment is actually positive. Surprisingly, given these findings, the best-fit model in Appendix 6.1 continues to feature the negative influence of transfers and of home ownership, but now includes a positive dependency ratio term. Estimating the real impacts of social security spending and home ownership in our normal manner suggests that these factors reduced male labour supply in the average OECD country by 7.7 and 8.9 percentage points respectively. OECD dependency rates in 1974 varied from 30.8 (Finland) to 41.9 (Ireland) per cent of the population, with a mean of 36.4. The estimated effect of the difference between the lowest value and the mean implies a positive boost to labour supply of 7.6 percentage points.

The findings reported in Figure 6.1(c) indicate that, by the early 1990s, cross-national variation in male labour supply is associated with a considerably wider range of factors than previously. We do not test for the influence of war impact because the age cohort which fought in World War II is now out of the labour force. However, this factor, which derived its strength from the somewhat lower participation levels of continental Western Europe, is now replaced by the strongly negative influence of the Catholic cultural impact variable and only somewhat less significant associations with Catholicism and European Community membership. For the first time, social security spending is significantly correlated with the participation rate, as are also the total outlays of government. Part-time employment remains, as in 1974, a significant factor and, indeed, is a little stronger than previously. Not surprisingly, under the circumstances of mass unemployment prevailing in the early 1990s, a negative association with male unemployment is now apparent and verging on statistical significance. Other expected relationships are missing. Home ownership, as in 1974, is not strongly correlated with outcomes in these simple bivariate terms. The effects of dependency and of tertiary enrolments are negligible and, contrary to Pampel and Weiss's (1983) modernization hypothesis, agricultural employment is associated with lower rather than higher levels of participation.

Despite all these changes in the factors associated with outcomes, Appendix 6.1 yet again features social security spending and home ownership in the best-fit model for the early 1990s, with Catholic cultural impact being the only other significant term. The estimated effects of the constant terms have, however, decreased as compared with 1974: to 4.3 percentage points in the case of social security and 5.0 points in the case of home ownership. Countries which are characterized by Catholic cultural impact are estimated to have 5.2 points lower male participation than countries which are not.

Correlations for the factors associated with change in the male labour force over time are to be found in Figure 6.1(d). Much the strongest influence is the negative impact of increasing levels of home ownership, with measures of religious influence also featuring prominently as factors accelerating the decline in the male participation rate. For the first time, there is evidence compatible with a discouraged worker effect, with a negative association between changes in male participation and changes in the rate of male unemployment. For the first time also, there are signs of an occupational structure effect, with a significant negative relationship between changes in the size of the service sector and changes in the participation rate, and an almost significant positive relationship between changes in the size of the agricultural sector and changes in the participation rate. Contrary to the proposition that adverse labour market trends are largely shaped by the changing role of government, there are no significant correlations between changes in the public expenditure variables and changes in male labour supply. However, the negative association with public consumption expenditure is very nearly significant and, somewhat counter-intuitively, suggests that male labour supply was declining most rapidly where governments were most increasing their spending on goods and services. Almost certainly this is a case of a causal misspecification, with the true implication of the finding arguably being that countries in which the decline in the male labour force was a source of major concern were precisely those which tended to utilize public consumption expenditure as a mechanism of job creation. The successful model for change in Appendix 6.1 is consistent with previous ones in including a negative term for home ownership. In addition, there are significant negative terms for Catholic cultural impact and change in services employment. Change in home ownership increased the estimated decline in male labour supply by 5.0 percentage points, Catholic cultural impact by 3.8 points and change in services employment by 3.4 points.

Analysis

The most interesting of our findings concerning the post-war evolution of male labour supply relates to the constant factors, social security spending and home ownership. Before discussing them, however, we comment briefly on some other aspects of the models. One seeming anomaly is the way in which, despite being the factor most strongly correlated with outcomes in both 1960 and 1974, war impact does not feature in our best-fit equations. Almost certainly, that is because the effect is mediated through social security spending, with high levels of disability resulting from war service leading to high levels of transfers, which provide the income streams required to remain outside the labour force. A further possible anomaly arises from the dependency ratio effect in 1974. This result must be regarded as somewhat suspect just because, if the burden of dependency argument applies at one date, one might expect that it would apply at all dates. Given the information available, it is not possible to be definitive about this result beyond noting that it is a joint artefact of the two cases at the extremes of the dependency distribution, Finland and Ireland. Without these countries in the analysis, social security and home ownership provide a model no less adequate than that for 1960. Lastly, while commenting on seemingly anomalous results, it is worth pointing out that the services effect in the change model is probably a symptom rather than a cause. Clearly, it is not the shift into services which leads to labour force withdrawal, but rather shifts out of agriculture and manufacturing which render the skills of, particularly older, workers redundant.

Another aspect of the findings which deserves comment is the emergent relationship between labour force withdrawal and Catholic cultural impact. The point of interest here is the manner in which cultural values come to impinge on labour market behaviour. Examination of the relationships between the independent variables suggests that part of the answer is to be found in part-time employment, which is correlated with Catholic cultural impact at –0.70 in 1974 and –0.56 in the early 1990s. The 1990s figure is, however, markedly reduced by the presence of two outliers, Finland and the Netherlands, without which the correlation would be no less than –0.89. Focusing on the recent labour market experience of the Netherlands tells us something of the mechanisms involved here. Until the early 1980s, the Netherlands was right at the bottom of the OECD distribution for levels of part-time employment, with the main impediments to the creation of such jobs lying in social security contributions thresholds and a tax system which severely penalized households substituting towards part-time work. Faced by extremely high levels of unemployment in the early 1980s, the Netherlands replaced contributions thresholds with a sliding scale and transformed the tax treatment of part-time working, leading to an increase in part-time jobs from 4.4 per cent of the total in 1973 to 35.0 per cent in the early 1990s and to a decline in unemployment unrivalled by any other country in the OECD (for data, see OECD, 1996a).

The argument, then, is that one way in which Catholic social policy values are translated into labour market outcomes is via regulations linking labour supply to the funding mechanisms of the welfare state, with the 'just wage' doctrine serving as an underlying premise for the view that only full-time jobs are proper jobs. Such regulations include those determining whether the incomes of husbands and wives are taxed jointly or separately and whether there are thresholds in the social security contributions system favouring full-time work, as well as those governing relative tax liabilities on full-time and part-time earnings. Calculations from OECD data for the late 1970s show that, in each of these respects, Catholic countries were significantly more likely to have regulations favouring full-time over part-time work (data from OECD, 1990, 166). So, just as the contributory mechanism was the key to understanding the distinctive political economy of the Catholic welfare state (see pp. 160–61), the wider tax system of which it is a part is one of the crucial links between Catholic social policy and labour market behaviour. These regulations may have been largely irrelevant to male labour supply when men had no aspirations to work anything less than full-time, but with the rise of mass unemployment, under circumstances when part-time work has become a means of preserving a toe-hold in the labour market, they are of much greater importance. Given that, for most women, part-time employment has been the key to combining domestic responsibilities with labour force participation, this mechanism is likely to be no less pertinent to our understanding of the post-war development of female labour supply.

Clearly the strongest findings concerning male labour supply are the consistently negative impacts of social security spending and home ownership. Whilst these findings underline the relevance of a life-cycle account, they are not necessarily incompatible with other explanations. Income streams from social security and the reduced need for income resulting from home ownership should be seen as factors influencing the choices available to those contemplating labour force withdrawal for whatever reasons. With an alternative income stream available or with a reduced need for income, there is a real possibility of leaving the labour force. Without such advantages, there is none. In this sense, labour market inactivity is truly a reflection of available resources and, therefore, of income levels, but only of income levels as they have been transformed into institutional arrangements allowing individuals the option of leaving the labour force.

The impacts of social security and home ownership apply most obviously in respect of voluntary choices to withdraw from the labour market through early retirement. A pension – public or private – plus a house free of mortgage allow retirement on reasonably comfortable terms. However, the same kind of logic applies to the choices confronting a worker who becomes unemployed. Becoming a discouraged worker has costs and it is only where the individual can meet them that he or she can afford to become inactive. The normal image of the discouraged worker is, of course, of one who perforce must rely on the income of others within the household. However, for older workers with resources there are other choices, with early retirement on an income stream below that which would have otherwise been optimally chosen prominent among them. It may also be that, for older home owners, there are real costs attached to the job search process which is the penalty of remaining in the labour market. These costs – financial and emotional – may reduce individual mobility (see Oswald, 1996), giving those with some choice a reason to prefer withdrawal to job search. The same logic would suggest that, for those who own their own homes, but do not have an income adequate to leave the labour force, there may be a reason to prefer unemployment to mobility in search of a new job. This is a proposition which will be examined in the later section on the factors associated with cross-national variation in unemployment rates.

The final point that should be made relates to the proposition that the rise of big government is implicated in emergent distortions of post-war labour markets. The evidence provided by our findings suggests that, in so far as such effects can be discerned, they have been with us throughout and are actually declining in importance. In 1960, the estimated real impact of social security spending for the average OECD country was a reduction in male labour supply of 5.9 percentage points, in 1974 the figure was 6.5

points and, in the early 1990s, only 4.3 points. More sophisticated commentators than those usually found amongst the ranks of the critics of big government might also note that levels of home ownership are also strongly influenced by public policy, with governments in many Western nations using tax incentives and a wide range of other mechanisms to facilitate house purchase (Heidenheimer, Heclo and Adams, 1990; Castles, 1997b). In encouraging home ownership, these governments are sometimes represented as building the foundations of a privatized and non-statist society, but their interventions, no less than those of the social security state, have been amongst the factors leading to the post-war decline in male labour supply. The truth is that where institutional arrangements exist which permit labour force withdrawal, individuals will avail themselves of such opportunities irrespective of whether those arrangements are public or ostensibly private.

FEMALE LABOUR FORCE PARTICIPATION

The huge post-war growth in female labour force participation is at one and the same time a return to the past and a major social and economic departure with genuine emancipatory potential. It is a return to the past because, in the context of pre-industrial societies, women's work outside the home has been the norm of human history, as it remains the norm in Third World agrarian economies. Indeed, it was the era of industrialization, allowing first the wives of the middle classes and, for a brief period in the early post-war decades, the wives of the affluent working classes, the luxury or penance of domesticity unalloyed by labour, which was the real historical aberration (see Hudson and Lee, 1990). The truly significant departure of recent decades has been the transformation by which a majority of women in most Western nations have become, for the first time, a part of the cash economy, completing the process of labour market commodification set in motion by the rise of modern capitalism centuries earlier. Women had, of course, worked for cash before, but usually only before marriage or childbirth, or under circumstances where women's wages were an alternative to family destitution. Now, for the first time, most women, and even, in some countries, most married women, had autonomous access to financial resources potentially independent and separable from the household budget. This is an aspect of post-war economic change which, by altering the balance of power within the household, has created the potential for a complete transformation of gender-based relations in modern societies. In this section, we examine the factors associated with the growth of female labour force participation in the post-war era. In sections in the next chapter which explore the factors associated with post-war changes in patterns of fertility and divorce, we look at some of the consequences that have already followed from this development.

Data

An obvious place to start is with contrasts between trends in male and female labour supply. In a period between 1960 and 1993 in which male labour force participation decreased by 14.1 percentage points, female labour force participation increased by 18.7 points. To dispose of a persistent myth, there was absolutely no connection between these trends, with the correlation between change in male and female labour supply being a minuscule –0.06. Moreover, while the decline in male participation was reasonably evenly spread across the period as a whole, the growth in female labour supply was most pronounced towards the end of the period. Finally, while the trend of male labour supply was slightly divergent, the trend of female participation was quite strongly convergent. Admittedly, the absolute gap between the extremes of the female labour supply distribution had only been closed a little with the passing of time, from the 45.7 percentage points separating Finland and Portugal in 1960 to the 37.4 points separating Denmark and Ireland in 1993. However, the extent of the transformation is indicated by the fact that Ireland, the country at the bottom of the distribution in 1993, had a participation rate that would have been close to the mean in 1960 and by the fact that, by 1993, there remained only four OECD countries with participation rates of less than 50 per cent.

In 1960, family of nations patterns were not particularly pronounced. The countries with outstandingly the highest levels of participation were Finland and Japan, defeated nations of World War II still in the business of post-war reconstruction and rapid economic growth. Otherwise, the only noticeable regularity is the relative lack of employment equality in the English-speaking nations, possibly exemplifying a tendency for early affluence to promote female labour force withdrawal. By 1974, the single family of nations resemblance was that all members of the Scandinavian group exceeded the mean, with three of the four countries in the OECD vanguard for female participation. The 1974 rearguard was a mixed bag in family terms, consisting of Ireland, Italy, the Netherlands, Greece and Spain. The group was, however, uniformly Catholic and, with the exception of the Netherlands, uniformly poor. The period of massive growth in female labour supply over the following two decades was simultaneously a period in which astonishingly strong family of nations patterns appear. Scandinavia remains at the top of the distribution with all the countries in the 70 per cent plus bracket, the English-speaking nations, bar Ireland, come next with figures in the 60 to 70 per cent range, the nations of continental Western Europe, bar Italy, are to be found in a band from 60 to 50 per cent, while the countries of Southern Europe,

Table 6.2 Levels of and change in the female labour force as a percentage of the female population aged 15–64, 1960–93

Country	1960	1974	1993	Change 1960–93
Australia	34.1	48.7	62.3	28.2
Canada	33.7	48.5	65.3	31.6
Ireland	34.8	34.2	40.9	6.1
New Zealand	31.3	41.1	63.2	31.9
UK	46.1	54.3	65.3	19.2
USA	42.6	52.3	69.1	26.5
Denmark	43.5	63.2	78.3	34.8
Finland	65.6	65.5	70.0	4.4
Norway	36.3	50.0	70.8	34.5
Sweden	50.1	64.9	75.8	25.7
Austria	52.1	52.8	58.5	6.4
Belgium	36.4	42.4	53.9	17.5
France	46.6	50.6	59.0	12.4
Germany	49.2	50.6	60.7	11.5
Italy	39.6	34.1	43.3	3.7
Netherlands	26.2	29.7	55.8	29.6
Greece	41.6	32.6	43.6	2.0
Portugal	19.9	51.2	61.3	41.4
Spain	26.0	33.0	42.8	16.8
Switzerland	51.0	54.0	57.9	6.9
Japan	60.1	52.4	61.8	1.7
Mean	41.3	47.9	60.0	18.7
Correlation with 1960		0.62	0.33	–0.62
Coefficient of variation	27.50	22.13	17.61	

Sources and notes: Data from OECD, *Historical Statistics,* Paris, various years. The figure reported in the final column is the percentage point change over the entire period.

plus Italy, but minus Portugal, are located in the 40 per cent range. Switzerland and Japan, having both started out the post-war period well above the OECD mean, were, by the early 1990s, adjacent to it. No pattern is apparent in the figures for change over time. That is, however, scarcely surprising, given that what appears to be happening is a shift from positions in a distribution seemingly unrelated to the historical and cultural factors defining the families of nations identified in this study to a pattern in which these factors were paramount. Within each family grouping, there were countries that had to make far greater adjustments than others to conform to this pattern.

Hypotheses

As in the case of male labour supply, we would expect that cross-national variation in female labour force participation would variously reflect the forces of economic, social, political and public policy transformation in the post-war era. We have already noted an inverse correlation between wartime involvement and male labour supply in the early post-war decades. We would expect female labour supply to be positively related to wartime involvement, because of the need for widows and the wives of the disabled to find employment to support their families. Where the tasks of post-war reconstruction were particularly onerous, there may also have been greater demand for women workers. It might also be expected that high participation levels would be associated with higher levels of income, variously conforming with the assumptions of those who might be inclined to see income levels as proxies for wage levels (Killingsworth and Heckman, 1986) and of those arguing that economic modernization has been a source of decreasing gender inequality (see Wilensky, 1968; Semyonov, 1980). It should be noted, however, that there must be some causal ambiguity about links between female participation rates and measures of both real GDP per capita and real GDP per worker, the former because, other things being equal, the higher the overall level of employment the higher will be per capita income, and the latter because any tendency for women to work in low-productivity industries would be likely to lead to an inverse relationship between female labour supply and real GDP per worker.

Income levels are not the only way in which female labour supply has been linked to the process of socio-economic modernization. Indeed, the causal mechanism most frequently identified is change in the occupational structure, with the standard account suggesting a U-shaped pattern of development. Agricultural employment is traditionally associated with the employment of women, although national statistics do not always capture this effect, counting a large part of their work output as that of male peasant proprietors. Manufacturing, on the other hand, has not been regarded as providing favourable employment opportunities for women, with most commentators suggesting that the decisive shift in female labour supply has been associated with the post-war expansion of services employment (see Sorrentino, 1983; OECD, 1984; Bakker, 1988).

We also have some reason to expect that female participation levels will be influenced by religious differences. In our analysis of the factors associated with male labour supply, we noted that, in Catholic countries, social policy doctrines were linked to labour supply via tax regulations favouring full-time over part-time employment. Given that part-time work has a far greater role in the employment of women than of men, there is reason to expect that this impact will be even stronger in the case of female than of male labour supply. However, whether the relationship will be manifest in a positive relationship with the availability of part-time work or a negative one with the measures of Catholic influence is difficult to predict. The assumptions of the Catholic breadwinner model concerning an appropriate gender-based division of labour are built into a host of policy arrangements, including the availability of child care places, the integration of work and school hours, taxation arrangements relating to part-time work and expectations concerning the role of women in the care of the sick and the elderly, all of them creating impediments to female labour force participation. We do not have the data to compare these arrangements for the post-war period as a whole and, in their absence, it may well be that measures of Catholic influence will serve as proxies for their combined effects.

Contrary to the initial hypothesis from which we started in the last section, that strong trade unions and corporatist institutions might be conducive to labour market strategies favouring male interests, the literature which has discussed the determinants of female labour supply has tended to take the alternative view: that high levels of union density and the existence of encompassing institutions to regulate class conflict are likely to be associated with higher levels of female participation (see Ruggie, 1984; Schmidt, 1993). As noted in Chapter 3, theorists of the 'power resources' school have tended to argue that the hegemony of the working class movement is likely to be associated with measures of gender equality, with Social Democratic parties seeking to promote women-friendly policies and their opponents being more resistant to, and sometimes attempting to reverse, such initiatives. Thus, as in the case of male labour supply, the assumption is that any link between party politics and female labour force participation is one mediated by policy.

This brings us back to the argument that changing patterns of labour supply are substantially a function of the growth of big government. However, in the case of female labour supply, the standard hypothesis concerns the role of government as employer and as service provider rather than as provider of transfers. Public sector provision of services in health, education, child and age care has been the major source of new job opportunities for women in the post-war era (OECD, 1982; Paukert, 1984; Esping-Andersen, 1990). At the same time, the growth of child care services has been absolutely crucial in allowing married women to combine work and motherhood (Norris, 1987; Gornick, Meyers and Ross, 1997). For the most part, these services fall under the heading of public consumption expenditure. Given the very strong links between this category of spending and both democratization and Left incumbency established in Chapter 4, we would regard evidence of a positive association between the public consumption budget and female participation as a clear demonstration of the contribution made by politics to gender equality in the labour market. Having argued that government's role as service provider is the crucial one for female labour supply, it should be noted that certain kinds of transfer are also relevant and, in particular, those which provide parental benefits to workers who maintain their labour force status. However, the only available data (see OECD, 1996d) on cash benefits to families conflate such spending with transfers designed to provide women who have the left the labour force to have children with a source of income. Unfortunately, this makes it rather improbable that there will be a clear relationship between such benefits and levels of female participation.

Apart from factors more broadly implicated in the process of post-war transformation, we also focus on a number of hypotheses more specific to labour market behaviour. Several of these involve respecifications of arguments previously encountered in the discussion of male labour supply. The logic of the proposition that the utilization of the work force is likely to increase where rates of dependency are high suggests the possibility that the dependency argument will apply to female as well male labour supply. Both theory and research findings suggest that the discouraged worker effect is likely to be more pronounced for women than for men (see Bowen and Finegan, 1969; Bakker, 1988), and we therefore test to see whether there is a negative relationship between female labour supply and female unemployment. Consideration is also given to the role of education. Human capital theory suggests that the demand for women workers will be, in some part, a function of their levels of educational attainment (Norris, 1987). In order to test this proposition, we have calculated ratios of women to men in both schools and tertiary education (data from UNESCO, 1995 and earlier dates), with the hypothesized relationship being that the higher these ratios, the higher will be levels of female participation.

Finally, we examine the role of a factor without any parallel in the male labour force literature. Until recently, it has been a standard assumption of the literature that female participation is inversely related to child bearing and the tasks of child rearing, implying a link between the post-war decline in fertility and the growth of female labour force participation (see Sorrentino, 1990; Blau and Ferber, 1992). The causal links implied by this relationship can be seen as reciprocal, with a decision to participate amounting to a decision to delay fertility and a decision to have children serving effectively as a decision to leave the work force. Comparative evidence emerging towards the latter part of the period has, however, called the relationship into question or, at least, implied that it may be historically contingent. The contemporary contrast between relatively high levels of fertility in the Scandinavian countries of high female labour supply and the much lower levels of fertility in the Southern European countries of weaker female participation (see Table 7.2 below) has been attributed to the presence of women-friendly policies in the former, including parental benefits, access to day care and flexible working conditions (Gustavsson and Stafford, 1994), and the difficulty of combining work and child care in the latter, leading to a widespread decision to delay or forgo fertility (see Esping-Andersen, 1996). The possibility that there has been a change in the relationship between fertility and female labour supply is discussed briefly in this section and more fully in Chapter 7.

Findings

Figure 6.2(a) shows the correlations between female labour supply in 1960 and the various factors discussed above. Only three factors prove to be significantly associated with outcomes: fertility and Catholicism negatively and war impact positively. Public consumption is also positively related to outcomes and only just misses out on being significant. All these relationships are as hypothesized, but those with the occupational structure uniformly contradict the U-shaped development hypothesis, with manufacturing employment positively related to labour supply and agricultural and services employment negatively related. It is possible that these somewhat perverse findings are a result of testing a thesis about change over time in individual nations with cross-sectional data.

Turning to Appendix 6.2, the best-fit model for 1960 contains four terms: war impact, fertility, Catholic cultural impact and the gender ratio in primary and secondary schooling, with fertility and Catholic cultural impact having a negative influence and war impact and the gender ratio a positive one. All relationships in the model are as hypothesized. Estimates

(a) 1960

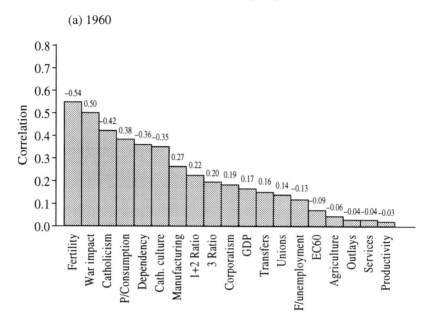

(b) 1974

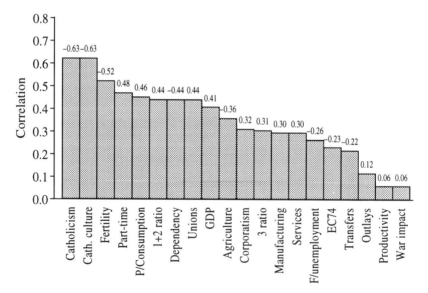

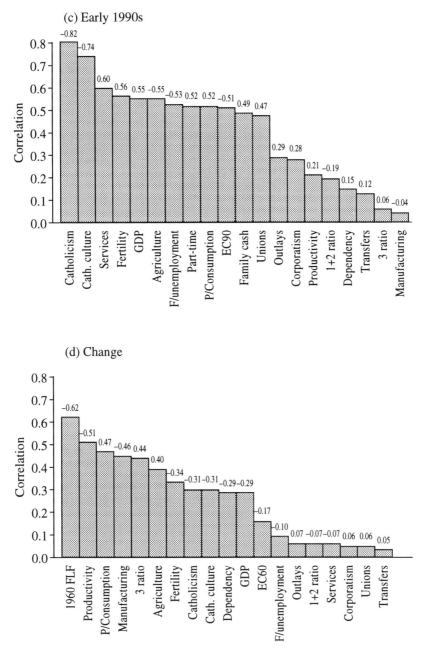

Figure 6.2 Bivariate tests: female labour force participation (1960, 1974 and early 1990s and change over time)

of the real impact of these terms suggest that countries which lost the war had participation rates 7.2 percentage points higher than countries which were victorious and that Catholic countries had a participation rate 9.2 percentage points lower than Protestant countries. Calculating the estimated difference between an average country and one at the bottom of the distribution suggests a negative impact of fertility of around 9.7 percentage points and a positive impact of the gender ratio of about 7.3 points.

Figure 6.2(b) shows that by 1974 there were many more significant relationships than previously. The strong negative associations with measures of Catholic influence and of fertility are replicated, but now part-time employment, civilian public consumption expenditure, the school gender ratio, union density and real GDP per capita are all positively and significantly correlated as well. Each of these factors is associated with labour supply in the manner hypothesized. Manufacturing and services employment are now positively correlated to outcomes and agricultural employment negatively. Contrary to our hypothesis, dependency is negatively and significantly associated with female labour supply. The 1974 model presented in Appendix 6.2 is consistent with its predecessor in including negative terms for both Catholic cultural impact and fertility. However, war impact and educational equality are replaced by the positive influence of civilian public consumption and the unexpectedly negative impact of services employment. The estimated effect of Catholic cultural impact has increased to 14.6 percentage points, while the average difference made by fertility has declined to 5.6 percentage points. The estimated average difference made by services employment is considerable at 14.0 percentage points, while the, sometimes offsetting effect of civilian public consumption expenditure is 8.4 points.

The negative association between female labour force participation and Catholicism reported in Figure 6.2(c) is the strongest correlation for the full sample of 21 countries reported in this book to date. Services employment, fertility, real GDP per capita, part-time employment, public consumption expenditure, family cash benefits and union density are all positively and significantly associated with higher levels of gender equality in the labour market. The major reversal in the nature of the relationship between fertility and female participation underlines the radical changes taking place in the cross-national distribution of both female labour supply and fertility during the post-war decades. Agricultural employment, female unemployment and EC membership are negatively and significantly associated with outcomes. The early 1990s model in Appendix 6.2 contains three terms, indicative of the negative influence of Catholicism and of female unemployment and the continuing positive impact of civilian public consumption. Calculating on our normal basis, a country with the average level of Catholic adherence had a level of female labour supply estimated to be 7.6 percentage points lower than the least Catholic nation, whilst the average effect of public consumption spending was to raise the participation level by an estimated 7.4 percentage points. On average, female unemployment made for a participation level 4.2 percentage points lower than it would otherwise have been. However, for a country like Spain, with extremely high levels of female unemployment, the estimated effect is much larger.

Possibly the most interesting aspect of the findings reported in Figure 6.2(d) is that the strongest correlation with change over time is the catch-up term for labour supply in 1960. Positive and significant findings for change in public consumption expenditure and increasing gender equity in tertiary education are as hypothesized. However, other significant findings require interpretation. The negative association between productivity growth and increased female labour supply would seem to invite explanation in terms of the low productivity growth of the service sector were it not for the fact that there is actually a tiny negative relationship between the growth of labour supply and the growth of services employment. This suggests that we should probably be looking for an explanation of the reported association in terms of a more general tendency for women to be concentrated in low-productivity jobs across the economy. The signs attached to the correlations for agricultural and manufacturing employment are somewhat confusing. In the case of agriculture, the positive sign implies that female participation was increasing most in countries where agricultural employment was decreasing least; these were, in fact, countries in which services employment had been dominant for the longest period of time. In the case of manufacturing, the negative sign indicates that female labour force participation was increasing most where manufacturing was declining most rapidly. Both findings are, therefore, quite compatible with the strong positive association between services employment and female participation reported for the early 1990s.

Despite the appearance of a number of novel significant relationships in Figure 6.2(d), the change model identified in Appendix 6.2 is largely consistent with what has gone before. Female participation has grown more slowly in countries in which Catholicism was strong and more rapidly in countries where public consumption expenditure has been growing fastest. The average effect of Catholicism was a reduction in participation of 9.7 points and the average public consumption effect was an increase in participation of 6.3 points. The only other factor of significance was catch-up. However, it mattered a great deal, with an estimated effect for the average OECD country of no less than 20.4 percentage points. The magnitude of this effect is a topic for the analysis which follows.

Analysis

An interesting question with which to start the analysis is why the labour supply pattern of the early post-war period was so different from the way it is now. We shall have more to say on this later, but the beginnings of an answer are to be found in the findings concerning war impact and fertility. The big mystery of the early period is why the English-speaking countries, which were later to be amongst the leaders of the push for gender equality in the labour market, started out from such a relatively low level of participation. The answer is simply that these countries experienced less wartime disruption to their demographic and economic structures than did the countries of continental Western Europe, and it was also these countries which set the pace in the 'baby boom' of the late 1950s and the 1960s. While the majority of English-speaking countries were predominantly Protestant in their religious beliefs, this was insufficient to counteract the influence of these factors.

By 1974, the core pattern of post-war female labour supply was clearly established, with measures of Catholic influence negatively associated with outcomes and public consumption spending positively associated. In these terms, the distinct family of nations patterns observable can quite readily be accounted for. The Scandinavian countries were Protestant and the leaders in public consumption spending, the English-speaking countries were Protestant but, in general, relatively low spenders on welfare state services, and the countries of continental Western and Southern Europe were both Catholic and relatively low spenders on public consumption, preferring to finance their welfare states by the transfers route. Here, indeed, are Esping-Andersen's three worlds of welfare capitalism as translated into labour market behaviour, but defined at least as much by religious belief as by the impact of partisan public policy (cf. Esping-Andersen, 1990, 144–61).

The effects of religion are extremely strong: 9 percentage points in 1960, 14 points in 1974 and, estimating the difference between an overwhelmingly Catholic nation like Belgium and a highly Protestant one like Sweden, 14 points in the early 1990s and 18 points for change over time. That these measures have more influence than any of the single policy impacts associated with them, such as the extent of part-time employment or, early in the period, gender equity in education, suggests strongly that the cultural and social policy influence of Catholic beliefs is mediated by many factors, some of them, almost certainly, not featuring in this analysis.

Examining the relationships between the independent variables which are included in this analysis, we find significant relationships between Catholicism *circa* the early 1990s and part-time employment (–0.66), services employment (–0.59), GDP per capita (–0.55), agricultural employment (0.46) union density (–0.44) and female unemployment (0.42). Looking at the findings in Figure 6.2(c), it will be seen that all these factors are themselves significantly associated with labour supply in such a manner that makes it reasonable to assume that the measure of Catholic influence is picking up on aspects of their joint impact. Moreover, although Catholicism is not significantly associated with public consumption expenditure, it is strongly related with one of its components, family services (–0.66), which in turn is strongly positively correlated with the female participation rate (0.70). So the story again appears to be one of nations characterized by a distinctive Catholic political economy, which serves to shape multiple aspects of the policy milieu and which results in substantial impediments to full labour market equality for women.

There are at least three apparent anomalies in our findings. First, there is the significant negative association between female labour supply and dependency levels in 1974, which was precisely the date at which that term featured positively in the best-fit model for male labour supply. This implies a traditional story of the consequences of dependency, with males seeking greater earnings in the labour market and women staying out of the labour market to undertake caring work. Second, there is the fact that services employment is negatively related to female labour supply in 1974. This may be seen as reflecting a situation in which service sector growth in countries other than those in which public consumption expenditure was high remained primarily in areas unfavourable to women's employment. From the mid-1970s onwards, however, even private sector service growth tended to be primarily in welfare-related areas, so that this effect had disappeared by the early 1990s.

A third anomaly is the fact that, in the early 1990s, fertility appears as a factor positively associated with female labour supply. The correct interpretation here would seem to be that the poor labour market prospects for women in some countries have caused them to reduce their fertility as part of their employment search strategy, while both fertility and female participation have increased in other countries as a result of policies facilitating the employment of married women. Referring back to the 1974 dependency finding, it is clear that by the 1990s the majority of women no longer find staying out of the labour market to have children a viable option. These are issues which will be discussed further in the next chapter.

The only influence greater than religion is the catch-up effect manifested in the change model. As in the case of both health and education expenditure previously, a coefficient close to 1.0 is indicative of a transformation which has, effectively, compensated for all the sources of cross-national difference existing at the beginning of the period. In other words, the contemporary world of female labour force participation is one which has been exclusively shaped by the forces impacting on it since 1960 and owes virtually nothing to an inheritance from the past. In the case of health and education, catch-up of these dimensions was interpreted in terms of programme maturation. To a considerable extent, a similar story applies here, with early 1990s female participation rates in the Scandinavian countries, bar Norway, less than 10 percentage points below prevailing male rates and other countries doing as well as might be expected given a Catholic culture and a relative lack of state services employment.

It is, however, also worth thinking in terms of the forces pushing the catch-up process. Clearly, whatever they might be, they are not the factors considered in this analysis, for otherwise they would show up as significant terms in the change model. A convincing explanation requires that we locate a force which would impact on countries more or less in inverse proportion to the extent of their labour market gender inequality at the beginning of the period. Although unprovable with the data at our command, the most promising candidate for such a force is the impact of post-war feminist ideas, which might be expected to have had an effect in direct proportion to the disadvantages confronted by women in the labour market and other spheres. Such an interpretation would suggest that feminism had played a major role in dispelling attitudes, values and codes of conduct which in many countries had denied married women access to labour market opportunities, and in creating a society in which the normative assumption of participation was well on the way to becoming as strong for women as for men.

We conclude by considering the role of big government and the welfare state in the post-war growth of female labour supply. As we noted at the beginning of this chapter, it is a standard critique of the thrust of post-war public policy that it has undermined the incentive to work. In the case of female labour supply, this is clearly untrue. In all the correlations reported in Figure 6.2, we found no significant association between female participation and either total outlays of government or social security transfers, in these respects confirming the finding that cross-national comparison provides no evidence of an 'association between levels of welfare state provision and female participation rates' (Rubery, 1988, 279). The exception is, of course, public consumption expenditure, but this, as we have clearly demonstrated, is a factor which increases women's participation rather than reduces it. Even were we to offset the lower male participation brought about by transfers with the increased female participation brought about by public consumption, the net balance in both 1974 and the early 1990s would be positive. The equation is, of course, more complicated than this. In particular, the shift to a more female work force has been associated with an increase in part-time work. Nevertheless, it is quite clear that the view that the growth of the state has reduced the incentive to participate is far too simplistic.

UNEMPLOYMENT

For those who criticize the growth of big government on the ground that it undermines the will to work, the acid test is unemployment. In the decades since 1960, unemployment has grown right across the OECD, but it started out as more of a problem in some countries than in others and grew more in some countries than in others. The story offered to the unsophisticated is that, as the state has grown, so too has the problem of post-war unemployment and that where the state has grown most the problem has become greatest. This story has never been particularly compelling because, for much of the post-war period, it has been so obviously contradicted by the experience of some of the biggest welfare states – in particular, Austria, Norway and Sweden – which have conspicuously succeeded in combining high levels of social expenditure and consistently low levels of unemployment. The story as it is told for the more sophisticated is that what really makes a difference to unemployment levels is the design of the unemployment benefits system. If benefits are easily available, replace a substantial proportion of earnings and are of long duration, then, so the argument goes, there will be a tendency to prefer leisure plus benefits to work plus earnings or, perhaps more realistically, for those who are unemployed to have reduced incentives to search for work. So, according to this view, what matters is not big government as such, but whether it translates into a benefits system which rewards unemployment. However, whether this factor is, indeed, a major cause of the deterioration in labour market performance in the post-war period can only be established through a broader review of the factors impacting on cross-national differences in post-war unemployment rates.

Data

The data presented in Table 6.3 are unlike those in other comparative tables in this book in being averaged over periods of between seven and five years. That is because unemployment rates are subject to rapid upward change and are cyclical in character. Since, in any one year, countries will be at different points in the cycle, single-year comparisons will tend to obscure underlying structural differences between them. In the period between 1960–66 and 1974–79, the average OECD unemployment

Comparative public policy

Table 6.3   Levels of and change in the average rate of unemployment as a percentage of total labour force, 1960–66 to 1990–94

Country	1960–66	1974–79	1990–94	Change 1960/66– 1990/94
Australia	1.9	5.0	9.5	7.6
Canada	4.9	7.2	10.2	5.3
Ireland	4.9	7.6	15.0	10.1
New Zealand	–	–	9.1	–
UK	1.4	4.2	8.4	7.0
USA	5.1	8.3	6.4	1.3
Denmark	1.7	6.1	9.0	7.3
Finland	1.4	4.4	12.0	10.6
Norway	1.0	1.8	5.6	4.6
Sweden	1.5	1.9	5.2	3.7
Austria	2.0	1.7	3.6	1.6
Belgium	2.1	5.7	9.2	7.1
France	1.2	4.5	10.5	9.3
Germany	0.7	3.4	6.9	6.2
Italy	4.9	6.6	11.1	6.2
Netherlands	1.0	4.9	6.8	5.8
Greece	5.0	1.9	8.5	3.5
Portugal	–	6.0	5.1	–
Spain	2.2	5.3	19.3	17.1
Switzerland	–	–	2.6	–
Japan	1.3	1.9	2.4	1.1
Mean	2.5	4.7	8.4	6.4
Correlation with 1960		0.55	0.29	–0.12
Coefficient of variation	67.02	45.12	47.87	

Sources and notes: Data are averages for the periods indicated and are drawn from OECD, *Historical Statistics*, Paris, various years. The figure in the final column is the percentage point change from the first to the last period. – indicates the absence of data for part or all of a particular period.

rate almost doubled and it almost doubled again in the period between 1974–79 and 1990–94. The first of these changes represents the shift from the high point of the 'Golden Age' of post-war capitalism to the economic crisis following the first oil shock. The second represents the extent to which labour market performance had deteriorated over two decades in which the entry into each successive recession was, for most countries, at a higher level of unemployment than for the previous cycle.

Unemployment is quite unlike the aspects of labour market functioning that we have already examined in that cross-national differences start out very large, and although diminishing somewhat, stay relatively large. Of all the policy outcomes analysed in this book, only divorce rates manifest higher coefficients of variation than rates of unemployment. In the 1960–66 period, five countries – Canada, Ireland, the USA, Italy and Greece – had levels of unemployment more than twice as high as any other countries in the OECD. In the aftermath of the first oil shock, there were no longer any countries so completely set apart from the rest, but, with the exception of Greece, this same grouping had rates of unemployment between 40 and 75 per cent above the average. By the early 1990s, the major change at the top end of the distribution was that the USA had ceased to be the OECD country with the highest level of unemployment and was now somewhat below the mean. Canada, Ireland and Italy, all high-unemployment nations throughout, were now joined by Finland, France and Spain.

These patterns amongst the high-unemployment nations are clearly not families of nations patterns. At first sight, the same appears to be true of the low-unemployment countries. A number of countries have been consistently below the OECD mean throughout the post-war period. They include Norway, Sweden, Austria, Japan and, despite the absence of OECD data for the entire period, Switzerland as well. As revealed by the data in Table 6.3, the nearest approach to a family resemblance was in Scandinavia for the period 1960–66, when all four countries were below the OECD mean. This was no longer true either in 1974–79 or in 1990–94, with Denmark and Finland variously close to the mean or well above it. In fact, however, Scandinavia's reputation as an area of low unemployment is not wholly apocryphal. Throughout the 1980s, Finland's unemployment rate was well below the OECD mean and, for a period during the latter part of the 1980s, Denmark's rate was also somewhat below the mean. Thus, for considerable parts of the post-war era, Scandinavia has some legitimate right to be described as an area of generally low unemployment.

Cross-national patterns of post-war unemployment are a curious mixture of stability and change. As already noted, some high-unemployment countries – Canada, Ireland and Italy – remained high-unemployment countries throughout, and some countries – Norway, Sweden, Austria and Japan – were exemplars of full employment throughout. On the other hand, the labour market experience of certain countries changed quite dramatically. The USA went from having the highest rate of unemployment to one below the mean. Greece, which started out as a high-unemployment nation in the 1960s, became, if the OECD dataset is reliable on this point, a low-unemployment country in the latter half of the 1970s, and by the 1990s had become a country of average unemployment. At the other end of the distribution, Spain went from being an average unemployment country in the 1960s to being a major outlier in the 1990s, with a rate of unemployment somewhat over twice the OECD average, while Finland, an exemplar of Scandinavian full-employment policies throughout the 1980s, became, by the mid-1990s, an OECD unemployment black spot. Neither patterns of stability nor those of change obviously conform with the trajectories of development of big government and the welfare state identified in previous chapters. Nor do they resemble the kinds of patterns located in our discussion of male and female labour supply earlier in this chapter. It seems quite probable, then, that in order to account for cross-national differences in levels and changes of unemployment, we may need to pay attention to factors which have not featured prominently in our analysis so far.

Hypotheses

Four of our standard economic and social variables are considered here. Earlier research (Glyn and Rowthorn, 1988; Korpi, 1991) has suggested a negative relationship between productivity growth and unemployment and this is tested for by looking at the association between unemployment rates and growth in real GDP per worker in the preceding period. It is also relevant to examine the proposition that unemployment is likely to be higher in those countries that are most exposed to international trade. The argument that state intervention has been in some part a response to economic vulnerability (Cameron, 1978; Katzenstein, 1985) is premised on the view that the state must step in to prevent fluctuations caused by trade exposure. A positive relationship between trade exposure and unemployment would suggest that such intervention has not always been wholly successful.

Comparative research on the correlates of post-war unemployment has also suggested that there is likely to be a strong negative relationship between unemployment and industrial employment. This relationship has been variously attributed to the impact of structural factors impeding the reassimilation of workers made redundant by economic downturn (Glyn and Rowthorn, 1988) and to the influence of industrial employment in reducing female labour supply (Mumford, 1989; Castles and Mumford, 1992). In our findings, we report the degree of association between unemployment and the relative employment shares of agriculture, manufacturing and services. Finally, we seek to assess whether religious differences have any impact on unemployment. Earlier analysis in this chapter has suggested a strong tendency for labour supply to be lower in Catholic countries, with the probable causal mechanism located in disincentives to part-time employment resulting from the tax treatment of part-time incomes in such countries. Since the availability of part-time work is also likely to be a factor reducing unemployment levels, we test for the degree of association between measures of Catholic influence, the share of part-time employment in total employment and rates of unemployment.

There are also important potential links between political factors and unemployment. Both Left and Right claim to have policy answers to unemployment, the Left through job creation schemes and active labour market policy and the Right via a more flexible or market-oriented approach to wage determination and working conditions. In many cases, the cross-national data to test for the effects of such policies are not available, so we explore the degree of association between labour market performance and partisan strength in order to establish whether such claims have any substance. Because unemployment is a cyclical phenomenon and one which has increased most spectacularly in recent decades, we do not utilize our standard cumulative measures of partisan incumbency. Rather our assumption is that labour market performance will reflect partisan influences over no more than one or two decades. The measures of partisanship used to derive our unemployment findings are, therefore, those found in the first three columns of Tables 3.3 and 3.4, with the 1974 to early 1990s reading of partisan strength doing double duty as a predictor of the average level of unemployment in 1990–94 and of change over the entire period.

The other aspects of politics which are clearly relevant to unemployment concern the role of trade unions and the institutionalization of class conflict. Economists see wages as the price paid for labour and see wage increases as a factor reducing the demand for labour. Since the main function of trade unions is wage bargaining, it may be argued that the successful use of union power will lead to higher unemployment. However, under certain circumstances unions may keep their demands within the bounds of employer capacity to meet such wage increases from productivity growth. It has been suggested that such circumstances are most likely to arise where union participation in processes of corporatist intermediation creates a predictable environment for investment decisions and some guarantee that wage claims will not be pursued in such a way as to damage wider economic interests (see Schmidt, 1982; Olson, 1982;

Bruno and Sachs, 1985; Layard, Nickell and Jackman, 1991). Despite strong correlations between corporatism and various measures of the extent of big government and the welfare state, nowhere in this study to date have we located any decisive link between the regulation of class conflict and policy outcomes. Labour market performance is the area where theory suggests that such an influence should be paramount.

Our findings also report on two other variables familiar from earlier discussion. They are European Community membership and levels of home ownership. In recent years, it has been commonplace to suggest that moves towards European integration are likely to have adverse employment effects (Streek and Schmitter, 1991; Leibfried and Pierson, 1995). Amongst possible mechanisms are the fact that EC membership rules out many of the strategies used by the smaller non-EC countries to bolster employment in the 1970s and 1980s (Therborn, 1986, 52–3) and the way in which membership in Community institutions, such as the European Monetary System, limits autonomous monetary policy initiatives (Kurzer, 1991). Turning to home ownership, it will be recalled that our earlier analysis in this chapter clearly demonstrated this factor's consistent negative impact on male labour supply throughout the post-war period. This outcome was attributed both to the positive effect of completed purchase on voluntary decisions to retire early and to the negative effect of home ownership on job-search mobility. The implication of the hypothesis to be tested here is that the mobility reducing effects of home ownership also lead to higher rates of unemployment.

Two more variables are specific to economic theories concerning the causes of unemployment. We test to establish whether there is a relationship between rates of unemployment and of inflation. Hibbs's (1977) early work on the political economy of macro-economic policy was premised on an inverse Phillips-curve relationship between these two variables, implying that full employment and monetary stability are basically incompatible aims of economic policy. However, work by Friedman (1977, 463), which sought to interpret post-oil shock developments in certain Western nations, suggested the possibility of inflation and unemployment 'mutually reinforcing' each other in a process which came to be known as stagflation. The measure of inflation used here is the average change in the consumer price index (data from OECD, 1996a) over the same span of years for which we measure unemployment rates.

We also test for a link between increased real wages and unemployment. In research on differences between the trajectories of unemployment in Australia and the USA, Gregory has noted that 'a simple macro neoclassical model would look to a different path of real wage changes in each country, relative to labour productivity, as the source of the larger unemployment increases in Australia' (Gregory, 1993, 62). Generalizing this argument to our wider cross-national context suggests that we should seek to relate levels of and changes in unemployment to changes in real earnings. Unfortunately, problems of data availability make this impossible for earlier periods, but we can use OECD (1996a) data to produce a measure of average annual change in real wages in manufacturing from 1979 to 1993. In our findings, we seek to establish the degree of relationship between this measure and both average levels of unemployment in the period 1990–94 and change in unemployment over the post-war period as a whole.

Finally, we turn to hypotheses relevant to our broad theme of how big government and the welfare state impinge on post-war labour market outcomes. We have already noted that the more unsophisticated critics of post-war state interventionism imply that high levels of state spending are associated with high levels of unemployment. For the record, there is not one single significant correlation between unemployment and the big aggregates of taxing and spending or the components of welfare spending for any time-point in the dataset. Nor is there any significant correlation for change over time. However, we would not expect to encounter such relationships and we would not expect them to make much sense if we did. The point is that unemployment is more likely to impact on taxes and expenditures than vice versa and to do so in quite conflicting ways, with some countries paying out huge sums in transfers because of high levels of unemployment and others paying out not necessarily much smaller sums on public sector job creation with the aim of containing the rise of unemployment.

Here, we examine two rather more specific mechanisms of public sector intervention and non-intervention in the labour market. First, using recently available data on expenditures explicitly targeted at active labour market intervention (see OECD, 1996d), we seek to establish whether such policies do, in fact, serve to reduce the incidence of unemployment. Since such data are only available for the period from 1980 onwards, this hypothesis can only be tested for the early 1990s time-point. We also seek to establish whether the design of unemployment benefits systems influences levels and changes in unemployment. That high replacement rates and long duration of benefit entitlement are factors increasing the incidence of unemployment is strongly argued by Layard, Nickell and Jackman (1991, 49–50), but is much more cautiously assessed by the OECD (1991, 199–226). In seeking a measure that is usable for all three periods under examination here, we roll all aspects of system design into a single indicator by dividing total benefit expenditure as a percentage of GDP by the percentage of those unemployed, thereby creating a measure of benefit per unemployed person (data on benefit expenditure from Varley, 1986 and OECD, 1996d; data on unemployment from OECD, 1996a). Those who see the role of state spending as strongly implicated in declining post-war labour market performance would expect this indicator of benefit generosity to be significantly and positively associated with both levels and changes in unemployment.

Findings

Figure 6.3(a) reveals six factors which are significantly correlated with unemployment outcomes in the period 1960–66. Corporatism, manufacturing employment, Left incumbency and inflation are all associated with lower levels of unemployment, while home ownership and Catholicism are linked to higher levels. All these relationships are in the directions hypothesized. However, contrary to hypothesis, the generosity of unemployment benefits is negatively, although negligibly, associated with unemployment levels. The best-fit model reported in Appendix 6.3 contains three terms: manufacturing employment, corporatism and trade union density. For a country with an average level of manufacturing employment, unemployment is an estimated 2.4 percentage points lower than for a country at the bottom of the manufacturing employment distribution. Calculating on the same basis, an average corporatism score reduces the estimated unemployment level by 1.5 percentage points, while an average degree of trade union density is associated with an unemployment level 1.4 percentage points higher.

Compared with the earlier period, the correlations for 1974–79 shown in Figure 6.3(b) are disappointingly weak. As previously, both corporatism and Left incumbency are negatively and significantly associated with the level of unemployment, but no other factors show up as strongly related to outcomes. It should be noted, however, that the weakness of these results is largely an artefact of the extremely low reported level of unemployment in Greece in the period 1974–79. Given that Greece had the second highest level of unemployment in the OECD in the period 1960–66, there must be at least some question of the validity of that country's unemployment data for the 1970s. Excluding Greece, the correlations for corporatism and Left incumbency are of greater magnitude, being –0.70 and –0.55 respectively. Moreover, the relationships with home ownership and manufacturing employment also become significant, the former positively and the latter negatively. Since these four factors were also those most strongly associated with 1960–66 unemployment levels, the story, leaving the Greek case to one side, seems to be one of relatively little change.

Not surprisingly, given the weakness of the correlations for the full sample, the best-fit model in Appendix 6.3 has very limited explanatory power, with corporatism the only significant predictor of unemployment levels. Excluding Greece from the analysis, the influence of corporatism becomes appreciably stronger, manufacturing employment re-enters the picture and trade exposure emerges as a marginal factor positively associated with unemployment. This variant of the model is reported in the notes to the relevant model in Appendix 6.2 and provides the basis for our estimation of the magnitudes of the real effects on unemployment. On this basis, a country with an average corporatism score had an unemployment rate 1.7 percentage points lower than a country at the bottom of the distribution. The employment-enhancing effects of manufacturing were much diminished, reducing unemployment in the average OECD nation by only 1.0 percentage point. An average level of international trade increased unemployment by 1.1 percentage points.

Figure 6.3(c) shows four significant correlations in the early 1990s. The positive link between home ownership and unemployment present throughout is now much the strongest relationship, while corporatism continues to be significantly negatively associated with outcomes. Part-time employment has become a factor significantly associated with lower levels of unemployment, while European Community membership is linked to higher levels. Our two measures of the effects of state intervention, active labour market spending and benefit generosity, do not seem to be related to outcomes to any appreciable extent. Left incumbency, which was significantly and negatively associated with outcomes in both 1960–66 and 1974–79, is now negligibly and positively related to unemployment levels. Correspondingly, the relationship between unemployment and Right incumbency has become a negative one, although remaining somewhat below the level of statistical significance.

Despite this, the negative impact of Right incumbency is the strongest term in the early 1990s model in Appendix 6.3. Other new factors featuring in the model are home ownership and the growth of real earnings, both of them positively linked to outcomes. Finally, as in each of the previous models, corporatism features as a strong negative influence on the unemployment level. The estimated effects of corporatism, Right incumbency and home ownership are of similar magnitude; making differences to the unemployment rate of 3.8, 3.6 and 3.4 percentage points respectively. The estimated impact of the average real earnings is only marginally smaller at 2.8 percentage points.

According to Figure 6.3(d), there are four factors significantly associated with post-war change in unemployment. Changes in real earnings, in levels of home ownership and in services employment are positively

(a) 1960–66

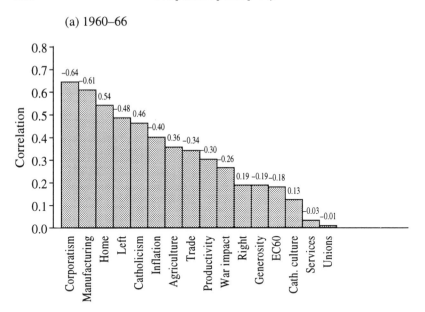

(b) 1974–79

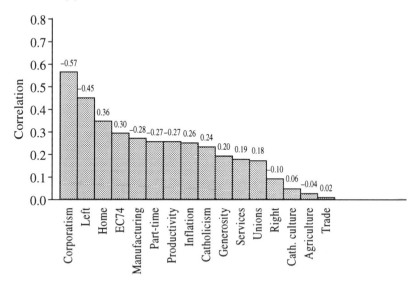

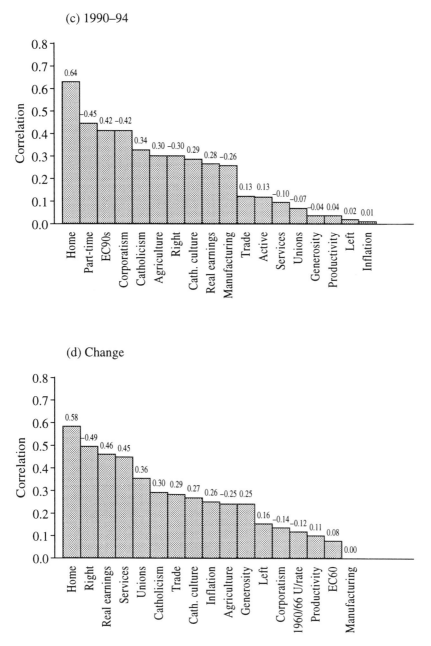

Figure 6.3 Bivariate tests: average unemployment (1960–66, 1974–79 and 1990–94 and change over time)

related to increasing unemployment, while Right incumbency is associated with somewhat better labour market performance. Despite marked cross-national differences in changing patterns of benefit generosity over the post-war period, there is no sign that this is an important factor shaping unemployment outcomes. A difference between these findings and the earlier ones for levels of unemployment is that corporatism no longer features as a significant predictor of successful labour market outcomes. Nevertheless, corporatism reappears as part of the successful change model in Appendix 6.3, along with a negative term for Right incumbency and a positive one for change in real earnings. On our standard basis for estimating the real effects of these factors, corporatism and Right incumbency have almost identical impacts, the first implying a rate of increase in unemployment lower by 3.8 percentage points and the second by 3.9 points. The unemployment-enhancing effect of increasing real wages is of comparable magnitude at 4.3 percentage points. The findings for change largely replicate those for levels of unemployment in the early 1990s, which is scarcely surprising given that these measures are themselves correlated at the 0.91 level.

Analysis

The story for the first two periods is relatively straightforward. In effect, the unemployment pattern for the 1960–66 period consisted of two virtually discrete groupings, high- and low-unemployment nations. High-unemployment nations had two things in common: their labour markets were not organized along corporatist lines and their manufacturing sectors were relatively weak. The positive finding for trade union density is much more fragile and solely dependent on the inclusion of Italy, a country in which union militancy was unconstrained by corporatist discipline. Basing our conclusions on findings excluding the anomalous Greek case, it would appear that this basic pattern of outcomes was little altered in the immediate fallout from the first oil shock. By the second half of the 1970s, the distinction between high- and low-unemployment nations was no longer as clear-cut, but corporatist institutions and a strong manufacturing sector remained the keys to successful labour market performance. The fact that, in the aftermath of the first oil shock, it was the countries that were the most dependent on international trade that were the most prone to unemployment comes as no surprise. It is worth noting, however, that, as in the majority of instances where international trade has figured significantly in our findings, this is a result which is wholly dependent on the Irish case. Overall, these results underline the extent to which the outstanding labour market performance of most OECD countries in the 'Golden Age' of post-

war capitalism depended on the conjunction of a highly dynamic manufacturing sector and an institutional structure capable of managing the
distributional struggles of an industrial society.

By the early 1990s, Germany was the only nation in the OECD with
more than 25 per cent of its active population employed in manufacturing and, as the sector progressively relinquished its role as the dynamic
source of employment growth, it ceased to be a discernible influence on
cross-national variation in unemployment. Corporatist institutions still
seemed to offer superior labour market performance, but otherwise the
factors now leading to better outcomes were those making it easier for
employers and employees to adjust to changing circumstances. This
clearly applies to the positive relationship between changes in real earnings and unemployment. The demand for labour had now seemingly
become much more price-sensitive than it had been in the 'Golden Age'
and governments finding ways of making reduced earnings growth politically acceptable could clearly reap rewards in reduced unemployment
queues. Interpreting the early 1990s finding of a positive relationship
between home ownership and unemployment in terms of obstacles to job
search similarly implies that the removal of factors impeding labour
market adjustment could pay dividends in reduced unemployment levels.
The home ownership finding should be regarded with some caution, however, since it is solely dependent on the inclusion of the Swiss case. In the
absence of that term, the early 1990s model is wholly robust and almost
identical to the change model in Appendix 6.3.

The most obvious interpretation of both the corporatism and the Right
incumbency effects is that these are factors which in different ways – via the
encompassing behaviour of trade unions or through pressure on wages
levels – serve to reduce real earnings levels. However, the lack of any significant correlation between either of these variables and real earnings growth,
together with the strong impact of a distinct real earnings term in both the
1990s and the change models, suggests that this is not the case. Rather it
would appear that these factors impact on labour markets by influencing
their mode of functioning: in the case of corporatism, by establishing some
stability of expectations based on a settlement of distributional issues at an
industrial or wider societal level and, in the case of Right incumbency, by
underwriting efforts by employers to create the basis for a more flexible or
market-determined operation of labour markets.

The problem is that stability and flexibility are not characteristics
which it is easy to combine, which is why we find a moderately strong
inverse relationship between corporatism and Right incumbency (–0.54)
and a strong empirical tendency for low-unemployment countries to
have one or other characteristic, but not both. The location of such pat-

terns in the data is not particularly novel. Calmfors and Driffill (1988) have suggested that, whilst strong corporatist institutions facilitate encompassing trade union behaviour, weak institutional co-ordination allows labour markets to clear in the manner presupposed by neoclassical theory. On the partisanship side of the equation, Alvarez, Garrett and Lange (1991) have argued that this U-shaped relationship between labour market institutions and unemployment is reinforced by party politics, with the two most successful combinations occurring when leftist governments are allied with encompassing unions or when rightist governments encounter very weak unions.

Our own account, however, is somewhat different, since, for our sample of nations, a linear specification of the influence of corporatist institutions performs better than a curvilinear one and there is no interactive effect between corporatism and Right partisanship. This latter implies that, despite the empirical tendency for high and low corporatist countries to cluster with high and low degrees of Right incumbency, the optimum scenario for low unemployment should be a combination simultaneously maximizing both of these characteristics, creating, in terms of the interpretation offered here, a situation in which stability of expectations can co-exist with labour market flexibility. In pure form this combination occurs nowhere, but the nearest approaches are Japan with a middle level of corporatism and a very high level of Right incumbency, Germany with a moderately corporatist labour market and a rather more right-wing complexion of government than most, and Switzerland with a still more institutionally regulated labour market than Germany, but with a rather more fragmented right-wing presence in politics. In these countries, which would be most commentators' choice as the post-war era's star macro-economic performers, the factors militating against unemployment are reinforcing, where elsewhere they have been, to various degrees, offsetting, leaving the success or failure of real wages policies to determine cross-national unemployment relativities.

CONCLUSION

This inquiry into the factors shaping post-war labour market outcomes has been framed in terms of a debate on the ways in which the growth of big government has impinged on the structure of incentives which make labour markets function efficiently. Previous sections of the chapter showed that the effects of increased income transfers in facilitating male exit from the labour market were somewhat outweighed by the effects of increased public consumption expenditure in promoting female entry to the labour market. That leaves a judgement of the role of state intervention in post-war labour markets substantially dependent on the manner in which the growth of government has impacted on unemployment.

However, there is little indication in our findings of any direct links between public policy and unemployment outcomes. At no point was there any significant connection between benefit generosity and the percentage unemployed. Nor, in the 1990s, was there a link between active labour market spending and lower unemployment levels. Admittedly, there may be indirect connections. There is a reasonably strong negative relationship (–0.73) between Right incumbency and benefit generosity, so it could be that where the Right is associated with favourable outcomes this is one of the reasons why. There is also a marginally significant positive relationship between corporatism and active labour market spending (0.40), which might go part of the way in accounting for these countries' capacity to counter the forces making for unemployment growth. Clearly, however, one cannot mount a strong case for the decisive influence of state intervention on effects which only occur in conjunction with other independently significant factors.

The only other potential candidate for an adverse labour market impact stemming from state intervention would be if we could somehow link trends in earnings growth to the size and growth of the state. However, such connections are by no means obvious. Countries with weak earnings growth include small welfare states, such as the USA, Australia and Canada, but they also include big welfare states such as Sweden, the Netherlands and Belgium. Countries with high earnings growth include big welfare states, such as Finland and Austria, but they also include small welfare states, such as the United Kingdom and Japan. So we are left with a story in which, of the two factors negatively linked to unemployment, one – corporatism – is strongly associated with big government and the welfare state (see Figures 4.2 and 5.1) and the other – Right incumbency – is still more strongly associated with the small state (see Appendices 4.1, 4.2 and 5.1), while the factor which is positively linked to outcomes – the growth in real earnings – is seemingly totally unrelated to the size of government. The factors influencing unemployment are either largely offsetting or unconnected to the interventionist role of the state. So, contrary to the view that the general emergence of high unemployment levels is an indictment of the growth of big government in the post-war era, the sad truth seems simply to be one of an incapacity of most governments in the period following the end of the 'Golden Age' of capitalism to find policy instruments capable of delivering desired macro-economic outcomes.

APPENDIX 6.1 MALE LABOUR FORCE MODELS

1960	Coefficient	Standard error	t-value
Intercept	118.609		
1960 social security transfers	−1.153	0.236	4.893
1960 home ownership	−0.299	0.059	5.052

Adj. R^2 = 0.612

Sources and notes: 1960 social security transfers from Table 5.1; 1960 home ownership from Table 7.1. 20 cases in regression.

1974	Coefficient	Standard error	t-value
Intercept	72.295		
1974 social security transfers	−1.247	0.202	6.185
1970 home ownership	−0.353	0.064	5.525
1974 dependency rate	1.341	0.293	4.578

Adj. R^2 = 0.691

Sources and notes: 1974 social security transfers from Table 5.1; 1970 home ownership from Table 7.1; 1974 dependency rate is the percentage of the population of 13 years and under plus the percentage of the population of 65 years and over calculated from OECD (1993a). 20 cases in regression.

1993	Coefficient	Standard error	t-value
Intercept	104.154		
Catholic cultural impact	−5.173	1.598	3.238
1993 social security transfers	−0.594	0.177	3.349
Early 1990s home ownership	−0.167	0.064	2.611

Adj. R^2 = 0.613

Sources and notes: Catholic cultural impact from Table 2.7; 1993 social security transfers from Table 5.1; early 1990s (1990) home ownership from Table 7.1. 20 cases in regession.

1960-1993 Change	Coefficient	Standard error	t-value
Intercept	0.443		
1960–early 1990s change in services employment	–0.443	0.17	2.601
Catholic cultural impact	–3.815	1.808	2.111
Early 1960s–early 1990s change in home ownership	–0.251	0.102	2.451

Adj. R^2 = 0.661

Sources and notes: 1960–early 1990s (1993) change in services employment from Table 2.4; Catholic cultural impact from Table 2.7; early 1960s–early 1990s (1990) change in home ownership from Table 7.1. 21 cases in regression.

APPENDIX 6.2 FEMALE LABOUR FORCE MODELS

1960	Coefficient	Standard error	t-value
Intercept	−62.438		
War impact	3.612	1.458	2.478
Catholic cultural impact	−9.211	3.031	3.039
1960 total fertility	−11.092	2.857	3.883
1960 1+2 gender ratio	2.748	1.109	2.477

Adj. R^2 = 0.655

Sources and notes: War impact from Table 2.1; Catholic cultural impact from Table 2.7; 1960 total fertility from Table 7.2; 1960 1+ 2 gender ratio denotes female students as a percentage of total primary and secondary grade school enrolments and is calculated from UNESCO, *Statistical Yearbook,* Paris, 1970. 21 cases in regression.

1974	Coefficient	Standard error	t-value
Intercept	97.277		
1974 Services employment	−0.735	0.263	2.795
Catholic cultural impact	−14.646	3.607	4.061
1974 Civilian public consumption expenditure	1.142	0.46	2.48
1974 total fertility	−9.713	3.245	2.993

Adj. R^2 = 0.623

Sources and notes: 1974 services employment from Table 2.4. Catholic cultural impact from Table 2.7; 1974 civilian public consumption expenditure from Table 4.3; 1974 total fertility from Table 7.2. 21 cases in regression.

1993	Coefficient	Standard error	t-value
Intercept	57.428		
Catholicism	−0.161	0.032	4.952
Early 1990s civilian public consumption expenditure	0.974	0.286	3.412
Early 1990s female unemployment	−0.554	0.2	2.774

Adj. R^2 = 0.804

Sources and notes: Catholicism from Table 2.7; early 1990s (1993) civilian public consumption expenditure from Table 4.3; early 1990s (1993) female unemployment rate from OECD, (1996a). 21 cases in regression.

1960–93 Change	Coefficient	Standard error	t-value
Intercept	59.558		
1960 female labour force	−0.953	0.123	7.764
Catholicism	−0.205	0.037	5.545
1960-Early 1990s change in civilian public consumption expenditure	1.115	0.436	2.558

Adj. R^2 = 0.811

Sources and notes: 1960 female labour force as in Table 6.2; Catholicism from Table 2.7; 1960–Early 1990s (1993) civilian public consumption expenditure from Table 4.3. 21 cases in regression.

APPENDIX 6.3 UNEMPLOYMENT MODELS

1960–66	Coefficient	Standard error	t-value
Intercept	5.257		
1960 manufacturing employment	–0.157	0.05	3.162
1960 Trade union density	0.032	0.013	2.53
Corporatism	–1.125	0.269	4.184

Adj. R^2 = 0.624

Sources and notes: 1960 manufacturing employment from Table 2.4; 1960 trade union density from Table 3.2; corporatism from Table 3.5. 17 cases in regression.

1974–79*	Coefficient	Standard error	t-value
Intercept	4.662		
Corporatism	–1.249	0.435	2.873

Adj. R^2 = 0.287

Sources and notes: Corporatism from Table 3.5. 19 cases in regression. *Re-estimating this model without Greece produces the following result: 1974–79 average unemployment = 7.944 + 0.026 (0.012) 1974 international trade –0.168 (0.073) 1974 manufacturing employment –1.748 (0.356) corporatism (figures in parentheses are standard errors). Adj. R^2 = 0.649. For discussion of the re-estimated model, see text.

1990–94	Coefficient	Standard error	t-value
Intercept	5.061		
1974–early 1990s Right cabinet seats	–0.124	0.022	5.61
Corporatism	–2.913	0.72	4.043
1990 home ownership	0.113	0.042	2.678
1979–93 change in real earnings	1.693	0.59	2.872

Adj. R^2 = 0.783

Sources and notes: 1974–early 1990s (1994) Right cabinet seats calculated from the same source as Table 3.4; corporatism from Table 3.5; 1990 home ownership from Table 7.1; 1979–93 change in real average earnings is the annual average change in real wages in manufacturing from OECD (1996a). 20 cases in regression.

1960/66–1990/94 change	Coefficient	Standard error	t-value
Intercept	9.269		
1974–early 1990s Right cabinet seats	–0.133	0.023	5.771
Corporatism	–2.903	0.609	4.77
1979–93 change in real earnings	2.602	0.596	4.368

Adj. R^2 = 0.734

Sources and notes: 1974–early 1990s (1994) Right cabinet seats calculated from the same source as Table 3.4; corporatism from Table 3.5; 1979–93 change in real average earnings is the annual average change in real wages in manufacturing from OECD (1996a). 18 cases in regression.

7. Public policy and the personal

INTRODUCTION

This chapter starts from two propositions. The first is that, during the post-war era, the arena of domestic and family life, which we here describe as the realm of the personal, has been no less subject to fundamental change than any other area discussed in this book. Taking as illustrations the topics to be discussed in this chapter, in the three or so decades following 1960, home ownership levels in the OECD nations have increased by almost 20 per cent, fertility rates have declined by somewhat over 40 per cent and divorce rates have increased by no less than 200 per cent. If home, hearth, children and marriage are the bedrock of human existence, then the post-war period has seen a dramatic transformation in the geomorphology of contemporary societies. The second proposition is that the realm of the personal is inescapably an arena of public policy. It would, indeed, be strange if, in an era when democracy has elevated the satisfaction of citizen demands to the highest law, the state did not concern itself with the preoccupations closest to the hearts of ordinary people (see Rose, 1989). Yet the idea that personal concerns are also public policy concerns is not a wholly familiar one. That is because, in such areas, the modern state treads warily. In the realm of the personal, governments do not generally seek to procure policy objectives via their own agency, but rather by establishing the ground rules or parameters of individual behaviour. In the realm of the personal, individuals are confronted by state-made incentives and prohibitions rather than by injunctions and massive bureaucracies. For this reason, it is often easy to forget the extent to which the personal realm is publicly structured.

Yet, while the idea of the personal realm as an arena of public policy is relatively unfamiliar, the notion that, during the post-war years, the state has impinged on the personal is a commonplace of political rhetoric. The distinction is largely one between intended and unintended effects. The critique of post-war state interventionism is often regarded as being at its most telling where it involves an assertion that, by reducing incentives to thrift and by weakening the bonds of marriage, big government and the welfare state have undermined the functioning of the family as the basic economic and social unit. Without that necessarily being anyone's deliberate intention, the role of the modern state in offering social protection 'from cradle to grave' is seen as having rendered the traditional verities of the domestic sphere obsolete. Such critiques are, of course, deeply morally charged, but rest on empirical assertions which can be tested. Broad categories of explanation for the transformation in the arena of domestic and family life include the economic, social and political forces that have been so influential in shaping post-war public policy generally, specific policy choices designed to alter the ground rules for personal conduct and the unintended consequences of big government. This chapter may be regarded as an attempt to disentangle which of these alternative accounts best fits the facts.

HOME OWNERSHIP

Using home ownership as an initial prism through which to focus on the factors shaping the personal realm may seem a somewhat strange choice. While the state was initially reluctant to play a major role in the housing sector, by mid-century governments in most industrialized nations had assumed a responsibility for the existence of an adequate housing stock for the majority of the population and at least some responsibility as providers of last resort for the housing needs of the poor (see Heidenheimer, Heclo and Adams, 1990). For this reason, housing policy has quite often been regarded as an integral aspect of the modern welfare state to be analysed along with income transfers, health and education. But the incidence of home ownership is a rather different matter, since, ostensibly, it represents a measure of the capacity of individuals to obtain shelter for themselves and their families without the intervention of the state. Although, as we shall see, the notion that the state is unconcerned with tenure choice is quite unrealistic, such a perception has shaped both academic and political characterizations of developments in housing markets during the post-war era. For those who have seen the proper role of the state in the housing arena as an ameliorative one, owner-occupation has been regarded as, at best, a residual category and, at worst, a factor leading to serious distortions of desirable housing outcomes (see Kemeny, 1981). For those favouring market solutions, wider home ownership has been seen as the basis for the creation of a property-owning democracy, in which the need to finance payments over the long term serves as the in-built motivational source for resistance to the further extension of the tax state. It follows that an assessment of the factors which have shaped levels and changes in the incidence of owner-occupied housing in the OECD countries is highly relevant to at least one aspect of the question of how far public policy has encroached on the realm of the personal over the course of the post-war decades.

Data

Adequate cross-national data on home ownership levels have only become available in recent years. Even so, there are important deficiencies in what we know. We do not have cross-tabulations of ownership data by house size, room numbers or available amenities, so comparisons of the extent of owner-occupation cover an extremely wide range of types of accommodation. Possibly still more important, we only have information for a small number of countries on one of the most crucial dimensions of home ownership; namely, the extent to which the equity in homes is actually owned by the householder. There are likely to be major differences in the extent to which mortgages are paid off, depending on how long owner-occupation has been the prevailing form of tenancy, with a country like Australia, in which home ownership has been the dominant form of tenure for much of this century, having an outright ownership level amongst the old of no less than 70 per cent, while the United Kingdom, a new aspirant to the title of a property-owning democracy, has a level of only 46 per cent (Whiteford and Kennedy, 1995, 79). There are likely to be still bigger differences between countries where mortgage financing is the prevalent mode of home acquisition and countries where self-construction of dwellings on owned land has been a common practice, as in Southern Europe (see Castles and Ferrera, 1996, 172–3) and, until quite recently, in Ireland.

It is important to note that the data reported in the 1970s column of Table 7.1 are, for the most part, figures for the beginning of that decade. This dispels the impression that might otherwise arise of a process of change that took place mainly in the latter decades of the post-war period. With only a few exceptions – the decline in ownership which took place in Japan in the 1960s and the increases which took place in Ireland, Italy and Portugal in the 1960s, Spain in the 1970s and the United Kingdom in the 1980s – change has tended to be both gradual and continuous. With the exception of only three nations – Japan, Switzerland and Canada – change was in the same direction: towards an expansion in ownership tenure and a decline in rental forms. In this process, countries became more alike, but not hugely so, judging by a decline in the

Table 7.1 Levels of and change in home ownership as a percentage of household tenure, 1960–early 1990s

Country	Early 1960s	1970s	Early 1990s	Change: 1960–early 1990s
Australia	63	67	70	7
Canada	66	60	64	–2
Ireland	60	71	81	21
New Zealand	69	68	71	2
UK	42	49	68	26
USA	64	65	64	0
Denmark	43	49	51	8
Finland	57	59	67	10
Norway	53*	53	59	6
Sweden	36	35	42	6
Austria	38	41	55	17
Belgium	50	55	62*	12
France	41	45	54	13
Germany	29*	36	38	9
Italy	45	50	67	22
Netherlands	29	35	44	15
Greece	67	71	77	10
Portugal	45*	57	58	13
Spain	51†	64	76	25†
Switzerland	34*	28	30	–4
Japan	71	59	61	–10
Mean	50	53	60	9
Correlation with 1960		0.91	0.77	–0.40
Coefficient of variation	27.44	24.09	22.12	

Sources and notes: Main data source is Hedman (1994). Additional data indicated by * are from Choko (1993). Data for New Zealand are from the censuses of 1961, 1971 and 1991.

† The 1960 data-point for Spain is from Oswald (1996). It is possible, however, that this figure may not be wholly consistent with other figures in the table. Although the Spanish figures for home ownership rates were used in the computations elsewhere in this book in order to maximize case numbers, the calculations in this section for both 1960 and change over time omit the Spanish case. Tests show that neither the inclusion nor exclusion of Spain in these instances influences the significance of terms in the relevant models in Appendix 7.1.

The figure reported in the final column is the percentage point change over the entire period. Data for the early 1960s are from the nearest reported data-points to 1960; for the 1970s from the nearest reported data-point to 1974; and for the early 1990s from the nearest data-points to 1990.

coefficients of variation shown in Table 7.1 of just over 20 per cent. This moderate convergence in tenure forms was accompanied by only a modest degree of catch-up. It was, however, of sufficient dimensions to diminish greatly the dramatic contrast between the countries of the New World and the Old apparent early on in the post-war period (see Castles, 1998). In 1960, the non-European OECD countries had average home ownership rates of 66.6 per cent, while the average for the European countries was a full 20 percentage points lower; three decades later, the average for the non-European countries was virtually unchanged, but the gap between Old World and New had narrowed to 8.1 percentage points.

In reality, this contrast between the New World and the Old is something of an oversimplification. A family of nations analysis suggests that there was throughout a tendency for high home ownership rates to be concentrated in countries with either extremely modern or very traditional occupational structures. The English-speaking countries of the New World fall into the first category, while the countries of Southern Europe, Ireland and, initially, Japan, fall into the second. At the beginning of the period, there were also clear family clusters elsewhere in the distribution, with the countries of continental Western Europe being characterized by much the lowest average levels of ownership and those of Scandinavia in an intermediate position. This pattern had changed little by the early 1970s, but by the early 1990s the distinctiveness of these latter groupings had disappeared, with just a few isolated countries – Sweden, Germany and the Netherlands – resisting the general trend towards majority home ownership. In this, they were joined by Switzerland, which, since the 1970s, has been the OECD country with much the lowest level of owner-occupied housing (for one account of the reasons, see McGuire, 1981, 181–2).

In terms of change, the countries of continental Western Europe have constituted the most distinctive family grouping, with a growth trend in owner-occupation consistently at or above the OECD average. However, the country manifesting the most spectacular change has unquestionably been the United Kingdom, which started out with ownership levels more typical of the continental European pattern than of the other English-speaking countries, and ended with ownership levels in excess of those in both Canada and the USA. Nor is there any doubt about the extent to which this shift was policy-driven, with privatization of council housing a key plank of Margaret Thatcher's 1979 election platform (see Forest and Murie, 1985, 97–109). That Ireland is presently the OECD country with the highest level of owner-occupation is partly a function of long-term government support for small farm proprietorship, but also owes much to a similarly motivated campaign to sell off a level of public housing stock which was second only to that of the United Kingdom.

Hypotheses

Turning to possible explanations for cross-national variation in home ownership levels, there exist some *prima facie* grounds for exploring the degree of association between tenure types and most of our standard repertoire of economic and social factors. There is no reason to suppose that wartime destruction of housing stock would have had a direct effect on the incidence of tenure types. However, there can be no doubt that a major stimulus to immediate post-war public intervention in the housing field was the need for massive reconstruction of war-damaged urban centres, leading, under circumstances of post-war shortages of building materials, to an emphasis on mass housing for rental rather than individual housing for private consumption. The explanatory potential of levels and changes in real income and productivity is no less obvious, given the extent to which ownership is dependent on the existence of an income stream sufficiently large to save over the medium to long term. If the substantial increase in OECD home ownership levels in these years was not in some way connected with the dramatic growth of the post-war economy, it would, indeed, be highly surprising.

Other measures of socio-economic modernity seem no less potentially relevant. A schematic, but by no means wholly inaccurate, historical account would suggest that private owner-constructed housing was a characteristic of pre-industrial peasant proprietorship, largely superseded, under circumstances of industrialization and urbanization, by a shift to mass housing for rental, which has, in more recent times, given way to a preference by service employees for owner-occupation in the suburbs. Such an account makes sense of the fact that, for much of the post-war period, there was a higher incidence of private housing in the modern, service economies of the English-speaking New World and the rural economies of Ireland, Japan and Southern Europe than in the manufacturing nations of continental Western Europe and Scandinavia. Finally, on empirical grounds alone – because, on every other occasion that we have located a strong similarity in the continental European family of nations, it has turned out to be associated with the prevalence of Catholic beliefs and culture – we also test to see whether religious differences have had any bearing on tenure patterns.

There is also every reason to suppose that class politics and ideological partisanship will be related to housing policy stances. In contradistinction to labour market outcomes, where parties either do not have distinctive positions or, as in the case of unemployment, claim to have identical goals, political parties in the post-war era have been strongly identified with quite different views on the state's responsibilities in respect of housing. Parties of the Left and their allies in the trade union movement have tended to see housing as an important welfare state issue, with the removal of the causes of housing poverty high on socialist agendas of welfare reform. In contrast, traditional conservatism has tended to see home ownership as intrinsically valuable in giving individuals a stake in their own society. More recently, the New Right has taken the view that homelessness stems largely from individual inadequacy and has concentrated on addressing the housing needs of the broad mass of the population through programmes offering greater access to and affordability of private housing. These differences suggest that long-term Right incumbency is likely to have been associated with high levels of home ownership and that strong unions and long-term Left incumbency are likely to have been associated with low levels. Kemeny's (1992) view that collective housing forms have been preferred to private ownership in nations manifesting strong corporatist arrangements is basically another version of the same story, given that, for Kemeny, the societal consensus on which corporatism rests is an outcome of long-term labour movement hegemony. It is possible, however, that whatever class and partisan differences in tenure forms may have existed in the early post-war decades may have diminished considerably in recent years as Left parties have recognized owner-occupation's increasing appeal to the median voter (see Papadakis and Taylor-Gooby, 1987, 152–9).

Our focus on the extent to which post-war state intervention has impacted on the realm of the personal also requires us to examine possible links between the incidence of home ownership and policy activity by the state. Such activity includes deliberate attempts to favour certain types of housing tenure at the expense of others. To cope with housing shortages or to reduce the incidence of poverty associated with homelessness, governments in many OECD countries became the builders and owners of low-cost rental housing stock on a major scale in the early post-war years. Such public housing programmes have varied in size from the 1 or 2 per cent of housing stock typical in North America to the 30 per cent plus figure for the United Kingdom. In addition, a number of governments – conspicuously those in continental Western Europe and Scandinavia – have heavily subsidized non-profit housing associations and co-operatives with a similar set of objectives.

Using United Nations Economic Commission for Europe data (1986) and data from a variety of national sources, we have compiled a measure of the percentage of dwellings completed by public and/or non-profit agencies at and around the dates figuring in our analysis, with the assumption being that the greater the role of the public and non-profit sector, the lower is likely to be the incidence of owner-occupied housing.

In 1960, the OECD average for non-private dwelling completions was 19.5 per cent of the total, with Sweden, the Netherlands, the United Kingdom and Austria all in excess of 40 per cent; in the early 1970s, the average had increased marginally to just over 20 per cent, but, by the early 1990s, it had declined to a mere 10.8 per cent. In a further attempt to capture the extent of the government's bias towards collective, non-private, provision, we have also devised a simple dummy variable based on Donnison's (1967) well-known distinction between 'comprehensive' and 'supplementary' housing strategies. The former strategy, which Donnison argues is most developed in France, Germany, the Netherlands, Norway and Sweden, emphasizes the state's responsibility for the housing needs of the community as a whole and is, therefore, hypothesized to be inversely related to the extent of private ownership.

The policy measures elaborated here are not ideal for our purposes, because they are, essentially, indicators of degrees of commitment to a strong public presence in the housing market and can only be linked to the incidence of private ownership through a logic of opposites. What we really require is a direct measure of the efforts made by many OECD governments – and, these days, by no means only right-wing ones – to encourage home ownership through a wide range of policy instruments, including mortgage interest tax relief, regulated and/or subsidized interest rates, mortgage guarantee schemes and easy-access schemes for first-time, low-income, purchasers. Sadly, no such measure exists, and my reading of the comparative housing policy literature suggests that there are insufficient data to construct a valid indicator of government support for owner-occupation for more than around half the OECD member nations even for the most recent period, with data still scarcer for earlier time-points (for the most comprehensive and up-to-date survey of policy instruments favouring owner-occupation, see Hedman, 1994, 103–16). Given that there are strong reasons for believing that the countries that have been most active in promoting home ownership are also likely to have been those least active on the public housing front, it is arguable that we should regard any evidence of an inverse relationship between owner-occupation and a commitment to a public role in housing as possibly understating the real degree to which deliberate policy action has shaped the incidence of housing tenure.

Apart from the deliberate policy actions of government in the housing arena, there is also the question of whether home ownership trends have been affected by manifestations of the post-war growth of big government. We test for this possibility using our standard procedure to examine whether there is any association between levels and changes in ownership and levels and changes in total government outlays, public consumption expenditure and social security transfers. As noted in discussing hypotheses relevant to the growth of government and the welfare state in Chapter 4, it has been suggested that, where cultural pressures in favour of home ownership are strong, voters may resist the tax imposts required to build an extensive welfare state edifice (Kemeny, 1980 and 1981). A more benign variant of this argument sees saving for home ownership and public provision of earnings-related pensions as alternative mechanisms of life-cycle redistribution, with the reduced need for income in old age resulting from owner-occupation leading to a lesser demand for generous welfare state provision for the aged (Castles and Ferrera, 1996; Castles, 1998).

Although our earlier findings demonstrated strong inverse relationships between home ownership and most dimensions of taxing and spending in the immediate post-war decades, the ownership term failed to feature in any of the best-fit models in Chapters 4 and 5. One possible reason for that might be that the hypothesized trade-off between ownership and public welfare expenditure has worked primarily the other way around (see Schmidt, 1989), with a heavy commitment of national resources to public purposes making it difficult for any but the most affluent of tax-payers to contemplate the high costs of private ownership. Articulated in this way, the hypothesis would seem to fit with the observed tendency of continental European and Scandinavian welfare states to manifest low ownership rates in the early post-war decades, but to show some signs of catch-up as increasing income levels allowed a larger percentage of the population to purchase housing at the same time as paying their dues to the welfare state.

Finally, we examine two more specific mechanisms related to the finance of house purchase. First, we use the measure of change in real earnings introduced in Chapter 6 as a more focused way of establishing the link between increasing income levels and increasing levels of home ownership. The hypothesis is that increasing real wage levels encourage new entrants into the private housing market because they provide an enhanced capacity to save. As previously, we only possess adequate cross-national data for this measure for the most recent period and so can only test this hypothesis for the early 1990s and for change over time. Second, we test if there is a relationship between inflation and levels and changes in the extent of owner-occupied housing. Under circumstances of rapidly increasing price levels, mortgage repayments tend to decline as a proportion of income, while the net value of housing assets purchased tends to increase as a direct function of inflation. The overall result is to reward house purchasers over tenants and mobile owner-occupiers over stationary ones and to effect a major transfer of wealth from lenders to borrowers (see Headey, 1978, 27; Maclennan, 1982, 188–93). According to this hypothesis, it is far from coincidental that the three countries with the greatest increases in home ownership levels – the United Kingdom, Italy and Ireland – were simultaneously amongst the countries with the highest sustained levels of post-war inflation and that the two countries in which the change in ownership levels was least – Japan and Switzerland – were the amongst the nations with the lowest levels of inflation.

Findings

According to Figure 7.1(a) there are seven factors significantly correlated with the level of home ownership in 1960. These correlations are all negative and fall into three distinct categories: measures indicative of specific policy stances in the housing field (that is, non-private dwellings completed and comprehensive housing strategy), measures capturing aspects of the growth of government (that is, social security transfers and the outlays of government) and measures tapping various aspects of the social and political context of tenure choice (that is, manufacturing employment, corporatism and Christian Democratic incumbency). Although, in this instance, the relationships are not significant, it is interesting to note that ideology and outcomes are linked in the manner hypothesized, with the Left negatively associated with ownership levels and the Right positively.

The best-fit model reported in Appendix 7.1 contains three terms – manufacturing employment, Catholic cultural impact and non-private dwellings completed – all with negative coefficients. In substantive terms, the really big effect is that of manufacturing employment, which, for the average OECD country, reduces private ownership by an estimated 19.7 percentage points. The estimated impact of non-private investment in dwelling construction is a third of that size, with an average reduction in ownership levels of 6.6 percentage points. Catholic cultural impact is, of course, a dummy variable, so the notion of an average effect is meaningless, but the difference between a country categorized in this manner and one which is not is 12.5 percentage points.

Contrasting the findings of Figures 7.1(a) and (b) shows that all the correlations significant in 1960 remain significant a decade later and that, in general, the magnitude of the relationships is little changed. There are, however, a number of additional factors significantly associated with outcomes. Links with ideological partisanship have become stronger and the association with the Left, but not the Right, is now of significant proportions. As a counterpoint to the continuing negative connection with

(a) 1960

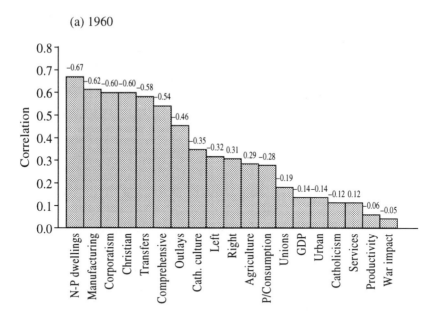

(b) 1970s

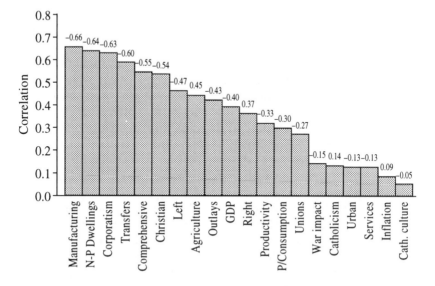

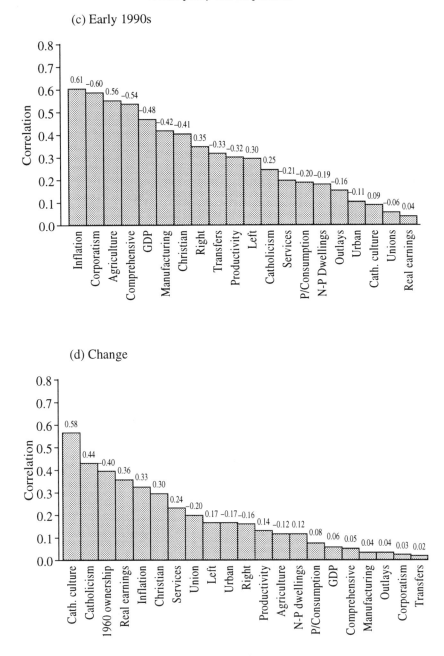

Figure 7.1 Bivariate tests: home ownership rates (1960, 1970s and early 1990s and change over time

manufacturing employment, agricultural employment is now positively and significantly associated with private ownership. It is presumably this link with agriculture in the poorer countries of Southern Europe that accounts for the marginally significant negative relationship with GDP per capita, which contradicts the hypothesis that access to private housing is likely to be a function of income levels. Despite the fact that the main correlations are largely unchanged, the 1970s model reported in Appendix 7.1 is markedly different from that for 1960. Manufacturing employment represents the only element of continuity, but the links with Catholic cultural impact and non-private dwellings are replaced by negative relationships with corporatism and comprehensive housing policy. Comparing countries at the bottom of the distribution and those with average values, manufacturing employment makes an estimated difference of 12.7 percentage points and corporatism of 5.9 points. Comprehensive housing policy is a dummy variable, with countries in this category having an estimated 9.6 percentage points lower home ownership than countries in the supplementary category.

The picture for the early 1990s as shown in Figure 7.1(c) is a mixture of continuity and change. Continuity is represented by the continuing significant negative associations with corporatism, comprehensive housing policy, Christian Democratic incumbency and manufacturing employment. Change is apparent in the fact that inflation has now become a strong and positive predictor of outcomes, that the links with agricultural employment and GDP are now stronger than those with manufacturing employment, and that non-private dwelling construction is no longer connected to outcomes to any noticeable degree. Further changes include the fact that measures of the growth of big government are no longer correlated with tenure type and that Left incumbency has become positively, although not significantly, associated with ownership levels. The early 1990s model in Appendix 7.1 contains only two terms and accounts for only just over half the cross-national variation. The most significant term is for the positive impact of inflation, which, calculating in the normal way, made for an estimated average increase of ownership of 9.7 percentage points. The estimated effect of corporatism was to reduce ownership levels by an average of 8.2 percentage points.

According to Figure 7.1(d) only three factors are significantly correlated with changes in home ownership levels over time. A moderately strong positive association with Catholic cultural impact and a modest one with Catholicism are clearly picking up on the substantial growth of owner-occupation in Southern Europe, Ireland and the countries of continental Western Europe. The same story is also told by the marginally significant negative relationship between the initial level of ownership in 1960 and change thereafter. Both earnings growth in the 1980s and inflation levels over the post-war period as a whole are positively associated with outcomes at a level somewhat below that of statistical significance. However, both of these terms feature as important predictors in the change model in Appendix 7.1, along with the positive impact of Catholic cultural impact and the negative influence of change in manufacturing employment. The latter finding needs interpreting in light of the general post-war OECD decline in manufacturing employment, so that the story is of greater increases in private home ownership in those countries in which manufacturing was declining most precipitously. The estimated average effects of real earnings growth, inflation and change in manufacturing employment are 5.7, 8.9 and 11.5 percentage points respectively. The positive impact of Catholic cultural impact is 14.2 percentage points which, given that the negative effect of the same variable in the 1960 model was 12.5 percentage points, means that Catholic nations now had marginally higher home ownership levels than the rest of the OECD.

Analysis

Earlier we noticed that the level of non-private dwelling construction was almost halved in the two decades following 1970. The underlying reason for this retreat from a public role in the direct provision of housing is immediately apparent in our findings. Above all, the impetus to public intervention in the immediate post-war decades was the rise of manufacturing as the dominant source of employment growth in the latter years of the 'Golden Age' of capitalism. The growth of industry on a mass scale necessarily involves the relocation and housing of populations on a corresponding scale and, arguably, manufacturing employment here stands as a surrogate for a measure of urbanization which was conceded to be inadequate for the purposes of cross-national comparison (see discussion in Chapter 2). Under circumstances aggravated in many countries by wartime damage and post-war shortages of building materials, it was necessary for governments to play a major part in catering for the housing needs of those migrating to the factory centres of Western Europe, both from rural hinterlands and from Southern Europe and former colonial dependencies. But, as we observed in Chapter 2, the high point of manufacturing as a source of employment in OECD countries was between 1960 and the mid-1970s. With manufacturing on the decline in the years following the first oil shock, demand for mass housing in new locations decreased, and with it much of the rationale for an activist role for the state as a direct provider of housing.

Apart from the hugely influential role of manufacturing in the earlier periods, the two factors revealed by Figures 7.1(a) to (d) as consistently associated with outcomes throughout are corporatism and Christian Democratic incumbency. Whilst these factors may, at first glance, seem strange bed-fellows, the empirical link is undoubted, with a strong tendency for Christian partisanship to flourish in the same countries of continental Western Europe – Austria, Belgium, Germany and the Netherlands – in which class conflict has been most muted. Since the key to electoral success for Christian Democratic parties has been to dissolve the class antagonisms that feed ideological partisanship, the connection is almost certainly much more than accidental. Examination of the correlations between the independent variables also reveals significant positive associations between corporatism and a comprehensive housing policy stance and between corporatism and the completion of non-private dwellings in both the earlier periods, suggesting greater consistency in the models than appears on the surface and indicative of a strong tendency for countries seeking to minimize class conflict to pursue policies focusing on the housing needs of all classes of citizens.

An apparent anomaly in the findings for 1960 is the strong negative link between home ownership and Catholic cultural impact. This seems odd, given that Christian Democratic incumbency is far more strongly correlated with outcomes than is Catholic cultural impact. However, the reason for the non-appearance of Christian Democracy in the successful model is that the Christian Democratic countries all have high levels of non-private dwelling construction, so that it is this latter policy characteristic, shared by these nations and certain countries in Scandinavia, which is singled out as the common antecedent of exceptionally low ownership levels.

That leaves the question of why Catholic countries should, in general, have had lower levels of owner-occupation than other OECD nations in the early post-war years. Whilst Catholic policy initiatives are generally of a kind which seek to mute class antagonisms, there would appear to be nothing intrinsic in Catholic beliefs which would suggest a preference for non-private forms of tenure. Indeed, the subsequent significant growth of ownership levels in these countries suggests that what we are dealing with here is not a matter of preferences, but of historical contingencies. That a majority of these countries were situated in the area which was simultaneously the cockpit of hostilities in World War II and the epicentre of the post-war manufacturing boom is clearly a part of the explanation for the earlier trend. The end of post-war housing shortages and the shift to services employment in these countries from the 1970s onwards helps to account for their catch-up in recent decades.

Catholic catch-up apart, the story of post-war growth in home owner-ship is quite easy to tell. The decline in manufacturing from the mid-1970s onwards implied a lesser need for mass housing and fostered a shift to the suburbs, while increases in real earnings and the fillip given to mortgage borrowing by inflation account for other aspects of the change. The influ-ence of real earnings suggests that the demand for home ownership, as for any other consumption good, tended to increase with increasing real income levels. By the early 1990s, specific measures of housing policy stance no longer feature as part of the best-fit model, although the persistence of the corporatism term may be indicative of the extent to which the co-operative housing forms typical of such countries had become institu-tionalized over half a century. Clearly, in most of the countries where immediate post-war government intervention in the housing sector had led to a substantial level of direct public ownership, there was a much lesser reluctance to roll back the boundaries of the state. However, even in corpo-ratist nations, there has been a marked decline in the degree of state activism in the field of direct housing provision, as governments of all com-plexions have sought to cope with the housing needs of the poor through standard income transfer mechanisms, such as housing allowances, rather than by direct subsidies to housing production (see Heidenheimer, Heclo and Adams, 1990, 110–18).

The massive retreat from policies designed to promote a non-private housing sector has been accompanied by an equivalent decline in linkages between the size of the state and the extent of owner-occupation. In the early post-war period, as Kemeny has argued, public expenditure and home ownership were strongly inversely related, but, over time, these rela-tionships have weakened and there is no indication in our findings that the growth of home ownership has proceeded more slowly in those countries in which the public sector has expanded most strongly. Thus, precisely con-trary to the views of those who have seen the rise of big government in the post-war era as forcing back the boundaries of the personal, what has hap-pened in the arena of housing provision has been a process of disengagement and declining influence. Indeed, the prevailing policy stance has become one of a benign neglect of the whole area. Housing is no longer on the front-burner of political concern, as it was in the early post-war decades. Welfare state responses are now largely restricted to systems of housing allowances and rental supplements, while, in the area of home ownership, the state tries to juggle the cost of subsidies to owner-occupation with the electoral risk of abandoning them. Whatever else the housing story proves, it proves that the rise of big government is not ineluctable. Governments got into the housing business reluctantly and they do not appear to be too concerned that, in this area at least, the latter part of the post-war era has seen a decline in their responsibilities.

FERTILITY

Fertility is one of those arenas in which we must be constantly aware that the cross-national methodology we employ only allows us to arrive at conclusions about the factors associated with aggregates of behaviour and not about the forces shaping individual decisions. However, from a policy perspective, it is aggregates that matter. Governments are not generally interested in the number of children born to particular families, but are deeply concerned that population neither increases so rapidly that it is a drain on a nation's resource base nor declines so precipitously that it imperils national viability. The former has been the 'population problem' for most Third World nations in the contemporary era. The latter is likely to be the 'population problem' for the vast majority of advanced nations in the years ahead.

Nor is it only in regard to policy concerns that aggregates matter. Most policy solutions are likely to have the same character: they are not targeted at individual families, but designed to alter the decision-making parameters of whole populations so as to tip the balance in favour of desired outcomes. Legalizing contraceptive devices allows all individuals in a given population to avail themselves of their use if they so wish. Establishing entitlements to parenting benefits allows those women who so wish the option of combining labour force participation and maternity. In the realm of the personal, as we have already noted, most governments seek to constrain their citizens rather than to compel them. Finally, if the post-war growth of the state has been a factor undermining the fabric of family life and, hence, altering the parameters within which the fertility choices of individual families are made, the only way we can find out is by looking at differences in national aggregates. Whilst it is certainly arguable that the links between fertility and economic and social factors may be better established by analysis at the individual level, that is not the case where the imputed role of the state is as the undifferentiated context for citizen behaviour. Here, as elsewhere in this volume, the only available strategy is cross-national analysis of aggregate outcomes.

Data

At present levels of mortality, the rate of fertility at which a population will replace itself is slightly below 2.1 children per woman. According to Table 7.2, in 1960, at the height of the so-called 'baby boom' in the West, the average fertility rate of the countries under examination here exceeded the replacement rate by a substantial margin, with only Japan falling below that level. In 1974, however, the average fertility rate was

Table 7.2   Levels of and change in total fertility rates (average number of children per woman aged 15–44), 1960–93

Country	1960	1974	1993	Change: 1960–93
Australia	3.48	2.02	1.87	–1.61
Canada	3.90	1.88	1.66	–2.24
Ireland	3.73	3.72	1.93	–1.80
New Zealand	4.24	2.58	2.10	–2.14
UK	2.69	1.81	1.76	–0.93
USA	3.65	1.84	2.04	–1.61
Denmark	2.54	1.90	1.75	–0.79
Finland	2.71	1.62	1.82	–0.89
Norway	2.90	2.10	1.86	–1.04
Sweden	2.13	1.89	2.00	–0.13
Austria	2.69	1.74	1.48	–1.21
Belgium	2.58	1.80	1.62	–0.96
France	2.73	1.93	1.65	–1.08
Germany	2.36	1.51	1.28	–1.08
Italy	2.41	2.30	1.21	–1.20
Netherlands	3.12	1.66	1.58	–1.54
Greece	2.28	2.40	1.34	–0.94
Portugal	3.01	2.60	1.46	–1.55
Spain	2.86	2.79	1.24	–1.62
Switzerland	2.44	1.70	1.48	–0.96
Japan	2.00	2.05	1.46	–0.54
Mean	2.88	2.09	1.65	–1.23
Correlation with 1960		0.37	0.55	–0.90
Coefficient of variation	21.06	24.38	16.23	

Sources and notes: Data for 1960 and 1974 are from World Health Organization, *World Health Statistics Annual*. WHO, Geneva, 1993. Data for 1993 from Monnier and Guibert-Lantoine (1996). The figure reported in the final column is the decline in the average number of children per woman aged 15–44 between 1960 and 1993.

almost exactly 2.1, with only six countries exceeding that figure. By 1993, the average had declined to 1.65, with New Zealand now the only OECD country able to maintain its population level in the long term without migration from outside. This means that the majority of Western states face drastic population decline in coming decades. Indeed, a recent paper suggests that, given the maintenance of 1995 fertility rates over a span of 100 years, Italy's population will be only 14 per cent of what it is now, with corresponding figures of 15, 17 and 28 per cent for Spain, Germany and Japan respectively (McDonald, 1997, 2).

It might be argued that, on the record of the figures in Table 7.2, there is no particular reason to assume that fertility rates will be unchanging. As indicated by a correlation of only 0.37 between fertility outcomes in 1960 and 1974, there is no other area of policy discussed in this book in which change in the character of the cross-national distribution has been as great as in the case of fertility. However, whilst that changeability is amply confirmed by an even smaller correlation between 1974 and 1993 fertility rates of just 0.07, the general trend has been towards a continued reduction in fertility and, hence, towards an aggravated prospect of population decline. The other noteworthy feature of the statistical summary in Table 7.2 is the correlation of –0.90 between initial fertility level and change over time, indicative of catch-up on a scale greater than for any other of the policy outcomes featuring in this analysis. The post-war story, therefore, is not merely one of a strong downward trend in fertility, but of a decline in almost exactly inverse proportion to the level of fertility at the beginning of the period. Over more than three decades, these changes were conducive to some degree of convergence amongst nations, but, as indicated by the reduction in the coefficient of variation, of a quite surprisingly modest nature.

Turning to the families of nations patterns revealed by the data in Table 7.2, we find a picture no less changeable than that shown in the summary statistics. In the immediate post-war years, the cluster of nations in which fertility rates were consistently highest was the overseas English-speaking family. Other groupings did not have distinct fertility profiles and it is interesting to note that the poorest OECD countries were to be found at both the high (Ireland, Portugal) and the low (Greece and Japan) ends of the distribution. By the mid-1970s, the pattern had been radically transformed. Ireland was now the country in which fertility was highest, but, otherwise, the grouping at the high end of the distribution was constituted by the countries of Southern Europe. Apart from New Zealand, with a continuingly high rate of fertility, the overseas English-speaking nations now clustered somewhat below the mean. While the tail of the distribution remains indistinct in family of nations terms, a number of the countries in which fertility was lowest were to be found in continental Western Europe.

In families of nations terms, the story is at its clearest towards the end of the period. In the 1990s, all the countries in both the English-speaking and Scandinavian groups have values above the mean and all the countries in the continental Western and Southern European groups have values at or below the mean. The latter grouping, together with Italy, now constitutes a distinct Mediterranean region of exceptionally low fertility. In respect of change over time, the overseas English-speaking family of nations, in which the early post-war 'baby boom' had boomed most loudly, was the grouping in which fertility declined most drastically in absolute terms. The Scandinavian family of nations was that in which fertility decline had been least pronounced.

Hypotheses

The classical account of the determinants of fertility behaviour is to be found in a 'demographic transition theory' which links the decline of fertility to the process of socio-economic modernization (for a review of the literature, see van de Kaa, 1996). In its broadest formulation, the theory suggests that the forces of modernization lead to a reduction in disease and mortality, making it possible for families to reduce their fertility without any consequent decline in the number of children surviving until maturity (for a recent exploration of these themes, see Chesnais, 1992). This focus suggests the potential relevance of a number of the factors discussed in Chapter 2, including levels of economic development, changing occupational structure and urbanization, all of which we might expect to be negatively associated with fertility rates. The same applies to education, which has been regarded as a crucial aspect of the modernization process, conducive both to a widening of horizons beyond the ambit of the family and to a knowledge of the birth control techniques required to limit family size (Andorka, 1978, 259–65). We test this hypothesis with data on the percentage of the female population enrolled in primary and secondary education (data from UNESCO, *Statistical Yearbook*, various years).

A huge volume of post-war research has both elaborated and contested the demographic transition perspective. Of particular interest have been models which have analysed fertility choices in terms of a micro-economic logic of consumer demand (see Fulop, 1977; Becker, 1991). Because such models hypothesize that the demand for children is in principle akin to the demand for consumption goods, they imply the possibility that increased income will have a positive impact on fertility. Although such an account conflicts with the long-run trend towards smaller family size in advanced countries, it does offer potential insights into the immediate post-war fertility increase in many Western countries and into the fact that this 'baby boom' was most pronounced in the wealthiest nations. Within the micro-economic framework, it has been possible to reconcile the view that consumption is a direct function of income with the fact of long-term fertility decline through arguments which suggest that, as income rises, other goods are likely to be substituted for children or that quality of children (that is, the costs attached to child rearing) will be substituted for increased quantity (Hawthorn, 1980, 285). In effect, these models leave open the question of the relationship between income and fertility likely to be observed at any particular time.

Research in the demographic transition mode has also been challenged by findings which point to the significance of factors relating to cultural heritage, language and the historical experience of particular populations defined by nationality or by region (see Coale and Watkins, 1986). Here we consider three such factors – religious belief, wartime experience and home ownership – which in varying degrees cut across the socio-economic modernization dimension of the post-war transformation. The potential influence of religious belief on fertility rates has been a traditional preoccupation of demographers, a routine hypothesis being that Catholic families will be larger either because of a stronger commitment to traditional values or because of specific religious injunctions against contraceptive use. The evidence of numerous survey studies of national populations is quite mixed (Andorka, 1978, 298–324), but substantial differences in the extent of Catholic adherence across the OECD area (see Table 2.7 above) make this a natural hypothesis to test in a cross-national context. Major historical events, such as war, can also deeply influence population outcomes. The high mortality rates and markedly decreased male life expectancy in Central and Eastern Europe following the fall of communism are contemporary instances (Standing, 1996, 235). In what follows, we test to see whether there is evidence of a comparable fertility decline amongst populations experiencing or brought up in the shadow of the traumas of World War II. Finally, under this heading, we consider the possibility that cultural preferences for home ownership may be a source of differential fertility behaviour. This hypothesis rests on the argument that the cramped living conditions characteristic of much of the mass housing stock built for rental in the early post-war years was not conducive to large families.

A factor widely recognized as a crucial determinant of fertility rates is the extent of female labour force attachment (Kupinsky, 1977; Blau and Ferber, 1992). In our discussion of female participation, we noted that the general consensus of the literature was of an inverse and reciprocal relationship between labour force attachment and fertility, but that more recent data, demonstrating the co-existence of high levels of participation and fertility in Scandinavia and some of the English-speaking nations, suggested that this relationship might no longer hold. There has been some speculation as to the reasons for such a change. Earlier, we noted the potential role of feminist ideas in dispelling a cultural inheritance which had denied women access to the labour market. Esping-Andersen (1996, 7–8) implies a change of a similar character, when he points out that 'women's economic independence [has become] a defining element of postindustrial society'. Starting from a family-centred rather than a labour market perspective, McDonald (1997) has argued that traditional breadwinner models of the family have been progressively giving way to 'partnership' models in which roles and responsibilities for paid work and parenting are shared. All of these views have in common the supposition that there has been a fundamental transformation in the underlying parameters of women's choice between work and family: where once work was a subsidiary priority and organized to fit in with family obligations, now family is, at best, a priority of co-equal importance to be organized around women's work and career aspirations.

Under such circumstances, what is likely to determine a woman's fertility behaviour is her capacity to find ways of combining work and maternity, with the default options being to work without having children or to delay fertility until such time as these priorities can be better reconciled. This is where the welfare state comes in both as a provider of employment, often with superior maternity conditions attached, or as a provider of maternity and/or parental benefits. The former category of benefits is, of course, a traditional kind of population policy measure, with the goal being to induce women to withdraw from the labour force in order to have children. Parental benefits are one of the newest categories of income transfers, and are explicitly designed to make it possible for women to combine continuing labour force affiliation with childbearing and child rearing activities. This new variant of population policy was first adopted in Hungary in 1967 (Andorka, 1978, 296) and was introduced in Sweden in 1974. With varying degrees of generosity, such benefits are now available in a majority of OECD nations (see OECD, 1995a).

Unfortunately, it is as yet impossible to disaggregate national accounts statistics in such a way as to separate out different categories of family cash benefits, so here, apart from our standard measures of the growth of big government, our main indicator of the impact of state intervention on fertility behaviour is a measure of the replacement rate of family cash payments in different nations. This variable, for which data are only available for the early 1990s, is constructed by dividing the percentage of GDP spent on child benefits by the percentage of the population constituted by children under the age of 13 years (data from OECD 1993a and 1996d). Countries spending 0.10 or more per cent of GDP for each per cent of the population below this age include Sweden (0.15), Finland (0.14), Austria (0.13), Norway (0.13), Belgium (0.12), France (0.11) and Denmark (0.10). This mixture of Social Democratic, Scandinavian and French-speaking nations suggests that welfare state generosity to children derives not only from modern employment-focused motives, but also from more traditional natalist objectives.

Apart from female labour force participation itself and the measure of child benefit generosity, we include in our analysis a number of other variables with some relevance to the possible transformation of the relationship between women's work and fertility. In discussing female labour force participation, we earlier suggested that our measures of Catholic influence might stand as proxies for policies, ranging from the tax treatment of part-time work to the availability of day care places, facilitating or hindering female labour force participation. This implies the quite radical possibility that, given the transformed trade-off between work and family, Catholic influence may actually serve as a deterrent to high fertility, with women viewing policies which make it difficult to continue employment after childbirth as reasons for not having children at all or, at least, for limiting family size. We also explore the association between two labour market variables which may condition the possibility of women combining work and family. One is the availability of part-time employment, which may be seen as the ideal vehicle for combining work and family roles and hence as a likely positive influence on fertility. The other is female unemployment, which, in so far as it creates further obstacles to the realization of women's work aspirations, may be regarded as a factor deterring women from embarking on maternity.

Finally, we turn to the possibility that technological innovation may have influenced family size in the post-war period via the development and diffusion of access to reliable clinical and supply methods of contraception (the pill, condom, diaphragm, IUD, and so on). Whilst demographers tend not to regard contraceptive practice as amongst the ultimate sources of fertility decline, differences in the effectiveness of traditional and modern methods mean that, during the period of transition from one to the other, the nature of the practices adopted in different countries is likely to have had a major effect on fertility levels (van de Kaa, 1996, 404). In order to test for this possibility, we have devised a simple measure of contraceptive practice. Because data are not available for the 1960s, and because, by the 1990s, clinical and supply methods were very widely diffused throughout the OECD, this measure is used only for the mid-1970s, when national diversity was at its greatest. The measure employed here involves a simple scale, with a value of 0 for countries with legal barriers to the dissemination of contraceptive devices (Ireland and Spain), of 1 for countries in which contraceptive practice was primarily of a traditional character (Belgium, France, Italy, Portugal) and of 2 for countries in which more than 50 per cent of contraceptive use involved clinical and supply methods (all the remaining OECD countries, bar Greece, for which no data are available) (data from United Nations, 1984, 1989a, 1989b). Our hypothesis is that there is likely to be a strong inverse relationship between this measure and OECD fertility levels in the mid-1970s.

Findings

Cross-national studies of the factors associated with socio-economic modernization are generally at their most persuasive when the contrast is between large numbers of countries at highly disparate levels of development. Sometimes, however, such relationships cannot be located in sub-sets of nations with more similar attributes (see Castles and McKinlay, 1979, 184; Castles, 1997a, 150–51). Certainly, were we to judge the validity of demographic transition theory only on the basis of findings for the OECD nations *circa* 1960, we would find that paradigm seriously wanting. Figure 7.2(a) shows that, instead of measures of modernization being negatively associated with fertility outcomes as the theory suggests, levels of real GDP per worker, services employment and female educational enrolment are all positively and significantly related to fertility rates. Moreover, although at levels well below that of statistical significance, the relationships between fertility and real GDP per capita, agricultural employment and urbanization have signs opposite to those implied by the modernization paradigm. Turning to factors which do not feature as part of the transition model, we do find some relationships which conform with our earlier hypotheses. As previously established, there is a significant inverse relationship between fertility and female labour force participation and, in addition, there is a positive and significant association with home ownership. Finally, we note a negative correlation with wartime experience, which is only marginally below the level of statistical significance.

Appendix 7.2 reports a three-factor model of fertility outcomes in 1960 in which productivity and home ownership are positive terms and female labour supply a negative one. Gauging the real impact of these factors in our usual way by estimating the difference in outcomes between a nation at the OECD mean value and one at the bottom of the distribution, the estimated effects of real GDP per worker and of home ownership are fertility rates respectively 0.47 and 0.42 of a point higher than they would otherwise be. For the average OECD country, the estimated effect of female labour force participation is a fertility rate 0.58 of a point lower than it would otherwise be.

(a) 1960

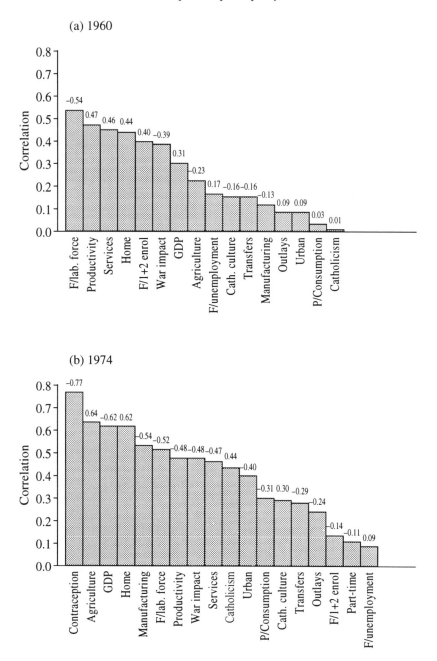

(b) 1974

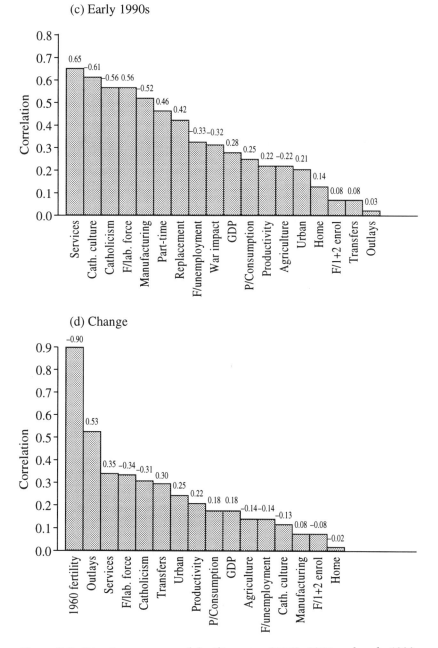

Figure 7.2 Bivariate tests: total fertility rates (1960, 1974 and early 1990s and change over time)

By the mid-1970s, the association between the indicators of socio-economic modernization and fertility rates had been utterly transformed. The findings in Figure 7.2(b) indicate a picture almost completely in conformity with the postulates of demographic transition theory. Agricultural employment is now strongly positively associated with fertility levels, while real GDP per capita, real GDP per worker, manufacturing employment, services employment and urbanization are all negatively and significantly associated with outcomes. Of possible measures of modernity, only the negative relationship with educational enrolment is of negligible magnitude, almost certainly because by this date gender-related differences in school enrolments were much diminished. There are also a number of new factors which emerge as important. Contraceptive practice obviously made a huge difference between these countries in the mid-1970s, tying in with an emergent positive relationship between fertility levels and Catholic influence. Under the surface of transformed socio-economic relationships and culturally related differences in the take-up of contraceptive technology, there remain some points of continuity, with home ownership and female labour force participation linked to outcomes in much the same ways as they had been in 1960, and with the apparent negative influence of wartime experience actually slightly greater than it had been previously.

The model for 1974 identified in Appendix 7.2 contains four factors. Having previously been positively associated with outcomes, productivity is now a negative factor. The terms for female labour supply and home ownership remain as before. Quite surprisingly, given that our focus is on outcomes three decades down the track, the negative association with wartime experience emerges as the single most significant parameter of cross-national fertility difference in this period. Real GDP per worker is associated with a fertility rate estimated to be 0.40 of a point lower in an average OECD country than in one at the bottom of the productivity distribution. Home ownership makes a positive difference of 0.30 of a point and female labour force participation a negative one of 0.33 of a point. Fertility rates in the former Axis countries are estimated to be 0.20 of a point lower than in those nations occupied during the course of the war, 0.41 of a point lower than in the countries which were victorious and 0.61 of a point lower than in those countries which had remained neutral.

Figure 7.2(c), providing correlations for the early 1990s, demonstrates changeability on a scale comparable to that of the preceding period. Most of the modernization variables again have reversed signs, although many have now ceased to be of significance. The big exception is manufacturing employment, which continues to be strongly negatively associated with fertility. Services employment, on the other hand, has reverted to the positive correlation that it manifested in 1960 and has actually become the strongest factor identified in Figure 7.2(c). Other changes are no less dramatic. Having previously been consistently, negatively and significantly correlated with fertility, female labour supply is now positively and significantly associated with outcomes. The measures of Catholic influence make reversals of almost similar magnitude. On a somewhat more modest scale, both home ownership and wartime experience cease to be associated with early 1990s fertility rates. New positive correlates of fertility rates in the early 1990s are the extent of part-time employment and the replacement rate of family benefits.

The early 1990s model to be found in Appendix 7.2 is quite unlike those which preceded it and challenges many of the standard hypotheses in the field. The model does contain a modernity term, but it is indicative of the negative impact of manufacturing employment, and can only be interpreted as conforming with the demographic transition theory if we wholly ignore the fact that the real contrast is with the high levels of fertility associated with services employment. Moreover, flying in the face of all orthodoxy concerning cultural influences on family size, Catholic cultural impact now features as a negative predictor of outcomes. In the model identified in Appendix 7.2, the nearest thing to a conventional finding is the positive effect of high family cash replacement rates. A country with the OECD average level of manufacturing employment has an estimated fertility rate 0.18 of a point lower than the country with the lowest level. Countries in the Catholic cultural impact category are estimated to have fertility rates 0.22 of a point lower than countries which are not. The average family cash benefit replacement rate leads to an estimated outcome 0.15 of a point higher than it would otherwise be.

Figure 7.2(d), summarizing correlations with change in fertility rates, features the huge catch-up effect already discussed previously. Otherwise, the only significant factor is change in outlays. Given the strong tendency of the rhetoric critical of the growth of big government to view state intervention as a factor undermining traditional family values, it is interesting to note that this finding is positive: that increased outlays of government go along with relatively weak post-war fertility decline. Although not significant, the signs on most of the socio-economic terms contradict the implications of demographic transition theory, with increasing modernization associated with lesser rates of decline in fertility. Similarly conflicting with standard cultural interpretations of demographic change, measures of Catholic influence are associated with greater rates of decline. Understandably, it is the catch-up term which dominates the change model in Appendix 7.2. The only other term is for the negative impact of Catholic adherence. The huge extent of the overall post-war decline in OECD fertility levels is amply testified to by the fact that, for every child born to a family in 1960, the catch-up effect implies an estimated decline in fertility of 0.75 of a point. For the average OECD nation, the Catholicism term implies a further reduction in fertility of 0.19 of a point.

Analysis

Given that the cross-national methodology employed here does not give us explanatory purchase on individual fertility choices, and that the nations examined here do not span anything like the full range of levels of socio-economic development, it would be inappropriate to seek to use these findings as the basis for a critique of theoretical approaches to fertility change. Rather our intention here is the far more modest one of trying to make sense of some of the more anomalous aspects of the fertility behaviour manifested in OECD countries in the post-war period, and of commenting on the implications of these findings for our broader theme of the impact of state intervention in the realm of the personal.

From a demographic transition viewpoint, the findings for the mid-1970s represent the one point at which theory and reality are congruent, with the findings for 1960, the early 1990s and change over time revealing a world seemingly quite out of kilter with the predictions of theory. Such a perspective can, however, be turned on its head. Thus, the post-war story of this group of countries, *defined by their already achieved modernity*, may be seen as exhibiting a substantially consistent relationship between modernization and fertility, disturbed only by the anomaly of the mid-1970s. This leads us to focus on the question of why the 1970s should be different, and the answer appears quite obvious: because cross-national variation at that time was hugely influenced by the differential adoption of modern contraceptive practices.

Evidence supporting such an interpretation is to be found in the re-estimated model in the notes to the 1974 equation in Appendix 7.2. In this equation, the contraceptive practice term features as much the most significant predictor of fertility behaviour in the model, replacing both real GDP per capita and female labour force participation. This suggests that the fertility flip-flop of the mid-1970s is largely a function of the early dissemination of clinical and supply methods of contraception in those countries which were most affluent and in which female labour supply was greatest. Such an account makes sense because it supplies the mechanism by which the generally positive relationship between modernity and fertility was restored in the early 1990s. As clinical and supply methods were further disseminated to poorer countries and countries in which control over fertility might be a key to women entering the labour force on a major scale for the first time, the pre-existing cross-national pattern was reasserted, although in a somewhat more muted form and at a much lower average level of fertility. This story also makes sense of the overall pattern of fertility change in these countries in the post-war period, with the universal adoption of modern methods of contraception the key to the simultaneous downward trend and compression of cross-national differences.

A further anomaly in our findings is the fact that wartime experience only appears as a predictor of fertility some three decades after the termination of hostilities in Europe. This anomaly is seemingly compounded if we examine the scatterplots of the relationship for each of the periods under review here. In both 1960 and the early 1990s, a strong inverse relationship is also apparent, but only if we exclude the five neutral nations from the sample. Paradoxically, however, in 1974, the year in which the term actually features in the fertility model, the relationship is only strong because the neutral nations are included in the analysis. The clue to what is going on once again lies in what is out of the ordinary in the mid-1970s, with the fertility levels in the former Allied powers going down because they were rich nations in the vanguard of contraceptive practice, and the fertility levels in three of the neutral nations – Ireland, Portugal and Spain – elevated by the fact that they were in the rearguard of modern contraceptive use. So, in a manner somewhat analogous to the mid-1970s disruption of the positive relationship between modernization and fertility, one might wish to view the relationship between war impact and fertility as a consistent pattern temporarily obscured by stronger factors. On the other hand, given that much of the explanatory action in 1974 concerns the high-fertility behaviour of three neutral nations, the pattern does not seem to be particularly well explained in terms of the effects of war-induced trauma in defeated populations. This is a matter which cannot be taken further on the basis of the evidence available here.

The final issue of interpretation we address concerns the great transformation in the relationship between women's labour force participation and fertility that occurred between the mid-1970s and the early 1990s. While the positive influence of female participation does not feature directly in the 1990s model, it seems clear that it is this effect that is being picked up both by the negative association with Catholic cultural impact and by the positive one with the family cash replacement rate. We know from our earlier findings concerning female labour force participation that this variable is extremely strongly inversely correlated with measures of Catholic influence. An examination of the relationships amongst the independent variables also reveals a more modest positive association of 0.53 between female labour supply and the generosity of replacement rates. So the story of fertility rates in the 1990s is precisely in line with the expectations of those who would argue that women's choices between family and work are now governed by a trade-off logic which reverses the priorities of the past. What our findings demonstrate is that, where mothers find it difficult to obtain work – where parenting benefits are unavailable, where there are few part-time jobs, where female unemployment is high and where Catholic beliefs are associated with policies and practices inimical to female employment – women no longer readily embrace family and fertility as an alternative. Rather, the response is increasingly to defer fertility, because children, in the absence of family-friendly policies, are seen as yet another obstacle to the achievement of women's legitimate career aspirations.

This is an account very different from that generally informing the critical rhetoric on the role of the modern state. In our findings there are no signs that state intervention has undermined the role of the family in reproducing the next generation. On the contrary, it is where state provision is at its most generous that fertility is the highest and it is where the outlays of government have increased most strongly that fertility rates have been most resistant to decline. Indeed, given that, for the majority of Western nations, the continuation of existing fertility levels implies population decline on a quite unacceptable scale, it may well be that a greater investment in population policy is the only key to long-term national survival. In this context, it is worth considering the implications of the family cash replacement rate term in the early 1990s equation. At the present time, governments in the OECD countries provide an average level of support to children equivalent to 0.072 per cent of GDP for every 1 per cent of the population below 13 years of age. According to the early 1990s model, trebling the generosity of that support would lead to an estimated increase in fertility of 0.34 of a point, at an estimated cost to the average OECD nation of somewhat in excess of 2.75 percentage points of GDP in additional child benefits. OECD governments, in recent decades, have tended to be obsessed by the public expenditure burdens imposed by population ageing and are not likely to relish the thought of family policy spending on such a scale. However, there is every prospect that they will be forced to think in such terms as they become more aware of the problems facing them at the other end of the demographic spectrum.

DIVORCE

In this final section on the ways in which public policy has impacted on the realm of the personal, we turn to the subject of divorce. Although they are frequently confused, and not least by the critics of the supposedly corrosive effects of the growth of government on family life, it is important to stress that divorce and marital breakdown are not identical phenomena. Marriages cease to function and couples separate even in – indeed, particularly in – nations in which divorce is illegal or difficult to obtain. Divorce, however, is a response to marital breakdown, involving the legal dissolution of marriage and the legalized possibility of remarriage.

The high divorce rates of most contemporary Western societies are anathema to social conservatives because they serve as a symbol of the breakdown of traditional mores concerning the regulation of family life. The state is seen as implicated in this process for at least two reasons. First, it is governments that have changed the laws which have made it possible to divorce. Between the mid-1960s, when the liberalization of the British law was given the imprimatur of the Church of England (Mortimer Commission, 1966), and the early 1980s, there was a vast wave of divorce law reform across the OECD countries, culminating in no-fault provisions in legislation across the English-speaking world and much of Northwestern Europe. Attributing the escalation in the divorce rate to the greater ease with which divorce could be obtained, critics saw increased legal permissiveness as one of the main factors undermining the sanctity of marriage. Second, the growth of big government and of the welfare state has been seen as facilitating divorce by providing the economic support necessary for single parents to support children outside the traditional two-parent household. According to this view, where once individuals had to think long and hard before leaving a marriage, the availability of state benefits now makes marital bonds relatively painless to sever. Thus, because it has reduced the legal and financial obstacles to the dissolution of marriage, the state stands accused of unravelling the very fabric of the realm of the personal: the integrity of family life.

At the beginning of the substantive analysis in this book, we argued that it was not our task to address normative issues other than by offering evidence concerning the causes and consequences of the human behaviour presupposed in normative accounts. That remains our position here. Whether an increasing divorce rate threatens the moral integrity of the family is beyond the scope of this discussion. On the other hand, the view that the huge post-war growth in the divorce rate is attributable to the permissiveness of laws and to the growth of the 'nanny' state puts forward a variety of propositions open to empirical testing. Although focusing on cross-national differences in divorce rates once again involves looking at the aggregate outcomes of individual decision processes rather than at the processes themselves, there is no real choice as to the appropriate methodology for exploring such propositions. Laws are nationally specific and so too are welfare state arrangements. The only way in which we can address these issues is through cross-national analysis.

Data

The summary statistics in Table 7.3 demonstrate the extent of the increase in OECD divorce rates over the post-war period. Between 1960 and 1974, divorce rates more than doubled; over the period as a whole, they have very nearly tripled. Unlike many of the processes of post-war development explored in this book, divorce rates have not manifested any kind of a catch-up tendency. The strong positive correlation between 1960 and 1993 divorce rates suggests a strong resemblance in cross-national distributions of outcomes more than three decades apart. Indeed, a marginally significant positive term for the relationship between the 1960 rate and subsequent change is indicative of a distribution in which countries were moving further apart. It is noticeable, however, that these tendencies were more pronounced at the bottom of the distribution than at the top. In other words, the countries that started out with exceptionally low divorce rates in 1960 tended to have exceptionally low divorce rates in the early 1990s, but, with the important exception of the USA, there was less continuity amongst the nations initially characterized by high divorce rates. Finally, examination of changes in the coefficients of variation shows us that there was considerable and continuing divergence in cross-national divorce rates. Of all the policy outcomes discussed in this study, only unemployment manifests a comparable diversity, which is conceivably why it is these outcomes that are so often singled out as the most egregious symptoms of the malfunctioning of contemporary societies. Dramatic contrasts breed dramatic rhetoric!

Although the picture is not completely clear-cut, it is possible to identify some reasonably distinct family of nations patterns from the very beginning. In 1960, the USA was in a class of its own, with a divorce rate more than three times the OECD mean. Otherwise, however, it was the Scandinavian nations bar Norway which were at the top of the distribution, with the majority of English-speaking and continental Western European nations in the middle. In this latter grouping, Austria and Germany had the highest divorce rates, with Switzerland's comparable level also suggesting some commonality amongst the German-speaking nations. The nations of Southern Europe clustered towards the bottom of the distribution, along with Ireland and Italy, two countries which, in 1960, had no legal provision for the dissolution of marriage. Although there was a considerable rise in the divorce rate in most countries between 1960 and 1974, there was little change in this ordering. What change there was – the shift of Canada and the United Kingdom from the bottom half to the top half of the distribution – made the English-speaking family more diverse in the character of its outcomes than previously.

Table 7.3 Levels of and change in divorce rates (final decrees per 1000 of the population), 1960–93

Country	1960	1974	1993	Change: 1960–93
Australia	0.65	1.31	2.74	2.09
Canada	0.39	2.00	2.71	2.32
Ireland	0	0	0	0
New Zealand	0.69	1.47	2.65	1.96
UK	0.51	2.29	3.01	2.50
USA	2.24	4.62	4.60	2.36
Denmark	1.42	2.60	2.50	1.08
Finland	0.82	2.13	2.42	1.60
Norway	0.66	1.29	2.54	1.88
Sweden	1.20	3.33	2.48	1.28
Austria	1.13	1.41	2.04	0.91
Belgium	0.50	1.03	2.09	1.59
France	0.61	1.11	1.89	1.28
Germany	0.81	1.59	1.93	1.12
Italy	0	0.32	0.39	0.39
Netherlands	0.49	1.41	2.00	1.51
Greece	0.30	0.41	0.69	0.39
Portugal	0.08	0.08	1.22	1.14
Spain	0	0	0.59	0.59
Switzerland	0.89	1.27	2.17	1.28
Japan	0.74	1.04	1.51	0.77
Mean	0.67	1.46	2.01	1.34
Correlation with 1960		0.87	0.79	0.42
Coefficient of variation	78.76	77.02	51.51	

Sources and notes: Data from United Nations, *Demographic Yearbook*, New York, various years. The figure reported in the final column is the increase in the number of divorces per 1000 of the population over the period as a whole. Where the divorce rate is reported as zero, the country concerned had no legal provision for divorce at the time.

By the early 1990s, however, family of nations patterns were very clear indeed. The USA remains the country with much the highest divorce rate, but the countries following in its immediate wake are now all English-speaking nations. The Scandinavian grouping occupies a distinct second place in the distribution, followed by the continental Western European nations, which continue to manifest higher rates than their Southern European cousins. The only countries to depart from this pattern are Ireland and Italy, and they make up the bottom of the distribution. In Ireland, it was only in the mid-1990s that it was possible to obtain the referendum majority needed to overturn a constitutional prohibition on divorce, while Italy, which had legalized divorce in 1970, continued to have the most restrictive law in Europe, stipulating a minimum of five years' legal separation as a prior condition for the legal dissolution of marriage. Change over time was also quite clearly patterned. The English-speaking countries bar Ireland were those in which divorce increased most spectacularly. Southern Europe, including Italy, was the region in which change was least pronounced.

Hypotheses

As in all our previous analyses, the first step is to test whether wartime experience had any influence on outcomes in the immediate post-war decades. Turning to the possible impact of post-war socio-economic development, we find that much of the research in this area has been more concerned with factors seen as influential in accounting for the general trend towards increased divorce rates with those associated with cross-national differences. In particular, there has been emphasis on the way in which widespread attitudinal changes stemming from the processes of economic modernization and of secularization have contributed to the declining stability of marriage in the post-war era (see Goode, 1963, 81; Ambert, 1980, 54–7; Price and McKenry, 1988, 7). However, from our viewpoint, the fact that modernization has been so widely identified as the basic source of post-war change in marital relations clearly invites examination of the possibility that cross-national differences in divorce rates and divorce rate trends may be a function of the diversity of socio-economic development in different countries.

We test for this possibility by exploring the association between divorce rates and our standard inventory of social and economic variables, including measures of income, occupational structure and urbanization. Earlier research by Castles and Flood (1993), based on a comparison of 17 OECD countries (the countries in this study minus Japan and Southern Europe) has demonstrated significant positive correlations between such variables and average divorce rates in the periods 1961–68 and 1976–83 and divorce rate change between these periods. Research by Lye (1989, 308–37), based on comparisons of US metropolitan areas and European regions, notes a strong association between divorce rates and the extent of services employment and speculates that this is probably because such employment stands as a proxy for the degree of women's employment opportunities (ibid., 451).

The view that secularization trends are important in understanding the growth trajectory of marital break-up is premised on the notion that the post-war period has seen a widespread erosion in the religious values upholding marriage. As noted in Chapter 2, we do not possess anything like adequate data on the post-war decline in religiosity in the OECD nations. However, given that commentators are widely agreed that secularizing trends have made greater inroads in Protestant than in Catholic milieux (see Chester, 1977; Halem, 1980), it seems quite appropriate to make use of our variables measuring the extent of Catholic influence in different nations as a kind of inverse measure of the extent of such trends. The idea that cultures informed by Catholicism and Protestantism should have radically different attitudes to divorce is, in any case, clearly justified by appeal to the historical record, with Reformation theology explicitly rejecting the principle of the indissolubility of marriage, whilst simultaneously defining family law as a matter of civil rather than ecclesiastical jurisdiction (see Rheinstein, 1972).

Virtually all accounts of the post-war increase in divorce rates underline the huge significance of the changing social and economic position of women, with declining fertility rates and increasing levels of female labour force participation seen as key parameters. Reduced fertility is a factor potentially conducive to higher divorce rates because women are less bound by obligations to nurture large families (see Norton and Glick, 1979, 16). High levels of female labour force participation, and, in particular, the widespread labour force participation of married women, are crucial (Phillips, 1988; Price and McKenry, 1988), because they create the basis for economic independence after the termination of marriage as well as the basis for greater autonomy within marriage. In a more explicitly economic modelling of the relationship between female participation and marital instability, Becker (1991) sees the economic advantages derived by women from the traditional household division of labour progressively diminished by the possibility of higher returns from market earnings.

In what follows, we explore both of these hypotheses, although noting the possibility of some degree of reciprocal causation. Reduced fertility could, in part, be a result of an increased tendency to early termination of marriage, and increased female labour force participation is likely to be, at least to some degree, a function of the need of divorced women to earn a living. On the whole, however, reverse causality is likely to be of only limited significance. Despite the substantial increase in divorce rates in recent decades, there are few countries in which the proportion of the divorced population is of sufficient magnitude to account for more than a modest part of the post-war decline in fertility. Moreover, the econometric evidence which points to increased hours of work following divorce suggests that this effect makes only a relatively minor contribution to overall female labour supply (see Peterson, 1989, 55–70).

The argument that cross-national differences in divorce rates can be explained by the relative permissiveness or liberality of national laws can only be tested by reference to typologies of the laws governing marital causes. As far as we are aware, there have been only two attempts to characterize divorce law provisions on a scale sufficiently wide to permit comparative analysis. The typology developed by Lye (1989), which covers 14 countries, is, however, seriously flawed. In part, this is because it fails to include countries in which the inhibiting effect of legal provisions or their absence has been most evident (Ireland, Italy) and, in part, it is because it was elaborated for a time-point (1980) at which much of the cross-national differentiation in legal forms had already disappeared as a consequence of divorce law reform. The typology developed by Castles and Flood (1993) includes countries which do not make legislative provision for divorce and provides separate categorizations of the liberality of the law in 1960 and in 1976. According to this categorization, countries with no-fault provisions or permitting both contested and uncontested divorce on the grounds of separation score 3, countries permitting uncontested divorce on the basis of mutual consent or of no more than three years of separation score 2, countries with still more restrictive legislation score 1 and countries with no divorce legislation score 0 (for more details, see Castles and Flood, 1993, 299). For the purposes of this inquiry, we have coded data on the liberality of divorce laws for the years 1960, 1974 and the early 1990s and extended the number of countries to the 21 covered in this study.

In the Castles and Flood study, the liberality of the law was shown to be much influenced by social and economic factors, including the size of the non-agricultural labour force, the extent of Catholic adherence and the extent of female labour supply, but was, nevertheless, an independently significant factor contributing to divorce outcomes. The replication of such findings in this somewhat wider study could be interpreted as an indication that, in this area of law reform, the state had served as a filter of economic and social forces and, therefore, had played a role in reshaping the parameters of marital behaviour. It should be emphasized, however, that such a role, even if demonstrated, should not necessarily be interpreted in terms of a rhetoric of permissiveness – of laws bringing about divorces which would not otherwise occur. Laws for the dissolution of marriage do not force people to divorce; they stipulate the circumstances under which they may seek relief from their marriage vows. Thus, in so far as the laws of divorce constrain behaviour, their more obvious effect is to prevent individuals from having recourse to legal remedies for marital breakdown.

The argument that the growth of the welfare state is a factor implicated in the post-war growth of divorce is much contested in the literature, with conflicting findings emerging from studies using survey data to explore possible links between the availability of benefits to single mothers and children and the increased incidence of divorce (see Hart, 1976; Moles, 1979; Albrecht, Bahr and Goodman, 1983). Our problem with testing such hypotheses is the lack of adequate cross-national data on the extent and value of such benefits. In the absence of such data, we can only use our broader aggregate measures of the size of government, together with indicators of replacement rates and spending levels for family cash benefits. These latter are only available for the early 1990s. Although family cash benefits include benefits going to both married and divorced parents, they almost certainly capture much of the variance in the generosity of the welfare state to potential divorcees. Their use provides the best test available of the hypothesis that the rise of big government has been a major factor contributing to the massive growth of marital break-up in recent decades.

Findings

Figure 7.3(a) points to eight significant correlates of divorce in 1960, all with signs as hypothesized. Of the modernization measures, income per capita and per worker are strongly and positively linked to outcomes, while the positive association with services employment and the negative one with agricultural employment are somewhat less marked. Our two main measures of religious belief are moderately strongly and inversely related to divorce rates, but there is no specific Christian Democratic incumbency effect. The liberality of divorce laws is moderately and positively associated with outcomes, while the positive correlation for female labour force participation is more modest. Of the findings for the three aggregates of public spending, the only one worth even a second glance is that for public consumption expenditure, with the positive sign possibly deriving from the association between this type of expenditure and female welfare state employment.

(a) 1960

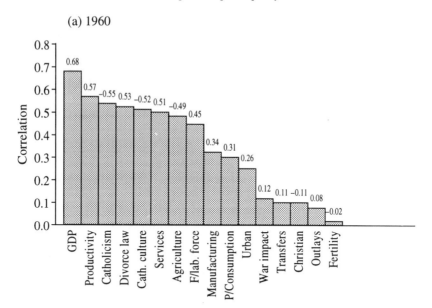

(b) 1974

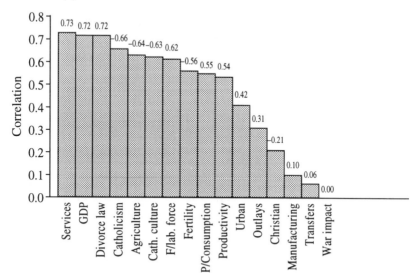

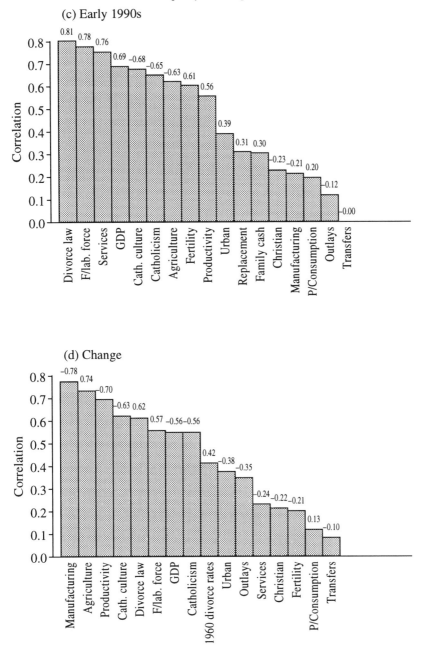

Figure 7.3 Bivariate tests: divorce rates (1960, 1974 and early 1990s and change over time)

Despite the complexity of these findings, the model identified in Appendix 7.3 contains only two terms indicative of positive links with both GDP per capita and the liberality of the law. The GDP effect is the stronger of the two, leading to a divorce rate estimated to be 0.54 of a point higher in a country with the average OECD level of GDP per capita. With a category measure like the liberality of the divorce law, averages convey very little. In 1960, Britain's divorce law was amongst the most restrictive in Europe and thus scores only 1 on our measure, while the divorce laws of the Scandinavian countries permitted contested divorce on the basis of no more than three years of separation and score 3 on the liberality index. The 1960 equation suggests that this diversity of legal provision made a difference of around 0.40 of a point as between British and Scandinavian divorce rates.

Figure 7.3(b) shows that, by 1974, not only had the range of significant correlates of divorce increased, but that, in many cases, the degree of association had become much stronger. Of the seven most significant factors in 1960, six remain so in 1974. Only in the case of productivity is there any decline in the strength of the relationship, while all the other factors have become more salient. Services employment is now marginally the strongest correlate of the divorce rate, narrowly followed by GDP per capita and the liberality of the law. New factors to emerge as statistically significant are fertility, public consumption expenditure and urbanization. The increased association with public consumption expenditure is again compatible with previous findings of an increasing link between such spending and female labour supply. Appendix 7.3 identifies services employment and female labour force participation as the only significant terms in the 1974 model. Calculating in our normal way, the model suggests that the divorce rate was 1.51 points higher in a country with the OECD average level of services employment and 0.86 of a point higher in a country with the average level of female labour force participation.

According to Figure 7.3(c), the same seven factors that featured as most significant in 1974 are again most significant in the early 1990s. The three strongest factors are the liberality of the law, female labour force participation and services employment, all with extremely strong positive correlations. There are a number of points of special interest in Figure 7.3(c). First, fertility remains significant, but has changed signs, manifesting the same changeability as demonstrated in the findings for fertility in the previous section. Second, the level of public consumption spending now has only the most minuscule connection with outcomes, even though female labour supply, with which it is strongly associated, has markedly increased in salience. Third, our more specific tests of the proposition that welfare state benefits to families lead to higher divorce rates do not produce any significant results. Neither the replacement rate of family cash benefits nor their cost are even modestly related to outcomes. The early 1990s model which appears in Appendix 7.3 again highlights the positive influences of services employment and of female labour force participation, but, completely contrary to expectations, includes a negative term for public consumption expenditure. In real terms, female labour force participation is now the strongest effect, making an estimated average difference of 1.24 points. The positive impact of services employment is estimated to be 0.74 of a point and the negative influence of civilian public consumption is 0.56 of a point.

Not all the findings reported in Figure 7.3(d) are quite as they seem. The strong negative relationship for change in manufacturing and the strong positive one for change in agricultural employment have to be interpreted in terms of the major declines in these categories of employment over the post-war period. So what these correlations are telling us is that it was the countries in which manufacturing declined most (which happen to be those which experienced the greatest post-war shift into services) and the countries in which agriculture declined least (which happen be those in which the transition to a services society had taken place earliest) in which the post-war divorce rates were increasing most rapidly. These findings are wholly in line with expectations and with our previous findings. The negative relationships with both productivity change and per capita GDP change appear to contradict the modernization thesis by suggesting that it was those countries which modernized most rapidly that experienced the least increase in divorce rates. However, here we need to remember that changes in income are measured in terms of growth rates, which are generally greatest in those countries with the lowest initial income levels. So, once again, these correlations confirm a picture clearly established previously: divorce is most commonplace in the countries which are most economically advanced. The remaining significant findings in Figure 7.3(d) are less difficult to interpret: divorce rates increased least rapidly where Catholic influence was greatest and they increased most rapidly in those countries in which divorce law reform was the most radical and in which female labour supply was growing fastest. As previously noted, there was also a modest tendency for divorce rates to increase most rapidly in those countries which had the highest divorce rates in 1960.

The change model which appears in Appendix 7.3 identifies three significant terms. In order of statistical significance they are Catholic cultural impact, change in the liberality of the law and change in manufacturing employment. Countries in the Catholic cultural impact category manifested an increase in divorce rates estimated as being 0.58 of a point less than that occurring in countries not categorized in this manner. The maximum increase in liberality scores between 1960 and 1993 was 2, so the maximum estimated impact of divorce law reform was 0.63 of a point. Experiencing the average degree of decline in manufacturing employment (to be interpreted as the average shift from manufacturing to services employment) led to an estimated increase in the divorce rate of 0.43 of a point.

Analysis

These findings are more consistent than they appear on the surface. In each of the models, there is a term suggesting that economic modernization is crucial to divorce outcomes, with the impact picked up by GDP per capita in 1960 and by services employment in both 1974 and the early 1990s. As already noted, the negative term for manufacturing employment in the change equation is most appropriately interpreted as picking up the post-war shift from manufacturing to services, so that, from the 1970s onwards, the services employment theme is a constant of the analysis. Moreover, leaving aside the anomalous term relating to civilian public consumption in the early 1990s and the impact of divorce law reform on the change in the divorce rate, a further constant seems to be the fact that divorce occurs markedly less frequently in milieux shaped by the influence of Catholic beliefs. On the one hand, this may be seen in the consistently negative correlations between outcomes and our measures of Catholic influence and, on the other, in the strong negative correlations between these measures and both the liberality of the law in 1960 and female labour force participation thereafter. In addition, the change model shows that it was in the countries of Catholic cultural impact that post-war growth in divorce rates was least apparent. So a large part of the post-war divorce phenomenon can be seen as a function of economic and cultural modernity, with economic change providing the means by which women might become more independent in marriage (access to resources and access to job opportunities) and cultural parameters determining the legal and financial availability of the divorce option (the liberality of the law and the availability of women's work).

The anomalous negative relationship between public consumption expenditure and divorce rates in the early 1990s is a reflection of the degree to which the extraordinarily high divorce rate of the USA influences our findings. Because the USA has much the highest divorce rate amongst these countries and because it simultaneously exhibits nearly the lowest level of public consumption expenditure in the early 1990s, the equation implies a coincidence between the two phenomena. However, it seems most unlikely that this is a meaningful relationship, given that the association between the variables was both significant and positive in the mid-1970s (see Figure 7.3(b)). This earlier positive association was the one aspect of our findings that even tentatively suggested that big government might have something to do with marital break-up, although the causal connection implied is not the one generally alleged by critics of the state. Instead of welfare benefits subsidizing the financial costs of divorce, what we find is yet another instance of the factors associated with greater employment opportunities for women also being associated with higher rates of divorce. The obvious interpretation of this phenomenon is that female employment enhances the economic independence and personal autonomy of women, providing a material basis for a more equal partnership in marriage and a means of ending the partnership where such equality is denied.

Even disregarding the early 1990s negative finding as anomalous, the marked decline in the association between public consumption spending and the divorce rate shown in Figure 7.3(c) indicates that the state employment route to divorce is no longer of much importance. Today, it is not the Scandinavian social service states which manifest high divorce rates, but the countries of the English-speaking world. Of course, what both these families of nations have in common are high levels of services employment and female labour force participation, in Scandinavia underpinned by high levels of welfare state employment and in the English-speaking countries by the growth of private sector service jobs. However, since the English-speaking countries are characterized by low levels of welfare state spending, it makes very little sense to argue that it is the post-war growth of the 'nanny' state which has made these countries prey to such high levels of marital break-up in the 1990s.

That leaves the anti-statist case dependent on the view that permissive laws lead to permissive behaviour, with some ostensible support in the positive relationships between the liberality of the law and the divorce rate in 1960 and between the degree of post-war divorce law reform and divorce rate change thereafter. But such a view is not really persuasive. The 1960 finding seems far more compatible with the notion of the law as an obstacle rather than an encouragement to divorce. The divorce law term is significant not in accounting for the high divorce rates of countries like the USA, Denmark and Sweden, but rather in accounting for the exceptionally low divorce rates of countries such as Australia, Canada and the United Kingdom. As demonstrated in some historical detail in earlier work by Castles and Flood (1993), these latter were countries in which the highly restrictive British divorce legislation of 1857 prevailed with only minor modifications until well into the 1960s, preventing access to divorce on anything like the scale typical of countries at comparable levels of economic development. What the positive term for change tells us is that when these countries embraced law reform in the 1960s and 1970s, their divorce rates shifted to a point in the distribution more obviously congruent with their degree of economic and cultural modernization. In other words, what the divorce law term is demonstrating is not the effect of legal permissiveness, but the end of legal constraint and the victory of modernity.

CONCLUSION

With this analysis of the factors influencing divorce rates in the post-war period, we come not only to the end of our study of the role of public policy in the realm of the personal but also to the conclusion of our investigation of the ways in which the growth of big government has impinged on the workings of the economy and civil society. Summary of so much material and analysis is clearly out of the question, but it is worth emphasizing two points that emerge from our discussion.

The first is that the critics of big government are utterly correct in identifying the state as a major contributor to economic and social change during the post-war period. In the labour market, income transfers have made it possible for a substantial proportion of older men to withdraw, voluntarily or otherwise, from an active search for employment, while the expansion of public consumption spending has been amongst the more significant sources of the growth in female labour supply. In the realm of the personal, housing policies have influenced the mix of public and private tenure, while family cash benefits have been one of the few factors countering recent trends towards reduced birth-rates. Moreover, as we have just shown, it has been the policy activity of the state in effecting divorce law reform which has removed previously existing legal bars to the dissolution of marriage. The story, then, is that, for good or for evil, the post-war state has been an agent of transformation in an arena far wider than the mere payment of taxes and the receipt of benefits and services. Or, to put it another way, the realm of post-war public policy has been bigger than big government alone.

The second point is that almost nothing in the findings presented here supports the view that increased state intervention has reduced work incentives or undermined the integrity of family life. In the labour market, we noted that the effects of declining male labour supply and of increasing female participation almost exactly cancelled each other out and that there was little evidence that public spending programmes or the generosity of labour market entitlements had contributed to the post-war trajectory of unemployment growth. In the realm of the personal, big spending and taxing have not prevented an ever increasing proportion of the population saving on the scale necessary to become home owners, while, quite contrary to the thrust of the views of those who deprecate state intervention, it would seem that only a population policy based on taxpayer-funded family cash payments can stave off disastrous population decline. In contrast to this potential for increasing policy activism, our analysis of post-war divorce rates suggests that the state has given up its role as a buttress of religiously sanctioned moral values and that any relevance its role as a provider of welfare jobs and services may once have had has now disappeared. Thus, while the much expanded role of the modern state has had important reciprocal effects on economy and society, the evidence does not support the view that it has become the main source of contemporary social ills.

Apart from concluding the discussion of the ways in which the post-war state has impinged on the wider economy and society, this chapter also marks the final step in our analysis of the multiple arenas which define the ambit of modern public policy. Most of the objectives we set ourselves in Chapter 1 have now been accomplished. We have used a cross-national and interdisciplinary research strategy to explore the ways in which the economic, social and political changes of the post-World War II epoch have impacted on public policy outcomes in the advanced, industrial nations of Western capitalism. In the process, we have described the extent of public policy transformation in different nations and looked at the reasons why countries have experienced diverse outcomes. Finally, we have used our investigation of the outer limits of public policy as a way of exploring the claims of those who have been concerned with the adverse effects of the growth of government in the post-war era. Only one objective remains. In what has gone before, we have attempted to reveal the shapes contained in the tapestry of post-war public policy by focusing on its separate components. The time has now come to stand back and look at the picture in its entirety and ask whether these components reveal wider patterns. That is the task of our final chapter.

APPENDIX 7.1 HOME OWNERSHIP MODELS

Early 1960s	Coefficient	Standard error	t-value
Intercept	97.436		
1960 manufacturing employment	–1.279	0.265	4.829
Catholic cultural impact	–12.516	3.125	4.005
1960s public/non-profit dwellings completed	–0.341	0.097	3.508

Adj. $R^2 = 0.772$

Sources and notes: 1960 manufacturing employment from Table 2.4; Catholic cultural impact from Table 2.7; 1960s (1963) public/non-profit dwellings completed from United Nations Economic Commission for Europe, *Annual Bulletin of Housing and Building Statistics for Europe 1969*, 1970. 20 cases in regression.

1970s	Coefficient	Standard error	t-value
Intercept	95.058		
1974 manufacturing employment	–1.458	0.362	4.022
Corporatism	–4.502	1.94	2.321
Comprehensive housing policy	–9.614	4.117	2.335

Adj. $R^2 = 0.689$

Sources and notes: 1974 manufacturing employment from Table 2.4; corporatism from Table 3.5; comprehensive housing policy is a dummy variable (France, Germany, the Netherlands, Norway and Sweden scored 1; other cases scored 0) derived from Donnison (1967). 21 cases in regression.

Early 1990s	Coefficient	Standard error	t-value
Intercept	40.661		
corporatism	−6.217	2.221	2.799
1960–early 1990s average annual change in consumer price index	2.67	0.852	3.135

Adj. R^2 = 0.524

Sources and notes: Corporatism from Table 3.5; 1960–early 1990s (1990) average annual change in consumer price index from OECD, *Historical Statistics*, Paris, 1992. 21 cases in regression.

Early 1960s–early 1990s change	Coefficient	Standard error	t-value
Intercept	−22.002		
1960-early 1990s change in manufacturing employment	−0.938	0.24	3.911
Catholic cultural impact	14.162	2.709	5.227
1960-early 1990s average annual change in consumer price index	2.463	0.662	3.719
1979–89 change in real earnings	3.423	1.234	2.773

Adj. R^2 = 0.685

Sources and notes: 1960–early 1990s (1990) change in manufacturing employment (1990 value minus 1960 value) as a percentage of civilian employment calculated from the same source as Table 2.4; Catholic cultural impact from Table 2.7; 1960–early 1990s (1990) average annual change in consumer price index from source noted above; 1979–89 change in real average earnings is the annual average change in real wages in manufacturing from OECD (1996a). 19 cases in regression.

APPENDIX 7.2 TOTAL FERTILITY MODELS

1960	Coefficient	Standard error	t-value
Intercept	2.249		
1960 real GDP per worker	0.00005283	0.00001458	3.624
1960 female labour force participation	–0.027	0.007	3.803
early 1960s home ownership	0.02	0.006	3.367

Adj. R^2 = 0.647

Sources and notes: 1960 real GDP per worker from the same source as Table 2.2; 1960 female labour force participation from Table 6.2; early 1960s home ownership from Table 7.1. 21 cases in regression.

1974*	Coefficient	Standard error	t-value
Intercept	3.444		
War impact	–0.204	0.054	3.788
1974 real GDP per worker	–0.00003682	0.00001139	3.232
1974 female labour force participation	–0.018	0.006	3.035
1970s home ownership	0.012	0.005	2.26

Adj. R^2 = 0.732

Sources and notes: War impact from Table 2.1; 1974 real GDP per worker from the same source as Table 2.2; 1974 female labour force participation from Table 6.2; 1970s home ownership from Table 7.1. 21 cases in regression. *Re-estimating the model to include the contraceptive use dummy produces the following result: 1974 total fertility = 1.74 – 0.118 (0.057) war impact +0.014 (0.005) 1970s home ownership –0.419 (0.103) contraceptive use (figures in parentheses are standard errors). Adj. R^2 = 0.728. For discussion of re-estimated model, see text.

1993	Coefficient	Standard error	t-value
Intercept	2.192		
Early 1990s manufacturing employment	−0.032	0.01	3.163
Catholic cultural impact	−0.222	0.077	2.871
Early 1990s family cash replacement rate	2.345	0.854	2.747

Adj. $R^2 = 0.611$

Sources and notes: Early 1990s (1993) manufacturing employment from Table 2.4; Catholic cultural impact from Table 2.7; early 1990s family cash replacement rate calculated from OECD (1993a) and OECD (1996d). 21 cases in regression.

1960–93 change	Coefficient	Standard error	t-value
Intercept	1.13		
1960 total fertility	−0.755	0.063	11.922
Catholicism	−0.004	0.001	3.976

Adj. $R^2 = 0.887$

Sources and notes: 1960 total fertility from Table 7.2; Catholicism from Table 2.7. 21 cases in regression.

APPENDIX 7.3 DIVORCE RATES MODELS

1960	Coefficient	Standard error	t-value
Intercept	−0.431		
1960 real GDP per capita	0.0001399	0.00003669	3.812
1960 divorce law liberality	0.198	0.079	2.506

Adj. R^2 = 0.559

Sources and notes: 1960 real GDP per capita from Table 2.2; 1960 divorce law liberality from data in Castles and Flood (1993) with codings for additional countries supplied by the author. 21 cases in regression.

1974	Coefficient	Standard error	t-value
Intercept	−4.794		
1974 services employment	0.079	0.018	4.497
1974 female labour force	0.047	0.014	3.326

Adj. R^2 = 0.679

Sources and notes: 1974 services employment from Table 2.4; 1974 female labour force from Table 6.2. 21 cases in regression.

1993	Coefficient	Standard error	t-value
Intercept	−5.505		
Early 1990s services employment	0.074	0.022	3.336
1993 civilian public consumption expenditure	−0.074	0.033	2.231
Early 1990s female labour force	0.065	0.015	4.422

Adj. R^2 = 0.77

Sources and notes: Early 1990s (1993) services employment from Table 2.4; early 1990s (1993) civilian public consumption expenditure from Table 4.3; early 1990s (1993) female labour force from Table 6.2. 21 cases in regression.

1960–93 change	Coefficient	Standard error	t-value
Intercept	1.051		
1960–early 1990s change in manufacturing employment	–0.041	0.017	2.422
Catholic cultural impact	–0.585	0.172	3.412
1960–early 1990s change in divorce law liberality	0.317	0.114	2.77

Adj. $R^2 = 0.757$

Sources and notes: 1960–early 1990s (1993) change in manufacturing employment from Table 2.4; Catholic cultural impact from Table 2.7; 1960–early 1990s change in divorce law liberality calculated from data in Castles and Flood (1993) with codings for additional countries and time-points supplied by the author. 21 cases in regression.

8. Patterns of post-war public policy

The findings of comparative public policy research have always been a test-bed for exploring major questions concerning the factors shaping the role of the state. That is because such findings make it possible for us to move from the experience of particular nation-states to the experience of the state in general. In reality, the state in question is only the state as it functions in the countries of advanced industrialism, but that, of course, is the state that matters most for the majority of those who undertake such research. The energizing problematic for much of the earlier work in the field was a desire to evaluate the claim that the role of the modern state has been largely shaped by processes of socio-economic change. Patterns of policy outcomes as revealed by cross-national research were critical to this debate, with supposedly convergent trends towards big government heralded as proof positive that economic development was rapidly dissolving all prior sources of political and cultural differentiation. From the late 1970s onwards, the impetus for research changed, as scholars found evidence of continuing divergence in the policy outcomes of advanced democratic states and interpreted them as evidence for the proposition that politics matters. The wheel has now turned full circle, with the recent upsurge in interest in the consequences of a global economy making policy convergence towards a smaller state the crucial benchmark of the extent to which the autonomy of the nation-state has been undermined by the forces of international capital.

Although the subject-matter of comparative public policy research invites us to use the patterns revealed by cross-national analysis to address issues such as these, there has often been a marked disjunction between a narrow-gauge empirical focus and wide-ambit conclusions, with a tendency to extrapolate from findings concerning specific policy outcomes to the factors shaping the role of the state more generally. However, if there is one message of this book which should be clear by now, it is that such processes of inference are likely to be profoundly misleading. As we have seen, the causes and consequences of the policy actions of the state differ widely from one policy area to another and within particular areas over time. That means that any general characterization of post-war policy development requires a far wider range of evidence than has generally been deployed for that purpose. The object of this book has been to collect and analyse some of that evidence and the object of this chapter is to re-examine some of the big questions about the factors shaping the role of the state in its light. The fact that work in the comparative public policy mode has been prone to generalize on the basis of narrow findings has contributed to a debate in which opposed schools of thought have often argued vehemently for the explanatory primacy of favoured variables using evidence which more properly suggests that all these variables are in some way relevant. Seeking to characterize the post-war transformation on the basis of a far wider range of findings makes complete nonsense of the idea that a single explanatory key can unlock the mysteries of the contemporary state. The story told in this chapter is an amplification of the story told throughout: of multiple, complex, interconnected and ever changing patterns of public policy. In this, as in all realms of knowledge, 'the truth is rarely pure, and never simple' (Oscar Wilde, *The Importance of Being Earnest*, Act I).

DOES MODERNITY MATTER?

In Chapter 2, we outlined the main dimensions of post-war economic and social change in the OECD countries and noted that modernization theory saw these changes as interlinked aspects of a singular process of societal transformation leading ultimately to policy convergence amongst nations. However, in the final section of Chapter 3, we suggested that there were reasons for questioning the closeness of the linkages between aspects of the modernization process and, therefore, reasons to doubt that countries' policy profiles would necessarily become more alike. In contrast to the integrated account of post-war change offered by modernization theory, the story revealed by our analysis was of a modernity fractured by major political, demographic and cultural fault lines, crosscutting each other in different ways in different nations and, potentially, making for considerable policy diversity. Table 8.1, which summarizes the findings of the models in the appendices in Chapters 4 to 7 concerning the role of economic and social factors in shaping post-war policy outcomes, provides us with a means of assessing which of these pictures is the more realistic.

If economic development is seen as providing the fundamental dynamic of the modernization process, the evidence in Table 8.1 suggests a more muted impact than is usually implied by sociological accounts of the post-war transformation. With respect to indicators of the size and

Table 8.1 Economic and social determinants of policy outcomes

	1960s	1970s	1990s	Change
Outlays of government	RGDPPC (+) RGDPPC^2 (–) Cath. culture (+)	None	Trade (–)	Age structure (+)
Receipts of government	War impact (+) RGDPPC (+) RGDPPC^2 (–) Age structure (+)	RGDPPC (+) RGDPPC^2 (–) Age structure (+)	Age structure (+) Trade (–)	Age structure (+)
Civilian public consumption	None	None	None	None
Social security transfers	War impact (+) RGDPPC (+) RGDPPC^2 (–) Age structure (+) Cath. culture (+)	RGDPPC (+) RGDPPC^2 (–) Age structure (+) Cath. culture (+)	Trade (–) Christian (+)	Age structure (+)
Public health expenditure	Trade (–) Age structure (+)	None	RGDPPW (+)	None
Public education expenditure	Catholicism (–)	Catholicism (–)	Catholicism (–)	Catholicism (–)
Male labour force	None	None	None	Cath. culture (–)
Female labour force	War impact (+) Cath. culture (–)	Services Employment (–) Cath. culture (–)	Catholicism (–)	Catholicism (–)
Unemployment	Manufacturing employment (+)	None	None	None
Home ownership	Manufacturing employment (+) Cath. culture (–)	Manufacturing employment (+)	None	Manufacturing employment (–) Cath. culture (+)
Fertility	RGDPPW (+)	War impact (–) RGDPPW (–)	Manufacturing employment (–) Cath. culture (+)	Catholicism (–)
Divorce	RGDPPC (+)	Services employment (+)	Services employment (+)	Manufacturing employment (–) Cath. Culture (–)

Variables and sources: See appropriate appendices. Signs in parentheses indicate whether the finding is positive or negative.

growth of government and the welfare state, income measures feature in our findings on only six occasions. The most significant pattern is that captured by the curvilinear specification for social security transfers in both 1960 and 1974, and this is of sufficient magnitude to be reflected in findings for the receipts of government at both dates and for the outlays of government at the beginning of the period. But while this is an interesting pattern, it is not one which can easily be interpreted as demonstrating the role of modernity as a solvent of cross-national policy diversity. The curvilinear specification arises precisely from the fact that very rich countries behave quite differently in policy terms from moderately rich countries. We interpreted this in terms of a tendency for nations moving beyond the threshold of economic modernity prior to the World War II to develop institutionalized preferences for private forms of provision, because their initial experience of the problems associated with industrialization occurred at a time when they had access to only a limited repertoire of interventionist policy responses.

That leaves only the link between productivity and health spending in the 1990s as evidence for the proposition that the growth of the state is a function of the growth of the economy. However, while there is absolutely no question that the main force driving total health spending is the availability of economic resources, if our analysis is correct, the linkage only emerged in the arena of public policy as a consequence of a long-drawn-out political battle to extend public health cover to ever wider sections of the population. The story is not one of modernity shaping public policy, but of politics determining the form of modern social provision.

Economic development seemingly has had no direct effects on labour supply or unemployment, but has had a role in shaping the realm of the personal. In the case of fertility, the 1960 finding that family size is positively associated with productivity levels seemingly contradicts a demographic transition theory which itself is part of the wider modernization thesis. The finding is reversed in 1974 because affluence does, indeed, seem to have been a factor leading to the early adoption of clinical and supply methods of contraception. In the case of divorce rates, a strong positive relationship with economic development in the early post-war period is transformed into a comparably strong relationship with services employment thereafter. Given the close and consistent association between services employment and real GDP per capita shown in Appendix 3.1, this is the one instance where a story of the transformative power of economic modernity seems substantially consistent with the facts.

Where the economic development story is at its weakest is in directly accounting for the shape of the contemporary state and in explaining post-war policy transformation. In the early 1990s, health is the only arena of policy in which national affluence seems to be immediately relevant to levels of public spending. Despite the fact that post-war economic growth more than doubled the wealth of these nations in the three decades after 1960, there is no indication that the overall size of government or of its programmes grew as a direct consequence of this change. Moreover, economic growth seems to have had no direct effects either on labour market outcomes or on outcomes in the realm of the personal. Rather the role of the contemporary state and the trajectory of post-war transformation appear to have been more significantly influenced by other social and economic factors.

In the case of transfers and the major aggregates of spending and taxing, the most important factor is the positive impact of population ageing. Of almost comparable significance in the early period is the role of Catholic cultural impact, with the allied variable of Catholicism strongly associated with educational spending throughout. International trade emerges as a constraint on some aspects of spending in the early 1990s, but these findings remain tentative because of their dependence on the single extreme case of Ireland. In the labour market and in the realm of the personal, two factors are particularly prominent. Measures of religious difference again feature strongly, with a consistent impact on female labour supply and, seemingly, an influence on the pace of change in all areas bar unemployment. The other factor is manufacturing employment, which is associated with both home ownership and full employment in the earlier periods, with fertility in the early 1990s and with change in both home ownership and divorce rates over the period as a whole.

The big question is what these findings say about the impact of socio-economic modernity on the development of public policy. The role of religious difference is discussed in a later section, because it represents a relatively unchanging cultural parameter of policy development. The intellectual force of the modernization account as it relates to the post-war growth of the state is that it sees policy development as an immediate response to socio-economic transformation. Since our various measures of the relative influence of the major Christian denominations are either invariant or change very little over time, they cannot be regarded as part of that process.

The age structure of the population and manufacturing employment are quite different matters. Both have changed markedly in the post-war period and both have been widely regarded as integrally linked to the process of modernization. However, as revealed in Appendix 3.1, age structure has not been strongly associated with income levels at any time during the post-war period, while the strongish positive association between manufacturing employment and GDP in the early post-war years had dwindled to almost nothing by the 1990s. In the case of population ageing, the connection between population structure and modernization is almost certainly misconceived, being based on assumptions about the impact of modernity on fertility rates, which we have seen to be incorrect for this group of highly advanced countries. Because a number of the richest countries in the OECD experienced high levels of fertility in the early post-war years, their population structures have remained more balanced in subsequent decades and they have, in consequence, experienced lesser pressures for the expansion of transfers and services for the aged. In the case of manufacturing, industrial development was clearly the engine of initial economic growth, but economic level and occupational structure became less congruent as the early modernizers progressively shifted into service production.

So it would appear that modernity can be characterized by quite different age and occupational structures, with the former having major implications for public spending development and the latter for outcomes in the labour market and the realm of the personal. The story, then, is of a modernity with many mansions, with precise implications for policy depending on the factors determining different national routes to and through modernity. As we shall see, it is a story that becomes still more compelling when we also take account of the way in which cultural and political differences impact on policy development.

The account offered here is one which seems to fit quite well with our earlier notion of thresholds of modernity. We are far from arguing that economic development has been unimportant for post-war public policy development. Rather the point is that the economic differences amongst nations that still existed until the mid-1970s have given way to other influences precisely because all these countries have moved beyond the threshold of economic modernity. As we shall see in the next section, a similar argument can be advanced in terms of the effects of democratic participation. Seeing the role of economic development in this way has other implications. First, although policy outcomes are no longer a direct function of economic affluence, it is clear that the continuing viability of government programmes is underpinned by some minimum level of economic development or, perhaps more properly, by a minimum tax take dependent on a given level of economic development. An argument of those who see globalization as undermining the fabric of modern public policy is that given levels of national prosperity may generate declining tax revenues as global capital moves or threatens to move off-shore.

Second, it suggests that, whilst policy outcomes may be quite different in countries of comparable economic development, underlying whatever policy options are chosen, the question of economic resources will often loom large.

Rich countries may or may not be big spenders on public education, but, as we noted, there is a moderately strong tendency for countries with the highest levels of educational enrolments to be those which are most affluent. Similarly, whilst it is not income measures, but transfers spending levels, which predict withdrawal from the male labour force, our analysis shows that, for much of the period, it was the more affluent of the Western European nations which were providing transfers on the largest scale. Looked at in these terms, economic modernity may be regarded as a necessary, although not a sufficient, condition for much of the post-war transformation of the role of the state and its wider implications. That is why Wagner's law of increasing state activity often appears to fit the facts, even though, strictly speaking, it is demonstrably false. It is not true that, as nations become wealthier, there is a proportionate increase in the activity of the state, but it is certainly true that massive post-war economic growth in the countries of advanced capitalism has produced an environment in which governments have been able to pursue a much wider range of policy options than ever before.

WHEN AND WHY POLITICS MATTERS

Counterposed to the view that the main forces impacting on public policy development have been socio-economic in character has been the argument that politics matters. Within the 'politics matters' camp, there has been a division between those who see partisan ideology as the shaping force of modern policy development and those who regard the institutional structuring of the state and the broader polity as of greater significance. Table 8.2 summarizes our findings relevant to these issues. It should be noted that corporatism and trade union density were the only political variables hypothesized as being directly linked to labour supply outcomes, because it was assumed that any other ideological and institutional effects were likely to be mediated via policy variables. Such indirect effects were apparent in the ways in which high levels of transfers spending led to male labour force withdrawal and in which high levels of public consumption expenditure led to increased female labour supply. In respect of both fertility and divorce rates, it was assumed that all political effects would be indirect and, for that reason, these outcomes are not included in Table 8.2. The only potential evidence for an indirect effect in either case is the positive association between the family cash replacement rate and fertility for the early 1990s. In fact, the association between the family cash replacement rate and cumulative Left cabinet seats over the period 1950–93 is extremely strong (0.79), suggesting that, via this indirect route, political choice may also have had some degree of influence on fertility patterns.

Table 8.2 Institutional and ideological determinants of policy outcomes

	1960s	1970s	1990s	Change
Outlays of government	None	Turnout (+) Left (+) EC (+)	Turnout (+) Right (−) Constitution (−)	Right (−)
Receipts of government	None	Right (−)	Right (−) Constitution (−)	Right (−) Constitution (−)
Civilian public consumption	Turnout (+) Left (+)	Turnout (+) Left (+)	Left (+)	Left (+)
Social security transfers	None	Right (−)	Right (−) Federalism (−)	Right (−) Federalism (−)
Public health expenditure	None	Turnout (+) Left (+)	None	None
Public education expenditure	Right (−)	Turnout (+) Right (−)	Right (−) Constitution (−)	Right (−) Constitufion (−)
Male labour force	None	None	None	None
Female labour force	None	None	None	None
Unemployment	Corporatism (−)	Corporatism (−)	Right (−) Corporatism (−)	Right (−) Corporatism (−)
Home ownership	None	Corporatism (−)	Corporatism (−)	None

Variables and sources: See appropriate appendices. Signs in parentheses indicate whether the finding is positive or negative

Turning to direct effects on public expenditure, the first point to note is the existence of a distinct pattern over time. Leaving aside education and public consumption expenditure, where political influences are constant, the basic sequence is one of the irrelevance of politics in the earliest period, of strong turnout and mixed Left and Right incumbency effects in the mid-1970s and of their replacement by the negative influence of constitutional impediments and by more exclusive Right incumbency effects in the early 1990s. The findings for the final period are also replicated for change over time. This is the story of a major transformation. Where, in the early post-war period, political effects were restricted to a few aspects of service provision by the state, from the 1970s onwards, only the health sector is immune from political influences frequently exerted simultaneously through institutional and ideological channels.

Moreover, given the undoubted role of the political Left in extending public provision in the health arena, the one exception to the rule of a contemporary world of public policy substantially shaped by political forces is more apparent than real.

The contrast between a seemingly non-political world of public policy in the early 1960s and a highly politicized one thereafter is undoubtedly too extreme. Looking at the correlations in Figures 4.1–4.3 and 5.1–5.3, we find strong patterns of association between 1960 and 1974 expenditure outcomes on the one hand and electoral turnout and Left and Right incumbency on the other. The link with democratic participation is astonishingly consistent, with turnout the only variable in our entire data-set to be significantly related to every single aspect of spending at both of these time-points. Except in the case of early 1990s outlays, turnout ceases to be significantly related to outcomes after 1974, but both Left and Right incumbency continue to be strongly and consistently associated with spending levels. This suggests that what needs explaining is not the sudden emergence of politics as a force shaping policy development, but rather changes in the kinds of political factors that were most salient at different time-points. The changes of the greatest interest are the virtual disappearance of an electoral turnout effect, the increasing salience of partisan effects from the 1970s onwards, the emergence of a strong constitutional impediments effect in the 1990s and the shift from mixed incumbency effects to a more clear-cut dominance of the Right by the end of the period.

In discussing the potential impact of democratization in Chapter 3, we suggested that turnout effects which ceased with the end of authoritarian government in Southern Europe could probably best be interpreted in terms of these nations achieving a threshold level of democratic representation permitting the free expression of political views. We pointed out that such an interpretation conformed broadly with the views of those proponents of modernization theory who saw political development as being no less a part of the modernization process than corresponding changes in the economic and social structure. Alternatively, turnout effects persisting into the 1990s might be seen as more consistent with the argument that electoral institutions directly influence the policy process by exposing the political system to greater or less degrees of popular demand.

Reviewing our findings as a whole, the former interpretation seems the more compelling. On the one hand, the evidence for an electoral institutions effect is weak. The only significant term for the 1990s occurs in the outlays model, but as noted in the relevant analysis section, the term is of only marginal significance and insufficient by itself to warrant strong conclusions. On the other hand, the positive evidence for a political modernization effect is very strong. The vast majority of the significant links with turnout occur in the mid-1970s, at a time when all three Southern European nations had autocratic forms of government. Moreover, the significant terms in all the 1960 and 1974 equations disappear once the Southern European nations are excluded from the analysis. The story, then, is of a threshold effect in which the countries of Southern Europe were the last to establish the institutional structures making it possible for citizens to influence the activities of the state. Like economic development, democratic government is not a sufficient but a necessary condition for modern policy development. The extent of democratic representation does not determine what the activities of the state will be, but the fact that political institutions are representative ensures that their scope will be far greater than where they are not.

The stories of the increasing salience of partisan effects and of the emergence of a constitutional impediments effect can be told in conjunction. Our best clue as to what is taking place and why is the relative timing of events in relation to changes in the health of the post-war economy. The greater salience of socio-economic variables in the early period can be seen in terms of the dominance of resource and needs considerations in a period of relative scarcity. But, if our earlier interpretation is correct, by the mid-1970s most OECD countries had moved beyond a threshold of affluence, where public policy choices were less constrained than previously. Under these circumstances, it makes sense that differences in ideological preference would increasingly structure the choices that were made. Parties make promises to favour the interests of their own constituents and all variants of class theory suggest that the Left is more strongly committed to extending the bounds of the state than is the Right. Thus, by a fine paradox, it was precisely in a period in which commentators could discern an 'end of ideology' that remaining ideological differences began to matter more, because governments were less economically constrained in fulfilling their manifesto promises.

By the early 1970s, governments in most OECD countries had embarked on a huge range of public expenditure programmes. Although, clearly, there were now real differences between Right and Left, some expansion of spending was universal, fuelled by the need for parties of all complexions to appear responsive to popular demands. Moreover many programmes contained substantial in-built pressures for further growth, particularly through enhanced commitments to population groups, like the aged, which could only increase with the passing of time. The premise was that the fulfilment of such inertial spending commitments would be relatively painless in an era in which high rates of economic growth had become the normal expectation of governments and their economic advisers. Instead, the first oil shock heralded the end of the 'Golden Age' of Western capitalism, foreshadowing further expenditure expansion as programmed commitments increased relative to levels of income growth and as the new armies of the unemployed took up their entitlements from the state. Under these new circumstances, widely construed as a fundamental crisis of the welfare state, issues of spending and taxing constraints re-emerged. In partisan terms, the result was initially to exacerbate differences as major parties of the Right were the first to withdraw their loyalty from a Keynesian orthodoxy of public sector expansion. Over the past decade, most parties of the Left have also shifted their ground, but differences remain, not least because the embrace of New Right philosophy by the Left has been most ardent in those countries in which the Right has been historically dominant and, most conspicuously so, in the countries making up the English-speaking family of nations.

That leaves the question of why constitutional impediments also became more salient in this period. The probable answer is that while federal institutions and other forms of constitutional veto merely slow down expenditure development at times when there is a widespread consensus that growth is possible, they provide more potent weapons once the general consensus shifts the other way. In the 1960s and the early 1970s, the growth of government was marginally less expansive in federal than in unitary states, but since, on average, such nations started from a slightly higher base than the OECD norms for overall spending and taxing, and since, in some of these countries, there were expansive spending programmes at times when non-rightist governments were in office, this does not show up in 1974 measures of the size of government. However, in the two decades after the first oil shock, the federal nations and those scoring high on the constitutional structure variable progressively fell farther behind OECD averages, with particular restraint in the expansion of income transfers and tax revenues. Revenues may, indeed, be the key to the post-crisis salience of political institutions, since the existence of greater veto power over budgetary processes provides a principled and recurrent platform for questioning the continued viability of expenditure programmes right across the board. The story, then, is that politics mattered in the 1970s because of divergent preferences for policy action by the state and mattered thereafter because of divergent beliefs as to the desirability of a bigger state and divergent institutional means for containing its growth.

In the broad scheme of this changing pattern of political forces and policy development, the issue of the relative salience of Left and Right is scarcely a matter of great import. Whilst the issue has sometimes been contentious in the literature, the question turns largely on the spending performance of a rather small group of countries. Cumulative Left incumbency effects will be salient when spending is particularly pronounced in the four countries in which Social Democracy has been hegemonic in the post-war period: Austria, Denmark, Norway and Sweden. Cumulative Right incumbency effects will be salient when high spending is particularly pronounced in a group of countries in which the Right has been exceptionally weak for much of the post-war period: the Social Democratic countries plus Belgium, Finland and the Netherlands.

In the early period, the Social Democratic nations were in the forefront of public consumption spending, giving rise to a positive Left effect, while Belgium and the Netherlands joined Scandinavia in the vanguard of educational spending to produce a negative Right effect. In 1974, Social Democratic hegemony in public consumption expenditure was allied with some moderate Scandinavian expansion in transfers spending to produce a positive Left effect in the outlays model. In the transfers area itself, huge spending by Belgium and the Netherlands made for a Right incumbency effect. But these partisan effects are obviously asymmetrical: Left incumbency findings depend on the exclusivity of the Social Democratic nations, while Right incumbency findings reflect the commonality of a reasonably large sub-set of these seven nations. By the early 1990s, apart from Scandinavian leadership in state services expressed in a continuing Left incumbency effect on public consumption spending, commonality ruled over exclusivity.

So where does this leave the claim of the protagonists of the 'power resources' model that the fullest extension of social citizenship rights is dependent on working class mobilization and Social Democratic hegemony? What the overall pattern of our findings shows is that, while there is a strong association between Left incumbency and the development of large-scale programmes of public spending, there are also other political configurations which produce similar outcomes. Thus the error of the protagonists of the 'power resources' model is to see Social Democratic hegemony as being both a necessary and a sufficient condition for the emergence of the advanced welfare state, when a more appropriate conclusion would be to see it as, at best, a sufficient condition.

We conclude this section with three summary comments on the remaining political variables which feature in our analysis: trade union density, corporatism and the European Community. First, it is worth noting that the complete absence of significant terms for either trade union density or corporatism in our public spending models, despite correlations frequently as strong as those for Left or Right incumbency, tends to support the view that class conflict, whether institutionalized or otherwise, only impacts on the size of the state if mediated via partisanship. Second, the fact that corporatism has no role in shaping the taxing and spending characteristics of the post-war state, but features prominently in our understanding of labour market and housing policy, suggests that this variable captures a dimension of political behaviour somewhat different from partisanship. Partisanship is about the battle of diverse interests; corporatism is about the ground rules of the conflict. What corporatist countries have in common are institutional arrangements and/or solidaristic traditions which serve to counter the partisan pursuit of private interest when victory can only be achieved at the cost of broader collective goals. Ensuring that distributive conflict does not result in mass unemployment and making mass housing the first priority of immediate post-war housing policy can thus be seen as characteristically corporatist endeavours. Finally, the only signs of European Community effects in our findings are indicative of prior characteristics that member states had in common. Whatever effects membership may have had on public spending and on labour markets, they have either been too subtle or, perhaps, too recent to be demonstrated as gross divergences from broader OECD patterns.

ON PATTERNS OF CONVERGENCE AND CATCH-UP

Because the convergence or divergence of post-war policy outcomes has been seen as an important benchmark for the validity of theories of post-war public policy development, it is worth asking whether our overall findings reveal any clear patterns in this respect. Table 8.3 uses the coefficients of variation reported in the comparative outcomes tables in Chapters 4 to 7 to establish whether patterns of outcomes are convergent, divergent or unchanged over three periods: the 1960s–1970s (that is, beginning in 1960 and generally terminating in 1974), the 1970s–1990s (that is, in most cases, beginning in 1974 and terminating in the early 1990s) and the 1960s–1990s (that is, beginning in 1960 and terminating in the early 1990s). Since one obvious potential source of convergence is the economic modernization and democratization of the countries of Southern Europe, we have also calculated coefficients of variation for a sample of nations excluding these countries and in parentheses we indicate cases where the patterns displayed by this smaller sample differ from the trajectory of change manifested by the OECD as a whole. In the final column of Table 8.3, we offer a simple categorization of the degree of cross-national variation in policy outcomes remaining in the early 1990s.

The sub-period patterns revealed by Table 8.3 defy easy generalization in terms of convergence and divergence. In the 1960s–1970s period, divergent and unchanged trajectories somewhat outweigh convergent ones, but

Table 8.3 Patterns of convergence and divergence

	1960s–1970s	1970s–1990s	1960s–1990s	Status in 1990s
Outlays of government	Unchanged (C)	Convergent (U)	Convergent	Alike
Receipts of government	Divergent	Convergent (U)	Convergent (D)	Alike
Civilian public consumption	Divergent	Convergent (D)	Divergent	Different (VD)
Social security transfers	Convergent	Convergent	Convergent	Very different
Public health expenditure	Convergent	Convergent	Convergent	Alike (VA)
Public education expenditure	Unchanged (C)	Convergent (D)	Convergent	Different
Male labour force	Unchanged	Divergent	Divergent	Very alike
Female labour force	Convergent	Convergent	Convergent	Alike
Unemployment	Convergent	Divergent (C)	Convergent	Very different
Home ownership	Convergent	Convergent	Convergent	Different
Fertility	Divergent	Convergent	Convergent	Alike (VA)
Divorce	Unchanged (C)	Convergent	Convergent	Very different

Definitions and notes: Distributions are categorized as unchanged if the difference between coefficients of variation for two time-periods is 1.0 or less. Where a coefficient of variation increases by more than 1.0, the distribution is categorized as divergent; where it decreases by more than 1.0, it is categorized as convergent. Letters in parentheses indicate differences in patterns of convergence and divergence when the countries of Southern Europe are excluded from the comparison: U = Unchanged; D = Divergent; C = Convergent. Final column categorizations are derived from coefficients of variation for early 1990s outcomes as follows: Very alike = Below 15.00; Alike = 15.00–19.99; Different = 20.00–24.99; Very different = 25.00+. Letters in parentheses indicate differences in patterns of convergence and divergence when the countries of Southern Europe are excluded from the comparison: VA = Very alike; VD = Very different.

more convergence is evident when we exclude the countries of Southern Europe. In the 1970s–1990s there is a marked preponderance of convergent outcomes, but the balance swings back somewhat when Southern Europe is excluded. In the first period, the spending and taxing variables are evenly divided between divergence, convergence and a lack of change. In the second period, the patterns are universally convergent, but the even division re-emerges with the exclusion of Greece, Portugal and Spain. The pattern for the period as whole is more clearly convergent, irrespective of sample and irrespective of whether we are looking at measures of the size of the state or at outcomes in the labour market and the realm of the personal. The final column of Table 8.3 reveals that trajectories of policy change over three decades had left marked cross-national variation in a number of areas, including social security transfers, education, unemployment and divorce. Excluding the countries of Southern Europe from this latter comparison does not suggest that the continuing fact of substantial policy differences amongst OECD nations is attributable to outcomes in these nations.

The two accounts of public policy development which have posited convergent patterns of outcomes as demonstrations of their validity are modernization and globalization theory. If the former theory is articulated in terms of changing levels of economic development, it fits rather poorly with the trajectories of public expenditure change revealed in Table 8.3. The period when measures of income were converging most rapidly (see Table 2.2) was during the 1960s and early 1970s, when patterns of outcomes were least convergent. Moreover, as the pace of income convergence decreased from the 1970s–1990s, policy convergence became more general. Obviously lagged effects are possible, but have not been reported in the literature to date. Far more congruent with the periodization of the change trajectories observed here would be a modernization account premised on age structure effects alone. Table 2.6, presenting data on the age structure of the population, shows a modest divergence between 1960 and 1974 and a massive convergence between 1974 and 1993, which is far closer to the pattern of expenditure trajectories observed in Table 8.3. Such a conclusion is also broadly congruent with the strong age structure terms featuring in the social security transfers and outlays models and the rather more modest one in the receipts model.

Turning to the globalization thesis, it will be remembered that patterns of post-war trade as revealed in Table 2.3 have remained highly dissimilar and only minimally convergent across the entire post-war period, again implying a weak congruence with expenditure trajectories. It is, however, possible to argue that what matters about globalization is the perception of policy-makers that nations with extensive trade or capital flows will be punished by markets if they depart from the paths of financial rectitude. Such a perception might also be a factor making for convergence in taxing and spending outcomes. The problem in matching theoretical predictions and reality in this case is that globalization predicts a downward convergence in expenditure development, whereas the general trend manifested by the data in Chapters 4 and 5 was markedly upwards. It is fair to suggest that this is a quite weak test for the effects of globalization, which have, supposedly, emerged most strongly over the past 15 years or so. However, looking to routinely available OECD data (OECD, 1996a) shows very little sign of a marked downward trend in recent years.

Admittedly, between 1983 and 1993 the OECD average level of public consumption expenditure went down by 0.6 of a per cent of GDP, but average transfers spending increased by 1.3 percentage points. In the same period, total outlays of government went up by 1.5 percentage points and receipts of government by 1.4 percentage points. Thus it would seem that the final years of the post-war period have been characterized by a virtual stabilization of public spending levels after a quarter century or more of growth of big government and the welfare state.

This plateauing of OECD public expenditure development over the past decade or so itself requires some explanation. Several candidates suggest themselves. One is the response of governments to the end of the 'Golden Age' of economic resource growth; another is, indeed, the growing perception that the further growth of government has become difficult to combine with economic competitiveness. However, there is at least one further possible explanation for the plateauing effect that has the virtues of being compatible with the modest pattern of expenditure convergence actually observed over the post-war period as well as featuring prominently in our findings for each of the main programmes of post-war welfare state development. Health, education and transfers spending not only converged over the post-war period as a whole, but also manifested significant degrees of catch-up. In health and education, we interpreted these findings as indicative of a high degree of programme maturation and a similar diagnosis seems applicable to transfers, although to a much lesser degree.

The notion of programme maturation fits with an emergent plateauing of expenditure and with some limited degree of convergence, but also with some continuing cross-national variation. A major source of perceived cross-national diversity is that programmes in different nations are at different stages of maturity. Plateauing arises as countries complete their programme coverage and as entitlement levels rise to meet community expectations. Countries literally catch up because early adopters reach the plateau of their performance, whilst other countries continue to expand their coverage or entitlements. Once all programmes are mature, variation remains because those who designed the programmes in the first place had different objectives and adopted different mechanisms for programme delivery. That, in turn, is because notions of adequate coverage and proper standards are themselves moulded by ideological, institutional and cultural factors, which, as we have seen throughout this book, differ from country to country.

Most of these conclusions relating to trajectories of the size of the state can be replicated for outcomes in the labour market and the realm of the personal. Here too, convergence is more a feature of the later than of the earlier post-war years, although, here too, the broad tendency of development is also convergent. Although not always showing up in significant terms in all the relevant models, much of the analysis offered above suggests that the factor contributing most to growing similarity is the shift out of agricultural and manufacturing employment and into services employment. Even more than an ageing population, a services economy and a services society have become the OECD norm in the final decade of the Twentieth Century (see Table 2.4). Obviously, the factor which ensures that cross-national variation will not go away in these areas is the widespread influence of religious differences on trajectories of change. As we shall see in the next section, these are areas where culture matters a great deal.

Finally, we note that in respect of both female labour force participation and fertility, there are strong patterns of catch-up, no less suggestive of maturation effects than in the case of welfare state programmes. We interpreted the former as a victory for feminism and a major step toward redressing gender power differentials. The latter trend has more ominous portents. Post-war change in fertility rates represents a catch-up process which, according to the findings of Appendix 7.2, is only about three quarters complete. Since fertility is the one case of downwards convergence in our entire dataset, and since average fertility rates are already well below reproduction levels, continuation of such a trend is likely to have rather serious consequences.

CONCERNING FAMILY MATTERS

The purposes of this section are to identify the main family of nations patterns characterizing post-war public policy outcomes and to comment on the usefulness of a family of nations approach in comparative public policy analysis. The technique we have used for identifying such patterns has not been statistical, but has involved analysis of each of the cross-national distributions of economic, social political and policy data discussed in this book, with a view to locating instances in which the majority of nations in a given family grouping cluster relatively closely together. In Table 8.4, we adopt the somewhat more rigorous strategy of designating each family grouping as a dummy variable and calculating the correlation between that variable and each of the policy outcome variables featuring in our analysis. This makes it possible to establish instances where family groupings stand out at one end of the distribution or the other and to provide an indication of the relative strength of such effects. Such an analysis is an adjunct to, not a substitute for, identifying

Table 8.4 Families of nations and policy outcomes

	1960s	1970s	1990s	Change
Outlays of government	CW (Modest +) SE (Modest −)	CW (Modest +) SE (Strong −)	E-S (Modest −) SC (Strong +)	E-S (Moderate −) SC (Strong +)
Receipts of government	CW (Strong +) SE (Strong −)	SC (Moderate +) SE (Moderate −)	E-S (Modest −) SC (V. strong +)	E-S (Modest −) SC (Strong +)
Civilian public consumption	SC (Moderate +) SE (Moderate −)	SC (Moderate +) SE (Moderate −)	SC (Strong +)	SC (Moderate +)
Social security transfers	CW (E. Strong +) SE (Moderate −)	CW (V. strong +) SE (Moderate −)	E-S (Moderate −) SC (Modest +) CW (Modest +)	E-S (Modest −) SC (Moderate +)
Public health expenditure	SE (Modest −)	SC (Moderate +) SE (Strong −)	CW (Modest +) SE (Strong −)	None
Public education expenditure	SE (Strong −)	SC (Modest +) SE (E. strong −)	SC (V. strong +) SE (Modest −)	None
Male labour force	None	None	CW (Moderate −)	SE (Moderate −)
Female labour force	SE (Modest −)	SC (Strong +)	SC (Strong +) SE (Modest −)	None
Unemployment	E-S (Modest +)	E-S (Moderate +)	None	None
Home ownership	E-S (Moderate +) CW (Moderate −)	E-S (Moderate +) CW (Modest −)	E-S (Modest +)	None
Fertility	E-S (V. strong +)	SE (Modest +)	E-S (Moderate +) CW (Modest −) SE (Modest −)	E-S (Strong −) SC (Moderate +)
Divorce	SE (Modest −)	SE (Modest −)	SE (Modest −)	E-S (Moderate +)

Notes: Key to family groupings: E-S = English-speaking; SC = Scandinavian; CW = Continental Western Europe; SE = Southern Europe. Key to strength of relationships: Modest = 0.40 > 0.49; Moderate = 0.50 > 0.59; Strong = 0.60 > 0.69; V(ery) strong = 0.70 > 0.79; E(xtremely) strong = 0.80 > 90.

the presence of family clusters across the distribution. Clustering effects are no less significant when they occur in the middle of a distribution than when they occur at the extremes.

Looking at Table 8.4 in conjunction with Tables 8.1 and 8.2, it is possible to establish some degree of correspondence between significant family groupings and the economic, social, institutional and ideological variables which feature in our explanatory models. English-speaking countries are negatively associated with social security spending, receipts and total outlays towards the end of the period, because they tend to have high levels of Right incumbency. They also cluster as positive predictors of unemployment in the earlier period and home ownership throughout, because they tend to be characterized by low levels of manufacturing employment and to lack corporatist institutions. Scandinavian commonalities tend to be associated with ideological variables: with positive Left incumbency effects in the case of public consumption expenditure and negative Right incumbency effects for most other taxing and spending variables from 1974 onwards. It is also possible to discern Scandinavian similarities deriving from the way in which partisan incumbency has shaped the reach of the modern state, as in the consistent positive effect of public consumption expenditure on female labour supply. The affinities among the continental Western European family of nations are strongest in respect of social security transfers and outlays and seem most closely related to measures of religious difference. Finally, distinctive Southern European patterns of outlays, receipts and transfers are most pronounced in the early period, with the region's relative lack of economic modernity clearly the most relevant factor. The same factor appears to account for the region's low divorce rates throughout the period, while it is Southern Europe's high level of Catholic adherence that seems to be the key to its weak educational spending levels.

Another kind of families of nations effect has been prominent in our analysis, although it has not been labelled as such. The Catholic cultural impact variable groups nations on the basis of a significant aspect of their cultural experience, which is as old as the Reformation, but which has continuing resonances in diverse beliefs concerning social expenditure, education, divorce and most issues relating to family and gender. Catholic cultural impact is the variable in Table 8.1 which is associated with the widest range of outcomes, and the influence of religious difference is still more far-reaching if we regard the measures of Catholic adherence and Christian Democratic incumbency as capturing aspects of the same phenomenon. It must be emphasized that the division of our sample of nations on the basis of religious difference is not an alternative way of elaborating family affinities, but merely a simplification of the existing story. Religion may be a significant source of policy difference amongst the OECD nations, but it does not cut across our existing family groupings. Southern Europe plus continental Western Europe together make up the Catholic world of advanced democratic nations; the English-speaking nations together with Scandinavia plus Switzerland and Japan constitute the non-Catholic world.

Overall, post-war public expenditure can be seen either in terms of a four-family pattern or in terms of the supersession of one two-family pattern by another. As demonstrated by the findings concerning levels of social security transfers and the outlays and receipts of government in Table 8.4 and in Chapters 4 and 5, the crucial divide of the immediate post-war decades was between rich and poor Catholic nations, with economic development providing a dynamic of welfare development which distinguished the vanguard performance of continental Western Europe. The fact that, despite this clear differentiation, a Catholic cultural impact effect features in our models for both transfers and outlays at the beginning of the period is the result of a curvilinear specification of income effects, which takes account of the crucial impact of economic development in the Catholic nations during these decades. Our models capture the reality of both kinds of patterns.

Contemporary development and change over time reverses the pattern of the early post-war decades. What matters most now are political differences in the non-Catholic nations, with the left-wing Scandinavian nations becoming expenditure leaders and the right-wing English-speaking nations the laggards. This overall pattern of post-war development clearly has clear affinities with Esping-Andersen's account of the three worlds of welfare capitalism. His data are for 1980, at around the time of the transition from one set of patterns to the other, and his analysis excludes the countries of Southern Europe. Thus, his account of three worlds – a Social Democratic world of Scandinavia, in which consistently strong public consumption expenditure is conjoint with a moderately strong development of transfers, a 'conservative' world of continental Western Europe, built on strong transfers spending, and a 'liberal' English-speaking world, with weak welfare state development across the board – neatly captures the contemporary reality. The analysis here is only different in providing us with a picture of the ways in which the pattern is transformed over the post-war period as a whole.

Family of nations patterns relating to labour supply and the realm of the personal are probably more appropriately analysed in terms of two families of nations. These are areas in which beliefs matter more than economics or politics. Attitudes to issues of gender and the family have not been markedly different in the countries of continental Western European and Southern Europe, and have tended to contrast quite strongly with the more individualistic beliefs common to the non-Catholic nations. Again the story is one of a fractured modernity in which economic and cultural modernization are cross-cutting rather than complementary aspects of societal development. Since economic modernization is the shaping factor of the growth of the state in Catholic Europe and cultural modernization is what matters for gender and family concerns, family of nations patterns differ depending on the issue in question.

What we have attempted to demonstrate by summarizing these patterns of national affinity is that accounts resting on the families of nations metaphor can help us to reduce complex findings to understandable patterns of causation. Sometimes such accounts can also be of assistance in directing our attention to factors which are omitted from our explanations. Comparative analysis is generally at its strongest in deploying structural variables of the kind featured in this study. It has been much weaker in coming to grips with cultural, historical, linguistic and geographical parameters of national difference. Because the impact of such nation-centred variables is often better captured by qualitative research, such factors have frequently been neglected in systematic comparative analysis of the kind attempted in this study. But, as our discussion of the multiple policy impacts of religious differences clearly demonstrates, it is possible to devise measures for such parameters and they can play a significant role in systematic comparative analysis.

A family of nations approach highlights cases where researchers should be thinking in terms of nation-centred variables. A dramatic example is to be found in the discussion of state services in the final section of Chapter 5. In the model reported there (see note, p. 188), Left incumbency and trade union density were identified as factors very strongly associated with this category of spending. However, it turns out that the relationship between state services and our dummy variable for the Scandinavian family of nations is much greater still, accounting for more of the variation than both measures of working class mobilization put together. That leaves us with the question of what it is that accounts for the Scandinavian singularity in state services spending, but it also tells us where the answer must lie: namely, in other aspects of the Scandinavian experience still more closely associated with that singularity. Structural variables may capture part of that singularity – interestingly, Left incumbency features significantly in a model of state services in which the Scandinavian dummy is the strongest variable, but in which trade union density drops out – but the likelihood is that a fuller explanation will require nation-centred variables as well.

In this particular case, there are many possibilities – the influence of Lutheranism on Scandinavian conceptions of the role of the state, the impact of policy diffusion amongst the Scandinavian nations, unique forms of social solidarity resulting from long decades of Left hegemony (that is, a Social Democratic 'image of society') – but a hugely strong Scandinavian effect tells us that the first place we should be looking for a solution is in the nature of the Scandinavian experience. This does not, of course, mean that we should substitute research on particular areas for the systematic use of explanatory variables (Przeworski, 1987, 38–9). The question is one of the route we take to locating the nature of those variables. We can begin with structural variation or we can begin with patterns of commonality between nations. The point we are making is that sometimes these patterns are so strong that it makes sense to start from them.

THE FUTURE OF THE STATE

The story of post-war policy development has been one of a massive transformation. Government has more than doubled in size and its role as a provider of citizen needs has been hugely extended. However, in the 1980s, the last decade of the post-war period proper, the continuing growth and, indeed, in some instances, the continuing viability of big government and the welfare state have been called into question. This challenge is explicit in the New Right analysis of the 'over-mighty' state, which sees privatization of the service functions of the state as the only answer, and implicit in globalization theory, which views public spending and economic regulation as inimical to international competitiveness. We conclude our discussion by commenting briefly on the implications of our findings for the future of big government and the welfare state.

These comments can be brief because we do not believe the evidence for an imminent decline in the caring role of the state is very persuasive. Given our findings concerning the importance of Right partisan effects, the most obvious threat to the welfare state would come from a major shift in the ideological fault lines that have continued to characterize Western party systems for much of the post-war period. Such a shift seems likely to be slow in coming. As noted in Chapter 3, ideological polarization has scarcely declined and the 'unfreezing' of party systems is in its early stages. Moreover, arguments that the Left is in a long process of secular decline are invariably belied by the next day's news: who would have believed that only a few years before the turn of the millennium, Britain, France and Italy would all be ruled by reformist governments, two of them with the support of communist or former communist parties? Finally, it is worth remembering that, in most cases, our measures of partisan effects have been cumulative ones. This means that partisan effects increase gradually over time. By implication, it suggests that any radical dismantling of the welfare state will require much greater political change than any yet apparent and will have to occur over a time-span little shorter than that surveyed in this volume.

The other major threat to big government and the welfare state would arise if the prognostications of globalization theory proved accurate. As we have pointed out previously, our empirical findings on this topic are tentative. For transfers, outlays and receipts the extent of international trade did seem to be a factor making for lower expenditures in the early 1990s. However, these findings were dependent on the single case of Ireland and were not replicated for the public consumption meta-programme or its component elements, areas with no less relevance to issues of international competitiveness. We do not dismiss the possibility that globalization effects may become more apparent with the passing of time, but the fact that international trade expanded so markedly in the early post-war period, and financial flows over the past 15 years, with consequences for domestic policy which are as yet, at best, ambiguous, does suggest that such effects are unlikely to be as dramatic in the short to medium term as is often implied.

Against the view that the state is about to decline, we can set three countervailing points. First and foremost is the fact that post-war public policy development has been underpinned by economic and political modernity. Threshold levels of affluence and democratic representation do not directly shape the size of programmes, but they almost certainly guarantee that such programmes will continue to exist and that any process of radical reshaping will be slow. Pierson's (1995) story of New Right administrations in Britain and the USA seeking – and often failing – to dismantle welfare state programmes by stealth is the story of the power of democratic representation to frustrate ideologically motivated attacks on big government. Second is the connected point that a number of the more important government spending programmes can now be seen as having achieved maturity in the sense of offering complete coverage of relevant populations and offering entitlements meeting with contemporary community standards. As we have shown, this is a process now arguably complete in the arenas of health and education and on the way to completion in the area of income transfers. Full coverage and entitlements based on community standards are, of course, principles that could be altered, but probably not too easily within the structure of the democratic polity. More likely are threats posed by attempts to redefine the adequacy of coverage and the rationale for particular entitlement levels. This has been the strategy of cost-containing governments across the OECD, but it has neither been universally successful nor has it, so far, done much more than contain the rise in state expenditures.

The reason that cost-cutting in some programmes does not reduce the overall size of government brings us to our third point: there remain some factors which continue to provide a dynamic for further expenditure growth. Most conspicuous of these is, of course, population ageing, which our findings show to be a strong factor pushing the post-war expansion of outlays and transfers and a somewhat weaker one in the growth of the total receipts of government. Whether it shows up in our findings or not, it is also a factor deeply relevant to escalating health care costs. According to all demographic prognostications, the ageing of the population of the advanced democratic states is not a problem that will go away over the course of the next 50 years or so, although it is a problem that varies quite markedly from country to country. Governments in some nations have seen the solution to rising pension costs as the privatization of life-cycle redistribution via private superannuation, but a reform of this character has no obvious economic advantages and simply transforms the state's role into one of fiduciary guarantor of a contributory insurance scheme. The more fundamental problem, funding the costs of vertical redistribution for those unable to make adequate provision for old age over a lifetime of contributions, remains.

Governments in coming years may also face other demands for the expansion of the state. In terms of the analysis presented here, the issue of the greatest urgency is to take steps to reduce a widespread and massive fertility decline, which threatens the continued viability of populations and societies as well as states. If the post-war period has witnessed a trade-off between work and family life of the dimensions suggested here, governments will have to contemplate some very expensive population policy measures to reverse the tide. The nature of the policy changes required is quite clear: a shift towards a welfare state focused on the contemporary needs of women, providing them with the services and income required to combine maternity with labour force participation. In the short to medium term, such policies are likely to increase spending pressures. In the very long term, however, the reverse may be true. A crucial reason why populations are ageing, and a major reason why ageing problems are different in different nations, is that fertility rates have declined, and have declined more in some countries than in others. A population policy aimed at increasing fertility will eventually pay dividends in reducing the pressure of welfare spending on the old.

Assuming no providential quantum increase in the rate of economic growth, the most probable overall outcome of the tendencies rehearsed here will be a long era of continued attempts at programme containment in the face of population pressures for greater spending, which seem likely to escalate in coming years. The modern state, characterized by big government and extensive welfare provision, has been the product of post-war transformation and will not disappear in the near future. What will change, however, is which countries pursue what policy goals and to what extent. What our analysis has amply demonstrated is that cross-national patterns of policy outcomes are in a constant state of flux as they are shaped by a wide range of economic, social, cultural, political and policy factors, which themselves alter over time. Everything matters and nations are never the same. That is the substance and the challenge of comparative public policy analysis.

References

Albrecht, S.L., Bahr, H.M. and Goodman, K.L. (1983), *Divorce and Remarriage: Problems, Adaptations and Adjustments*, Westport, C: Greenwood Press.

Alesina, A. (1989), 'Politics and business cycles in industrial democracies', *Economic Policy*, **8**, 55–98.

Alvarez, R.M., Garrett, G. and Lange, P. (1991), 'Government partisanship, labor organization, and macroeconomic performance', *American Political Science Review*, **85** (2), 539–56.

Ambert, A.-M. (1980), *Divorce in Canada*, Ontario: Academic Press Canada.

Ambrosius, G. and Hubbard, W.H. (1989), *A Social and Economic History of Twentieth-Century Europe*, Cambridge, MA: Harvard University Press.

Anderson, D. (1991), 'Is the privatisation of Australian schooling inevitable?', in Castles, F.G. (ed.), *Australia Compared: People, Policies and Politics*, Sydney: Allen & Unwin.

Andorka, R. (1978), *Determinants of Fertility in Advanced Societies*, London: Methuen.

Anttonen, A. and Sipilä, J. (1996), 'European social care services: is it possible to identify models?', in Alestalo, M. and Kosonen, P. (eds), *Welfare Systems and European Integration*, University of Tampere: Department of Sociology and Social Psychology, pp. 35–59.

Archer, M.S. (1979), *Social Origins of Educational Systems*, London: Sage Publications.

Arrow, K.J. (1963), 'Uncertainty and the welfare economics of medical care', *American Economic Review*, **53** (5), 941–73.

Bakker, I. (1988), 'Women's employment in comparative perspective', in Jenson, J., Hagen, E. and Reddy, C. (eds), *Feminization of the Labour Force*, Cambridge: Polity Press, pp. 65–84.

Baldwin, P. (1990), *The Politics of Social Solidarity: Class Bases of the European Welfare State 1875–1975*, Cambridge: Cambridge University Press.

Barrett, D.B. (1982), *World Christian Encyclopedia: A Comparative Study of Churches and Religions in the Modern World AD 1900–2000* Nairobi: Oxford University Press.

Bartolini, S. and Mair, P. (1990), *Identity, Competition, and Electoral Availability: the Stabilisation of European Electorates 1885–1985*, Cambridge: Cambridge University Press.

Baumol, W. (1967), 'The macroeconomics of unbalanced growth', *American Economic Review*, **57** (2), 415–26.

Beck, N. and Katz, J.N. (1995), 'What to do (and not to do) with time-series-cross-section data in comparative politics', *American Political Science Review*, **89** (3), 634–47.

Becker, G.S. (1991), *A Treatise on the Family*, Boston: Harvard University Press, 2nd edn.

Bell, D. (1960), *The End of Ideology: The Exhaustion of Political Ideas in the Fifties*, Glencoe, IL: The Free Press.

Bernstein, E. (1909), *Evolutionary Socialism*, New York: Schocken Books.

Blau, F.D. and Ferber, M.A. (1992), *The Economics of Women, Men, and Work*, Englewood Cliffs, NJ: Prentice-Hall, 2nd edn.

Boskin, M.J. (1977), 'Social security and retirement decisions', *Economic Inquiry*, **15**, 1–25.

Boskin, M.J. and Hurd, M.D. (1978), 'Effect of social security on early retirement', *Journal of Public Economy*, **10**, 361–77.

Bowen, W.G. and Finegan, T.A. (1969), *The Economics of Labor Force Participation*, Princeton, NJ: Princeton University Press.

Boyer, R. and Drache, D. (eds), *States Against Markets: The Limits of Globalization*, London: Routledge.

Brennan, G. and Buchanan, J.M. (1980), *The Power to Tax: Analytical Foundations of a Fiscal Constitution*, Cambridge: Cambridge University Press.

Briggs, A. (1961), 'The welfare state in historical perspective', *Archives Européennes de Sociologie*, **II** (2), 221–58.

Brittan, S. (1977), *The Economic Consequences of Democracy*, London: Temple Smith.

Bruno, M. and Sachs, J. (1985), *Economics of Worldwide Stagflation*, Cambridge, MA: Harvard University Press.

Buchanan, J.M. and Wagner, R. (1977), *Democracy in Deficit*, New York: Academic Press.

Burkhart, R.E. and Lewis-Beck, M.S. (1994), 'Comparative democracy: The economic development thesis', *American Political Science Review*, **88** (4), 903–10.

Busch, A. (1993), 'The politics of price stability: why German-speaking nations are different', in Castles, F.G. (ed.), *Families of Nations: Patterns of Public Policy in Western Democracies*, Aldershot: Dartmouth, pp. 35–92.

Calmfors, L. and Driffill, J. (1988), 'Bargaining structure, corporatism and macroeconomic performance', *Economic Policy*, **6**, 13–61.

Cameron, D. (1978) 'The expansion of the public economy: a comparative analysis', *American Political Science Review*, **72** (4), 1243–61.

Cameron, D. (1984), 'Social democracy, corporatism, labour quiescence and the representation of economic interest in advanced capitalist society', in Goldthorpe, J.H. (ed.), *Order and Conflict in Contemporary Capitalism*, Oxford: Oxford University Press, pp. 143–78.

Cameron, D. (1986), 'The growth of government spending: The Canadian experience in comparative perspective', *Royal Commission on Economic Union and Development Prospects for Canada*, Toronto: University of Toronto Press, Research Studies, **31**, 21–51.

Castles, F.G. (1978), *The Social Democratic Image of Society*, London: Routledge and Kegan Paul.

Castles, F.G. (1982), 'The impact of parties on public expenditure', in Castles, F.G. (ed.), *The Impact of Parties*, London: Sage Publications, pp. 21–96.

Castles, F.G. (1989), 'Explaining public education expenditure in OECD nations', *European Journal of Political Research*, **17**, 431–48.

Castles, F.G. (1991), 'Democratic politics, war and catch–up: Olson's thesis and long–term economic growth in the English–speaking nations of advanced capitalism', *Journal of Theoretical Politics*, **3** (1), 5–26.

Castles, F.G. (1992), 'The dynamics of public policy transformation', in Alexander, M. and Galligan, B. (eds), *Comparative Political Studies: Australia and Canada*, Melbourne: Pitman, pp. 105–18.

Castles, F.G. (ed.) (1993), *Families of Nations: Patterns of Public Policy in Western Democracies*, Aldershot: Dartmouth.

Castles, F.G. (1994a), 'On religion and public policy: does Catholicism make a difference?', *European Journal of Political Research*, **25**, 19–40.

Castles, F.G. (1994b), 'Is expenditure enough? On the nature of the dependent variable in comparative public policy analysis', *The Journal of Commonwealth and Comparative Politics*, **32** (3), 349–63.

Castles, F.G. (1995) 'Welfare state development in Southern Europe', *West European Politics*, **18** (2), 291–313.

Castles, F.G. (1997a), 'On income inequality and democracy: seeking a viable data base', *Keizai Kenkyû* (*The Economic Review*), **48** (2), 143–54.

Castles, F.G. (1997b), 'On leaving the Australian labor force: an extended encounter with the state', *Governance*, **10** (2), 97–122.

Castles, F.G. (1998), 'The really big trade–off: Home ownership and the welfare state in the New World and the Old', *Acta Politica*, **33** (1).

Castles, F.G. and Ferrera, M. (1996), 'Home ownership and the welfare state: is Southern Europe different?', *South European Society and Politics*, **1** (2), 163–85.

Castles, F.G. and Flood, M. (1993), 'Why divorce rates differ: law, religious belief and modernity', in Castles, F.G. (ed.), (1993), *Families of*

Nations: Patterns of Public Policy in Western Democracies. Aldershot: Dartmouth, pp. 293–326.

Castles, F.G. and Mair, P. (1984), 'Left–right political scales: Some expert judgements', *European Journal of Political Research*, **12**, 73–88.

Castles, F.G. and Marceau, J. (1989), 'The transformation of gender inequality in tertiary education', *Journal of Public Policy*, **9** (4), 493–508.

Castles, F.G. and McKinlay, R. (1979), 'Does politics matter?: An analysis of the public welfare commitment in advanced democratic states', *European Journal of Political Research*, **7**, 169–86.

Castles, F.G. and Mumford, K. (1992) 'The vision of a full employment Australia'. in Argy, F. (ed.), *A Long Term Economic Strategy for Australia*, Vol. 2, Sydney: CEDA Information Paper no. 35, 74–99.

Chesnais, J.C. (1992), *The Demographic Transition: Stages, Patterns, and Economic Implications*, Oxford: Clarendon Press.

Chester, R. (ed.) (1977) *Divorce in Europe*, Belgium: Netherlands Interuniversity Demographic Institute.

Choko, M.H. (1993), 'Homeownership: from dream to materiality', in Hays R.A. (ed.), *Ownership, Control, and the Future of Housing Policy*, Westport, C: Greenwood Press, pp. 3–38.

Clark, C. (1957), *The Conditions of Economic Progress*, London: Macmillan, 3rd edn.

Coale, A.J. and Watkins, S.C. (eds) (1986), *The Decline in Fertility in Europe*, Princeton, NJ: Princeton University Press.

Compston, H. (1994), 'Union participation in economic policy-making in Austria, Switzerland, Belgium, the Netherlands and Ireland, 1970–1992', *West European Politics*, **17** (1), 123–45.

Compston, H. (1995a), 'Union participation in economic policy-making in Scandinavia, 1970–1992', *West European Politics*, **18** (1), 98–115.

Compston, H. (1995b), 'Union participation in economic policy-making in France, Italy, Germany and Britain, 1970–1993', *West European Politics*, **18** (2), 314–39.

Cooper, B., Kornberg, A. and Mishler, W. (eds) (1988), *The Resurgence of Conservatism in Anglo–American Democracies*. Durham, NC: Duke University Press.

Crepaz, M.M.L. (1992), 'Corporatism in decline? An empirical analysis of the impact of corporatism on macroeconomic performance and industrial disputes in 18 industrialized democracies', *Comparative Political Studies*, **25** (2), 139–68.

Crepaz, M.M.L. (1995) 'Explaining variation in air pollution levels: political institutions and their impact on environmental policy-making', *Environmental Politics*, **4** (3), 391–414.

Crosland, A. (1963), *The Future of Socialism*, London: Jonathan Cape.

Crouch, C. (1985), 'Conditions for trade union restraint', in Lindberg, L.N. and Maier, C.S. (eds), *The Politics of Inflation and Economic Stagnation*, Washington: The Brookings Institution, pp. 105–39.

Crozier, M., Huntington, S.P. and Watanuki, S. (1975), *The Crisis of Democracy: Report to the Trilateral Commission on the Governability of Liberal Democracies*. New York: New York University Press.

Daalder, H. and Mair, P. (1983), *Western European Party Systems: Continuity and Change*. London: Sage Publications.

Dahl, R. and Tufte, E. (1973), *Size and Democracy*, Stanford, CA: Stanford University Press.

De Swaan, A. (1988), *In Care of the State: Health Care, Education and Welfare in Europe and the USA in the Modern Era*, Cambridge: Polity Press.

Detsky, A.S., Stacey, S.R. and Bombadier, C. (1983), 'The effectiveness of a regulatory strategy in containing hospital costs: the Ontario experience, 1967–1981', *The New England Journal of Medicine*, **309** (3), 153–8.

Dogan, M. and Pelassy, D. (1990), *How To Compare Nations*, London: Chatham House, 2nd edn.

Donnison, D.V. (1967), *The Government of Housing*, Harmondsworth: Penguin.

Duncan, N.G. (1981), 'Home ownership and social theory', in Duncan, J.S. (ed.), *Housing and Identity: Cross–cultural Perspectives*, London: Croom Helm, pp. 98–134.

Dunleavy, P. (1989), 'The United Kingdom: Paradoxes of an ungrounded statism', in Castles, F.G. (ed.), *The Comparative History of Public Policy*, Cambridge, Polity Press, pp. 242–91.

Dunleavy, P. and O'Leary, B. (1987), *Theories of the State: The Politics of Liberal Democracy*, London: Macmillan.

Esping–Andersen, G. (1985), *Politics Against Markets. The Social Democratic Road to Power*, Princeton, NJ: Princeton University Press.

Esping–Andersen, G. (1990), *The Three Worlds of Welfare Capitalism*, Cambridge: Polity Press.

Esping–Andersen, G. (1993), 'Budgets and democracy: towards a welfare state in Spain and Portugal, 1960–1986'. in Budge, I. and McKay, D. (eds), *Expanding Democracy: Research in Honour of Jean Blondel*, London: Sage.

Esping-Andersen, G. (ed.) (1996), *The Welfare State in Transition*, London: Sage.

Esping-Andersen, G. and Korpi, W. (1984) 'Social policy as class politics in post-war capitalism: Scandinavia, Austria and Germany', in Goldthorpe, J.H. (ed.), *Order and Conflict in Contemporary Capitalism*, Oxford: Clarendon Press, pp. 179–208.

Esping-Andersen, G. and Sonnenberger, H. (1989), *The Demographics of Age in Labour Market Management*, Florence: European University Institute, Working Papers, 89/414.

Ester, P., Halman, L. and de Moor, R. (1993), *The Individualizing Society: Value Change in Europe and North America*, Tilburg, The Netherlands: Tilburg University Press..

Ferrera, M. (1996), 'The "Southern Model" of welfare in social Europe', *Journal of European Social Policy*, **6** (1), 17–37.

Flora, P. (1983), *State, Economy and Society in Western Europe*, vol. 1, Chicago: St James Press.

Flora, P. (1986), 'Introduction'. in Flora, P. (ed.), *Growth to Limits: The Western European Welfare States Since World War II*, Berlin: De Gruyter, vol. 1, xi–xxxvi.

Flora, P. and Alber, J. (1981), 'Modernization, democratization, and the development of welfare states in Western Europe', in Flora, P. and Heidenheimer, A.J. *The Development of Welfare States in Europe and America*, New Brunswick: Transaction Books, pp. 37–80.

Forest, R. and Murie, A. (1985), 'Restructuring the welfare state: privatization of public housing in Britain', in van Vliet-Huttman, E and Fava, S. (eds), *Housing Needs and Policy Approaches: Trends in Thirteen Countries*, Durham, NJ: Duke University Press, pp. 97–109.

Frieden, J.A. and Rogowski, R. (1996), 'The impact of the international economy on national policies: an analytical overview', in Keohane, R.O. and Milner, H.V. (eds), *Internationalization and Domestic Politics*, Cambridge: Cambridge University Press, pp. 25–47.

Friedman, M. (1977), 'Inflation and unemployment', *Journal of Political Economy*, **85**, 451–72.

Friedman, M. and Friedman, R. (1980), *Free to Choose*, New York: Avon Books.

Fuchs, V.R. (1990), 'The health care sector's share of the gross national product', *Science*, **247**, 534–8.

Fulcher, D. (1974), *Medical Care Systems*, Geneva: International Labour Office.

Fulop, M. (1977), 'A survey of the literature on the economic theory of fertility behavior', *American Economist*, **21** (10), 5–16.

Gemmell, N. (1993), 'Wagner's law and Musgrave's hypotheses', in Gemmell, N. (ed.), *The Growth of the Public Sector: Theories and International Evidence*, Aldershot: Edward Elgar, pp. 103–20.

Glyn, A. and Rowthorn, B. (1988), 'West European unemployment: corporatism and structural change', *American Economic Review*, Papers and Proceedings, May, pp. 194–9.

Goode, W.J. (1963), *World Revolution and Family Patterns*, New York: Free Press of Glencoe.

Goodin, R.E. and Dryzek, J. (1987), 'Risk sharing and social justice: the motivational foundations of the post-war welfare state', in Goodin, R.E. and Le Grand, J. (eds), *Not Only The Poor*, London: Allen & Unwin, pp. 37–73.

Goodman, R. and Peng, I. (1996), 'The East Asian welfare states: peripatetic learning, adaptive change, and nation-building', in Esping-Andersen, G. (ed.), *The Welfare State in Transition*, London: Sage.

Gordon, M.S. (1988), *Social Security Policies in Industrial Countries*, Cambridge: Cambridge University Press.

Gornick, J.C., Meyers, M.K. and Ross, K.E. (1997), 'Supporting the employment of mothers: Policy variation across fourteen welfare states', *Journal Of European Social Policy*, **7** (1), 45–70.

Gough, I. (1979), *The Political Economy of the Welfare State*, London: Macmillan.

Gould, J. (1982), *The Rake's Progress? The New Zealand Economy Since 1945*, Auckland: Hodder and Stoughton.

Gourevitch, P. (1986), *Politics in Hard Times: Comparative Responses to International Economic Crises*, Ithaca, NY: Cornell University Press.

Gray, G. (1991), *Federalism and Health Policy*, Toronto: University of Toronto Press.

Gregory, R.G. (1993), 'Aspects of Australian and US living standards: the disappointing decades 1970–1990', *Economic Record*, **69** (1), 61–76.

Gunther, R. (1980), *Public Policy in a No-Party State*, Berkeley, CA: University of California Press.

Gustavsson, S. and Stafford, F. (1994), 'Three regimes of childcare: the United States, the Netherlands, and Sweden', in Blank, R. (ed.), *Social Protection versus Economic Flexibility*, Chicago: University of Chicago Press, pp. 333–62.

Halem, L.C. (1980), *Divorce Reform: Changing Legal and Social Perspectives*, New York: The Free Press.

Hamermesh, D.S. and Rees, A. (1988), *The Economics of Work and Pay*, New York: HarperCollins.

Hart, R. (1976), *When Marriage Ends: A Study in Status Passage*, London: Tavistock.

Hawthorn, G. (1980), 'The paradox of the modern: Determinants of fertility on northern and western Europe since 1950', in Höhn, C. and Mackensen, R. (eds), *Determinants of Fertility Trends: Theories Re-Examined*, Liège: Ordina Editions, pp. 281–96.

Headey, B. (1978), *Housing Policy in the Developed Economy*, London: Croom Helm.

Heclo, H. (1974), *Modern Social Politics in Britain and Sweden*, New Haven, CT: Yale University Press.

Hedman, E. (ed.) (1994), *Housing in Sweden and International Perspective*, Stockholm: Bokverket.

Heidenheimer, A.J. (1981), 'Education and social security entitlements in Europe and America', in Flora, P. and Heidenheimer, A.J. (eds), *The Development of Welfare States in Europe and America*, New Brunswick: Transaction Books, pp. 269–304.

Heidenheimer, A.J. (1996), 'Throwing money and heaving bodies: heuristic callisthenics for comparative policy buffs', in Imbeau, L.M. and McKinlay, R.D., (eds), *Comparing Government Activity*, London: Macmillan, pp. 13–25.

Heidenheimer, A.J. (1997), *Disparate Ladders: Why School and University Policies Differ in Germany, Japan, and Switzerland*, New Brunswick, NJ: Transaction Publishers.

Heidenheimer, A.J., Heclo, H. and Adams, C.T. (1990), *Comparative Public Policy*, New York: St Martin's Press, 3rd edn.

Henrekson, M. (1993) 'The Peacock–Wiseman hypothesis', in Gemmell, N. (ed.), *The Growth of the Public Sector: Theories and International Evidence*, Aldershot: Edward Elgar, pp. 53–71.

Hibbs, D.A. (1977), 'Political parties and macroeconomic policy', *American Political Science Review*, **71** (4), 1467–87.

Hibbs, D.A. (1987), *The Political Economy of Industrial Societies*, Cambridge, MA: Harvard University Press.

Hicks, A. and Swank, D. (1984), 'On the political economy of welfare expansion', *Comparative Political Studies*, **17** (1), 81–119.

Hicks, A. and Swank, D. (1992), 'Politics, institutions, and welfare spending in industrialized democracies, 1960–1982', *American Political Science Review*, **86** (3), 658–74.

Higgins, J. (1981), *States of Welfare: Comparative Analysis in Social Policy*, Oxford: Basil Blackwell.

Hirst, P. and Thompson, G. (1996), *Globalization in Question*, Cambridge: Polity Press.

Huber, J. and Inglehart, R. (1995), 'Expert interpretations of party space and party locations in 42 societies', *Party Politics*, **1** (1), 73–111.

Huber, E., Ragin, C. and Stephens, J.D. (1993), 'Social Democracy, Christian Democracy, constitutional structure and the welfare state', *American Journal of Sociology*, **99** (3), 711–49.

Hudson, P. and Lee, W.R. (1990), 'Introduction', in Hudson, P. and Lee, W.R. (eds), *Women's Work and the Family Economy in Historical Perspective*, Manchester: Manchester University Press, pp. 2–47.

ILO (1949), *Systems of Social Security: New Zealand*, Geneva.

ILO (1958), *The Cost of Social Security*, Geneva.

Imbeau, L. (1988), 'Aid and ideology', *European Journal of Political Research*, **16** (1), 3–28.

Immergut, E. (1992), *The Political Construction of Interests: National Health Insurance Politics in Switzerland, France and Sweden, 1930–1970*, New York: Cambridge University Press.

Inglehart, R. (1997) *Modernization and Post–modernization: Cultural, Economic and Political Change in 43 Societies*, Princeton, NJ: Princeton University Press.

Inkeles, A. (1981), 'Convergence and divergence in industrial societies', in Attir, M.O., Holzner, B. and Suda, Z. (eds), *Directions of Change: Modernization Theory, Research and Realities*, New York: Westview Press, pp. 3–38.

Jackson, R.J., Jackson, D. and Baxter-Moore, N. (1986), *Politics in Canada: Culture, Institutions, Behaviour, and Public Policy*, Scarborough, Ontario: Prentice–Hall Canada.

Jahn, D. (1997), 'Environmental policy and policy regimes: explaining variation in 18 OECD-countries', mimeo, International Political Science Association, Seoul, 17–21 August.

Kaelble, H. (1989), *A Social History of Western Europe 1880–1980*, Dublin: Gill and Macmillan.

Kangas, O. (1991), *The Politics of Social Rights*, Stockholm: Swedish Institute for Social Research.

Katzenstein, P. (1985), *Small States in World Markets*. Ithaca, NY: Cornell University Press.

Keman, H. (1982) 'Securing the safety of the nation-state', in Castles, F.G. (ed.), *The Impact of Parties*, London: Sage Publications, pp. 177–21.

Keman, H. (1993), 'The politics of managing the mixed economy', in Keman, H. (ed.), *Comparative politics: New Directions in Theory and Method*, Amsterdam: VU University Press, pp. 161–90.

Kemeny, J. (1980), 'The political economy of housing'. in Wheelwright, E.L. and Buckley, K. (eds), *Essays in The Political Economy of Australian Capitalism*, Volume 4, Sydney: Australia and New Zealand Book Company, pp. 173–91.

Kemeny, J. (1981), *The Myth of Home Ownership*, London: Routledge and Kegan Paul.

Kemeny, J. (1992), *Housing and Social Theory*, London: Routledge.

Kerr, C. (1960), *Industrialism and Industrial Man*, Cambridge, MA: Harvard University Press.

Keg, V.O. (1949), *Southern Politics*, New York: Alfred A. Knopf.

Killingsworth, M.R. and Heckman, J.J. (1986), 'Female labour supply: a survey', in Ashenfelter, O. and Layard, R. (eds), *Handbook of Labor Economics*, Amsterdam: North–Holland, pp. 103–204.

King, A. (1975), 'Overload: problems of governing in the 1970s', *Political Studies*, **23** (2–3), 283–96.

King, G., Keohane, R.O. and Verba, S. (1994), *Designing Social Inquiry*, Princeton, NJ: Princeton University Press.

Kirchheimer, O. (1964), 'The waning of opposition', in Macridis, R. and Brown, B.E. (eds), *Comparative Politics*, Homewood, IL: Dorsey Press.

Kohl, J. (1981), 'Trends and problems in postwar public expenditure development in Western Europe and North America', in Flora, P. and Heidenheimer, A.J. (eds), *The Development of Welfare States in Europe and America*, New Brunswick, NJ: Transaction Books, pp. 307–44.

Korpi, W. (1978), *The Working Class in Welfare Capitalism*, London: Routledge and Kegan Paul.

Korpi, W. (1983), *The Democratic Class Struggle*, London: Routledge and Kegan Paul.

Korpi, W. (1989), 'Power, politics, and state autonomy in the development of social citizenship', *American Sociological Review*, **54**, 309–28.

Korpi, W. (1991), 'Political and economic explanations for unemployment: a cross-national and long-term analysis', *British Journal of Political Science*, **21** (3), 315–48.

Kudrle, R.T. and Marmor, T.R. (1981), 'The development of welfare states in North America', in Flora, P. and Heidenheimer, A.J. (eds), *The Development of Welfare States in Europe and America*, New Brunswick, NJ: Transaction Books, pp. 81–121.

Kupinsky, S. (1977), *The Fertility of Working Women: A Synthesis of International Research*, New York: Praeger Publishers.

Kurzer, P. (1991), 'Unemployment in open economies: the impact of trade, finance and european integration', *Comparative Political Studies*, **24** (1), 3–30.

Lane, J.-E. and Ersson, S. (1990), *Comparative Political Economy*, London: Pinter Publishers.

Larkey, P.D., Stolp, C. and Winer, M. (1981), 'Theorizing about the growth of government: a research assessment', *Journal of Public Policy*, **1** (2), 157–220.

Laver, M. and Hunt, B. (1992), *Policy and Party Competition*, London: Routledge.

Layard, R., Nickell, S. and Jackman, R. (1991), *Unemployment: Macroeconomic Performance and the Labour Market*, Oxford: Oxford University Press.

Lazear, E.P. (1986), 'Retirement from the labor force', in Ashenfelter, O. and Layard, R. (eds), *Handbook of Labor Economics*, Amsterdam: North-Holland, pp. 305–55.

Le Grand, J. (1982), *The Strategy of Equality: Redistribution and the Social Services*, London: George Allen and Unwin.

Lehmbruch, G. (1977), 'Liberal corporatism and party government', *Comparative Political Studies*, **10** (1), 91–126.

Lehmbruch, G. (1993), 'Consociational democracy and corporatism in Switzerland', *Publius*, **23** (2), 43–60.

Leibfried, S. (1993), 'Towards a European welfare state?', in Jones, C. (ed.), *New Perspectives on the Welfare State in Europe*, London: Routledge.

Leibfried, S. and Pierson, P. (eds) (1995), *European Social Policy: Between Fragmentation and Integration*, Washington, DC: The Brookings Institution.

Lijphart, A. (1968), 'Typologies of democratic systems', *Comparative Political Studies*, **1** (1), 3–44.

Lijphart, A. (1997), 'Unequal participation: democracy's unresolved dilemma', *American Political Science Review*, **91** (1), 1–14.

Lipset, S. M. (1959) 'Some social requisites of democracy', *American Political Science Review*, **53** (1), 69–105.

Lipset, S.M. (1976), 'Radicalism in North America: a comparative view of the party systems in Canada and the United States', *Transactions of the Royal Society of Canada*, series 4, vol. 14.

Lipset, S.M. and Rokkan, S. (1967), *Party Systems and Voter Alignments*, New York: The Free Press.

Lye, D.N. (1989), *The Rise of Divorce in Developed Countries Since 1960: A Comparative Study of Law, Opportunity and Values*, University of Pennsylvania doctoral thesis.

Mackie, T.T. and Rose, R. (1990), *The International Almanac of Electoral History*, London: Macmillan, 3rd edn.

Maclennan, D. (1982), *Housing Economics*, London: Longman.

Maddison, A. (1991), *Dynamic Forces in Capitalist Development*, Oxford: Oxford University Press.

Mair, P. and Castles, F.G. (1997), 'Revisiting expert judgements', *European Journal of Political Research*, **31** (1–2), 150–57.

March, J.G. and Olsen, J.P. (1989), *Rediscovering Institutions. The Organizational Basis of Politics*, New York: Free Press.

McDonald, P. (1997), 'Gender equity, social institutions and the future of fertility', *Working Papers in Demography*, Canberra: Research School of Social Sciences, no. 69, 1–25.

McGuire, C.C. (1981), *International Housing Policies: A Comparative Analysis*. Lexington, MA: Lexington Books.

McPherson, K. (1990), 'International differences in medical care practices', in OECD, *Health Care Systems in Transition: The Search for Efficiency*, Paris: OECD.

Milner, H.V. and Keohane, R.O. (1996), 'Internationalization and domestic politics: an introduction', in Keohane, R.O. and Milner, H.V. (eds),

Internationalization and Domestic Politics, Cambridge: Cambridge University Press, pp. 3–24.

MIRE (1997), *Comparing Social Welfare Systems in Southern Europe*, Mission Recherche, Ministère de l'Emploi et de la Solidarité, Paris.

Mitchell, B.R. (1992), *International Historical Statistics*, vols 1 and 2, New York: Stockton Press.

Moles, O.C. (1979), 'Public welfare payments and marital dissolution', in Levinger, G. and Moles, O.C. (eds), *Divorce and Separation: Context, Causes and Consequences*, New York: Basic Books, pp. 167–80.

Monnier, A. and de Guibert-Lantoine, C. (1996), 'La conjoncture démographique: L'Europe et les pays développés d'outre-mer', *Population*, 4–5, 1005–30.

Mortimer Commission (1966), *Putting Asunder: A Divorce Law for Contemporary Society*. London: SPCK.

Mumford, K. (1989), *Women Working: Economics and Reality*, Sydney: Allen & Unwin.

Musgrave, R.A. (1969), *Fiscal Systems*, New Haven, CT: Yale University Press.

Najman, J.M. and Western, J.S. (1984), 'A comparative analysis of Australian health policy in the 1970s', *Social Science and Medicine*, **18** (11), 949–58.

Newhouse, J.P., Anderson, G. and Roos, L.L. (1988), 'Hospital spending in the United States and Canada', *Health Affairs*, Winter, 6–16.

Norris, P. (1987), *Politics and Sexual Equality. The Comparative Position of Women in Western Societies*, Boulder, CO: Rienner.

Norton, A.J. and Glick, P.C. (1979) 'Marital instability in America: past, present and future', in Levinger, G. and Moles, O.C. (eds), *Divorce and Separation: Context, Causes and Consequences*, New York: Basic Books, pp. 6–19.

O'Connor, J. (1973), *The Fiscal Crisis of the State*, New York: St Martin's Press.

O'Connor, J.S. (1989), 'Welfare expenditure and policy orientation in Canada in comparative perspective', *The Canadian Review of Sociology and Anthropology*, **26** (1), 127–50.

OECD (1982), *Employment in the Public Sector*, Paris.

OECD (1984), 'The contribution of services to employment', in *OECD Employment Outlook*, Paris, pp. 39–54.

OECD (1987), *Financing and Delivering Health Care: A Comparative Analysis of OECD Countries*, Paris.

OECD (1989), *Education in OECD Countries 1986–87*, Paris.

OECD (1990), 'Employer versus employee taxation: the impact on employment', in *OECD Employment Outlook*, Paris, pp. 153–77.

OECD (1991), 'Unemployment benefit rules and labour market policy', in *OECD Employment Outlook*, Paris, pp. 199–236.

OECD (1993), *OECD Health Systems*, Paris, vol. I.

OECD (1993a), *OECD Health Systems*, Paris, vol. II.

OECD (1994), *New Orientations for Social Policy*, Social Policy Studies, no. 12, Paris.

OECD (1995 and earlier years), *Labour Force Statistics*, Paris.

OECD (1995a), 'Long–term leave for parents in OECD countries', in *OECD Employment Outlook*, Paris, pp. 171–202.

OECD (1996a and earlier years), *Historical Statistics*, Paris.

OECD (1996b and earlier years), *Economic Outlook*, Paris.

OECD (1996c), *Employment Outlook*, Paris.

OECD (1996d), *Social Expenditure Statistics of OECD Member Countries* (provisional version), Paris.

OECD (1996e), *Ageing in OECD Countries: A Critical Policy Challenge*, Social Policy Studies, no. 20, Paris.

OECD (1996f and earlier years), *Revenue Statistics*, Paris.

OECD (1996g), *Education at a Glance: OECD Indicators*, Paris.

OECD (1996h and earlier years), *National Accounts*, Paris.

OECD (1996i and earlier years), *OECD Health Database*, Paris.

Olson, M. (1982), *The Rise and Decline of Nations*, New Haven, CT: Yale University Press.

Oswald, A. (1996) 'A conjecture on the explanation for high unemployment in industrialised nations: Part I', *Warwick Economic Research Papers*, no. 75., University of Warwick.

Overbye, E. (1994), 'Convergence in policy outcomes: social security systems in perspective', *Journal of Public Policy*, **14** (2), 147–74.

Pampel, F.C. and Weiss, I. (1983), 'Economic development, pension policies, and the labour force participation of aged males', *American Journal of Sociology*, **89** (2), 350–72.

Pampel, F.C. and Williamson, J.B. (1989), *Age, Class, Politics, and the Welfare State*, Cambridge: Cambridge University Press.

Papadakis, E. and Taylor-Gooby, P. (1987), *The Private Provision of Public Welfare*, New York: St Martin's Press.

Paukert, L. (1984), *The Employment and Unemployment of Women in OECD Countries*, Paris: OECD.

Payne, J. (1979), 'Inflation, unemployment and left-wing political parties: a reanalysis', *American Political Science Review*, **73** (1), 181–5.

Peacock, A.T. and Wiseman, J. (1961), *The Growth of Public Expenditures in the United Kingdom*, Princeton, NJ: Princeton University Press.

Pempel, T.J. and Tsunekawa, K. (1979), 'Corporatism without labor? The Japanese anomaly', in Schmitter, P.C. and Lehmbruch, G. (eds), *Trends Towards Corporatist Intermediation*, Beverly Hills, CA: Sage, pp. 231–70.

Pencavel, J. (1986), 'Labor supply of men: a survey', in Ashenfelter, O. and Layard, R. (eds), *Handbook of Labor Economics*, Amsterdam: North-Holland, pp. 3–102.

Peters, B.G. (1991), *The Politics of Taxation: A Comparative Perspective*, Oxford: Blackwell.

Peterson, R.R. (1989), *Women, Work and Divorce*, Albany: State University of New York Press.

Pfaff, M. (1990) 'Differences in health care spending across countries: statistical evidence', *Journal of Health Politics, Policy and Law*, **15** (1), 1–67.

Phillips, R. (1988), *Putting Asunder: A History of Divorce in Western Society*, New York: Cambridge University Press.

Pierson, P. (1995) 'Fragmented welfare states: federal institutions and the development of social policy', *Governance*, **8** (4), 449–78.

Piven, F.F. and Cloward, R.A. (1972), *Regulating the Poor: The Functions of Public Welfare*, London: Tavistock Publications.

Price, S.J. and McKenry, P.C. (1988), *Divorce*, Berkeley, CA: Sage Publications.

Przeworski, A. (1985), *Capitalism and Social Democracy*, Cambridge: Cambridge University Press.

Przeworski, A. (1987), 'Methods of cross–national research, 1970–83: an overview', in Dierkes, M., Weiler, H.N. and Antal, A.B. (eds) *Comparative Policy Research: Learning from Experience*, Aldershot: Gower, pp. 31–49.

Przeworski, A. and Sprague, J. (1986), *Paper Stones: The History of Electoral Socialism*, Chicago: University of Chicago Press.

Rheinstein, M. (1972), *Marriage Stability, Divorce and the Law*, Chicago: Chicago University Press.

Rimlinger, G.V. (1971), *Welfare Policy and Industrialization in Europe, America and Russia*, New York: Wiley.

Rodrik, D. (1997), *Has Globalisation Gone Too Far?* Washington, DC: Institute for International Economics.

Rokkan, S. (1970), *Citizens, Elections, Parties*, Oslo: Universitetsforlaget.

Rose, R. (1984), *Understanding Big Government: The Programme Approach*, London: Sage Publications.

Rose, R. (1989), *Ordinary People in Public Policy*, London: Sage Publications.

Ross, A.M. and Hartman, P.T. (1960), *Changing Patterns of Industrial Conflict*, New York: John Wiley.

Rothstein, B. (1992), 'Labour–market institutions and working class strength', in Steinmo, S., Thelen, K. and Longstreth, F. (eds), *Structuring Politics: Historical Institutionalism in Comparative Analysis*, Cambridge: Cambridge University Press, pp. 33–56.

Rowthorn, B. and Glyn, A. (1990), 'The diversity of unemployment experience since 1973', in Marglin, S. and Schor, J. (eds), *The Golden*

Age of Capitalism: Reinterpreting the Postwar Experience, Oxford: Clarendon Press, pp. 218–66.

Rubery, J. (1988), 'Women and recession: a comparative perspective', in Rubery, J. (ed.) *Women and Recession*, London: Routledge and Kegan Paul, pp. 253–86.

Rudd, C. (1992), 'Controlling and restructuring public expenditure', in Boston, J. and Dalziel, P. (eds), *The Decent Society?*, Auckland: Oxford University Press, pp. 39–58.

Ruggie, M. (1984), *The State and Working Women*, Princeton, NJ: Princeton University Press.

Sax, S. (1990), *Health Care Choices and the Public Purse*, Sydney: Allen and Unwin.

Sbragia, A.M. (1992), 'Thinking about the European future: the uses of comparison', in Sbragia, A.M. (ed.), *Euro-Politics: Institutions and Policymaking in the 'New' European Community*, Washington, DC: The Brookings Institution, pp. 257–91.

Scharpf, F.W. (1991), *Crisis and Choice in European Social Democracy*, Ithaca, NY: Cornell University Press.

Schmidt, M.G. (1982), 'The role of parties in shaping macroeconomic policy', in Castles, F.G. (ed.), *The Impact of Parties*, London: Sage Publications, pp. 97–176.

Schmidt, M.G. (1986), 'Comment on "social expenditure and the political right"', *European Journal of Political Research*, **14**, 677–80.

Schmidt, M.G. (1993), 'Gendered labour force participation', in Castles, F.G., (ed.), *Families of Nations: Patterns of Public Policy in Western Democracies*, Aldershot: Dartmouth, pp. 179–237.

Schmidt, M.G. (1996a), 'When parties matter: a review of the possibilities and limits of partisan influence on public policy', *European Journal of Political Research*, **30**, 155–83.

Schmidt, M.G. (1996b), *Die parteipolitische Zusammensetzung von Regierungen in demokratischen Staaten (1945–1996)*, Heidelberg: Institut für Politische Wissenschaft.

Schmidt, S. (1989), 'Convergence theory, labor movements, and corporatism', *Scandinavian Housing and Planning Research*, **6** (2), 83–101.

Schmitter, P.C. (1974), 'Still the century of corporatism', *Review of Politics*, **36** (1), 85–131.

Semyonov, M. (1980), 'The social context of women's labor force participation: a comparative analysis', *American Journal of Sociology*, **86**, 534–50.

Shalev, M. (1983), 'The Social Democratic model and beyond: two "generations" of comparative research on the welfare state', *Comparative Social Research*, **6**, 315–51.

Simpson, M. (1990), 'Political rights and income inequality: A Cross-National Test', *American Sociological Review*, **55** (5), 682–93.

SIPRI (Stockholm International Peace Research Institute) (1996 and earlier years), *SIPRI Yearbook*, London: Oxford University Press.

Skocpol, T. (1985), 'Bringing the state back in: strategies of analysis in current research', in Evans, P.B. Rueschemeyer, D. and Skocpol, T. (eds), *Bringing the State Back In*, Cambridge: Cambridge University Press, pp. 3–37.

Sorrentino, C. (1983), 'International comparisons of labor force participation, 1960–81', *Monthly Labor Review*, **106** (2), 23–36.

Sorrentino, C. (1990), 'The changing family in international perspective', *Monthly Labor Review*, **113** (3), 41–58.

Standing, G. (1996), 'Social protection in Central and Eastern Europe: a tale of slipping anchors and torn safety nets', in Esping-Andersen, G. (ed.) (1996), *The Welfare State in Transition*, London: Sage, pp. 225–55.

Stearns, P.N. (1967), *European Society in Upheaval*, London: Collier-Macmillan.

Steinmo, S. (1995), 'Why is government so small in America?, *Governance*, **8** (3), 303–34.

Steinmo, S, Thelen, K. and Longstreth, F. (eds) (1992), *Structuring Politics: Historical Institutionalism in Comparative Analysis*, Cambridge: Cambridge University Press.

Stephens, J.D. (1979), *The Transition from Capitalism to Socialism*, London: Macmillan.

Stimson, J. (1985), 'Regression in space and time: a statistical essay', *American Journal of Political Science*, **29**, 914–47.

Streek, W. and Schmitter, P.C. (1991), 'From national corporatism to transnational pluralism: organized interests in the Single European Market', *Politics and Society*, **19**, 133–64.

Summers, R. and Heston, A. (1991), 'The Penn World Table (Mark 5)', *Quarterly Journal of Economics*, **106** (2), 327–68.

Therborn, G. (1987), 'Does corporatism really matter? The Economic Crisis and Issues of Political Theory, *Journal of Public Policy*, **7** (3), 259–84.

Therborn, G. (1986), *Why Some Peoples Are More Unemployed Than Others*, London: Verso.

Therborn, G. (1989), '"Pillarization" and "Popular Movements". Two variants of welfare state capitalism: the Netherlands and Sweden', in Castles, F.G. (ed.), *The Comparative History of Public Policy*, Cambridge, Polity Press, pp. 192–241.

Therborn, G. (1995), *European Modernity and Beyond: The Trajectory of European Societies, 1945–2000*, London: Sage Publications.

Thomas, J.C. (1979), 'The changing nature of partisan divisions in the west: Trends in domestic policy orientation in ten party systems', *European Journal of Political Research*, **7**, 397–413.

Tuohy, C.J. (1992), *Policy and Politics in Canada*, Philadelphia: Temple University Press.

United Nations (1984), 'Recent levels and trends of contraceptive use as assessed in 1983', Department of International Economic and Social Affairs, New York.

United Nations (1989a), 'Levels and trends of contraceptive use as assessed in 1988', *Population Studies*, no. 110, New York.

United Nations (1989b), 'Trends in population policy', *Population Studies*, no. 114, New York.

United Nations (1991), *World Urbanization Prospects*, New York.

United Nations Economic Commission for Europe (1986 and earlier years), *Annual Bulletin of Housing and Building Statistics for Europe*, New York: United Nations.

UNESCO (1995 and earlier years), *Statistical Yearbook*, Paris.

Urwin, D. (1981), *Western Europe Since 1945*, London: Longman, 3rd edn.

Van Kersbergen, K. (1995), *Social Capitalism: A Study of Christian Democracy and the Welfare State*, London: Routledge.

Van Arnhem, J.C. and Schotsman, J.G. (1982), 'Do parties affect the distribution of incomes? The case of advanced capitalist democracies', in Castles, F.G. (ed.) *The Impact of Parties*, London: Sage Publications, pp. 283–364.

Van de Kaa, D.J. (1996), 'Anchored narratives: The story and findings of half a century of research into the determinants of fertility', *Population Studies*, **50** (3), 389–432.

Varley, R. (1986), *The Government Household Transfer Base 1960–1984*, Paris: OECD.

Von Rhein-Kress, G. (1993), 'Coping with economic crisis: labour supply as a policy instrument', in Castles, F.G., (ed.) (1993), *Families of Nations: Patterns of Public Policy in Western Democracies*, Aldershot: Dartmouth, pp. 131–78.

Wallace, H. and Wallace, W. (eds) (1996), *Policy-Making in the European Union*, Oxford: Oxford University Press.

Wallerstein, M. (1989), 'Union growth in advanced industrial democracies', *American Political Science Review*, **83** (2), 481–501.

Weaver, R.K. and Rockman, B.A. (eds) (1993), *Do Institutions Matter? Government Capabilities in the United States and Abroad*, Washington, DC: The Brookings Institution.

Weber, M. (1968), *The Protestant Ethic and the Spirit of Capitalism*, London: Unwin University Books.

Weir, M. and Skocpol, T. (1985), 'State structures and the possibilities for "Keynesian" responses to the Great Depression in Sweden,

Britain and the United States', in Evans, P.B., Rueschemeyer, D. and Skocpol, T. (eds), *Bringing the State Back In*, Cambridge: Cambridge University Press, pp. 107–63.

Weller, G.R. and Manga, P. (1983), 'The development of health policy in Canada', in Atkinson, M.M. and Chandler, M.A. (eds), *The Politics of Canadian Public Policy*, Toronto: University of Toronto Press, pp. 223–46.

Western, B. (1995), 'A comparative study of working-class disorganization: union decline in eighteen advanced capitalist countries', *American Sociological Review*, **60** (2), 179–201.

Western, B. and Jackman, S. (1994), 'Bayesian inference for comparative research', *American Political Science Review*, **88** (2), 412–23.

Whiteford, P. and Kennedy, S. (1995), *Income and living standards of older people*, Department of Social Security, Research Report no. 34, London: HMSO.

Wildavsky, A. (1975), *Budgeting. A Comparative Theory of Budgetary Processes*, Boston: Little Brown.

Wildavsky, A. (1985), 'The logic of public sector growth', in Lane, J.-E. (ed.), *State and Market: The Politics of the Public and the Private*, London: Sage Publications, pp. 231–70.

Wilensky, H.L. (1968), 'Women's work: economic growth, ideology, structure', *Industrial Relations*, **7**, 235–48.

Wilensky, H.L. (1975), *The Welfare State and Equality*, Berkeley, CA: University of California Press.

Wilensky, H.L. (1981), 'Leftism, Catholicism, and democratic corporatism: the role of political parties in recent welfare state development', in Flora, P. and Heidenheimer, A.J. (eds), *The Development of Welfare States in Europe and America*, New Brunswick, NJ: Transaction Books, pp. 345–82.

Wilensky, H.L. and Lebeaux, C.N. (1958), *Industrial Society and Social Welfare*, New York: Russell Sage Foundation.

Woldendorp, J. Keman, H. and Budge, I. (1993), 'Political Data 1945–1990: Party Government in 20 Democracies', *Special Issue of European Journal of Political Research*, **24**.

Woldendorp, J. Keman, H. and Budge, I. (1998), 'Party Government in 20 Democracies (1990–1995)', *European Journal of Political Research*, **31** (1), pp. 1–118.

World Bank (1994), *Averting the Old Age Crisis*. New York: Oxford University Press.

World Health Organization (1993), *World Health Statistics Annual*, WHO, Geneva.

Index